MUTUAL
FUNDS

The *Robert W. Kolb Series in Finance* provides a comprehensive view of the field of finance in all of its variety and complexity. The series is projected to include approximately 65 volumes covering all major topics and specializations in finance, ranging from investments, to corporate finance, to financial institutions. Each volume in the *Kolb Series in Finance* consists of new articles especially written for the volume.

Each *Kolb Series* volume is edited by a specialist in a particular area of finance, who develops the volume outline and commissions articles by the world's experts in that particular field of finance. Each volume includes an editor's introduction and articles by experts that fully describe the current state of financial research and practice in a particular area of finance.

The essays in each volume are intended for practicing finance professionals, graduate students, and advanced undergraduate students. The goal of each volume is to encapsulate the current state of knowledge in a particular area of finance so that the reader can quickly achieve a mastery of that special area of finance.

MUTUAL FUNDS

Portfolio Structures, Analysis, Management, and Stewardship

John A. Haslem, Ph.D.

The Robert W. Kolb Series in Finance

John Wiley & Sons, Inc.

Library of Congress Cataloging-in-Publication Data:

Haslem, John A.
  Mutual funds : portfolio structures, analysis, management, and stewardship / John Haslem.
      p. cm. – (Robert W. Kolb series)
  Includes index.
  ISBN 978-0-470-49909-2 (cloth)
 1. Mutual funds.   2. Investments.   3. Portfolio management.   I. Title.
  HG4530.H3867 2009
  332.63'27–dc22
                                                                    2009013311
ISBN-13 978-0-470-49909-2

Printed in the United States of America

10 9 8 7 6 5 4 3 2 1

This book is dedicated to the experts who generously contributed their knowledge, and to Jane Haslem and our three families and seven grandchildren.

JOHN A. HASLEM

Contents

PART III   Fund Types and Comparative Performance, Efficient Markets, Asset Allocation, and Morningstar Analysis

Introduction

When the financial history of the United States is written, one chapter will necessarily be dedicated to mutual funds. This industry has been and continues to be one of the extraordinary growth stories in the history of American financial markets. Today, 96 million individual investors in 55 million households own mutual funds, representing 87 percent of total fund assets. In 1984, net fund assets totaled $370 million; today they are $10.4 trillion.

Several major forces explain most of this growth, but the first and essential force has been the demonstrated effectiveness of mutual funds as vehicles for providing individual investors with retirement incomes and financial wealth. Mutual funds provide individual investors (and all other investors) with investment performance and investment alternatives, objectives, and services traditionally reserved for institutional and large individual investors. Nonetheless, mutual funds also have numerous shortcomings in their management and regulation that could be removed through stewardship of fund management, increased investor knowledge, and more investor-friendly fund regulation.

This book brings together some of the finest minds in academia, investment management, and mutual fund management to discuss the nature and pros and cons of mutual funds. The focus explores mutual funds as investment vehicles and the approaches that will further improve and lessen the often-hidden pitfalls of fund investing. The result is an improved source of learning for university students and an increased ability of informed investors to make fund decisions that will make the experience much more rewarding and even simpler.

MUTUAL FUNDS

PART I

Mutual Funds: Nature, Regulation, and Costs

CHAPTER 1

The Nature of Mutual Funds

CONRAD S. CICCOTELLO, J.D., Ph.D.

Associate Professor and Director of Graduate Personal Financial Planning Programs, Georgia State University, Atlanta, Georgia

A s a first-year doctoral student at the Pennsylvania State University in 1990, I wrote my investments seminar paper on the performance of a sample of open-end mutual funds. My professor indicated that the paper was methodologically sound but suggested to me that finance academics did not really care about mutual fund performance (or, for that matter, about mutual funds, in general). So he advised that I examine something else in future research. Academics often lag what is of interest in the "real world," and I recall thinking that mutual funds were important, and likely to become more so over time. But as a doctoral student, one learns to do what one is told to do. So, I put down the mutual fund topic during the rest of my doctoral program, although my interest in funds never waned. Soon after entering the professorate in 1993, I restarted my formal research on mutual funds. That research continues to this day.

While I had suspicions in 1990 that mutual funds would become an interesting and important topic, I did not even come close to imagining then what has actually happened in the mutual fund universe over the nearly two decades since my first research effort as a doctoral student. At the time of my first study, there were a few hundred open-end mutual funds that held about $1 trillion total. Today, there are well over 10,000 funds holding about $10 trillion in wealth. A confluence of societal and corporate trends over this time, the biggest of which being the large-scale changeover from defined benefit to defined contribution retirement plans, has fueled the tremendous growth of assets held in open-end mutual funds.

There has also been explosive growth in academic research about mutual funds. Most of that research in finance examines fund performance issues, broadly addressing the question: Do mutual funds "beat the market"? More recently, there has been a growing stream of research on institutional and structural aspects of mutual fund services and providers (Sirri and Tufano, 1998). One might view this research as more oriented toward marketing, studying the intersection of the supply and demand for mutual funds as well as the growing segmentation of both sides of that fundamental equation. The broad growth in the demographics of individuals owning funds partly explains this research trend. Several decades ago, mutual fund ownership was concentrated among the affluent. Now funds are owned by a wide range of individuals across the income spectrum. Over the past two decades, open-end mutual funds have become the primary financial wealth accumulation vehicle in American society, especially for middle-market consumers and the "emerging affluent." Understanding mutual funds has thus become critical for social well-being. Nowhere is this decision more evident than in the choice of funds for an individual's retirement plan.

This chapter first provides an overview of the nature, structure, and services of open-end mutual funds. The goal of this chapter is to introduce the reader to the characteristics of the open-end fund as well as the competitive environment for investment products. This chapter also sets the stage for more detailed discussions of various aspects of mutual funds that are presented in subsequent chapters. This overview chapter highlights how the open-end fund is unique, and the advantages and disadvantages the product has for individual investors. The discussion focuses on the key attributes of open-end funds, with the individual investor's perspective in mind. Upon moving to Chapter 2, the reader should have a sense for the relevant factors necessary for understanding the open-end fund product and ultimately how these factors compare to those in alternative investment vehicles.

ATTRIBUTES OF THE OPEN-END MUTUAL FUND

Board of Directors

Open-end mutual funds are pooled investment products where a large number of individual investors can each own a "slice" of the investment pie. Stepping back from that general description, it is first important to understand how mutual funds are controlled. Most mutual funds are corporations or trusts that are managed by a board of directors, which consists of both inside and outside members. Inside members are typically officers of the investment adviser that manages the funds' assets while outsiders (independents) can come from various occupations and backgrounds (some are even college professors). The mutual fund board's primary responsibility is to protect the interests of the fund's shareholders, similar to the duty that a board of directors has in an operating company. One key task that the independent directors of a mutual fund board face is the negotiation of the investment advisory agreement, which takes place during the "15-c process" (named after a provision in the 1940 Investment Company Act [ICA]). Another key task of the independent directors is to approve and oversee the fund's independent auditors.

The board also technically oversees the other service providers of the funds, such as the distributor (who performs or oversees the actual transactions in fund shares with investors), transfer agent (who keeps shareholder records), and custodian (who holds the inventory of the fund's securities). Once the investment advisory agreement is signed, the investment management company typically manages the day-to-day aspects of the service providers above. As Gremillion (2005) states, a number of investment management companies perform some or even all of the distribution and transfer agent functions themselves while others outsource these functions. The inside members of the board, much like inside board members/officers of the corporation in an operating company, typically oversee the administrative service functions of the fund on a day-to-day basis.

The ICA requires that a mutual fund board have a majority of independent directors. In recent years, there have been proposals to strengthen the "independence" of mutual fund boards by requiring that three-quarters of all board members be independent and that the chairman of the board be independent. These governance proposals have been controversial, and are discussed in more detail in Chapter 2 in the context of current regulatory challenges.

Liquidity

Perhaps the most distinguishing attribute of the open-end mutual fund is its liquidity feature. In an open-end fund, the *fund itself* stands ready to buy and sell shares from investors at the fund's net asset value (NAV) each day (the fund is "self-liquidating"). For purposes of introduction, the reader can assume that NAV equates to fair market value of a share of the fund. So investors can generally buy or sell (redeem) shares of the fund for its fair market value each day, with the fund itself taking the opposite side of the transaction. This daily self-liquidating feature of the open-end fund is unlike the liquidity mechanisms in the competing investment structures. For example, compare the open-end fund to the closed-end fund. Investors have the ability to purchase or liquidate fund shares in closed-end funds, but the mechanism for exchange is typically trading the shares of the fund with another investor. As such, trading in closed-end funds is similar to trading a stock on an exchange (such as the New York Stock Exchange). In fact, many closed-end funds are listed on an exchange and traded similarly to stocks. In closed-end vehicles, purchases by investors do not add to total assets in the fund, nor do redemptions reduce the total assets in the fund. Thus in a closed-end fund, trades would most often take place with another investor and not the fund itself, unless the fund was repurchasing its own shares or selling new shares in as in a secondary equity offer. These are usually rare events and not the day-to-day reality.

Why is this self-liquidating feature of the open-end fund such a big deal? Having the fund standing ready to buy or sell shares from investors each day as opposed to transacting shares in a marketplace sounds like a somewhat trivial distinction. This feature, however, has probably been the single most troublesome regulatory issue surrounding open-end mutual funds since their birth in the 1920s. There are several reasons for this, but one relates to computation of the sale price, the fund's NAV, as mentioned earlier. Ciccotello et al. (2002) details the historical regulatory issues, which initially related to computation of the NAV so as to avoid allowing the purchase or sale of shares at a "stale price." In the past decade, in particular, large advances in technology have allowed for rapid order submission as well as an increase in the submission of bundled orders ("omnibus accounts") to funds. This has put a strain on the challenges present in calculating NAV so as to not provide those who trade an advantage in doing so (Edelen, 1999). Chapter 2 details some of the regulatory and operating issues associated with fund pricing and rapid trading.

Aside from technical issues with setting the correct NAV, the fund's self-liquidating feature can also have significant performance implications. Stepping back and thinking about how open-end fund performance is comprised is illustrative. Suppose that a stock fund has $500 million in assets today, and tomorrow $500 million of cash inflows arrive at the fund. The portfolio manager's job has just doubled in size, and the overall return of the fund is now a blend of the return on the existing assets and the return on the new assets. Presumably, these inflows start as cash equivalents (they are put into a money market type of account) and remain as such while the portfolio manager invests them into assets in the fund's particular investment objective. This would be stocks if the fund were a stock fund, bonds if it were a bond fund, and so on. Now reverse the process, and consider a $1 billion fund today where investors request $500 million in redemptions tomorrow. In this case, the portfolio manager might be in position where she might have to sell securities (such as stocks if the fund is a stock fund) in the portfolio to meet redemptions. Since the manager might have to sell securities to meet redemptions, open-end funds tend to hold securities that themselves are liquid in that they can be sold quickly and for fair value. In contrast, closed-end funds can hold illiquid securities in the portfolio since investors seeking to sell typically have to trade with other investors instead of redeeming assets from the fund itself.

So an open-end fund manager must not only select securities but also manages the portfolio with an eye toward daily flow into and out of the fund (Greene and Ciccotello, 2006). This aspect of portfolio management is unique to the open-end fund vehicle. The reader might suspect that these fund flow examples were concocted to overstate the point, but that is not really so. In recent years, both investment professionals and academics have become increasingly concerned with the performance and regulatory implications of "flow" into and out of mutual funds. The ability to buy and sell shares from an open-end fund is defined by the fund's prospectus. Some funds restrict trading either by limiting the number of trades an investor can make in a given period of time or by imposing a minimum length of time between trades. Other funds impose a redemption fee, which requires that a percentage of the sale (2 percent is typical) be returned to the fund for the privilege of trading. Allowing an investor to trade in excess of prospectus limits while enforcing those limits against other shareholders can violate the prospectus and lead to regulatory action. Such problems were at the core of the mutual fund market timing scandal that broke in September 2003 (Hulbert, 2003; Masters, 2003). Chapter 2 discusses in more detail the issues associated with violation of prospectus trading limits during the recent mutual fund market timing scandal.

More generally, the timing of inflows and outflows from open-end funds has been a hot topic for academic research over the past decade. As Edelen (1999) observes in his groundbreaking paper, flows into open-end funds can have a significant impact on performance. As Braverman, Kandel, and Wohl (2005) observe, investors tend to buy shares in open-end funds after stock market prices have increased in the sector (or asset class) where funds invest, and similarly, they tend to request redemptions after market prices have fallen in that sector. Thus, mutual fund investors tend to chase performance and often arrive "late to the party." Arriving late in a mutual fund context means buying shares after asset prices have already risen (and are more inclined to fall) or vice versa. Behavioral arguments suggest that investors would tend to herd by following the crowd—buying into sectors that have done well.

Also consider the actual portfolio management challenges associated with flows into and out of the fund on a daily basis. While mutual fund portfolio managers do have some discretion about how quickly to invest or divest from the fund's risky asset base of stocks (assuming a stock fund), poorly timed flows into funds can create a significant performance issue. Since the fund is a pooled investment vehicle with a self-liquidating feature, those investors who are not trading can be impacted by the trades of those investors who trade. Fund (in- and out-) flows have thus become a significant aspect both of the management of mutual funds, as just mentioned, and in the reporting of fund performance. Fund flows also set up a conflict between the interests of shareholders who might want to trade funds often and those who want to buy and hold funds. This regulatory issue surrounding trading and performance reporting is discussed in more depth in Chapter 2.

In the context of this overview chapter, the key takeaways are that liquidity in an open-end fund matters to fund management and performance.

All-Equity Capital Structure

Another attribute that distinguishes open-end funds from other pooled investment vehicles is that open-end funds have a very simple all-equity capital structure. Sections 12 and 18 of the ICA limit any type of borrowing and forbid the issuance of senior securities (bonds) by an open-end investment company (Gremillion, 2005, p. 22). Closed-end funds, by contrast, often rely on both debt and equity (common and preferred stock) capital. According to the 1940 ICA, a closed-end fund may have up to 33 percent of its assets financed with debt (leverage). This might seem like a manageable amount of leverage, but debt can create problems for closed-end funds, as the 2007–2008 meltdown in the auction rate market (where many closed-end funds had borrowed funds) illustrates (Gullapalli, 2008; Rappaport, 2008).

From the investor's perspective, the lack of leverage in an open-end fund has both costs and benefits. Prudent use of leverage can enhance the returns of stockholders in a firm or in a fund. However, a leveraged capital structure adds risk. The ICA does recognize this risk; that is why the law imposes debt limits on closed-end funds. But consider an example where a pooled investment vehicle is not subject to any leverage restrictions (one might call such an investment a hedge fund). If such a fund employed high leverage and also had restrictions on redemptions, an equity investor would be holding both an illiquid and a highly levered investment vehicle. Now assume that the fund's investment objective is to create value by buying and selling assets in a high-risk asset class with the accompanying high price volatility. The balance sheet risk of this fund is very high. The example fund has highly volatile assets, which may be illiquid themselves, a highly levered capital structure, and low liquidity for shareholders regarding shares of the fund itself. Falling asset prices can quickly lead to financial distress and large losses in shareholder value, as in the 2008 debacles with Bear Stearns hedge funds (Kelly, 2008) and, in the more distant past, Long Term Capital Management.

The open-end fund stands at the other end of the spectrum with regard to capital structure risk. Since the open-end fund must be unlevered, the returns to shareholders of the fund cannot be magnified (up or down) relative to the returns of the assets the fund holds. Together with the self-liquidating feature, the absence of leverage provides individual mutual fund investors with a low-risk investment structure, independent of the considerations about the nature of the investments held by the fund. Such a structure is especially valuable in the case of redemptions in a period of falling asset (stock) prices. An open-end fund manager might be forced to sell securities to meet redemptions in such an environment, but she would not be forced to sell securities in order to avoid breaking any covenants associated with debt the fund is carrying—because the open-end fund has no debt.

Despite the debt restrictions just discussed, some fund families have started to offer open-end funds that have the ability to take "short" positions in a portion of their portfolio. Short positions occur when the fund borrows securities and sells them into the market with the goal of buying them back later at a lower price. Investors should be wary of these types of funds (typically indentified by a title such as a 130/30 fund, indicating that up to 30 percent of the portfolio may be short positions). These funds may present higher risks than ordinary open-end funds due to the use of margin borrowing to hold short positions.

Portfolio Diversification

Open-end funds tend to hold a large number of securities within their given asset class (such as stocks, bonds, or cash equivalents) and investment objective. Even the most "focused" funds tend to hold at least 20 securities—the Janus 20 fund comes to mind as an example. Holding a large number of individual securities in one investment vehicle is a big plus for investors in funds. The single most powerful (Nobel Prize–winning) and useful idea in all of finance is that investment diversification has benefits (Markowitz, 1959). Holding an undiversified portfolio is a bad idea, as the investor is not rewarded for taking company-specific risks. The open-end mutual fund especially provides a powerful advantage for individual investors with smaller amounts of capital to invest, because the fund's diversification is provided for them at the most critical time—when they have the small amount of capital. Since younger individuals tend to have less capital to invest than older investors, diversification is also provided to protect their most critical investments—those with the longest time horizon for compounding.

Minimum investments in funds vary across investment managers. Typical entry-level investments might be $100,000 to $300,000, but employees entering a retirement plan (such as a 401[k]) typically do so with no required minimum. Employees make their first monthly contribution (with a match from the employer, it is hoped). Next month, the process continues. Without a pooled investment vehicle, an investor with a small amount of capital might choose to buy a single stock (a bad idea). Alternatively, an investor might be able to use a brokerage account to purchase a closed-end fund or exchange-traded fund each month as he accrues wealth for retirement. Such a strategy would address diversification needs but would require payment of a commission each month, unlike the open-end fund. Issues regarding choices of investment vehicles are discussed in more depth later in this chapter.

Professional Management

Successful negotiation of the investment advisory agreement results in a contract for the investment adviser's day-to-day management of the fund. The aspect of this task most frequently examined is the selection of securities by a portfolio manager—and the resulting fund performance. Clearly, the selection of securities is one key job of the fund manager. A vast body of academic literature explores mutual fund manager performance with evidence mixed about how and whether mutual fund managers can beat the market (Carhart, 1997). For readers of this chapter, the key point should be that all investment managers charge some fee for investment advisory services. Performance that investors experience is net of fees charged. The higher the fees, the better the portfolio manager must be, all else the same (Bogle, 2005; LaPlante, 2001).

Parsing the universe of open-end mutual funds into two classifications is useful for thinking about investment strategies and investment fees. Some funds are passively managed, meaning that their goal is to track the performance of a specific market index, such as the Standard & Poor's (S&P) 500. Portfolio managers of passively managed funds tend to trade fairly infrequently, and when they do so, it is to minimize the difference (tracking error) between the performance of the fund and that of the market index they track. Other funds are actively managed, meaning that their goal is to employ a manager-specific investment strategy to the fund's assets. Active management strategies come in numerous forms; some rely on fundamental analyses of value while others rely on technical indicators of value. As the names imply, active management tends to be more expensive than passive management, although even passively managed funds have a range of expenses (Haslem, Baker, and Smith, 2006).

The fundamental issue for investors, stated in academic terms, is whether active managers can earn their (higher) advisory fees. If the marketplace for mutual fund management were in a competitive equilibrium, one might expect that active fund management would result in obtaining information that translated into superior trading capability but that, net of the higher costs of active management relative to passive management, the returns of active and passively managed funds would be similar. The evidence on this point is mixed, although recently there has been more emphasis on questioning the growth of actively managed funds in the face of their relatively poor overall performance (French, 2008). Subsequent chapters in the book discuss the regulatory and performance aspects of mutual fund fees in greater detail.

Investor Services

Professional management of open-end mutual funds involves more than picking securities and managing fund inflows and outflows. These activities typically do not involve direct contact with investors, who are the ultimate owners of the fund. So if the portfolio manager herself does not interact with investors on a day-to-day basis, who actually services investors? There are a range of tasks, such as order processing, fund performance reporting, tax reporting, beneficiary designations, and even assistance in fund selection that fall under this category. One useful way to group these activities might be to think of them as investor servicing issues.

Fund-level personnel could handle investor servicing tasks, but the nature of these tasks might suggest that they could be efficiently executed by administrative personnel who serve several funds at once. Consider that most open-end mutual funds belong to a fund family (also called a fund complex). Fidelity is one example; T.R. Price is another. Families can provide economies of scale in the administration of investor servicing. Indeed, the roles and importance of fund families are growing areas of academic research (Ciccotello, Greene, and Walsh, 2007; Hechinger, 1999).

Reputation of fund families might be linked with investment style (Massa, 2003). For example, the Janus family built its reputation as a growth stock investment family. But some mutual fund industry observers believe that competitive advantage in the industry is becoming more closely linked with the quality and scope of investor servicing, since security selection is becoming increasingly commoditized by the growth in the number and variety of funds. With over 10,000 mutual funds run by highly sophisticated investment professionals, the view is that any security selection advantages that a particular investment adviser might have would tend to be short-lived.

Pozen (2002) argues that the move in the mutual fund industry is toward "open architecture," where an investor can have a choice of funds that transcend a single family through a servicing portal. Black, Ciccotello, and Skipper (2002) assert that brand in financial services is moving toward the distributor and away from the originator. These trends clearly bring marketing issues and the proper "boundary" of the mutual fund firm into the discussion. Similar to firms involved in the value chain for tangible goods, mutual fund families must consider matching their strategy and structure to best serve their target clients (Milgrom and Roberts, 1995).

Consider the marketing issues associated with starting a new open-end mutual fund. If an investment adviser has an investment strategy that she believes will be successful, that alone is not enough to start an open-end fund. Investors are needed. The investment adviser must attract capital in an environment where an investor has tens of thousands of choices. Moreover, that advisor must then address the management of the accounts of the capital she attracts. This is really a customer service or investor relations function, where the adviser herself (or her outsourced entity) actually has direct contact with the investor. In the increasingly competitive open-end mutual fund environment, some investment management companies may decide that they cannot perform both security selection and investor servicing functions well. Evidence of this choice is the growth in open-end fund distribution innovations, such as fund supermarket platforms (Reid and Rea, 2003). Similar to a supermarket for groceries, a fund supermarket offers a one-stop-shop for funds.

Beginning in 1992, the Charles Schwab No-Transaction-Fee (NTF) Supermarket offered investors the ability to choose from among the funds of many different investment companies (also called mutual fund families). With the fund supermarket, investors have the advantage of a unified account, which is helpful for tax administration and record-keeping purposes. Ciccotello, Miles, and Walsh (2006) find that smaller, more focused (as to investment objective) fund management companies tend to rely more on supermarket distribution than larger, less focused families. This trend is growing more noticeable over time and is consistent with arguments that the goal of these smaller fund families is to focus on security selection and outsource servicing.

Investor servicing is also becoming more important in an era of increased number of choices investors have with regard to "asset locations." The traditional asset location for a mutual fund was an ordinary, after-tax account. In that type of account, interest and dividends paid by the mutual fund and passed through pro rata to its investors trigger ordinary income for current-year tax purposes. At present, qualified dividends receive special tax treatment, but this is not guaranteed to continue. Realized capital gains (either long or short) also trigger current-year tax treatment. Unrealized capital gains become a "tax overhang" in the fund that might be realized at some future time. Tax efficiency in funds is a growing area of research and clearly intersects both investment management issues (since trading of securities has tax consequences) and investor servicing.

As complicated as that all might be, especially given the various tax results that individual investors might experience based on the days entered, stayed in, and left the fund in a given tax year, the current tax situation has become much more involved. Many investors now purchase funds through tax-deferred accounts, such as 401(k) accounts, Individual Retirement Accounts (IRAs), or Simplified Employee Pensions (SEPs). In this kind of tax-deferred asset location, fund distributions such as income and capital gains do not affect investors' current year taxes. Consider, however, that all monies that individuals eventually remove from the tax-deferred account itself are considered and taxed as ordinary income, as opposed to capital gains. The fundamental issue, identified by Horan (2002); Bergstresser and Porterba (2004); Dammon, Spatt, and Zhang (2004); and Reichenstein (2007), is that tax efficiency from the investors' perspective might indicate putting certain types of investments in certain types of asset locations. All else equal, from a tax efficiency perspective, bond funds are better placed in tax-deferred accounts. This is because the ordinary income from bond interest is shielded from tax in the tax-deferred account. Similarly, stock funds may be better located in taxable accounts because long-term capital gains tax rates are lower than those on ordinary income.

The story does not end with tax-deferred retirement accounts. There has been an explosion in education funding accounts, for example, 529 Plans, where capital contributed (and often held in mutual funds) receives preferential tax treatment when it is redeemed from the fund and used for educational purposes. Similarly, there is likely to be explosive growth of health savings accounts (HSAs), where funds taken from the account receive favorable tax treatment if used for medical expenditures. Again, it is likely that open-end funds will form a major investment within HSAs.

What responsibility does the mutual fund company have for all this? The recent research on asset location mentioned earlier suggests that the growth in the number of asset locations is triggering the need for more careful coordination of investments chosen and places (types of accounts) where those investments are made. This is creating a necessity for advice that links investments with tax and individual investor goals. Ultimately, what investors will have to do is convert their wealth, now largely held in mutual funds, to income that is needed to address specific goals. The process and efficiency of conversion from wealth to income is a major growth area for financial planning firms. For investment management firms, the decision will be the degree to which they focus on security selection as opposed to offering the potential array of broader investor service functions.

The danger for open-end funds in relying solely on security selection may be the eventual disconnect from the customer, as seen in the supermarket account. For example, Schwab mutual fund supermarket customers hold shares in the mutual funds from a large number of different fund families. These investors are Schwab customers, not the customers of the individual funds (Ciccotello et al., 2007). Often the fund itself may not even know the identity of the individuals who comprise the supermarket account. The interesting point in all of this is the consideration of brand loyalty. Suppose that financial products are like tangible goods. One goes to a supermarket (Kroger, e.g.) for one-stop shopping for groceries. It is convenient. On the shelves at Kroger are different brands of green beans, such as Del Monte. But Kroger also has its own brand of green beans, often less expensive than the name brand. How long will it be until the brand of the supermarket overtakes the name brand of the product?

MUTUAL FUNDS AND THE COMPETITIVE ENVIRONMENT

This chapter has discussed the major attributes of the open-end fund. The open-end fund offers the investor a range of desirable features, including liquidity, all-equity capital structure, diversification, professional management, and a range of investor services. To complete this introductory chapter, consider these attributes within the framework of an investor choosing a vehicle to accumulate wealth for some specified goal. Suppose that we have a young investor beginning her first job and wanting to begin saving for retirement. What choices does that investor have?

Employer-Sponsored Retirement Plans

First, let us discuss the context of an employer-sponsored retirement plan account, such as a 401(k), then move on to discussing the choices the investor might have in other types of accounts, such as an IRA or an ordinary after-tax brokerage account. In many employer-sponsored retirement plans, the investment choices are limited to open-end funds. Open-end funds have been popular for retirement plans because of their liquidity feature, along with the benefits offered by instant diversification and professional management. The latter two attributes are very valuable for those employees with small account balances, which is everyone when they enter a plan anew (they start with a zero balance).

Most 401(k)-type retirement participants make monthly contributions, often matched to some degree by employers. The open-end fund accepts these as inflows; there is no need to trade in as would have to happen in a market-traded vehicle. Moreover, if a participant wanted to reallocate money toward a more conservative strategy as she ages, the open-end fund allows that redemption (from the fund itself) and the reinvestment into another fund. Many 401(k)-type plans offer a broad menu, but the selection is often from open-end mutual products as opposed to market-traded vehicles, like closed-end funds. Typically, a sponsor would offer an employee the choice of one or more open-end fund families in which to invest.

Two trends are worth noting in the design of employer-sponsored retirement plans and the offerings of open-end products. The first is the movement toward "default" options in plans. Default is what happens if the investor does not take an action. The default option emerging in retirement plans are the target-date retirement funds. Although many fund families now offer such funds, one of the first to do it was Fidelity, with the Fidelity Freedom Funds. These funds spell out a target retirement date, say 2050, 2040, or 2030, or 2020. Based on an individual's age, say 25 in our example, she would be placed in (or could choose herself) a target-date 2050 plan, which would put her in retirement at age 67.

Target-date retirement funds allow investors to stay in the fund and not have to reallocate their investments as they age. As time progresses and the retirement date draws closer, the fund moves toward a more conservative asset allocation. So, a fund with a target retirement date of 2050 might hold mostly (85–90 percent) stocks, while a 2020 target-date plan might be more balanced between stocks and bonds (close to 50/50).

The second major trend in retirement plans is open architecture. What this means is that open-end funds are offered in a supermarket-type platform. While a single fund family or financial services firm might have baseline administrative duties for the plan, the individual who participates in the plan might be able to choose from the funds of literally hundreds of fund families. This is changing the relationship among fund providers, who now must often cooperate and share information in order to be listed on the platform offered by another fund provider acting as administrator for the plan. For investors who seek a wide variety of choices and investment strategies, this is a desirable platform. This structure raises the issues mentioned earlier regarding branding and recognition of funds.

Recall the earlier discussion of mutual fund attributes, including liquidity, all-equity capital structure, diversification, professional management, and investor services. Recent trends in the law increase the fiduciary duty of a retirement plan sponsor—think of this as the sponsor's duty to see that investors do not hurt themselves. The open-end fund provides plenty of advantages in this context that may help it keep its favorable position in the employer-sponsored retirement plan going forward.

After-Tax Accounts

The discussion now turns from employer-sponsored retirement plans to individual accounts, either tax deferred, such as IRAs, or "ordinary" after-tax accounts. In this environment, the individual has more flexibility in terms of investment vehicles. Limiting the discussion to products that allow investment in a portfolio of assets, as opposed to investing in a particular firm, such as IBM stock, for example, the individual could choose an open-end fund, a closed-end fund, an exchange-traded fund (ETF), or a hedge fund.

Compared to these alternatives, the open-end fund generally offers the most investor-friendly set of attributes. An open-end fund investor can trade each day with the fund acting as the counterparty. This contrasts with exchange-based trading in either the closed-end fund or the ETF. At the end of the spectrum is the hedge fund, which may offer the ability for investors to buy and sell only at specific points in time.

Regarding capital structure, the open-end fund and ETF essentially do not rely on borrowed funds. The closed-end fund may borrow, but only to certain limits prescribed by the 1940 ICA. Hedge funds really do not have any limits on the use of leverage, and through the use of derivatives they can magnify (up or down) their returns dramatically relative to the other investment vehicles discussed in this chapter.

All of these products offer diversification and professional management, but the range of investment strategies that the hedge fund can offer is arguably broader than any of the other three products. This is clearly where hedge funds attempt to make their market, in that they can do what other vehicles cannot.

In sum, outside of the typical employer-sponsored retirement plan, the open-end fund is in direct competition with several vehicles. The competitors tend to offer a riskier platform than the open-end fund, independent of the riskiness of the assets that the vehicle itself holds. Investors should consider the desirable attributes of the open-end fund structure in their decision. The open-end fund offers daily liquidity through the fund itself, diversification of investments, no risks associated with leverage, and professional management and services.

REFERENCES

Bergstresser, D., and J. Porterba. 2004. "Asset Allocation and Location Decisions: Evidence from the Survey of Consumer Finances," *Journal of Public Economics* 88: 1893–1915.

Black, K., C. Ciccotello, and H. Skipper. 2002. "Issues in Comprehensive Personal Financial Planning," *Financial Services Review* 11: 1–9.

Bogle, J. C. 2005. "The Mutual Fund Industry 60 Years Later: For Better or Worse?" *Financial Analysts Journal* 61: 1 (January/February): 15–24.

Braverman, O., S. Kandel, and A. Wohl. 2005. "The (Bad?) Timing of Mutual Fund Investors." Working Paper, Tel Aviv University.

Carhart, M. 1997. "On Persistence in Mutual Fund Performance, *Journal of Finance* 52: 57–82.

Ciccotello, C. S., R. Edelen, J. Greene, and C. Hodges. 2002. "Trading at Stale Prices with Modern Technology: Policy Options for Mutual Funds in the Internet Age." *Virginia Journal of Law and Technology* 7 (3): 6–37.

Ciccotello, C. S., J. Miles, and L. Walsh. 2006. "Should Investors Choose Funds from Focused Families?" *Financial Services Review* 15: 247–264.

Ciccotello, C. S., J. T. Greene, and L. Walsh. 2007. "Supermarket Distribution and Brand Recognition of Open-End Mutual Funds," *Financial Services Review* 16: 309–326.

Dammon, R., C. Spatt, and H. Zhang. 2004. "Optimal Asset Location and Allocation with Taxable and Tax-Deferred Investing," *Journal of Finance* 59: 999–1037.

Edelen, R. 1999. "Investor Flows and the Assessed Performance of Open-End Mutual Funds, *Journal of Financial Economics* 53: 439–466.

French, K. 2008. "Presidential Address: The Cost of Active Investing," *Journal of Finance* 63: 1537–1573.

Greene, J., and C. Ciccotello. 2006. "Mutual Fund Dilution from Market Timing Trades," *Journal of Investment Management* 4: 31–54.

Greene, J. T., and C. W. Hodges. 2002. "The Dilution Impact of Daily Fund Flows on Open-End Mutual Funds," *Journal of Financial Economics* 65: 131–158.

Gremillion, L. 2005. *Mutual Fund Industry Handbook: A Comprehensive Guide for Investment Professionals.* Boston: Boston Institute for Finance.

Gullapalli, D. 2008. "Closed-End Funds that Wield Leverage Expect Trading Delays," *Wall Street Journal*, February 15, C1.

Haslem, J. A., H. K. Baker, and D. M. Smith. 2006. "Are Retail S&P 500 Index Funds a Financial Commodity? Insights for Investors," *Financial Services Review* 15: 99–116.

Hechinger, J. 1999. "Fidelity's Rivals Help It Draw 'Supermarket Shoppers,'" *Wall Street Journal*, May 26, C1.

Horan, S. 2002. "After-Tax Valuation of Tax-Sheltered Assets," *Financial Services Review* 11: 253–275.

Hulbert. M. 2003. "Sometimes, Market Timing Pinches," *New York Times*, September 7, C9: 7.

Kelly, K. 2008. "Bear Probe May Center on Investor Call," *Wall Street Journal*, February 15, C1–C2.

LaPlante, M. 2001. "Influences and Trends in Mutual Fund Expense Ratios," *Journal of Financial Research* 24: 45–63.

Markowitz, H. 1959. *Portfolio Selection: Efficient Diversification of Investments.* New York: John Wiley & Sons.

Massa, M. 2003. "How Do Family Strategies Affect Fund Performance? When Performance Maximization Is Not the Only Game in Town," *Journal of Financial Economics* 67: 249–304.

Masters, B. A. 2003. "Spitzer Alleges Mutual Fund Improprieties," *Washington Post*, September 4, E01.

Milgrom, P., and J. Roberts. 1995. "Complementarities and Fit: Strategy, Structure, and Organizational Change in Manufacturing," *Journal of Accounting and Economics* 19: 179–208.

Pozen, R. 2002. *The Mutual Fund Business*. Boston: Houghton Mifflin.

Rappaport, L. 2008. "Auction-Rate Debt Market Faces Probe," *Wall Street Journal*, April 18, C1.

Reichenstein, W. 2007. "Implications of Principal, Risk, and Returns Sharing across Savings Vehicles," *Financial Services Review* 16: 1–17.

Reid, B., and J. D. Rea. 2003. "Mutual Fund Distribution Channels and Distribution Costs," *Investment Company Institute Perspective* 9 (July): 1–19.

Sirri, E., and P. Tufano. 1998. "Costly Search and Mutual Fund Flows," *Journal of Finance* 53: 1589–1622.

ABOUT THE AUTHOR

Conrad S. Ciccotello is an Associate Professor and Director of Graduate Personal Financial Planning Programs in the Robinson College of Business at Georgia State University. A graduate of Suffolk Law School and a member of both the Pennsylvania and the Supreme Court bars, Professor Ciccotello earned his Ph.D. in Finance in 1993 from the Pennsylvania State University. His primary research interests are in law and finance, with emphasis on financial intermediation, organization, and contracting. Professor Ciccotello's research on the financial planning profession has been cited in the Federal Register and his paper on market timing of mutual funds has been entered into the *Congressional Record* as Senate Banking Committee testimony. Professor Ciccotello currently serves as a Research Fellow in the TIAA-CREF Institute. He has provided expert testimony to the Retirement Committee of the Georgia Senate and served as an investment consultant to the University System of Georgia for the redesign of its defined contribution plan. Since 2004, Professor Ciccotello has been an independent director and audit committee chairman for the Tortoise Capital Advisors' Funds.

CHAPTER 2

Mutual Fund Regulation and Issues

CONRAD S. CICCOTELLO, J.D., Ph.D.
Associate Professor and Director of Graduate Personal Financial Planning Programs,
Georgia State University, Atlanta, Georgia

I recall attending a symposium at the Wharton School at the University of Pennsylvania in 2002. The symposium topic was delegated portfolio management, and I was to present a paper on mutual funds along with several other academics during the one-day conference. In attendance were invited academics, practitioners from mutual fund management firms (such as Vanguard and Fidelity), and some members of the financial media. Our lunchtime speaker was Jason Zweig, a well-known and insightful columnist from *Money* magazine.

During lunch, Jason presented the situation of a high-technology sector open-end fund that had $50 million in assets. That fund then had a spectacular year of performance, with a return of 100 percent on its asset base. Then, almost overnight, $2 billion of new capital flowed into the fund. The next year the fund returned a −75 percent on its asset base. Jason then asked the crowd (rhetorically) what the two-year average performance of the fund would be. Taking the simple average of the two years' returns would give (100 + (−75))/2, or 12.5 percent per year. This is what the "time-weighted" average performance would be and what disclosure of the fund's performance would indicate.

Jason next argued that such a measure was misleading, given the value implications suggested by the returns in the fund and the asset base during those returns. Weighting the returns by the beginning asset base each year would clearly show that doubling $50 million is more than offset by losing 75 percent of $2 billion. He suggested that the academics in the room should do more research on dollar-weighted returns and not take the lazy way out by simply using the simple time-weighted returns reported by funds and captured by electronic databases such as Morningstar. Imagine someone thinking that academics take the lazy way out!

But the academics were soon to have company. Jason next pointed to the investment managers in the room and suggested that advertisements of (superior) prior performance should be carefully considered in light of the tendency for investors to chase returns. The advertisement of good recent performance drives new investment into funds, which drives portfolio managers in that sector to buy stocks, which increases their prices, which in turn drives more investment into funds. This cycle ends with overinvestment and maybe even an asset bubble. Seems plausible, but what fund would want to advertise poor recent performance?

By this point in our lunch, the academics and practitioners were probably both feeling a bit sheepish about our roles in this unfortunate scenario. As Jason was about to finish, however, a question came from the back row of the seminar room (probably from one of those Wharton finance professors). In effect, the question was: What role do the financial press and media (like *Money* magazine) play in this unfortunate situation? The answer is that they often publish lists of "top" funds, and the "top" funds tend to be those that have done well recently. Investors, looking for ways to find the "best" funds with the least amount of effort, consult the rankings and send their money to the "top" funds. Hence, the circle is complete. Academia, the mutual fund industry, and the media combine to propagate poor fund investor choices.

I recall thinking about how complicated the issue of required disclosure is in the case of fund performance. The fund itself has a return, which it is required to report—call it the "time-weighted" return. The time-weighted return is what an investor who holds the fund (without buying or selling any shares) through the entire reporting period experiences. Other investors in that fund, however, might have a very different return from that reported depending on when (and with how much money) they entered and exited the fund during that same period of time. That return is the dollar-weighted return for *that investor*. In theory, every investor could have a different dollar-weighted return depending on when she put money into or took money out of the fund over a given time period. Time-weighted returns and dollar-weighted returns in funds do differ, and differ greatly, as recent research shows (Ciccotello, Greene, Ling, and Rakowski, 2008; Friesen and Sapp, 2007). If dollar-weighted returns differ by investor, however, how would a fund go about disclosing a meaningful dollar-weighted return? The broader policy issue is: What performance should a fund be required to disclose?

Required performance disclosure is but one of a number of challenging regulatory issues currently facing open-end mutual funds. This chapter provides an overview of the regulation of mutual funds before turning to a more detailed discussion of a few of the current regulatory issues that impact investors. While there are a range of current issues, a number of the recent regulatory challenges in open-end funds are linked to the ability investors have to buy and sell the fund each day at net asset value.

The chapter proceeds in this way: After offering some historical perspective on regulation and overall structure of regulation, it first tackles issues related to mutual fund (net asset value) pricing and trading policies. The next section analyzes recent issues involving mutual fund governance and its impact on issues such as fund expenses. The final section returns to the issue of performance disclosure.

HISTORICAL PERSPECTIVE

Since its beginnings around 70 years ago, the open-end fund industry has largely avoided *major* legal troubles until the past few years. To start the discussion, it is useful for the reader to understand what might explain such a long period of relative legal and regulatory calm. Some explanatory power would seem to be related to the open-end product's unique characteristics, namely its self-liquidating feature and its simple (all equity) capital structure. Open-end portfolio managers generally cannot use leverage (borrowed money) to magnify fund returns, and if investors are not happy with a fund's performance, they can redeem funds at net asset value (NAV) on a daily basis.

Many of the largest problems in finance, whether personal investments or corporate matters, typically trace to one or two basic issues: high leverage and/or (low) liquidity. The reader can take note of the 2008 implosion of the real estate market to find both aspects. Highly leveraged investors (e.g., those making a zero down payment on a house) bought highly illiquid assets (real estate). When the value of these assets began to fall, buyers were quickly in a negative equity scenario. Eventually, there were no buyers, and an economic catastrophe ensued. This panic soon spread to the stock market.

In the last few months of 2008, investors had a taste of stock market panic not unlike what happened in the Crash of 1929. Most major indexes lost about 40 percent over just a few months' time in late 2008, and daily stock price volatility was extremely high. A number of the titans of modern finance, including Lehman Brothers, Bear Stearns, and Merrill Lynch, have either failed or been forced to merge in order to avoid failure. The major automakers stand on the brink of collapse. Think about how much more frightening this would be if, in a period of rapidly falling stock prices, investors could not find any other investors with whom to trade.

Closed-end funds (those offering a fixed number of shares) were more popular than open-end funds until the Crash of 1929. Often closed-end funds would lever themselves. Many continue that practice to this day. During the Crash, investors suffered from a lack of disclosure about fund leverage combined with an inability to sell since the (closed-end) fund itself did not stand ready to purchase and redeem shares each day (as an open-end fund would have). A panic ensued.

In contrast, open-end funds must offer daily liquidity, so the funds themselves tend to hold more liquid securities than closed-end funds. Despite the panic, investors in open-end funds could redeem their shares from the open-end company. This brought investors comfort and arguably formed the foundation for the popularity of the open-end product that continues to this day. The stock market implosion of late 2008 has brought back some of the same types of investor behaviors as the Crash of 1929, so a historical perspective on regulation may take on a heightened level of interest for contemporary readers.

Following the Crash of 1929, the federal government began to put a structure into place to address the underlying problems in securities markets, including mutual funds. In the paragraphs that follow, this chapter lays out that fundamental structure as it applies to open-end funds. The goal is to give the reader a sense of the overall regulatory framework. The sections that follow focus in more detail on a few issues that have been of increased interest in the past few years.

REGULATION OF OPEN-END FUNDS

The Securities Act of 1933 pertains to open-end funds as it requires registration if the fund intends to offer shares to the public. The broad goal of this act was to protect investors from fraudulent sales and misrepresentations by those selling shares. The act requires funds to provide a prospectus that discloses the key aspects of the fund. Open-end funds also typically provide additional disclosure in a Statement of Additional Information. While some of the elements of required disclosure have been well settled for decades, several disclosure topics remain a lively topic of debate. As this chapter's introductory story illustrates, required fund performance disclosure is one area that is still controversial. Disclosures about fund management (advisory), marketing and distribution (12b-1) fees, and other costs (such as brokerage fees) also remain hot topics.

While there is lively policy debate about disclosure requirements in several areas, it is clear that funds' failure to follow their prospectus can be very costly. For example, some funds' selective failure to enforce trading restrictions spelled out in their prospectus was the major legal "hammer" in the mutual fund market timing scandal, which is discussed in more detail later in this chapter.

The Securities Exchange Act of 1934 also impacts open-end mutual funds. This act focuses on regulating the trading of securities, requiring various types of record keeping, qualifications, and business practices for broker-dealers. In open-end funds, these rules pertain mainly to funds' distributors and transfer agents. The latter are involved with a number of the interactions that a shareholder has with the fund, including account maintenance, processing of trades, dividend and capital gains payments, and document transfer (Gremillion, 2005, p. 233).

While the 1933 and 1934 Securities Acts apply to open-end funds as well as to other financial products, the Investment Advisory Act of 1940 targets the investment management industry more directly. The Investment Advisory Act requires those advising mutual funds to register with the Securities and Exchange Commission (SEC). The act also regulates the contract between the investment adviser and funds. Some of the key contractual provisions are those that specify a maximum contract length between adviser and fund (two years), those that give the fund the ability to terminate the agreement (with at least 60 days' notice), and those that require the approval of a majority of the outside directors for adviser–fund contract renewal. For those readers desiring more details, Gremillion (2005) is an excellent resource.

The Investment Company Act of 1940 is the major piece of legislation pertaining to open-end mutual funds. The SEC describes the scope and intent of the act quite nicely on its Web page (www.sec.gov/about/laws.shtml):

> *This Act regulates the organization of companies, including mutual funds, that engage primarily in investing, reinvesting, and trading in securities, and whose own securities are offered to the investing public. The regulation is designed to minimize conflicts of interest that arise in these complex operations. The Act requires these companies to disclose their financial condition and investment policies to investors when stock is initially sold and, subsequently, on a regular basis. The focus of the Act is on disclosure to the investing public of information about the fund and its investment objectives, as well as on investment company structure and operations. It is important to remember that the Act does not permit the SEC to directly supervise the investment decisions or activities of these companies or judge the merits of their investments.*

This quotation captures the overall philosophy of the Investment Company Act, which is based on disclosure. The emphasis is on those areas of operation where there could be a conflict of interest between the adviser and the investor. The next paragraphs highlight a few of those areas in the law. Some tie to the more in-depth discussion of contemporary issues in subsequent sections.

At the outset, the reader should recognize that the Investment Company Act carves out a special category for the open-end mutual fund. The open-end fund is deemed an open-end management company because of the investor's ability to redeem shares of the fund for cash upon request. This distinction matters as it goes to a fundamental characteristic of the open-end fund and one that distinguishes it from other investment structures: its self-liquidating nature. The open-end management company characterization also is important because the rules for open- and closed-end management companies (as well as for other types of investment companies) also differ in other dimensions.

The Investment Company Act of 1940 covers five primary areas of open-end operations: fund management, sales practices, investment advisory fees, fund capital structures, and financial statements and accounting (Sjostrom, 2006). Within each of these areas, particular sections are devoted to issues where there are potential conflicts of interest between fund management and investors. For example, section 10 requires the fund to provide detailed statements of its policies and structure. This section also outlines the requirement that at least 40 percent of the fund's directors not be "interested persons" in the fund. These are the "independent" directors. If the fund is to have various sorts of exemptions from other requirements under the act, then a majority (greater than 50 percent) of the directors must be independent.

Section 13 of the act gives shareholders the right to vote on certain matters, including a change in investment policy. Section 15 of the act requires a written investment contract, which is negotiated by the adviser and the independent directors. Section 17 prohibits affiliated transactions, so the advisers or other service providers cannot conduct financial transactions with the fund. This section also requires that securities be held in custody and that those who have access to securities or cash be adequately bonded. In addition, governance is accomplished by the section 12 requirement that the fund's annual reports be audited by an independent party. Usually this is an accounting firm (e.g., Ernst & Young). As was discussed in Chapter 1, open-end funds cannot issue senior securities (e.g., debt in an equity fund). That prohibition is contained in sections 12 and 18 of the act.

This sampling of provisions illustrates some of the ways that the 1940 Investment Company Act addresses conflicts of interest between investors and fund managers. For example, suppose that open-end funds could freely borrow money. If the fund manager were paid as a percentage of assets under management, perhaps the manager would be inclined to overleverage the fund and increase risk. Assessing the potential for a conflict of interest is a useful approach to consider any regulatory issue under the scope of the act.

Having built a foundation for open-end fund regulation, this chapter now turns to discussing a few regulatory issues that have been in the headlines in the recent past.

RECENT REGULATORY ISSUES IN OPEN-END FUNDS

The open-end mutual fund's self-liquidating feature, the ability for investors to buy and sell shares each day at NAV, has brought about several regulatory challenges. This feature sets up two kinds of investors in a fund: those who buy and sell (trade) a lot (even daily) and those who buy and hold funds for long periods (i.e., they might go years without trading). The fund management and regulatory challenges in open-end funds often involve striking a reasonable balance in the interests of these two groups. Consider for a moment that those who want to hold funds for long periods are "sheep" and those that want to trade funds daily are "wolves." Suppose further that those who want to trade in and out of the fund in short intervals harm fund performance and/or impose a burden on fund management. Ideally, the sheep need to be protected from the risks associated with wolves' behavior, or at least be adequately warned about them.

How could the sheep be protected from the wolves? One way is to limit trading, either via individual fund rules (such as those in a fund prospectus that limit number of round-trip [buy-and-sell] trades per year by an investor, e.g.) and/or by regulatory fiat, such as a mandatory fee imposed for sales of fund shares held for only short periods of time. These sound appealing until one recognizes that trading limits or costs reduce liquidity for all investors, even some of the "innocent" sheep who might want to trade based on a change in their investment circumstances. Plus limits on liquidity raise the cost for all investors to get out of the fund and, if high enough, could trap the investors with a poorly performing manager. Trading restrictions are one regulatory area where conflicts of interests between investors and fund managers, as well as those between investors themselves, remain an ongoing challenge.

NAV Pricing and Trading Policies

Every investment product structure has strengths and weaknesses, and the open-end fund is no exception. So where would the open-end fund be vulnerable? Consider the daily self-liquidation feature. The *fund itself* stands ready to buy and sell to individual shareholders at NAV each day. Consider that a fund can hold billions of dollars in assets, made up of thousands of individual accounts. Given its size alone, such a large fund presents an interesting target for fraud. What if an individual can take a small amount of money from a very large number of other individuals? In this case, the amount taken from each individual is so small as to make it unnoticeable or not worth pursuing a remedy even if noticed. If the target number of victims is large enough, then the scam artist can make a lot of money, even if the per-victim rate is very small.

The words *fund* and *target* were used in the same sentence on purpose. As Ciccotello, Edelen, Greene, and Hodges (2002) state: "Suppose that the calculated NAV were to deviate systematically and predictably from the value of the fund's underlying assets." Assume further that mutual fund trading technology allows rapid order submission for large numbers of shares each day. Together, these are a mix for trouble. If a trader could take systematic advantage of predictability in movements of a fund's NAV and trade large amounts of shares daily, that trader could trade at favorable prices. In the context of an open-end fund, that would translate into wealth taken by the trading shareholders and extracted from buy-and-hold shareholders. Hence, the one takes from the many, and typically in small amounts each day.

How could the NAV be biased? As it turns out, pricing of open-end fund shares is not a new problem, having vexed regulators from the birth of open-end funds in the 1920s. Many of the early problems were due to rules that priced the fund shares *before* the orders to buy or sell at that price were made (backward pricing). Responding to what it perceived to be widespread abuses that resulted from this practice, the SEC adopted Rule 22c-1 in 1968. Reversing what had been the norm (backward pricing), Rule 22c-1 requires funds to adopt a forward-pricing rule in which they sell or redeem shares at the NAV that is first computed *after* the order is received.

Backward pricing is an example of a broader issue of traders being able to buy or sell at a "stale" NAV. That is, the price at which the investor could buy or sell the fund (the NAV) did not reflect all market information when the trader executed the trade. So a stale price trader had an advantage somewhat like placing a bet on a horse race *after* watching the race. Problems with stale prices are worse in open-end funds that are domiciled in one location but hold assets that are traded on markets in other countries (Bhargava, Bose, and Dubofsky, 1998). Consider the situation with a U.S.-domiciled fund that holds international (say, stocks traded on Asian exchanges) assets. When the fund computes its price as of 4:00 P.M. Eastern Standard Time (EST), most Asian markets are closed. The prices of those Asian stocks have not changed to reflect market movements in the United States during that day. As such, they are "stale" prices (Chalmers, Edelen, and Kadlec, 2001). Academic research has shown that prices in international markets tend to follow U.S. moves the following day, thus opening up a pattern for trading in U.S. mutual funds that can "dilute" buy-and-hold shareholders while rewarding the stale price traders (Greene and Ciccotello, 2006; Greene and Hodges, 2002). The problem became extreme in the case when markets are highly volatile, as in the late 1990s in Asian markets. On Tuesday, October 28, 1997, the Hong Kong market index declined about 14 percent, following the previous day's decline on the New York Stock Exchange. Later on Tuesday, October 28, the New York market rallied. U.S. funds holding Hong Kong securities were now faced with a dilemma: Should they compute NAV from the Tuesday closing prices in Hong Kong? That would seem to be a stale price.

In that scenario, some funds concluded that the closing prices in Hong Kong did not represent "fair value" and calculated their funds' NAV based on another method. For the purposes of calculating value, the Investment Company Act of 1940 divides securities into two classes. Where securities have "readily available" market quotations, "current market value" should be used. Current market value is generally accepted to be a security's last quoted sales price on a national exchange. Where securities do not have a "readily available" market quotation, "fair value" should be used. The fund's board of directors has the power to determine "fair value" in good faith. As detailed in Ciccotello et al. (2002), the SEC has made a number of recent attempts to clarify the use of fair value in terms of both application and disclosure.

Fund Pricing and the (Late) Trading Scandal

On Labor Day weekend in September 2003, then New York Attorney General Elliott Spitzer broke the Canary trading scandal (Masters, 2003; *State of New York*, 2003). The Canary hedge fund attacked the open-end structure's self-liquidating feature in an innovative manner. While international funds were known to have vulnerability to market timing trades due to links between markets as just described, domestic funds (holding domestic securities) were thought to be (relatively) safe from market timing trades because their prices were not stale. At 4:00 P.M., for example, when the stock fund computed its NAV using closing prices, these were the 4:00 P.M. prices of the stocks in the fund. Among Canary's innovations were the alleged submissions of orders as late as 9:00 P.M. EST to buy or sell at the 4:00 P.M. price. Often the submissions of orders would relate to moves in the after-market (post–4:00 P.M.) futures market. In effect, Canary had transformed a domestic fund into an international fund in terms of staleness.

Being able to trade at 9:00 P.M. for a 4:00 P.M. price is valuable. The price move from 4:00 P.M. to 9:00 P.M. today can shed light on the market move tomorrow just as the movements in the U.S. stock market today can shed light on international stock market moves tomorrow. In a domestic fund, the odds of predicting the next day's market return (as either positive or negative) are roughly 50 percent, the flip of a fair coin, if one trades at 4:00 P.M. today. With the five-hour after-market advantage today, the odds of correctly predicting a positive or negative market return tomorrow become closer to 66 percent. If one conducts 100 round trips in a fund a year using $100M per buy order, and one is right 66 percent of the time (next day), this lucrative (although illegal) operation for the trader can be quite damaging to the buy-and-hold shareholder (Damato, 2003; Hulbert, 2003).

> Canary allegedly submitted late orders under several (false) pretenses, including masquerading as a qualified pension investor (which at that time could submit late orders due to the time lag for bundling all of the individual orders together). This abuse and the concern for the anonymity of bundled orders have led the SEC to adopt more stringent order submission guidelines. In December 2003 the SEC proposed: amendments dictating that an order to purchase or redeem fund shares would receive the current day's price only if the fund, its designated transfer agent, or a registered securities clearing agency receives the order by the time that the fund establishes for calculating its net asset value. The amendments are designed to prevent unlawful late trading in fund shares (See SEC, Amendments to Rules Governing Pricing of Mutual Fund Shares, 2003).

In sum, the rules surrounding enforcement of prospectus trading limits, fair valuation of fund shares, and timely order submission have become much more important in an era where large (and sometimes bundled) trades can be submitted electronically through various channels to the open-end fund (Ciccotello et al., 2002).

CURRENT REGULATORY ISSUES IN FUNDS

Board Governance

The mutual fund market timing scandal went beyond the escapades of the Canary hedge fund. Over the period from 2003 to 2006, regulators implicated a number of other late traders and mutual fund families in the scandal. In some of these cases, the mutual fund had made explicit special arrangements for certain investors to trade in excess of stated prospectus limits. Often this was done in exchange for that investor's agreement to put buy-and-hold (sticky assets) cash into other funds in the family. In other cases, the market timers had no explicit agreement with the fund but nevertheless traded in and out of funds by switching accounts or by taking on other "cloaking" devices. Regulators often alleged that these timers were "tolerated" by the family, although there were circumstances where timers were kicked out of funds (by the fund's "timing police") for their trading behavior. As a result of this timing phenomenon, fund families did (in general) step up their awareness of investor trading practices.

The market timing scandal was a big deal. Over $2 billion to date has been placed in settlement funds for disbursement to open-end fund shareholders who were harmed by market timing trades. Market timing was the largest scandal ever to hit the open-end fund industry, and it has had several regulatory spillovers. Recall that the major goal of the 1940 Act is to address areas of conflict of interest between investors and fund managers. Allowing preferential trading rights (in violation of prospectus limits) to some investors in return for sticky assets looks like such a conflict of interest.

The "timing" of the market timing scandal is also informative as to the nature of the conflict-of-interest issues at hand. Some of the leading "creative" investors with strategies to market time (or late trade in) funds made their pitch to funds in years 2001 and 2002. Recall that by late 2002, the market had dropped about 25 percent (based on the Dow Jones index) and over 50 percent (based on the Nasdaq index) since early 2000. Mutual funds advisory fees are normally assessed a flat percentage of assets under management. With declining asset values and flat percentage fees, the amount of money that the fund manager gets to manage the fund goes down—even if no investors pull their money out of the fund. If asset values fall 50 percent, then revenues to the fund manager are down significantly—indeed, exactly 50 percent if that management (advisory) fee is a flat percentage of assets. So a market timer's promises to add sticky assets to one fund in exchange for the ability to trade in excess of prospectus limits in another made for an interesting business proposition for some fund managers in this period, when management fees were down.

These market timing offers set off quite a struggle in some fund families between compliance personnel and marketing (sales) managers. The former argued that the deal would violate prospectus (harming buy-and-hold shareholders); the latter looked at more of the revenue upside—and perhaps thought that market timing in a domestic fund would not hurt shareholders anyway since the NAV was not stale. It is apparent in some cases that the sales side won the battle, although the war ended up being a different story.

For the reader, the important point is to see the clear conflict of interest between shareholders in the fund (especially those who buy and hold shares) and fund management in this matter. How could this happen? Why weren't shareholders' interests protected by the board of directors? One pressure point in the 1940 Investment Company Act to deal with conflicts of interest like this is the structure of the mutual fund board of directors. Recall from earlier in the chapter that most mutual fund boards have a simple majority of independent (disinterested) directors. Where were the independent directors in preventing these deals with late traders? In the aftermath of the scandal, the SEC promulgated changes requiring that three-quarters of the board be independent directors and that funds have an independent board chairman. The mutual fund industry did not agree with these changes, and litigation over them has taken place over the past few years. As of late 2008, the changes had not been implemented due mainly to legal procedural issues. Despite the legal holdups, some funds have voluntarily changed board structure to comply with the enhanced independence standards.

Would the enhanced independence standards be a net benefit for mutual fund investors? Added board independence certainly would seem to favor investor interests over those of fund management, although the costs of adding independent board members to get to a three-quarters independent position might be nontrivial—especially in small mutual fund families or funds. Director fees are paid by the funds themselves. Making the chairman independent would probably also require additional compensation and administrative support. Recent research does not provide a clear answer to whether the benefits would outweigh the costs; mixed evidence has been found regarding the relationship of fund board independence, fees, and fund performance (Kong and Tang, 2008; Meschke, 2007).

Board governance in a mutual fund has some unusual features relative to an operating company scenario. With an operating company, such as IBM or Microsoft, for example, the board of directors can hire and fire the chief executive officer (CEO) while keeping (in many cases) at least some of the rest of the company's officers to operate the firm in the interim. In a mutual fund, the board essentially hires or fires the entire operating company through renewal or nonrenewal of the manager's investment contract. While CEOs are often fired in operating companies, investment managers are very seldom replaced in mutual funds, perhaps due in part to the logistical issues associated with replacing all the functions that the manager controls. Consider also that mutual funds have a substitute governance mechanism: daily liquidity. If a shareholder does not like the policies or performance of the fund, she can sell out at NAV. But that investor does need to have adequate disclosure of what the performance and policies are in order to make an informed decision.

The real problem in the market timing case as it relates to governance may be that the timing arrangements were not disclosed to investors. As Ciccotello et al. (2002) argue, fund policies ought to make it clear to investors what type of trading environment is tolerated in the fund—for *all* investors. If the fund indeed wants to cater to wolves (market timers), then buy-and-hold shareholders (sheep) ought to know that. Some fund groups (e.g., Rydex) cater to investors who like to trade. As to the board structure issue, whether the fund's board knew about these arrangements and failed to act (to either stop them or compel their disclosure) or whether they were hidden from the board remain interesting questions. In either case, it seems likely that a more independent board would at least have been more likely to act (or discover the market timing side deals), although it is hard to argue that this more independent board structure would have provided a guarantee.

Fees

The market timing scandal also highlighted another area where there are potential conflicts of interest between fund investors and fund managers. The major cost in operating a mutual fund is the advisory fee, normally a percentage of assets under management. This is the charge levied by the adviser to manage the fund. The market timing scandal revealed that some funds were willing to sacrifice their investors' interests for higher fees. In some of the regulatory proceedings involving market timing, an advisory fee reduction schedule was included as part of the overall settlement. Fee reductions were often part of the deal when the New York Attorney General's office was involved with the case.

Aside from the settlements related to market timing, the issue of mutual fund fees has been debated by both academics and practitioners for a long while. In a provocative article, Freeman and Brown (2001) argue that open-end mutual fund investors are charged more for investment advisory services than are pension fund investors. Since the difference between the two groups of investors is primarily the governance mechanism, the authors assert that the costs differences are evidence of a failure of mutual fund boards to protect shareholders' interests when negotiating the advisory fee since pension funds have lower fees. Is the comparison a valid one? A number of class actions have been brought against mutual fund companies in recent years for excessive fees, seeking relief under Section 36(d) of the Investment Company Act of 1940. To this point, these cases generally have failed to bring any remuneration to investors. Section 36(d) is a high legal hurdle; in order to win, plaintiffs must show that fees must bear not reasonable relationship to performance. Also, courts typically have rejected comparisons between mutual funds and pension funds. Moreover, and unfortunately for plaintiffs, their counsel often has chosen to sue mutual fund families for excessive fees based on the fund's involvement in the market timing scandal. Some of these market timing funds and fund families have rather low fees (at least by comparison to other mutual fund families), a fact that makes a case for excessive fees tough to build.

The average advisory fee for an actively managed fund is about 0.68 percent (Gremillion, 2005). Mutual fund management can be highly profitable; indeed, the regulatory settlements in the market timing cases reduced fees by as much as a third in some cases. These settlements reinforced the belief that effective fund management could go on at lower cost to shareholders. Some of the controversy about the high cost of funds has sprung from fund managers' failing to pass along the benefits of scale economy to investors as funds have grown larger. Stated succinctly, mutual fund companies are not passing the economies of scale on to their customers as funds grow bigger in size. One way to accomplish this might be to have "break points" in fees, where the manager gets a lower percentage of the assets as a fee when the fund reaches a certain size. For example, a break-point fee schedule might be: 0.75 percent of assets for the first $1B under management and 0.65 percent of assets thereafter.

Fee defenders, however, point to the vast number of choices investors have, among both active and passive funds, and the liquidity of funds that permits relatively easy switching. The logic is that if fees are too high, investors will move their money. Moreover, unlike the undisclosed arrangements with market timers, advisory fees are disclosed, allowing for informed choice. Ongoing discussions about fee disclosure remain, however, and raise several issues and questions. First, there are a large number of funds from which to choose, making investors' basic search for a fund a non-trivial task. Even upon choosing a specific fund, can investors be expected to sort through the large volume of documentation to find the actual fees? Are fees disclosures reasonably transparent? For more in-depth discussion of these topics, the reader should consult Haslem (2003, 2004, 2006); Haslem, Baker, and Smith (2005, 2006); and Haslem, Smith, and Baker (2007).

Beyond the advisory fee issue, another concern regarding conflicts of interest involves charging investors for marketing and distribution (12b-1 fees) and other payments to the fund manager for preferential steering of fund business, such as brokerage services. Whether investors should be paying for fund marketing and distribution (Dukes, English, and Davis, 2006), or whether fund service provider "soft-dollar" payments to the fund manager made in exchange for business considerations remain issues hotly debated in the academic and professional literatures (Steil and Perfumo, 2003).

The market price declines in late 2008 do put an interesting perspective on fees, at least with regard to stock mutual funds. Over the past 25 years ending in 2008, stock prices have appreciated tremendously, adding greatly to the revenues of fund managers. Moreover, lots of new money flowed into stock funds as asset values appreciated, adding to the total assets under management. Much of this inflow over the past two decades is in retirement funds (in the form of 401[k] contributions). But in late 2008, stock markets worldwide lost about half their value, basically cutting revenues for many fund managers in half. So it appears that the markets have done what the lawsuits have generally failed to do: cut fund manager compensation. Moreover, investors followed their typical pattern and withdrew money from stock funds during late 2008, further decreasing fund manager revenue. Going forward, if depressed stock prices continue, it will be interesting to follow two issues regarding fees:

1. Will break points become more popular? Break points offer higher fees at lower asset values under management and reflect the notion of scale economy better than flat percentage fees.
2. Will lower fees drive consolidation in the mutual fund industry, as smaller and higher-cost families are unable to survive in the lower revenue environment?

Performance Reporting

The last section in this survey of current regulatory issues and mutual funds concerns the issue of performance reporting. As this chapter's opening story suggests, this issue presents some significant regulatory challenges. It is an interesting issue to use to summarize a chapter about regulation, however, as it also highlights the tension between the economy of presenting the performance of the mutual fund as a whole and the performance of the literally thousands of individual investors within that fund. This tension reflects the overall challenge with the disclosure-based rationale of the 1940 Act. If the demands for more complete and transparent disclosure also lead to an increase in the volume and complexity of disclosure, the net result of more disclosure could be negative. The SEC continues to wrestle with both the required elements of disclosure and the various methods of communication to shareholders (SEC, 2007).

Funds are required to report time-weighted performance for 1-, 5-, and 10-year periods, if they have been in existence that long (Jain and Wu, 2000). Funds must report at least 1-year's return ending with the latest calendar quarter. Jain and Wu (2000) observe that funds tend to advertise after periods of good performance and that performance does not persist postadvertisement. Performance reporting issues in open-end funds are especially interesting because of fund liquidity. Jain and Wu find that advertising funds attract large amounts of new money, which tends to arrive just in time to receive poor returns.

Consistent with the research by Jain and Wu, several researchers, including Friesen and Sapp (2007) and Ciccotello et al. (2008), have documented that time-weighted performance of funds is greater than dollar-weighted performance of funds. Recall that time-weighted performance is the return of the fund taken as a whole, measured over some period, such as a year. So if the NAV of the fund were $10 on January 1 and $15 on December 31, and the fund paid no dividends, its time-weighted return is 50 percent. An investor owning the fund at the beginning of the year and holding it throughout the year, without buying or selling any shares, earns the time-weighted return.

In contrast, dollar weighting considers the beginning and ending sizes of the fund as well as inflows and outflows during the period. Computing a fund's dollar-weighted returns is more complicated than computing time-weighted returns, and various methods have been applied (Ciccotello et al., 2008; Friesen and Sapp, 2007). Moreover, every investor buying or selling during the time period would have his or her own dollar-weighted return.

The differences in time–dollar-weighted fund returns are quite noticeable. In stock mutual funds, dollar-weighted returns are 15 percent lower than time-weighted returns (8.45 percent versus 10.29 percent on an average annual basis) over the sample period from 1929 through 2005. This means new money tends to flow into funds just before stock market returns decline and flow out of funds just before stock market returns increase. That causes a dollar-weighted return to be less than a time-weighted return. This pattern of returns is consistent with Jain and Wu's (2000) observation that funds with good recent performance tend to advertise and attract new money. In sum, open-end fund investors tend to chase recent performance, and flows into funds tend to be poorly timed (Edelen, 1999).

These time–dollar differences in performance are huge, and would seem to demand adequate disclosure to investors. Consider the fact that huge legal battles about mutual fund fees are occurring over 10 to 20 basis points in an annual fee, while the annual time–dollar performance difference stated above is 180 basis points. Given this large difference between what the required disclosure states as the return and what investors actually are earning, what should a fund be required to disclose and report in a prospectus?

Clearly there is no simple answer to this question, and the problem gets more complicated if one considers multiyear periods and returns. Some fund data firms, such as Morningstar, are considering the addition of dollar-weighted measures; the challenge is to establish a standard that will be simple enough to convey meaning but rigorous enough to have meaning.

In closing this chapter on fund regulation, performance reporting provides a useful example of a number of the regulatory issues impacting open-end funds. These issues generally tend to rest fundamentally on the open-end product's unique attribute: its self-liquidating feature. Because of the daily liquidity funds offer to investors, large amounts of inflows and outflows can happen each day. Investors tend to chase good performance, spurred on by fund advertisements and favorable financial media rankings. Modern technology has made trading in and out of funds very fast and simple. Forget the old days when one had to (snail) mail in a check to buy shares, with the transaction taking days if not weeks to clear. Now trading can be done electronically. The number of distribution channels in open-end funds has also grown dramatically (Reid and Rea, 2003), and some of these (such as mutual fund supermarkets) submit bundled orders such that the open-end fund may not even know the identity of the individual investors. Rapid trading has presented several challenges to fund management, the most fundamental of which is to ensure that the daily NAV is not calculated with any systematic bias that would allow a trader to take advantage. In addition, given the multiple distribution channels, enforcing trading limits, when they exist, is not a simple task.

In sum, the goal of the 1940 Act is to protect investors against conflicts of interest. Some of those interest misalignments are with fund management. What the contemporary issues suggest is that conflicts of interest can also exist between subgroups of investors, such as those who want to trade a lot and those who do not. Moving forward, regulation must consider the range of investors (and distribution channels) in open-end funds to harmonize a more complicated set of demands.

REFERENCES

Bhargava, R., A. Bose, and D. Dubofsky. 1998. "Exploiting International Stock Market Correlations with Open-End International Mutual Funds," *Journal of Business Finance & Accounting* 25: 765–773.

Chalmers, J., R. Edelen, and G. Kadlec. 2001. "On the Perils of Security Pricing by Financial Intermediaries: The Wildcard Option in Transacting Mutual Fund Shares," *Journal of Finance* 56: 2209–2236.

Ciccotello, C., R. Edelen, J. Greene, and C. Hodges. 2002. "Trading at Stale Prices with Modern Technology: Policy Options for Mutual Funds in the Internet Age," *Virginia Journal of Law and Technology* 7: 6–37.

Ciccotello, C., J. Greene, L. Ling, and D. Rakowski. 2008. "Timing and Scale Effects from Flows in Open-End Funds." Working Paper, Georgia State University.

Damato, K. 2003. "Timing at Mutual Funds Can Cost 2% a Year," *Wall Street Journal*, September 19, C1.

Dukes, P., P. English, and S. Davis. 2006. "Mutual Fund Mortality, 12b-1 Fees, and the Net Expense Ratio," *Journal of Financial Research* 29 (2): 235–252.

Edelen, R. 1999. "Investor Flows and the Assessed Performance of Open-End Mutual Funds," *Journal of Financial Economics* 53: 439–466.

Freeman, J., and S. Brown. 2001. "Mutual Fund Advisory Fees: The Cost of Conflict of Interest," *Journal of Corporation Law* 26: 609–673.

Friesen, G., and T. Sapp. 2007. "Mutual Fund Flows and Investor Returns: An Empirical Examination of Fund Investor Timing Ability," *Journal of Banking and Finance* 31: 2796–2816.

Greene, J., and C. Ciccotello. 2006. "Mutual Fund Dilution from Market Timing Trades," *Journal of Investment Management* 4: 31–54.

Greene, J. T., and C. W. Hodges. 2002. "The Dilution Impact of Daily Fund Flows on Open-End Mutual Funds," *Journal of Financial Economics* 65: 131–158.

Gremillion, L. 2005. *Mutual Fund Industry Handbook: A Comprehensive Guide for Investment Professionals.* Boston: Boston Institute for Finance.

Haslem, J. A. 2003. *Mutual Funds: Risk and Performance for Decision Making.* Oxford, UK: Blackwell Publishing.

Haslem, J. A. 2004. "A Tool for Improved Mutual Funds Transparency," *Journal of Investing* 13: 3 (Fall): 54–64.

Haslem, J. A. 2006. "Assessing Mutual Fund Expenses and Transaction Costs," *Journal of Investing* 15: 4 (Winter): 52–56.

Haslem, J. A., H. K. Baker, and D. M. Smith. 2005. "Excessive Mutual Fund Expenses also Mean Higher Risk and Worse Performance," *Journal of Indexes* 7: 4 (July/August): 40–41, 50.

Haslem, J. A., H. K. Baker, and D. M. Smith. 2006. "Are Retail S&P 500 Index Funds a Financial Commodity? Insights for Investors," *Financial Services Review* 15: 99–116.

Haslem, J. A., D. M. Smith, and H. K. Baker. 2007. "Identification and Performance of Equity Mutual Funds with High Management Fees and Expense Ratios," *Journal of Investing* 16: 1 (Spring): 32–51.

Hulbert. M. 2003. "Sometimes, Market Timing Pinches," *New York Times*, September 7, 9.

Jain, P., and J. Wu. 2000. "Truth in Mutual Fund Advertising: Evidence on Future Performance and Fund Flows," *Journal of Finance* 55: 937–958.

Kong, S., and D. Tang. 2008. "Unitary Boards and Fund Governance," *Journal of Financial Research* 31: 3 (Fall), 193–224.

Masters, B. 2003. "Spitzer Alleges Mutual Fund Improprieties," *Washington Post*, September 4, E01.

Meschke, F. 2007. "An Empirical Examination of Mutual Fund Boards." Available at SSRN: http://ssrn.com/abstract=676901.

Reid, B., and J. D. Rea. 2003. "Mutual Fund Distribution Channels and Distribution Costs," *Investment Company Institute Perspective* 9 (July): 1–19.

Securities and Exchange Commission, 2003. "Amendments to Rules Governing Pricing of Mutual Fund Shares." Available at www.sec.gov/rules/proposed/ic-26288.htm.

Securities and Exchange Commission. 2007. "Enhanced Disclosure and New Prospectus Delivery Options for Registered Investment Companies," *Federal Register* 72(230), November 30.

Securities and Exchange Commission. 2008. "How the SEC Protects Investors, Maintains Market Integrity." Available at: www.sec.gov/about/laws.shtml.

Sirri, E., and P. Tufano. 1998. "Costly Search and Mutual Fund Flows," *Journal of Finance* 53: 1589–1622.

Sjostrom, W. 2006. "Tapping the Reservoir: Mutual Fund Litigation Under Section 36(a) of the Investment Company Act of 1940," *Kansas Law Review* 54: 251–305.

State of New York v. Canary Capital Partners LLC, Canary Investment Management LLC, Canary Capital Partners LTD, and Edward J. Stern, 2003. Available at http://www.oag.state.ny.us/media_center/2003/sep/canary_complaint.pdf.

Steil, B., and D. Perfumo. 2003. *The Economics of Soft Dollar Trading*. New York: Efficient Frontiers, LLC.

Tang, D., and S. Kong. 2008. "Unitary Boards and Mutual Fund Governance," *Journal of Financial Research* 31 (3): 193–224.

ABOUT THE AUTHOR

Conrad S. Ciccotello is an Associate Professor and Director of Graduate Personal Financial Planning Programs in the Robinson College of Business at Georgia State University. A graduate of Suffolk Law School and a member of both the Pennsylvania and Supreme Court Bars, Professor Ciccotello earned his Ph.D. in Finance in 1993 from the Pennsylvania State University. His primary research interests are in law and finance, with emphasis on financial intermediation, organization, and contracting. Professor Ciccotello's research on the financial planning profession has been cited in the Federal Register and his paper on market timing of mutual funds has been entered into the *Congressional Record* as Senate Banking Committee testimony. Professor Ciccotello currently serves as a Research Fellow in the TIAA-CREF Institute. He has provided expert testimony to the Retirement Committee of the Georgia Senate and served as an investment consultant to the University System of Georgia for the redesign of its defined contribution plan. Since 2004, Professor Ciccotello has been an independent director and audit committee chairman for the Tortoise Capital Advisors' Funds.

CHAPTER 3

The Economics of Mutual Funds

DAVID M. SMITH, Ph.D., CFA
Associate Professor of Finance and Director of the Center for Institutional Investment
Management, the University at Albany (SUNY)

Investment companies, and mutual funds in particular, have become a dominant investment vehicle. Total investment dollars in mutual funds grew very slowly in the decades subsequent to passage of the Investment Company Act of 1940, but this was because the growth occurred on a very small base. According to the Investment Company Institute (ICI, 2009), the U.S. annual growth rate for open-end mutual fund net assets between 1940 and 2008 was 15.8 percent. Gremillion (2005) reports that by 1994, mutual fund assets had grown to a level that exceeded the total deposits in Federal Deposit Insurance Corporation–insured banks. Since then, mutual fund net assets have increased more than fivefold, and mutual funds are now owned by more than half of all U.S. households.

This chapter discusses the size and market concentration of the mutual fund industry, the market entry and exit of mutual funds, the benefits and costs of mutual fund size changes, principal benefits and costs of ownership from fund shareholders' perspective, and mutual fund governance.

SIZE AND STRUCTURE OF THE MUTUAL FUND INDUSTRY

The ICI (2009) reports that net assets of mutual funds worldwide have risen from $11.9 trillion at year-end 2000 to $19.0 trillion at year-end 2008. About 51 percent of these net assets are in U.S. mutual funds. The four other countries with more than 3 percent of the global total are Luxembourg (10 percent), France (8 percent), Australia (4 percent), and Ireland (4 percent). Although Luxembourg may appear an unexpected member on the list, Khorana, Servaes, and Tufano (2005) note that Luxembourg's strict bank secrecy laws have helped its mutual fund industry prosper. They find that the sizes of individual countries' fund industries are positively affected by the existence of regulatory requirements to start a fund and issue a prospectus, and negatively related to the amount of time or money required to set up a fund.

Based on data from Morningstar (2009), as of December 2008, the U.S. mutual fund industry was composed of 607 fund families (or complexes or sponsors) offering one or more open-end mutual funds to retail and/or institutional investors.

Industry membership has fluctuated between 638 families in December 2000 and 576 in December 2005. Despite constituent numbers that would suggest fierce competition, the industry is dominated by relatively few fund families. At year-end 1998, the top 10 mutual fund families had 48 percent of the total assets under management in the open-end fund market. By year-end 2008, the total share for the top 10 was 59 percent.

The largest mutual fund family in the United States is Vanguard, with about $1.1 trillion in assets under management at year-end 2008, followed by Fidelity Investments and American Funds with about $0.9 trillion and $0.7 trillion, respectively. Vanguard has the largest dollar amount of funds under passive management, while Fidelity has the largest amount actively managed.

This trend toward increased dominance by large fund families is also revealed using the Herfindahl Index, another measure of industry market share concentration. The Herfindahl Index is calculated by squaring the market share of each industry constituent and summing across all constituents. If one fund family has a virtual monopoly, the value would approach 10,000 (i.e., $\approx 100^2$). The theoretical minimum value for the Herfindahl Index reflects a scenario in which market share is uniformly distributed across industry constituents, and is calculated as 10,000 divided by the number of industry constituents. The Herfindahl Index for open-end mutual funds has risen from 380 in 1998 to 617 in 2008. If assets under management were uniformly distributed across families, the 2008 value would be 10,000 / 607 = 16.5. The Herfindahl Index is now 38 times the level of its theoretical minimum value, up from 23 times in 1998. All metrics point to increased industry concentration (see Exhibit 3.1).

Exhibit 3.1 Market Share Concentration among U.S. Mutual Fund Families Based on Assets under Management

Year	Number of Fund Families	Market Share for Top 10 Fund Families	Herfindahl Index (HI)	Actual HI Divided by Minimum Possible HI*	Active	Passive/ Semiactive
2008	607	59%	617	38	Fidelity	Vanguard[†]
2007	589	56%	576	34	Fidelity	Vanguard[†]
2006	578	54%	525	30	Fidelity	Vanguard[†]
2005	576	52%	486	28	Fidelity	Vanguard[†]
2004	582	53%	487	28	Fidelity	Vanguard[†]
2003	617	53%	469	29	Fidelity	Vanguard[†]
2002	612	51%	435	27	Fidelity	Vanguard[†]
2001	627	50%	436	27	Fidelity	Vanguard[†]
2000	638	51%	418	27	Fidelity[†]	Fidelity[†]
1999	630	50%	428	27	Fidelity[†]	Fidelity[†]
1998	615	48%	380	23	Fidelity[†]	Fidelity[†]

Source: Morningstar Principia, data as of December 31, 2008.
* Smallest possible Herfindahl index is calculated as 10,000 ÷ number of fund families.
[†] This fund family is the largest overall on the basis of assets under management.

MUTUAL FUND CREATION AND MORTALITY

Membership in the active mutual fund population is dynamic, as the number of mutual funds entering and exiting the scene has remained high. Khorana and Servaes (1999) examine 1,163 mutual fund starts over a 14-year period. They find that fund families are more likely to start a new fund if the fund's investment category objective is broad, if other funds with the same objective have high levels of capital gains overhang (potential tax liability), and if the family has other funds that are stellar performers. Fund starts are also related to the proportion of its mutual funds that the management company has in the lowest management fee level. Percent management fees typically are staggered according to the level of assets under management, with the lowest percent fee applying to the largest fund size. Starting a new fund for which the highest fee on the schedule applies—and to which investor flows are likely to come at the expense of one of the family's lower-fee funds—is consistent with fund family profit maximization (but not necessarily shareholder welfare).

Karoui and Meier (2008) show that new equity mutual funds often experience strong initial performance but returns tail off quickly. They examine 828 U.S. equity mutual funds that started between 1991 and 2005 and find that in the year immediately after their creation, funds tend to load up on small-cap stocks and bear high levels of unsystematic risk by holding industry-concentrated positions. The starting funds' average performance declines by 13 basis points per month between year 1 and year 2.

Mutual funds sometimes experience mortality, which occurs via either merger or liquidation. The former is far more frequent than the latter. Ding (2006) reports that between 1962 and 1999, 1,751 U.S. mutual funds—one in six in existence—were eliminated through merger. The two most common rationales for these mergers are (1) to take advantage of economies of scale and (2) to eliminate the weaker fund's inferior historical performance record. The three forms of merger, listed in order of decreasing prevalence, are merger of (1) two funds within one family, (2) two funds from different families, and (3) two share classes of one fund. In Ding's sample of 604 *equity* fund mergers, 330 involved a target that had the same investment style (e.g., aggressive growth) as the acquirer, while 274 were cross-style mergers. The latter figure appears to indicate a large proportion of shotgun weddings.

Jayaraman, Khorana, and Nelling (2002) examine the causes and consequences of mutual fund mergers. Using 742 mergers in a 39-month period between 2004 and 2007, they find that acquiring funds are larger and have higher premerger performance than target funds. After the merger, a certain degree of wealth transfer occurs, whereby the target fund's performance improves but the acquiring fund's performance deteriorates. Khorana, Tufano, and Wedge (2007) show that cross-family mergers are more likely if there exists a combination of poor target fund performance and a target fund board that has a large fraction of independent directors. For boards composed of 100 percent independent directors, the high merger incidence is particularly striking, even relative to boards that are 88 percent independent. Although target-fund shareholders tend to benefit from cross-family mergers, each target-fund board member stands to lose an average of $24,670 in annual director's fees if his or her board service is discontinued postmerger. Evidence suggests that as long as they are not compensated *too highly*, fully independent boards are more apt to take that step in the service of fund shareholders.

REGULATION

Mutual funds in the United States are subject to a variety of government regulations, among them requirements of the Securities Act of 1933, the Securities Exchange Act of 1934, and the Investment Company Act of 1940. Gremillion (2005) provides an excellent summary of the various legislative acts, their provisions, and the entities that administer them. The Securities Act of 1933 requires funds to register their share offerings and issue a prospectus to investors. The offering documents and proxy statements must be filed with the Securities and Exchange Commission (SEC), which was established under the 1934 Act. As noted in Chapter 4, funds are also subject to regulation that caps the fees charged to investors.

The SEC administers the 1940 Act, which covers mutual funds and other types of managed portfolios. The 1940 Act specifies the basic organizational and governance structure of mutual funds, as well as operational measures to protect investors. Among the provisions of the 1940 Act and its amendments is the requirement that fund directors be largely "independent." The most recent amendment in 2004 required that 75 percent of directors—including the chair of the board—be independent.

The National Association of Securities Dealers (NASD) regulates mutual fund advertising and brokers who sell fund shares. The Internal Revenue Service regulates the degree of portfolio concentration and the tax treatment of mutual funds. Funds must show, on a quarterly basis, that they are properly diversified. Funds must report all dividends received and capital gains realized, both of which are taxed at the fund shareholder level.

SCALE ECONOMIES: EXPENSES AND FEES

A spirited debate has occurred about the possible existence of scale economies in the mutual fund industry, at both the individual fund and family levels. *Economies of scale* mean that by increasing assets under management, a fund or fund family can spread fixed costs over a larger base and achieve higher profitability from each additional dollar of investor inflows. In a highly competitive industry, scale economies will eventually be reflected in a lower expense ratio charged to investors. As shown by Dellva and Olson (1998) and Haslem, Baker, and Smith (2007), fund performance net of fees is negatively related to expense ratios. Malhotra, Martin, and Russel (2007) note that if economies of scale in the industry are confirmed, investors should also have good reason to cheer mutual fund mergers.

Latzko (1999) examines individual mutual funds between 1984 and 1996, finding that the elasticity of expenses to fund assets is less than 1.0. This result holds across funds specializing in all classes of equity and fixed income investments. Latzko interprets this as supporting scale economies, although he finds that expenses decrease rapidly only until fund size reaches about $3.5 billion.

Researchers have also analyzed scale economies at the level of the fund *family*. Many fund families share research, trading, and client servicing resources across multiple funds. Thus, the fixed costs associated with those functions are often largely borne at the fund family level.

Analysis of the year-end 2008 Morningstar data reveals a negative relation between expense ratios and fund family assets managed using active strategies. This result is consistent with the existence of scale economies. Exhibit 3.2 shows that the average expense ratio for actively managed funds decreases monotonically across active assets under management quintiles, from 2.12 percent for Quintile 1, which contains the smallest fund families, to 1.05 percent for Quintile 5. A confounding effect is the possibility that larger families, such as Vanguard, have an abundance of low-cost index mutual funds. In order to facilitate an apples-to-apples comparison, Exhibit 3.2 leaves out assets and expenses for index funds, enhanced index funds, and funds of funds.

Makadok (1999) attempts to detect economies of scale in mutual fund families that offer money market funds. He notes that studies of industries typically assume that any benefits or costs of scale are similar for firms industry-wide. Yet as Makadok points out, certain fund family characteristics lead to savings arising from size while others do not. Thus, he finds it useful to estimate separately the magnitude of scale economies for each fund family.

Makadok shows that fund family weighted-average expense ratios are negatively related to assets under management, which suggests the presence of scale economies. He also hypothesizes that the expense ratio should be negatively related to average account size. Servicing each new client account involves incremental fixed costs. All else equal, the larger the average account size (i.e., the smaller the number of accounts given the assets under management), the smaller the total fixed costs and the lower the expense ratio the fund family can charge. Makadok's empirical evidence is consistent with this hypothesis and generally confirms the results of Baumol, Koehn, Goldfeld, and Gordon (1990). Dermine and Röller (1992) find similar effects for the French mutual fund industry, but they observe negative scale economies for large fund firms and conclude that there existed an optimal size at that time of about 3 billion French francs.

Malhotra et al. (2007) examine economies of scope. Some fund families elect to keep a focused product line while others provide investment opportunities in a broad array of market sectors. Malhotra et al. find that the extent to which fund families specialize in strategies has an impact on fees to investors. They report that fund families with a higher degree of "focus" tend to charge lower fees. They define *focus* as the difference between the number of funds offered by the family and the

Exhibit 3.2 Average Expense Ratio by Fund Family Size (Assets under Management); Funds of Funds and (Enhanced) Index Funds Excluded

Fund Family Assets	Quintile 1	Quintile 2	Quintile 3	Quintile 4	Quintile 5
Family Assets ($ millions)	$9	$64	$328	$1,687	$39,870
Expense Ratio	2.12%	1.49%	1.28%	1.17%	1.05%

Source: Morningstar Principia, data as of December 31, 2008.

number of different objectives those funds have, all divided by the number of funds offered by the family. Thus, a family offering 10 funds that have four distinct objectives would have *focus* = (10 – 4) / 10 = 0.6. Malhotra et al. calculate a mean value for focus between 1998 and 2003 of 0.75, with a standard deviation of 0.23. In the case of Vanguard, Fidelity, and American Funds for 2008, the focus values are 0.83, 0.88, and 0.62, respectively.

SCALE DISECONOMIES: FUND RETURNS

Substantial anecdotal evidence indicates that as fund size grows, generation of a positive alpha is less likely. Chen, Hong, Huang, and Kubik (2004) empirically examine the size–performance relation for mutual funds between 1962 and 1999. Irrespective of whether they measure performance using market-adjusted returns, beta-adjusted returns, a three-factor model, or a four-factor model, they find that individual fund performance is negatively related to beginning-of-period assets under management. Their results appear to be driven by the fact that buying larger amounts of illiquid stocks can become exponentially more costly as portfolio size rises. Hence, the performance–size relation is most dramatic for small-cap funds.

Edelen, Evans, and Kadlec (2007) report that Chen et al.'s finding of a negative relation between performance and fund size is almost entirely accounted for by fund portfolio trading costs. Funds with relatively large trade sizes experience diseconomies of scale to a much greater extent than do funds with small trade sizes. Trading costs are often generated not by manager discretionary trades but by trades necessitated by fund investor flows.

Relying on an *assumption* of negative returns to scale, Berk and Green (2004) provide a theoretical explanation for why the average mutual fund does not out-perform its benchmark index. In their model, a manager who has achieved superior performance attracts new investors. The new fund investors invest after redeeming their shares in other, underperforming funds. As the volume of investment in her fund increases, the superior manager finds it difficult to achieve the same high returns given the increasing portfolio scale, which causes the fund's alpha to decrease toward zero. Nonetheless, the more superior the manager, the larger the fund will become prior to the time that the return reaches a competitive level. Consequently, the superior manager's compensation will be higher than that of an inferior manager because her fund size is larger.

BENEFITS OF MUTUAL FUND INVESTING TO FUND SHAREHOLDERS

The benefits of mutual funds to investors are varied. Several of the most notable benefits are discussed next.

Diversification

Mutual fund portfolios reflect a much greater degree of diversification than is typically found in individual stock portfolios. Shawky and Smith (2005) show that the average number of stocks held in equity mutual fund portfolios is about 90, with roughly one-third of the total value in the top 10 stocks. For retail investors in particular, diversifying a portfolio of individual stocks to this level can be a costly and inefficient process. The costs include brokerage fees associated with buying relatively small amounts of many different stocks as well as the record-keeping associated with owning enough names to effectively eliminate unsystematic risk.

Professional Portfolio Management

Related to the diversification advantage, ownership of mutual funds brings professional portfolio management services to fund shareholders. Most professional portfolio managers bring experience at monitoring the entire feasible set of investments, making economically justified decisions about buying and selling individual stocks, and ensuring that each portfolio complies with the characteristics described in the fund's prospectus. This includes structuring the portfolio to set risk and expected return at an appropriate level. Balanced fund and fund-of-funds managers also rebalance the portfolio in a timely way when the stock–bond mix deviates from the target allocation.

Professional portfolio management sometimes serves the investor extraordinarily well. Kosowski, Timmermann, Wermers, and White (2006) find that some managers of growth mutual funds are truly exceptional stock pickers who exhibit remarkably persistent high performance even after fees are deducted. Kosowski et al. designed their bootstrap tests to account for the possibility that good luck drives the results, and they find that it does not. For income funds, they report evidence of managerial luck but not exceptional stock-picking success. Berk and Green's (2004) model would explain that the outperforming funds will attract prodigious investor flows, causing their returns to revert to the population mean but leaving the extraordinary managers well compensated through high-dollar fees.

Ready Access to Asset Classes and Market Sectors

By sharing portfolio management costs with fellow fund shareholders, investors gain access to financial markets in an economical way. Further, many mutual funds can be bought directly from the fund family, obviating the need to use brokers and pay their fees. In many cases, investors can avoid loads in this way as well.

Mutual funds provide investors with exposure to a wide array of asset classes. They offer a broad opportunity set, including security types, industry sectors, and geographic sectors. Certain securities, such as those trading on nondomestic exchanges, may be difficult for individual investors to buy directly. Mutual funds provide a means of ownership, albeit indirect.

The use of mutual funds designed to invest in a specific market industry sector or capitalization range, or by using a certain style, can help investors keep their portfolios balanced within an asset class. For example, many investors are unlikely to know whether a particular stock belongs under the mid-cap value or large-cap growth classification, although the distinction greatly influences eventual returns. Style-adherent mutual funds allow investors to more easily maintain target allocations across these various dimensions.

Finally, certain mutual funds impose screens that help them to invest in a "socially responsible" way. Negative screens often include prohibitions against investments in "sin" businesses such as alcohol, gambling, and tobacco. Socially or politically based constraints sometimes include avoidance of companies that produce guns and armaments, companies deemed to be hostile toward labor unions, and companies associated with nations that have poor human-rights records. A common positive screen requires investment only in companies that have a commitment to environmentally friendly business practices. Mutual fund managers can screen for the relevant criteria more efficiently than most individual investors can.

In March 2009, there were 73 distinct U.S. equity mutual funds that Morningstar designated as socially responsible, with $61.5 billion in total assets, up from $8.3 billion at the end of 2000. Despite the increasing popularity of such funds, Girard, Rahman, and Stone (2007) show that between 1984 and 2003, socially responsible fund managers have underperformed their active-fund peers in diversification, selectivity, and market timing.

DRAWBACKS OF MUTUAL FUND INVESTING

Open-end mutual funds also have some drawbacks, which are discussed next.

Persistent High Fees in Some Families

One drawback is that the benefits of cost-efficient investment are sometimes realized by the fund company and not shared with fund shareholders. Expense ratios, for active management in particular, are sometimes in excess of 3 percent per year. Some funds impose Rule 12b-1 distribution fees of up to 1 percent annually on their shareholders, and shareholders also have to pay sales loads of up to 8.5 percent on certain classes of funds. This matter is discussed in detail in Chapter 4, on fees and expenses.

Underperformance Relative to Index Funds

Another important drawback is that the average, actively managed mutual fund underperforms benchmark indexes and passively managed funds. Berk and Green's (2004) model and several empirical studies provide strong support for the notion that active mutual fund managers have stock-picking talent and earn persistent positive excess returns gross of fees. Unfortunately, net of fees the picture darkens, and superior fund managers capture for themselves most of the alpha that remains.

Tax Inefficiency

A further drawback of open-end mutual funds is their tax inefficiency. The relatively high turnover for actively managed funds is costly to fund shareholders in terms of transaction costs as well as in creating short-term taxable gains. Moreover, the redemption decisions of other investors can trigger tax liabilities for the fund shareholders left behind. Although the number and size of tax-efficient mutual funds are growing fast, many investors in actively managed funds continue to see a wide gap between their pre-tax and after-tax returns.

Inadequate Disclosure

Mutual fund information transparency has improved in certain ways (e.g., the more frequent disclosure of portfolio holdings), but disclosure has lagged in other areas. One prime area is portfolio trading costs. Edelen et al. (2007) find, in confirmation of Wermers' (2000) results, that the magnitude of mutual fund trading costs is approximately equal to the expense ratio. Even for those investors who know that trading costs are not included in the expense ratio, this number is certainly higher than most imagine. Mahoney (2004) contends that the U.S. regulatory approach to mutual funds focuses excessively on board composition and compensation and too little on disclosure to investors. He notes that some view the current levels of fees as evidence of a lack of investor sophistication in assessing fund costs. Mahoney advocates a General Accounting Office (2000) recommendation that mutual funds disclose, on each investor's quarterly statement, the *total dollar amount* of expenses deducted from the investor's account during the period.

Mutual funds disclose their portfolio holdings relatively infrequently, and even then, fund shareholders have a rightful concern about window dressing. Between 1985 and 2004, the Securities and Exchange Commission (SEC) required mutual funds to disclose portfolio holdings semiannually. Starting in May 2004, quarterly disclosure was mandated. Examining the period before mandatory quarterly disclosure, Ge and Zheng (2006) report that many mutual funds voluntarily disclosed their holdings quarterly. They find that the effects of more frequent disclosure are asymmetric. For the top-performing 20 percent of funds, those disclosing quarterly had lower performance than those disclosing semiannually. For the bottom-performing 20 percent of funds, those disclosing semiannually had lower performance than those disclosing quarterly. Ge and Zheng conclude that top-performing funds may lose some informational advantage through increased disclosure. They state that poor-performing funds may suffer from agency costs that are greater than any informational value managers hold. They conclude that more frequent disclosure is appropriate for these funds.

In a related study, Kacperczyk, Sialm, and Zheng (2008) show that the difference between fund shareholders' actual returns and the returns implied by funds' most recently disclosed fund portfolio holdings are large and systematic over time. This return gap, which derives from portfolio managers' unobserved actions, is also useful in predicting subsequent fund performance. Specifically, the decile of funds with the highest return gap subsequently outperforms the market by 1.2 percent, while the lowest-return-gap decile of funds *underperforms* by 2.2 percent.

FINANCIAL BARRIERS TO MUTUAL FUND INVESTING AND REDEMPTION

Mutual fund load charges are discussed in Chapter 4. Apart from this cost, many mutual funds impose a barrier in the form of the minimum initial investment amount. Incremental costs arise in servicing each new investor's account, and fund companies want to avoid taking on accounts whose fees do not cover those costs.

At year-end 2008, the median retail class fund required an initial investment of $1,000, although 513 retail funds require no minimum initial investment. Over 500 retail class funds have a minimum investment of $25,000 or more. The median retail fund's investment required to start an individual retirement account (IRA) is only $250. The presumption of mutual funds is that an investor's initial IRA investment will be followed by many subsequent investments. If these do not materialize and the account balance remains low, fund companies often charge account maintenance fees.

For institutional class funds, the minimum investment is as high as $250 million. At year-end 2008, over 500 funds had minimums of $50 million or higher. The median institutional class fund required a $100,000 initial investment.

Redeeming shares is not always a cost-free process for investors. As noted in Chapter 4, deferred load charges are frequently found on class-B fund shares. In addition, many mutual funds charge redemption fees, particularly for redemptions that occur in the few months immediately following the share purchase. Quick in-and-out trading by fund shareholders can greatly complicate the fund flows-and-investment balancing job of portfolio managers, can be administratively costly for the mutual fund family, and can be potentially damaging to the after-tax returns of fellow fund shareholders. Mutual funds impose redemption fees to discourage investors from using funds as trading rather than investment vehicles.

Exhibit 3.3 gives some perspective on the current prevalence and size of redemption fees in the United States. Almost one-fourth of equity funds (defined as distinct funds with 80 to 100 percent of the portfolio invested in U.S. common stocks) impose a redemption fee of some type. Most common is to charge a 2 percent fee if redemption occurs within one month of the shares' purchase, although across all holding periods, 2 percent remains the predominant fee amount.

Exhibit 3.3   U.S. Equity Mutual Fund Redemption Fees

Holding Period	Minimum Fee	Mean Fee	Median Fee	Maximum Fee	Number of Funds
0–15 days	1.00%	1.85%	2.00%	2.00%	132
0–1 month	0.50%	1.61%	2.00%	2.00%	235
0–2 months	1.00%	1.65%	2.00%	2.00%	89
0–3 months	0.50%	1.54%	2.00%	2.00%	106
0–6 months	0.25%	1.46%	1.50%	2.00%	44
0–1 year	1.00%	1.60%	2.00%	2.00%	5
Unlimited	0.02%	0.34%	0.50%	0.50%	3
Total with redemption fees	0.02%	1.64%	2.00%	2.00%	614
Funds with no redemption fees					1,933

Source: Morningstar Principia, data as of December 31, 2008.

MUTUAL FUND GOVERNANCE AND AGENCY PROBLEMS

Weak mutual fund governance is probably the most pernicious drawback for many fund investors. As the governance of public corporations has increased in prominence over the past decade, so has the topic of mutual fund governance. In their discussion of mutual fund board characteristics, Tufano and Sevick (1997) provide a lucid description of the structure of open-end mutual funds in the United States:

> Mutual funds are legal entities with no employees. Fund shareholders entrust their money to a fund. The fund is overseen by a board of directors (or trustees), which then outsources all management activities, including security selection (investment management), distribution, fund administration, custody, and accounting. This organizational structure, in which each fund has a separate, legally empowered board, differs from that of other corporations as well as from mutual funds in other countries. Were this practice applied to a firm like General Motors, there would be a different board of directors for each model of car GM sold, elected by the purchasers of that make of autos. (p. 324)

Tufano and Sevick (1997) note that setting fees that are not "excessive" is the main legal role of the board pursuant to the Investment Company Act of 1940. This role has been confirmed by the legal decisions subsequent to its passage. Siggelkow (1999) adds that SEC Rule 12b-1 requires boards to vote annually on the imposition of 12b-1 fees and to discontinue them if they are determined not to be in fund shareholders' best interests. His empirical results suggest that many boards have not taken this provision seriously enough and that investors should probably avoid funds that charge 12b-1 fees.

Tufano and Sevick (1997) analyze whether a mutual fund's fees are related to its board's characteristics. They find that lower fees to investors are associated with boards that are smaller and that have a larger proportion of independent directors. Lower fees are also observed in funds whose board members serve on other boards within the fund family. Tufano and Sevick emphasize that their results should not be overinterpreted to imply that certain board structures *produce* low fees. They raise the possibility that fund families with low fees gravitate toward certain types of board structures.

Evaluation of mutual fund governance involves at least two major components: whether the corporate culture of the fund family fosters a sensible investment and communication process that is client-centered, and whether the fund's board members are well positioned to act in shareholders' interests.

Morningstar provides grades of corporate culture (A through D) and board quality (A through C). Morningstar Principia (2009) describes the corporate culture evaluation process as answering four questions:

1. Is the fund company focused on investing or gathering assets?
2. Does the fund company foster a thoughtful, repeatable investment process?
3. Is the fund company straightforward with investors through clear, pertinent disclosure and responsible marketing?
4. Do talented investors spend their careers at this fund firm?

The board quality evaluation process involves answering three questions:

1. Does the board consistently act in shareholders' best interest?
2. Do the independent directors have meaningful investments in the fund? To earn the maximum score here, at least 75 percent of a board's independent directors must have more money invested in the funds they oversee than they receive in aggregate annual compensation for serving on the board.
3. Is the board led by an independent chairman, and are 75 percent of the directors independent?

Exhibit 3.4 shows the number of fund families, as of December 2008, that received various Morningstar grades for corporate culture and board quality. Families receiving grades of "A" in both criteria for all their funds include Clipper, FPA, Longleaf Partners, and Selected Funds.

Freeman (2007) argues that mutual fund industry governance in general has failed. If boards of directors acted in their designated capacity as fiduciaries, mutual fund fees would reflect competitive pricing. Freeman says that if prices were at competitive levels, they would be much lower than they are now.

As evidence of the noncompetitive state of mutual fund pricing, one can consider the prices that mutual fund advisers charge non–mutual fund clients for identical services. For example, Freeman (2007) found that the mutual fund family then known as Alliance Capital managed equity portfolios for other fund companies and retirement systems and charged 10 to 24 basis points per year while at the same time charging its own open-end mutual fund shareholders 93 basis points. As another example, he cites Senate testimony by New York Attorney General Eliot Spitzer, who stated that Putnam Investments admitted to charging its retail fund shareholders 40 percent higher advisory fees than it charged for identical services to its institutional clients.

Freeman (2007) notes that investors (and by extension, the board members who represent their interests) should consider the average expense ratio for index funds as a reasonable baseline for the cost of operating a mutual fund. Chapter 4 in this volume shows that the average expense ratio for retail class equity index funds is 0.21 percent. Mutual funds' pricing power is evidenced by the fact that their average expense ratios continue to be multiples of that baseline level.

Exhibit 3.4 Number of Mutual Fund Families Receiving Morningstar Grades for Corporate Culture and Board Quality

Corporate Culture Grade	Board Quality Grade		
	A	B	C
A	5	10	1
B	1	8	10
C	2	6	2
D	1	2	5

Source: Morningstar Principia, data as of December 31, 2008.

Khorana, Servaes, and Wedge (2007) study the extent of portfolio manager ownership of shares in the mutual funds they manage. At year-end 2004, the average dollar investment of managers of 1,406 U.S. mutual funds in their own funds was $96,663. The median manager held no shares at all in his fund. Twenty-five percent of managers held stakes larger than $50,000. Khorana et al. find a positive relation between mutual fund performance and managerial holding. Each 1–basis point increase in managerial holdings is associated with a 3–basis point higher excess return. Based on their findings, the authors recommend that investors inquire about portfolio managers' ownership of the funds they manage.

FUND MANAGER TOURNAMENT BEHAVIOR

Relatively minor differences in returns across mutual funds often produce large differences in investor flows. Chevalier and Ellison (1997) find that funds exhibiting annual outperformance of 20 percent attract next-year flows that are twice the level for funds that outperform by 15 percent. They find a negative effect, though much weaker, for funds that are the very worst performers. Sirri and Tufano (1998) also report a strong relation between mutual fund performance and investor flows, but it is asymmetric. Funds that outperform receive high inflows while funds that underperform do not experience the same degree of outflows. The relation is stronger for funds that charge high fees. Sirri and Tufano comment that high fees likely indicate a vigorous fund marketing effort, which is apt to bring investor attention to a fund. Weak performance is never advertised by the fund family, so relatively unsophisticated investors may not be primed to react to those results.

In view of the high sensitivity of investor flows to the degree of outperformance and given that portfolio manager compensation typically is linked to assets under management, managers have strong incentives to outperform by a large margin. Numerous authors have examined how mutual fund performance during the first months of the year affects portfolio managers' risk-taking behavior during the balance of the year. Schwarz (2009) summarizes the sometimes-conflicting results of past studies, and makes a key methodological contribution that reconciles those results. Examining funds between 1990 and 2006, he confirms the findings of the original Brown, Harlow, and Starks (1996) study: Low-performing managers from the year's first half consistently increase their risk levels in the second half. The Brown et al. (1996) and Schwartz (2009) results reveal manager behavior consistent with a multi-stage tournament, in which their primary objective is to maximize personal compensation. This aim can be achieved when a manager betters her position relative to other managers, attracting increased investor flows and assets under management.

FUND FAMILY MARKETING AND CROSS-SUBSIDIZATION

Gaspar, Massa, and Matos (2006) report striking results about mutual fund families' steps to enhance overall family profits by favoring certain of their funds at the expense of others (cross-subsidization). Specifically, they favor funds that carry high fees and funds with past outperformance. In terms of attracting flows, it is much more valuable for a mutual fund family to have one star fund and one laggard fund than to have two average-performing funds. Therefore, families have incentives to nurture the star funds, or at least to encourage investor flows into high-fee funds.

One mechanism by which this is done is to allocate superior opportunities, such as hot initial public offerings, to more favored funds. Another is to conduct cross-trading between more favored and less favored funds such that more favored funds do not have to bear the price-pressure cost normally imposed by open market transactions. The net benefit to more favored funds over less favored funds averages 0.7 to 3.3 percent per year between 1991 and 2001. The authors note that despite all the reputed benefits of crossing trades, regulators and investors should be concerned about intrafamily cross-trades creating problems that are known to arise with self-dealing.

CONCLUSIONS

The mutual fund industry worldwide has grown dramatically in recent years. In the United States, industry market share has become much more concentrated in the past decade, with almost 60 percent of assets under management now invested with 10 fund families.

The process of mutual fund creation and mutual fund mortality takes place continuously. For a fund, mortality typically occurs by being merged into another fund. This process tends to be economically beneficial to target fund shareholders but less so for acquiring-fund shareholders. Cost savings through scale economies are not sufficient to offset other negative impacts of mergers. The target's board structure is an important determinant of whether a merger takes place.

Government regulation is a major feature in the U.S. mutual fund industry. The business process is influenced primarily by the Investment Company Act of 1940 and its amendments. The Act stipulates that mutual funds register with the SEC, maintain board independence, and that the board must vote on all major contracts. Other regulations come from the Securities Act of 1933, the Internal Revenue Service, and self-regulatory organizations.

Economies of scale, at least to a point, are evident in mutual fund families. Fees charged to investors are generally lower for larger funds. Portfolio managers, however, find it more difficult to maintain superior investment performance as fund size grows. Performance is often hindered by high trading costs, which can be triggered by both discretionary trades as well as investor fund flows.

Mutual funds provide individual investors with numerous benefits, including ready diversification, professional portfolio management, and inexpensive access to asset classes and market sectors. Among the drawbacks to mutual funds are noncompetitive fee levels, tax inefficiency, a general failure to outperform benchmark indexes, and poor disclosure policies. Mutual fund investors also face barriers to purchasing and selling shares. These take the form of minimum initial investment levels and redemption fees, respectively. Given that mutual funds are designed as investment vehicles rather than trading vehicles, most investors do not find these barriers to be prohibitive.

Mutual fund governance is one of the issues that affects investment results most profoundly. Fund boards are responsible for hiring the portfolio manager and negotiating management fees. The board is required to attest that the fees are not excessively high and otherwise to act in fund shareholders' interests. Evidence suggests that boards that have even more than the SEC's mandated 75 percent of independent directors tend to perform better for investors. On average, portfolio management fees do not appear to be set as if the market is competitive, and management companies frequently charge far higher fees to open-end mutual funds than they do to other institutional investors for equivalent services.

Evidence suggests that achieving higher profitability through maximization of fund flows is extremely important to mutual fund families. Among the ways to increase flows is by taking steps to become a star fund. Managers tend to adjust their late-year risk taking in order to make the list of top funds. There is also evidence supporting the idea that fund families use weak funds in various ways to subsidize strong ones, possibly to help the strong funds reach the top tier. Finally, to the extent that the portfolio manager owns shares in the fund, it is a clear plus for shareholder performance.

REFERENCES

Baumol, W. J., M. F. Koehn, S. M. Goldfeld, and L. A. Gordon. 1990. "The Economics of Mutual Funds Markets: Competition versus Regulation," *Rochester Studies in Economics and Policy Issues*. Boston: Kluwer.

Berk, J. B., and R. C. Green. 2004. "Mutual Fund Flows and Performance in Rational Markets," *Journal of Political Economy* 112: 6 (December): 1269–1295.

Brown, K. C., W. V. Harlow, and L. T. Starks. 1996. "Of Tournaments and Temptations: An Analysis of Managerial Incentives in the Mutual Fund Industry," *Journal of Finance* 51: 1 (March): 85–110.

Chen, J., H. Hong, M. Huang, and J. D. Kubik. 2004. "Does Fund Size Erode Mutual Fund Performance? The Role of Liquidity and Organization," *American Economic Review* 94: 5 (December): 1276–1302.

Chevalier, J., and G. Ellison. 1997. "Risk-Taking by Mutual Funds as a Response to Incentives," *Journal of Political Economy* 105: 6 (December): 1167–1200.

Dellva, W., and G. Olson. 1998. "The Relationship between Mutual Fund Fees and Expenses and Their Effects on Performance," *Financial Review* 33: 1 (February): 85–103.

Dermine, J., and L.-H. Röller. 1992. "Economies of Scale and Scope in French Mutual Funds," *Journal of Financial Intermediation* 2: 1 (March): 83–93.

Ding, B. 2006. "Mutual Fund Mergers: A Long-Term Analysis." Working Paper, University at Albany.

Edelen, R. M., R. Evans, and G. B. Kadlec. 2007. "Scale Effects in Mutual Fund Performance: The Role of Trading Costs." Working Paper. Downloaded from http://papers.ssrn.com/sol3/papers.cfm?abstract_id=951367.

Freeman, J. P. 2007. "John Freeman's Working Paper Responding to the Advisory Fee Analysis in AEI Working Paper #127, June 2006, 'Competition and Shareholder Fees in the Mutual Fund Industry: Evidence and Implications for Policy' by John C. Coates IV and R. Glenn Hubbard." Working Paper, University of South Carolina.

Gaspar, J.-M., M. Massa, and P. Matos. 2006. "Favoritism in Mutual Fund Families? Evidence on Strategic Cross-Fund Subsidization," *Journal of Finance* 61: 1 (February): 73–104.

Ge, W. and L. Zheng. 2006. "The Frequency of Mutual Fund Portfolio Disclosure," Working Paper, downloaded from http://papers.ssrn.com/sol3/papers.cfm?abstract_id=557186.

General Accountability Office. 2000. *Mutual Fund Fees: Additional Disclosure Could Encourage Price Competition.* Washington, DC: Author, GAO/GGD-00-126.

Girard, E., H. Rahman, and B. Stone. 2007. "Socially Responsible Investments: Goody-Two-Shoes or Bad to the Bone?" *Journal of Investing* 16: 1 (Spring): 96–110.

Gremillion, L. 2005. *Mutual Fund Industry Handbook: A Comprehensive Guide for Investment Professionals.* Boston: Boston Institute of Finance Series, John Wiley & Sons.

Haslem, J. A., H. K. Baker, and D. M. Smith. 2007. "Identification and Performance of Equity Mutual Funds with Excessive Management Fees and Expense Ratios," *Journal of Investing* 16: 2 (Summer): 1–20.

Investment Company Institute. 2009. *Investment Company Fact Book: 49th Edition.* Washington, DC: Investment Company Institute, www.icifactbook.org.

Jayaraman, Y., A. Khorana, and E. Nelling. 2002. "An Analysis of the Determinants and Shareholder Wealth Effects of Mutual Fund Mergers," *Journal of Finance* 57: 3 (June): 1521–1551.

Kacperczyk, M., C. Sialm, and L. Zheng. 2008. "Unobserved Actions of Mutual Funds," *Review of Financial Studies* 21: 6 (November): 2379–2416.

Karoui, A., and I. Meier. 2008. "Performance and Characteristics of Mutual Fund Starts." Working Paper, HEC Montréal.

Khorana, A., and H. Servaes. 1999. "The Determinants of Mutual Fund Starts," *Review of Financial Studies* 12: 5 (Winter): 1043–1074.

Khorana, A., H. Servaes, and P. Tufano. 2005. "Explaining the Size of the Mutual Fund Industry around the World," *Journal of Financial Economics* 78: 1 (October): 145–185.

Khorana, A., H. Servaes, and L. Wedge. 2007. "Portfolio Manager Ownership and Fund Performance," *Journal of Financial Economics* 85: 1 (July): 179–204.

Khorana, A., P. Tufano, and L. Wedge. 2007. "Board Structure, Mergers and Shareholder Wealth: A Study of the Mutual Fund Industry," *Journal of Financial Economics* 85: 2 (August): 571–598.

Kosowski, R., A. Timmermann, R. Wermers, and H. White. 2006. "Can Mutual Fund 'Stars' Really Pick Stocks? New Evidence from a Bootstrap Analysis," *Journal of Finance* 61: 6 (December): 2551–2595.

Latzko, D. 1999. "Economies of Scale in Mutual Fund Administration," *Journal of Financial Research* 22: 3 (Fall): 331–339.

Mahoney, P. G. 2004. "Manager-Investor Conflicts in Mutual Funds," *Journal of Economic Perspectives* 18: 2 (Spring): 161–182.

Makadok, R. 1999. "Interfirm Differences in Scale Economies and the Evolution of Market Shares," *Strategic Management Journal* 20: 10 (October): 935–952.

Malhotra, D., K. R. Martin, and P. Russel. 2007. "Determinants of Cost Efficiencies in the Mutual Fund Industry," *Review of Financial Economics* 16: 4 (December): 323–334.

Morningstar Principia Pro. January 2009.

Philips, C., and F. Kinniry Jr. 2009. "The Active-Passive Debate," *Journal of Indexes* 12: 2 (March/April): 10–17.

Schwarz, C. G. 2009. "Mutual Fund Tournaments: The Sorting Bias and New Evidence." Working Paper. Downloaded from http://papers.ssrn.com/sol3/papers.cfm?abstract_id=1155098.

Shawky, H. A., and D. M. Smith. 2005. "Optimal Number of Stock Holdings in Mutual Fund Portfolios Based on Market Performance," *Financial Review* 40: 1 (November): 481–495.

Siggelkow, N. 1999. "Expense Shifting: An Empirical Study of Agency Costs in the Mutual Fund Industry." Working Paper, University of Pennsylvania (Wharton).

Sirri, E., and P. Tufano. 1998. "Costly Search and Mutual Fund Flows," *Journal of Finance* 53: 5 (October): 1589–1622.

Tufano, P., and M. Sevick. 1997. "Board Structure and Fee-setting in the U.S. Mutual Fund Industry," *Journal of Financial Economics* 53: 3 (December): 321–355.

Wermers, R. 2000. "Mutual Fund Performance: An Empirical Decomposition into Stock-Picking Talent, Style, Transaction Costs and Expenses," *Journal of Finance* 55: 4 (August): 1655–1695.

ABOUT THE AUTHOR

David M. Smith is Associate Professor of Finance and Director of the Center for Institutional Investment Management at the University at Albany, State University of New York. He conducts research on corporate finance and investments and is author of more than 20 published articles. Dr. Smith is Associate Editor (finance and accounting) for the *Journal of Business Research*. He serves on boards or committees for the Index Business Association, CFA Institute, and the Institute of Certified Management Accountants. Dr. Smith is the recipient of several teaching and research recognitions, including the SUNY Chancellor's Award for Teaching Excellence and the Financial Planning Association's Financial Frontiers Award. He holds the Chartered Financial Analyst (CFA), Certified Financial Manager (CFM), and Certified Management Accountant (CMA) designations. Dr. Smith earned bachelor's and doctoral degrees in Finance from Virginia Tech.

CHAPTER 4

Mutual Fund Fees and Expenses

DAVID M. SMITH, Ph.D., CFA
Associate Professor of Finance and Director of the Center for Institutional Investment Management, the University at Albany (SUNY)

The fees and expenses paid by mutual fund investors take multiple forms. Some charges are deducted from the fund's value in clear view of the investor. For other charges, the amount is disclosed yet they are deducted out of the investors' sight. The magnitude of certain charges is essentially invisible to fund investors.

The total monetary costs paid by mutual fund investors include front-end and deferred loads, operating expenses, account fees, and trading costs. The expense ratio consists of management fees, Rule 12b-1 fees, and "other" expenses. "Other" expenses may include transfer agent fees, securities custodian fees, shareholder accounting expenses, legal fees, auditor fees, and independent director fees. Some of the account fees investors bear can include switching fees, redemption fees, and account maintenance fees. Trading costs include brokerage fees, bid–ask spreads, and market impact costs.

The purpose of this chapter is to describe the various fee and expense categories associated with mutual funds and their consequences for investors.

LOADS

Mutual fund loads come in two main forms: front-end loads and deferred loads. Front-end loads are paid when the investor initially buys shares of the fund. Deferred loads, also known as contingent deferred sales loads or back-end sales charges, are paid when the investor sells shares of the fund. Analysis of the Morningstar Principia database (2008) as of December 2007 reveals that just under 20 percent of U.S. mutual funds charged a front-end load, and just under 30 percent of U.S. mutual funds charged a deferred load. About 0.3 percent of funds had both. Almost 52 percent of open-end mutual funds in the United States were "no-load funds," meaning they did not charge loads of any kind.

For mutual funds with loads, the load levels are disclosed to investors as a percent of the fund's net asset value. For example, the Fidelity Advisor Small-Cap Fund's class A shares have a front-end load charge of 5.75 percent. An investor who writes a check for $10,000 to buy these class A shares will experience an immediate $575 reduction in his account balance as a result of the front-end load. Although

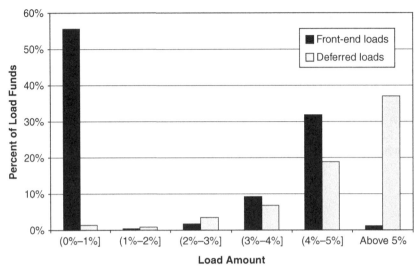

Exhibit 4.1 Load Amounts for U.S. Mutual Funds that Have Front-End or Deferred Loads (December 31, 2007)

the load itself is 5.75 percent, a return of 6.10 percent would be required to restore the investor's $10,000 wealth starting from the new $9,425 account balance.

Exhibit 4.1 shows that among mutual funds with front-end loads, over half charge loads of 1 percent or less. Of funds with deferred loads, over half charge loads above 4 percent. Mutual fund companies typically use the revenue from front-end loads to compensate brokers and financial advisers for helping to arrange the investor's purchase of mutual fund shares.

The Financial Industry Regulatory Authority (FINRA) allows front-end loads to be a maximum of 8.5 percent. As of December 2007, only five U.S. mutual funds charged 8.5 percent. Even so, not all investors will have to pay the published load percentage. Funds customarily offer concessions when investors are willing to commit large amounts. Investment levels that trigger decreases in loads are known as breakpoints. Exhibit 4.2 shows that in the case of the Fidelity Advisor Small-Cap fund's class A shares, breakpoints occur at $50,000, $100,000, and other levels, potentially resulting in dramatically reduced front-end loads.

Exhibit 4.2 Example of Breakpoints for Front-end Load: Fidelity Advisor Small Cap, Class A Shares

Amount Invested	Front-end Load
$0–49,999	5.75%
$50,000–99,999	4.50%
$100,000–249,999	3.50%
$250,000–499,999	2.50%
$500,000–24,999,999	2.00%
$25,000,000 and up	0.00%

According to the Investment Company Institute (ICI), the organization that represents the mutual fund and exchange-traded fund (ETF) industry, front-end loads weighted by mutual fund assets averaged 5.6 percent in 1980 and fell to 1.2 percent in 2007. The ICI attributes this decline to the dramatic increase in popularity of low-cost mutual funds in employer-sponsored retirement plans. The data of Barber, Odean, and Zheng (2005) suggest that despite the long-term decrease in the proportion of assets in funds with front-end loads, the drop was dramatic between 1980 and 1990 and negligible through the 1990s. According to Morey (2003) the explosion of fund classes in the mid-1990s was accompanied by a brief resurgence in the proportion of funds with loads.

Deferred loads have not enjoyed the same dramatic decline as front-end loads. Morey (2002) shows that between 1992 and 2001, the percent of U.S. diversified equity mutual funds with deferred loads more than tripled, to above 30 percent. Barber et al. (2005) suggest that investors have become more alert about the costs of investing and particularly savvy about avoiding up-front fees. They speculate that mutual funds have responded by increasing expense ratios and deferred loads.

Chordia (1996) argues that investor redemptions of mutual funds impose costs on fellow investors. He then implies that by imposing a deferred load, a mutual fund can create—or perhaps attract—more patient investors. Thus, the fund will have less need to maintain high cash balances to service redemptions and will be relatively unaffected by cash drag (see Hill and Cheong, 1996). Morey (2002) notes that if investors are patient, the fund should also be able to invest in less liquid securities that have higher expected returns. Examining the composition of deferred load funds, Morey finds that in the period after 1995, these funds do not maintain lower cash balances or invest in less liquid stocks than do no-load funds. He concludes that on average, any advantage of the deferred-load structure is not being exploited by managers. Another key disadvantage is that deferred-load funds tend to have much higher expense ratios than either front-end load or no-load funds.

Investors find it particularly costly to sell deferred-load mutual fund shares soon after investing. Typically, the magnitude of a deferred load decreases steadily throughout the investor's holding period. If the investor waits a few years, the load can go to zero. Exhibit 4.3 shows that in the case of the Eaton Vance Large-Cap Value fund's class B shares, the load amount declines by 1 percent per year after the fund has been held for two years. After eight years, the shares convert to A (front-load) shares, which have a much lower expense ratio than the B-class shares.

Exhibit 4.3 Example of Schedule for Deferred Load: Eaton Vance Large-Cap Value, Class B Shares

Holding Period	Deferred Load
0–2 years	5%
2–3 years	4%
3–4 years	3%
4–5 years	2%
5–6 years	1%
6 years and longer*	0%

* In year 8, B shares convert to A shares.

The decreased prevalence of front-end loads, even for retail class funds, is likely due to mounting evidence of underperformance by load funds relative to no-load funds. Contrary to the results of most researchers, Hooks (1996) reports that load equity mutual funds significantly outperformed no-load funds in the 15 years ending June 1993. Morey (2003) examines the out-of-sample performance of equity funds from 1993 to 1997. Using four performance measures and adjusting for load amount, he finds that no-load funds dramatically outperform funds that have either a front-end or a deferred load. Surprisingly, according to two of the performance measures, no-load funds slightly outperform load funds even *before* loads are subtracted. The mere presence of a load, rather than its amount, appears to be the more important performance determinant. Morey joins Dellva and Olson (1998) in counseling investors interested in maximizing performance to avoid load funds. For investors who do not have performance maximization as the primary objective, they recommend using load funds only if the service advantage over no-load funds clearly warrants it.

EXPENSES

A mutual fund's expense ratio reflects the amount required to cover the recurring costs of operating the fund. Expenses have both fixed and variable components. The largest component is the management fee that compensates the portfolio manager. For small mutual funds, the management fee is usually a specified percent of the assets under management, and it can be viewed by investors as a variable cost. For larger funds, the fee tends to be fixed, according to Gao and Livingston (2008).

In the case of funds of funds, including some target date and life cycle funds, investors can face two layers of expenses. The first layer is for the individual mutual funds held by the fund of funds. The second layer contains a management fee for the fund of funds itself. Some funds of funds waive the second layer of fees for investors. One example is Vanguard's STAR fund, which owns 11 diverse Vanguard mutual funds. The STAR fund passes through the expenses from its own holdings but does not charge its own management fee.

Published expense ratios are equal to the mutual fund's annual operating expenses divided by average daily assets. Expenses are typically charged to investors on a daily basis. Thus, for a fund that charges an annual expense ratio of 1.5 percent, the net asset value would decrease by 1.5 percent times 1/365 at the start of each day.

Exhibit 4.4 contains summary information on U.S. mutual funds as of December 2007. The simple (i.e., arithmetic or equally weighted) average expense ratio for U.S. common stock mutual funds is 1.34 percent. If expenses are weighted by assets under management, the average falls to 0.79 percent. The simple and weighted averages for corporate/general bond funds are 1.13 percent and 0.71 percent, respectively. The lowest expense ratios are found among money market funds, followed by bond funds and then common stock funds.

Institutional class mutual funds have consistently lower expense ratios than retail class funds. For actively managed funds, the difference in annual expenses between the institutional and retail classes is about 40 basis points for all but money market and U.S. Treasury bond funds. For index funds, the difference ranges between 10 and 20 basis points.

Exhibit 4.4 Average Annual Expense Ratios for Index Funds and Actively Managed Open-End Mutual Funds: Asset-Weighted and Simple (Arithmetic) Means for Institutional Class and Retail Class Funds

Fund Type Based on Morningstar Category	Index Funds				Actively Managed Funds					
	Institutional Class		Retail Class		Institutional Class		Retail Class		Grand Total	
	Asset-weighted Mean	Simple Mean	Asset-weighted Mean	Simple Mean	Asset-weighted Mean	Simple Mean	Asset-weighted Mean	Simple Mean	Asset-weighted Mean	Simple Mean
U.S. stocks	0.10%	0.33%	0.21%	0.86%	0.52%	0.91%	0.94%	1.49%	0.79%	1.34%
Large cap	0.09%	0.32%	0.19%	0.80%	0.43%	0.80%	0.87%	1.40%	0.73%	1.25%
Mid cap	0.12%	0.32%	0.26%	0.85%	0.74%	1.00%	1.11%	1.58%	1.01%	1.43%
Small cap	0.13%	0.35%	0.32%	1.02%	0.79%	1.08%	1.18%	1.68%	1.02%	1.52%
Non-U.S. stocks	0.15%	0.45%	0.15%	1.20%	0.53%	1.14%	0.72%	1.75%	0.63%	1.59%
Bonds										
Munis	n.a.	n.a.	n.a.	n.a.	0.31%	0.59%	0.72%	1.14%	0.65%	1.08%
Treasuries	0.24%	0.47%	0.21%	0.44%	0.47%	0.60%	0.56%	1.13%	0.54%	1.02%
Corporate/General bonds	0.09%	0.20%	0.20%	0.39%	0.51%	0.69%	0.89%	1.28%	0.71%	1.13%
World bonds	n.a.	n.a.	n.a.	n.a.	0.58%	0.83%	0.99%	1.45%	0.86%	1.32%
Money market										
Munis	n.a.	n.a.	n.a.	n.a.	0.22%	0.34%	0.28%	0.47%	0.27%	0.45%
Taxable	n.a.	n.a.	n.a.	n.a.	0.24%	0.36%	0.42%	0.80%	0.36%	0.64%

Source: Morningstar Principia, data as of December 31, 2007.
* n.a. indicates not applicable.

Expenses of equity mutual funds vary widely. Haslem, Baker, and Smith (2008, 2009) show that about one-third of all actively managed institutional and retail equity mutual funds in the United States have expense ratios more than 1 standard deviation from the mean. Although this is expected for any normally distributed variable, 1 standard deviation is economically large: 33 basis points for institutional funds and 46 for retail funds. More than 5 percent of all funds' expense ratios are more than 2 standard deviations above or below the mean. The difference between ±2 standard deviations in expense ratio is 1.84 percent. Thus, two funds with identical returns gross of expenses yet expense ratios four standard deviations apart will have a 20 percent disparity in portfolio values after a 10-year holding period.

How have expenses changed over time? Average expense ratios in the U.S. mutual fund industry varied between about 0.5 and 1.5 percent over the past 50 years, depending on how they are measured. As Barber et al. (2005) show, for U.S. diversified equity mutual funds, the asset-weighted expense ratio in the late 1960s fluctuated between 0.5 percent and 0.6 percent, and rose steadily toward 1 percent in the early 1990s. Exhibit 4.5 contains a graph of ICI (2008) data for the period since 1993, which indicates that expense ratios have declined in recent years. The simple average expense ratio rose from 1.43 percent in 1993 to 1.64 percent in 2002, and fell to 1.46 percent in 2007. The asset-weighted average expense ratio fluctuated around 1 percent until 2004, when it began falling and reached 0.86 percent in 2007.

The expense–versus–performance link is one of the most widely studied topics in the investments field. Ennis (2005) proposes a model that shows the relation among active mutual fund manager skill, expense ratio, and the likelihood of investor success. Success can be defined as desired, such as earning a positive alpha over time relative to a benchmark index. Assuming an expense ratio of zero (i.e., the portfolio manager declines to accept a fee for her efforts), the investor's likelihood

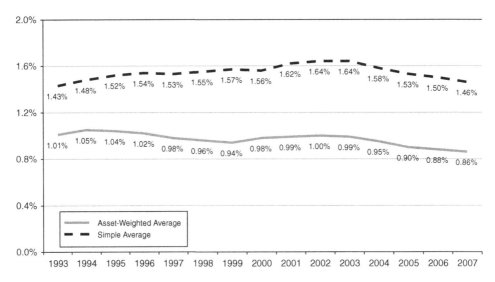

Exhibit 4.5   U.S. Equity Mutual Fund Expense Ratios, 1993–2007
Source: Investment Company Institute.

of success is equal to the active portfolio manager's likelihood of success. With the imposition of fees, the investor's likelihood of success diverges from the portfolio manager's. For example, assuming a 1.5 percent expense ratio, employing a manager with an 80 percent likelihood of success produces only a 46 percent likelihood of success for the investor. Only when the likelihood of portfolio manager success nears 100 percent do they substantially converge. The higher the expense ratio, the greater is the degree of divergence and the higher managerial skill must be in order to create convergence. The upshot of Ennis's model is that in order for active mutual fund investing to have a reasonable chance of success, manager skill should be high *and* expenses should be low.

Empirical tests have found that the path to better performance is paved with low-cost funds. For equity mutual funds, Dellva and Olson (1998) find a strong negative relation between expenses and four mutual fund performance measures. They reach this conclusion while holding constant for fund size, load, cash holding, beta, dividend yield, and turnover. Haslem et al. (2008) show the frequency with which actively managed equity mutual funds outperform the relevant Russell indexes, by expense ratio class. Although only one-third to one-half of all funds outperformed the benchmark indexes over 1- to 15-year periods, less than one-quarter of mutual funds outperformed when they had expenses 1 or more standard deviations above the mean for their categories.

Wermers (2000) examines the actual holdings of actively managed mutual funds and finds that the chosen stocks outperform benchmark indexes by 1.3 percent per year from 1975 to 1994. However, considering the expense ratio, transaction costs, and cash drag, Wermers finds these factors sufficient to explain the typical 1 percent net-of-fees underperformance of actively managed funds. Thus, equity mutual fund managers are good stock pickers on average, but the expense ratio and portfolio turnover costs often prove an insurmountable hurdle to beating a passive approach. The Wermers study contains some of the more optimistic conclusions in the literature about the value of active mutual fund management. Even given these results, it is hard to justify recommending high-expense-ratio funds to investors who have the alternative of obtaining exposure to a market sector through low-cost index funds.

Dellva and Olson (1998) also examine the determinants of equity mutual fund expense ratios. They find that lower expenses are associated with larger fund size, older age, and lower cash holdings. Higher expenses are associated with higher portfolio turnover and the fund's status as having an international focus or a 12b-1 fee.

As stated earlier, mutual fund expenses comprise management fees, Rule 12b-1 fees, and "other" expenses. The next sections consider each of these components.

MANAGEMENT FEES

As noted in Haslem, Baker, and Smith (2007), a 1970 amendment to the Investment Company Act of 1940 states that independent directors have a fiduciary duty with respect to the reasonableness of mutual fund fees. Independent directors are not to approve increases in management fees, even with shareholder approval, if the increases provide no shareholder benefit. Further, a majority of independent directors must approve any changes in advisory contracts, and they are "under duty" to request all information that is reasonably necessary to evaluate those contracts.

In his 2004 chairman's letter to Berkshire Hathaway shareholders, Warren Buffett expresses his views about the role of mutual fund boards and management fees:

> [Mutual fund] directors and the entire board have many perfunctory duties, but in actuality have only two important responsibilities: obtaining the best possible investment manager and negotiating with that manager for the lowest possible fee. When you are seeking investment help yourself, those two goals are the only ones that count, and directors acting for other investors should have exactly the same priorities. Yet when it comes to independent directors pursuing either goal, their record has been absolutely pathetic.

Haslem et al. (2008, 2009) show that typical management fees for actively managed U.S. institutional and retail equity funds are between 75 and 80 basis points per year. For both institutional and retail funds, they find that the managers of mutual funds that outperformed their relevant Russell benchmark indexes over 1-, 5-, 10-, and 15-year periods currently receive higher management fees than their underperforming peer managers.

A related but rarely used type of structure is an incentive fee. According to Elton, Gruber, and Blake (2003), only 1.7 percent of mutual funds (that hold 10.5 percent of aggregate assets) employ incentive fees. Such fees are intended to encourage portfolio managers to outperform the funds' benchmark indexes. Incentive fees have fixed and variable components, with the variable component providing a symmetric reward and penalty around the benchmark's performance. Elton et al. find that mutual funds with incentive fees tend not to have to make reward payouts, because manager performance rarely merits such a payment. Funds with incentive fees do outperform matched funds without such fees. The authors caution that this may be due to the motivational effects of the structure, or because superior managerial talent is drawn to funds that have incentive plans. Elton et al. also report that incentive fees appear to increase the risk-taking behavior of portfolio managers.

RULE 12B-1 FEES

Rule 12b-1 fees are among the most controversial in the mutual fund world. The fees, paid by current investors, are permitted under Rule 12b-1 of the Investment Company Act of 1940. Proceeds received from 12b-1 fees are intended as compensation for financial advisers and for marketing and advertising. Such fees were designed to provide incentives for financial advisers to promote growth in fund assets through new flows from their clients. With the fund's management and other fees spread over a larger number of dollars, the expense ratio should decline, providing a benefit to existing investors as well. According to the ICI (2007), 32 percent of stock mutual funds, 35 percent of bond mutual funds, and 15 percent of money market mutual funds charge 12b-1 fees.

How effectively do 12b-1 plans achieve their stated objectives of growing assets and decreasing fees to preexisting investors? Neither Trzcinka and Zweig (1990) nor Chance and Ferris (1991) find a relation between the existence of 12b-1 plans and mutual fund asset growth. In contrast, Barber et al. (2005) find a strong positive relation for 1993 to 1999, and Walsh (2004) confirms this for 1998 to 2002. Thus, the more recent research supports the notion that mutual funds with 12b-1 fees have higher growth than funds without such fees. The next question is whether fund shareholders derive benefit from the increased portfolio size.

Walsh (2004) examines this question and finds that the overall expense ratio decreases as fund size increases, but 12b-1 fees are very sticky. The size of the expense ratio decrease is not nearly as large as the magnitude of the unchanging 12b-1 fee. Moreover, the gross returns of 12b-1 funds are no higher than the returns for non-12b-1 funds, and some evidence suggests they are lower. This confirms in principle Malhotra and McLeod's (1997) earlier result for returns *net* of expenses. Walsh concludes: "These results highlight the significance of the conflict of interest that 12b-1 plans create. Fund advisers use shareholder money to pay for asset growth from which the adviser is the primary beneficiary through the collection of higher fees" (p. 18).

Although the original intent of Rule 12b-1 was to promote a fund's asset base and give existing fund shareholders access to lower expenses due to economies of scale, fund companies themselves do not tend to spend distribution fee revenue on advertising. The ICI (2005) surveyed its members in 2004, finding that 52 percent of fees are spent on shareholder services (with over 90 percent of this going to broker-dealers and bank trust departments); 40 percent are spent to pay financial advisers for initially directing the fund shareholder to the fund (with two-thirds as reimbursement of advance compensation received from an underwriter and one-third as ongoing compensation); 6 percent are paid to fund underwriters; and 2 percent of funds are spent for advertising.

Rosella and Pugliese (2007) note that mutual fund boards are required to reauthorize 12b-1 fee plans on an annual basis. They also cite evidence that even large and closed funds tend to maintain the plans after the apparent need to gather new assets has passed. Rosella and Pugliese hypothesize that investment advisors have become greatly dependent on 12b-1 fee revenue from mutual funds and will switch clients out of an otherwise appropriate fund purely because that fee has been discontinued. Some have speculated that the situation is so acute that mutual fund boards reauthorize the 12b-1 fee plans so that financial advisers will not instruct clients to migrate to other funds.

Given that 12b-1 fees are intended to induce growth in fund size through new investment, investors should expect that closed funds will not levy 12b-1 fees. Surprisingly, many closed funds do. Consider Exhibit 4.6, which shows that according to Morningstar Principia as of December 31, 2007, 116 mutual funds listed as closed had a 12b-1 fee. Of these, 102 funds were closed to new investors only. Fourteen funds were closed to all investors, with three each offered by DWS Scudder, Hartford, and Oppenheimer. As the rightmost column of Exhibit 4.6 indicates, the estimated total revenue from 12b-1 fees paid by investors of closed funds in 2007 is over $300 million. Of this, about $10 million is paid by fund shareholders who are not permitted to invest further in their own funds. First Eagle funds generated by far the highest estimated total 12b-1 fees, $48 million, with Julius Baer, Lord Abbett, and Van Kampen each having more than $20 million.

Exhibit 4.6 Mutual Fund Families Charging 12b-1 Fees for Funds that Are Closed

Fund family	Number of funds charging 12b-1 fees and closed . . .			Revenue from 12b-1 for funds closed . . .		
	. . . to new investors	. . . to all investors	Total	. . . to new investors	. . . to all investors	Total
AIM Investments	12	0	12	$16,009,270	$0	$16,009,270
Alger	1	0	1	$530,000	$0	$530,000
Aston		1	1	$0	$518,000	$518,000
BlackRock	5	1	6	$1,508,400	$793,000	$2,301,400
Calamos	1	0	1	$722,250	$0	$722,250
Champlain Funds	1	0	1	$826,250	$0	$826,250
Columbia	1	0	1	$248,750	$0	$248,750
Credit Suisse	1	0	1	$64,000	$0	$64,000
Delaware Investments	1	0	1	$1,121,700	$0	$1,121,700
Dreyfus	1	0	1	$931,420	$0	$931,420
Dreyfus Founders	5	0	5	$823,820	$0	$823,820
DWS-Scudder	4	3	7	$3,572,860	$335,600	$3,908,460
Eaton Vance	2	0	2	$5,135,750	$0	$5,135,750
Evergreen	2	0	2	$2,528,000	$0	$2,528,000
Farm Bureau	5	0	5	$171,500	$0	$171,500
Fidelity Investments	1	0	1	$19,132,500	$0	$19,132,500
First Eagle	3	0	3	$48,064,500	$0	$48,064,500
Franklin Templeton Investments	5	0	5	$15,152,830	$0	$15,152,830
Gabelli	3	1	4	$2,771,500	$10,750	$2,782,250
GE Asset Management		1	1	$0	$9,000	$9,000
Goldman Sachs	2	0	2	$9,814,250	$0	$9,814,250
Hartford Mutual Funds	1	3	4	$768,500	$5,905,750	$6,674,250
Hotchkis and Wiley	1	0	1	$81,750	$0	$81,750
ING Funds	8	0	8	$12,531,200	$0	$12,531,200
Janus	1	0	1	$3,997,750	$0	$3,997,750
JennisonDryden	2	1	3	$1,758,200	$661,000	$2,419,200
JP Morgan	1	0	1	$1,143,250	$0	$1,143,250
Julius Baer	1	0	1	$27,261,500	$0	$27,261,500
Legg Mason	1	0	1	$1,285,000	$0	$1,285,000
Lord Abbett	3	0	3	$26,837,850	$0	$26,837,850
Metropolitan West Funds	1	0	1	$150,250	$0	$150,250
MFS	1	0	1	$9,257,500	$0	$9,257,500
Morgan Stanley	2	0	2	$224,960	$0	$224,960
Munder	1	0	1	$31,000	$0	$31,000
Nationwide	2	0	2	$1,549,750	$0	$1,549,750
Oppenheimer Funds	2	3	5	$12,756,510	$1,736,500	$14,493,010
Phoenix	2	0	2	$1,596,000	$0	$1,596,000
Pioneer	1	0	1	$562,500	$0	$562,500

Exhibit 4.6 *(Continued)*

Fund family	Number of funds charging 12b-1 fees and closed . . .			Revenue from 12b-1 for funds closed . . .		
	. . . to new investors	. . . to all investors	Total	. . . to new investors	. . . to all investors	Total
Quaker	1	0	1	$7,000	$0	$7,000
Rainier	1	0	1	$9,124,000	$0	$9,124,000
Royce	1	0	1	$8,446,250	$0	$8,446,250
RS Funds	1	0	1	$5,478,750	$0	$5,478,750
State Street Global Advisors	1	0	1	$6,417,000	$0	$6,417,000
STI	1	0	1	$35,250	$0	$35,250
Touchstone	1	0	1	$94,000	$0	$94,000
Van Kampen	6	0	6	$21,017,250	$0	$21,017,250
Veracity Funds	1	0	1	$259,250	$0	$259,250
William Blair	1	0	1	$13,004,500	$0	$13,004,500
Grand Total	102	14	116	$294,806,270	$9,969,600	$304,775,870

Source: Morningstar Principia, data as of December 31, 2007.

"OTHER" EXPENSES WITHIN THE EXPENSE RATIO

This catchall component of expenses can include transfer agent fees, securities custodian fees, shareholder accounting expenses, legal fees, auditor fees, and independent director fees. Transfer agent fees are paid to the entity that conducts crucial back-office functions, such as fund shareholder record keeping, calculation of interest, dividends, and capital gains, and the mailing of account and tax statements to fund shareholders. The custodian is responsible for keeping the mutual fund securities safeguarded and partitioned from other assets. Major banks frequently serve in this role. Accounting expenses relate to the mutual fund's internal record keeping. Auditor fees are paid to an external party that reviews the company's books. As for legal fees, funds require professional assistance in preparing disclosure documents and negotiating investment advisory agreements with the fund's portfolio manager, among other matters.

Independent director fees are paid to the fund's trustees for serving on the board and on board committees. As Birdthistle (2006) notes, in many cases all the mutual funds for a particular adviser have the same board members, which means that the fees for board members can be spread over multiple funds and all those funds' shareholders. While having the same board members for multiple funds can create efficiencies, it also raises potential governance issues that are beyond the scope of this chapter.

LOAD VERSUS EXPENSE RELATION

Livingston and O'Neal (1998) advocate that mutual fund investors take a holistic approach to evaluating fund charges. They point out that the proliferation of fund classes over the past 15 years has created a confusing mix of loads and distribution fees. This presents a challenge to investors who want to evaluate the relative merits of gaining access to a portfolio via the various classes. Livingston and O'Neil examine the virtues and drawbacks of three archetypical fund class structures: Class A shares have a front-end load of 5.75 percent and a 0.25 percent annual distribution (Rule 12b-1) fee; Class B shares have a 5 percent deferred load that decreases to 0 percent after eight years, plus a 1 percent annual distribution fee that decreases to 0.25 percent after eight years; Class C shares have a 1 percent deferred load that decreases to 0 percent after one year, plus a perpetual annual distribution fee of 1 percent. Assuming an annual return of 10 percent and reinvestment of dividends, Livingston and O'Neal show that the Class C shares have the lowest cost if the investment is held for up to eight years, while the Class A shares have the lowest cost for holding periods greater than eight years.

In a later study, Houge and Wellman (2007) observe that the explosion of share classes continues. They note a particular increase in new classes of funds that have much higher total fees than the funds' preexisting classes. Whereas prior to 1990 load funds charged lower expenses than no-load funds, the compensatory relation no longer holds. Houge and Wellman find that load funds, both equity and fixed income, have expenses that are about 50 basis points higher than no-load funds. For equity funds newly launched between 2000 and 2004, the premium is 1.19 percent and for bond funds it is 0.60 percent. According to the authors, this finding reflects the mutual fund industry's skill "at segmenting customers by level of investment sophistication . . . and to use this ability to [charge higher fees] to less knowledgeable investors" (p. 14).

DISTRIBUTION CHANNEL

Bergstresser, Chalmers, and Tufano (2009) show that the distribution channel through which investors obtain their mutual fund shares has an enormous impact on the fee and expense structure for a mutual fund investment. The two main distribution channels are through a broker and through direct purchase of shares from the fund company. Whether measured using a simple or asset-weighted average, the 12b-1 fees, the expense ratios net of 12b-1 fees, and loads are substantially higher for equity, bond, and money market funds obtained through the broker channel. In fact, Bergstresser et al. find that even before accounting for distribution fees, the funds obtained through the broker channel underperformed those obtained through the direct channel. The authors conclude that the broker channel provides no tangible benefit for mutual fund investors and that any value must come from intangible sources that they are unable to identify.

ETFs AND CLOSED-END MUTUAL FUNDS

Investors can enjoy many of the advantages of open-end mutual funds by using exchange-traded funds (ETFs) or closed-end mutual funds. Like open-end funds, the cost of using these alternative instruments includes an expense ratio.

With rare exceptions, ETFs are passive investments designed to track market or sector indexes. One of the chief selling points of ETFs is that expenses are often

Exhibit 4.7 Index Mutual Funds versus ETFs: Lowest Expense Ratios Available for Investments under $10,000

Morningstar Category	Fund Type	Expense Ratio	Fund Name
Large-cap Value	Mutual fund	0.21%	Vanguard Value Index Fund
	ETF	0.11%	Vanguard Value ETF
Large-cap Blend	Mutual fund	0.09%	E*TRADE S&P 500 Index Fund
	ETF	0.07%	Vanguard Total Stock Market ETF
Large-cap Growth	Mutual fund	0.22%	Vanguard Growth Index Fund
	ETF	0.11%	Vanguard Growth ETF
Mid-cap Value	Mutual fund	0.26%	Vanguard Mid Cap Value Index Fund
	ETF	0.13%	Vanguard Mid Cap Value ETF
Mid-cap Blend	Mutual fund	0.09%	Fidelity Spartan Extended Market Fund
	ETF	0.08%	Vanguard Extended Market ETF
Mid-cap Growth	Mutual fund	0.26%	Vanguard Mid Cap Growth Index Fund
	ETF	0.13%	Vanguard Mid Cap Growth ETF
Small-cap Value	Mutual fund	0.23%	Vanguard Small Cap Value Index Fund
	ETF	0.12%	Vanguard Small Cap Value ETF
Small-cap Blend	Mutual fund	0.14%	Vanguard Tax-Managed Small Cap Fund
	ETF	0.10%	Vanguard Small Cap ETF
Small-cap Growth	Mutual fund	0.23%	Vanguard Small Cap Growth Index Fund
	ETF	0.12%	Vanguard Small Cap Growth ETF

Source: Morningstar Principia.

lower than those of open-end mutual funds tracking the same benchmark index. Exhibit 4.7 compares, for the nine Morningstar equity-style categories, expense ratios for the least expensive open-end mutual funds and ETFs as of December 31, 2007. For comparability, only retail class mutual funds are considered, and the minimum initial purchase requirement must be $10,000 or less. In every case, the ETF expense ratio is lower than the paired mutual fund's by at least 1 basis point and sometimes as much as 13. With only two exceptions, Vanguard offers the lowest-expense mutual fund *and* ETF in each category. Of course, the brokerage fees investors must pay to acquire ETF shares can more than offset the lower expense ratio.

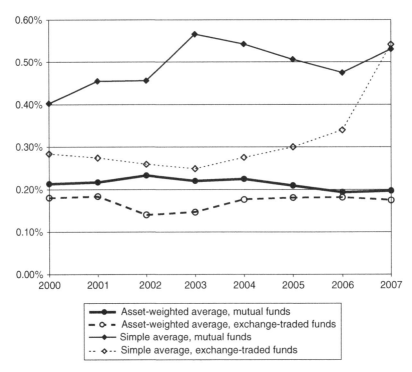

Exhibit 4.8   Average Annual Expense Ratios for Equity ETFs and Equity Index Mutual Funds, 2000–2007
Source: Morningstar Principia.

Exhibit 4.8 shows the trend between 2000 and 2007 of U.S. domestic equity ETF versus index mutual fund expense ratios. The graph includes only funds that Morningstar classifies in one of its nine style box cells. The simple (arithmetic) average expense ratio for ETFs has remained substantially lower until the most recent year, when it was actually above that of open-end mutual funds. Increasingly, investment product providers have introduced ETF specialty funds that provide exposure to equity market niche areas while somewhat deemphasizing expense minimization. Weighted-average expense ratios for ETFs and open-end funds are much lower than simple averages, hovering around 20 basis points for the past eight years. Comparing the two types of averages leads to the conclusion that both ETFs and open-end index mutual funds are most popular with investors who aim to track indexes at a low cost.

For closed-end mutual funds, the data and research available to investors are relatively sparse. Academic studies have focused mainly on explaining the persistence of market discounts and premiums relative to funds' net asset values (NAVs). Thus, investors using closed-end funds to gain exposure to a market sector experience holding period returns not only from the usual sources but also from changes in the funds' discounts and premiums. This additional source of unpredictability complicates the investment decision and makes some investors leery of using closed-end funds. Moreover, as with ETFs, closed-end fund investments require the payment of brokerage fees, and closed-end fund expense ratios are similar in magnitude to those of actively managed open-end funds.

Russel and Malhotra (2008) report average expense ratios of 1.18 to 1.31 percent for several hundred U.S.-based closed-end funds between 1994 and 2002. Domestic funds' expenses are lower, but the average is always above 1 percent. The average expense ratio for international closed-end funds in 2002 was 1.81 percent. Given both the brokerage fees and annual expenses, closed-end funds tend to be an expensive form of mutual fund investment.

TAXES

A discussion of the cost of mutual fund investing would be incomplete without some acknowledgment of tax-related costs. In the United States, taxable investors in mutual funds are liable for ordinary income taxes on fund distributions of dividends and interest. Ordinary income taxes are also due when fund shares are sold for a gain after a holding period of one year or less. Capital gains taxes are due if fund shares are sold for a gain after holding for longer than one year.

The mutual fund tax scenarios noted earlier are no different from those for individual stock and bond investments. However, mutual fund taxation is unique in that the fund can make distributions of capital gains to investors at any time, regardless of how long investors have held the fund shares. Thus an investor buying mutual fund shares can quickly face a tax liability if the fund sells some of its holdings for a gain, even though the investor has not benefited from that gain. Typically, funds plan their sales so as to minimize the tax liability on distributions, and some funds advertise that tax minimization is a prime objective.

Sometimes mutual funds must distribute gains that came about because the fund needed to sell part of its portfolio to meet investor orders to liquidate shares. It is in instances such as this that the "mutual" aspect of mutual funds becomes most apparent: The selling decisions of fellow mutual fund investors directly affect the capital gains distributions and resulting tax expenses of each remaining investor. Thus, it is important not to overlook the fact that open-end mutual fund investing carries a potential tax liability associated with fellow investors' decisions to cash in fund shares.

FEES AND EXPENSES INTERNATIONALLY

Khorana, Servaes, and Tufano (2009) report the costs to mutual fund shareholders in 20 countries as of 2002. Total annual shareholder costs, including amortized loads for an assumed five-year holding period, average 1.39 percent for bond funds and 2.09 percent for equity funds.

Exhibit 4.9 shows countries clustered in quartiles according to the Khorana et al. (2009) calculations of management fees and estimates of total shareholder cost. The exhibit contains aggregate figures for bond and equity funds. The United States has much lower management fees and total costs than any other country listed, by a factor of 2 in many cases. France, Germany, and Luxembourg are in the lowest quartile for both management fees and total costs. Countries in the highest quartile—Canada, Denmark, Finland, and Norway—all have total costs in excess of 2.30 percent per year. For bond funds, Denmark's estimated total annual cost is the highest, at 1.91 percent. For equity funds, Canada's is the highest, at 3.00 percent.

Exhibit 4.9   Annual Management Fees and Total Mutual Fund Shareholder Costs* in 2002: For Aggregated Bond and Equity Funds Available for Sale to Investors in the Countries Listed

Management Fees	Quartile I (0.80–0.89%)	Quartile II (0.93–1.00%)	Quartile III (1.05%–1.17%)	Quartile IV (1.20%–1.70%)
	Belgium	Austria	Australia	Canada
	France	Netherlands	Italy	Denmark
	Germany	Spain	Sweden	Finland
	Luxembourg	Switzerland	United Kingdom	Norway
Total Shareholder Costs	Quartile I (1.41–1.80%)	Quartile II (1.84%–1.98%)	Quartile III (2.03%–2.21%)	Quartile IV (2.30%–2.55%)
	Australia	Austria	Netherlands	Canada
	France	Belgium	Spain	Denmark
	Germany	Italy	Sweden	Finland
	Luxembourg	Switzerland	United Kingdom	Norway

Source: As reported by Khorana, Servaes, and Tufano (2009).
*Total shareholder costs include expenses plus amortized load assuming a 5-year holding period. For reference, U.S. figures are 0.43 percent for management fees and 1.04 percent for total shareholder costs.

Other countries' investors face even higher fees. Babalos, Kostakis, and Nikolaos (2009) find that the average expense ratio for Greek equity mutual funds is well above those countries covered by Khorana et al. In 2006, the respective arithmetic and asset-weighted average expense ratios for mutual funds in Greece were 3.88 percent and 3.27 percent. For both Jensen and Carhart alphas, Babalos et al. find a strong negative relation between expense ratio and performance.

CHARGES NOT INCLUDED IN THE EXPENSE RATIO

There is an assortment of investment costs that some investors face and others escape entirely. The fees levied on investors vary across mutual fund families and account types. One expense that all investors must bear is trading costs.

Some mutual fund families charge investors small fees for switching out of one fund within the family and into another. Such fees can be charged even by funds that do not have a front-end or deferred load. Also, investors who maintain an account balance below a certain threshold are subject to periodic charges for "account maintenance" by some mutual fund families. Moreover, due to Securities and Exchange Commission Rule 22c-2, funds are permitted to levy redemption fees of up to 2 percent. This feature is intended to discourage short-term trading, or at least to compensate the fund for the costs of rapid trading. This measure came in response to the 2003 mutual fund market-timing scandal.

Trading costs are perhaps the least-visible large cost for mutual funds. Such costs are almost never disclosed to investors with the degree of prominence given to the expense ratio or even to the portfolio turnover ratio (which clearly influences trading costs). Karceski, Livingston, and O'Neal (2004) conducted a comprehensive study of trading costs. They point out that the total amount of brokerage commissions—and explicit trading costs—is typically "buried" in the fund's Statement of Additional Information (SAI). For example, in American Mutual Fund's 2007 83-page SAI, the total brokerage fees (about $15 million) paid in the past three fiscal years are disclosed in a paragraph on page 30. For 1989 to 1993, Livingston and O'Neal find that the mean brokerage commissions per year are 0.28 percent of the net assets of equity mutual funds, and the median is 0.21 percent. Not surprisingly, they find that the magnitude is highly dependent on portfolio turnover. Karceski et al. report that the simple (asset-weighted) average brokerage commissions paid by equity mutual funds in 2002 were 38 (18) basis points. For actively managed funds, the average for commissions was 39 (21) basis points, and for index funds, it was 7 (2) basis points.

Karceski et al. (2004) also studied implicit trading costs. Implicit trading costs include the bid–ask spread and market impact costs. Market impact costs tend to be significant for institutional investors such as mutual funds because they trade large amounts of securities in markets of varying liquidity. Thus, the buy and sell orders of mutual funds can move the securities' market prices, which results in the fund transacting at prices that are inferior to those at which a retail investor might trade. Implicit trading costs are not readily observable, and finance researchers use various means to estimate them. Karceski et al. estimate the simple (asset-weighted) average implicit trading costs paid by equity mutual funds in 2002 to be 58 (24) basis points. For actively managed funds, the average for commissions was 60 (27) basis points, and for index funds, it was 17 (5) basis points.

In sum, mutual fund investors pay the costs of brokerage commissions triggered by securities transactions on the part of the portfolio manager. Investors in certain mutual funds must also pay fees when they transact in the fund shares. Although brokerage commissions are not communicated prominently and fund redemption fees occur only when investor trading occurs, potential investors should not ignore these fees because they are nontrivial in size.

PARTITIONING ACTIVELY MANAGED MUTUAL FUND FEES BASED ON ALPHA AND BETA SEPARATION

Given the relatively low cost of buying no-load index mutual funds, investors do well to seek beta exposure to a market via this economical means. Investors are reluctant to pay active mutual fund managers high fees to produce a positive alpha, only to find that the managers' portfolios track the benchmark closely. Numerous studies have observed that actively managed mutual funds' returns have high correlations with relevant benchmark indexes, behavior that some have dubbed "index hugging."

Miller (2007) proposed that most actively managed equity mutual funds can be thought of as having two components, or shares. The first component is the passive share, which mimics the benchmark index. The second component is the active share, which reflects the manager's efforts at beating the benchmark index. In Miller's approach, the passive share is determined first, and the size, cost, and benefits of the active share are inferred from this.

Exhibit 4.10 Active Share, Active Expense Ratio, and Active Alpha, Oppenheimer Main Street Fund: Class A

Year	Audited Expense Ratio (C_F)	R-squared (R^2)	3-year Alpha (α_F)	Weight of Active Share (W_A)	Active Expense Ratio (C_A)	Miller's Active Alpha (α_A)	Vanguard S&P 500 Expense Ratio (C_I)
1997	0.99%	91%	−2.77%	24%	3.50%	−10.94%	0.20%
1998	0.90%	95%	−3.62%	19%	3.99%	−18.57%	0.19%
1999	0.90%	95%	−2.51%	19%	4.04%	−12.67%	0.18%
2000	0.90%	95%	−1.45%	19%	4.04%	−6.99%	0.18%
2001	0.90%	94%	−0.64%	20%	3.75%	−2.46%	0.18%
2002	0.86%	94%	−0.20%	20%	3.55%	−0.28%	0.18%
2003	0.97%	97%	−0.01%	15%	5.46%	0.96%	0.18%
2004	0.93%	97%	0.44%	15%	5.19%	3.97%	0.18%
2005	0.92%	98%	0.05%	13%	6.10%	1.66%	0.18%
2006	0.92%	97%	−0.36%	15%	5.13%	−1.38%	0.18%
2007	0.89%	97%	−0.56%	15%	4.93%	−2.72%	0.18%

Source: Based on Miller (2007).

Miller (2007) derives a method for determining (1) the weight of a mutual fund's active share, (2) the annual expense ratio associated with the active share, and (3) a performance measure associated with the active share. The only inputs required are the actively managed fund's expense ratio, the expense ratio for a mutual fund that tracks the market index, and the R-squared from the regression of the actively managed mutual fund returns on market index returns. Exhibit 4.10 contains those inputs as well as the derived values using Miller's approach, for the Oppenheimer "Main Street fund," Class A shares. As of December 31, 2007, the Main Street fund size was almost $11 billion, and the Class A shares had $7.6 billion invested.

The variables in Exhibit 4.10 are discussed next. C_F is the reported expense ratio for the actively managed mutual fund, and C_I is the annual reported expense ratio for the Vanguard Standard & Poor's (S&P) 500 index fund, which is the largest and oldest open-end index mutual fund (established in August 1976). R^2 shows the proportion of the fluctuations in the three-year monthly return for the Main Street fund that is explained by the returns on the S&P 500 index. If the two return series are perfectly positively correlated—if they go up and down perfectly in sync—the R^2 is 1.00 (or 100 percent). Note also that the R^2 is the square of the correlation coefficient: R. The alpha for the actively managed mutual fund is given as α_F. Alpha is the extent to which the actively managed mutual fund's actual return differs from the expected return based on the fund's beta.

Many mutual funds, including the Main Street fund, attempt to achieve returns in excess of the returns on a benchmark stock index. The S&P 500 index is one of the more commonly used benchmark stock indexes. Managers who attempt to beat the index usually overweight and underweight the individual securities comprising the benchmark index. Due to the intensive analysis required, active management is relatively expensive.

Miller (2007) shows that the R^2 as reported by Morningstar (and based on three years of monthly returns) is all that is necessary to calculate the weight of the portfolio's active share (w_A). The formula is:

$$w_A = \frac{\sqrt{1 - R^2}}{R + \sqrt{1 - R^2}}$$

It is useful to consider an example. Let us say that an actively managed mutual fund has an R^2 of 96 percent relative to its benchmark index. This fund's active share weight would be:

$$w_A = \frac{\sqrt{1 - R^2}}{R + \sqrt{1 - R^2}} = \frac{\sqrt{1 - 0.96}}{0.98 + \sqrt{1 - 0.96}} = 0.169 \approx 17\%$$

Thus, one can think of this fund as being 17 percent actively managed and 83 percent passively managed. Miller reports in his Table 1 that the institutional and retail funds in his sample have average active shares of 15 to 16 percent. Under this situation, the passive (indexed) share of the portfolio is about 84 to 85 percent.

As noted, the cost of passive investing, or indexing, is denoted C_I. The fund's total expense ratio C_F is composed of a weighted average of the expense ratios for the passive and active shares of the portfolio: $C_F = (W_I \times C_I) + (W_A \times C_A)$, where W_I is equal to $(1 - W_A)$. The active expense ratio C_A for each fund is calculated as:

$$C_A = C_I + \frac{(C_F - C_I)}{W_A}$$

Continuing the example, the actively managed mutual fund has an active weight of 17 percent. Assume its expense ratio C_F is 1.5 percent and the expense ratio for indexing, C_I, is 0.18 percent. The active expense ratio for this fund is calculated as:

$$C_A = C_I + \frac{(C_F - C_I)}{W_A} = 0.0018 + \frac{(0.015 - 0.0018)}{0.17} = 7.94\%$$

This active expense ratio of 7.94 percent represents the cost of the active mutual fund manager's services purely from attempting to beat the benchmark index. This, combined with a passive expense ratio of 0.18 percent, constitutes C_F, the fund's total expense ratio of 1.5 percent:

$$C_F = (W_A \times C_A) + (W_I \times C_I) = (0.17 \times 7.94\%) + (0.83 \times 0.18\%) \approx 1.50\%$$

Knowing the weight for the mutual fund's active share and also the associated cost, one can now estimate the performance for the active share. As many investors do for entire funds, Miller (2007) uses alpha (α_A) as the active share's performance measure. Miller notes that assuming an alpha of 0 percent for a zero-expense index fund, the alpha for an index fund should be the negative of the index fund expense ratio, $-C_I$. Alpha for each fund's active portion (shown in the exhibit as "Miller's active alpha, α_A") can be determined by knowing only (1) the actively managed mutual fund's overall alpha, (2) the cost for an index mutual fund, and (3) the R^2 between the actively managed fund's returns and the returns on the benchmark index. The active alpha α_A is calculated as:

$$\alpha_A = \alpha_F + \frac{R(\alpha_F + C_I)}{\sqrt{1 - R^2}}$$

Exhibit 4.10 for the Main Street fund indicates that the active expense ratio is between 3.5 percent and 6.1 percent. The active expense ratio would have been even higher if the overall fund's expense ratio C_F had not been as low as it is.

Further examining the exhibit: The fund's overall expense ratio is ticking downward over the years, and its R^2 relative to the S&P 500 Index is rising. The fund's active share is between 13 and 24 percent, which spans the 15 to 16 percent average that Miller found. All else equal, higher is better, assuming that (1) investors buying this fund want to employ managers who are trying to beat the index, and (2) managers doing the active investing are able to beat the benchmark index over time.

For the Main Street fund, evidence suggests that investors are being charged a full active management fee while the fund's other characteristics more closely reflect a passive index fund. The expense ratio for the active share is never lower than 3.5 percent, and this contributes to an alpha for the active share that is negative in all but three years. In short, the fund's stock-picking activities have failed to add value over the years.

CONCLUSIONS

As discussed in other chapters, mutual funds offer many advantages to investors. However, the sources of mutual fund fees and expenses are many, and the magnitude is potentially large. Charges to investors include front-end loads, deferred loads, operating expenses, trading costs, and various account fees. Operating expenses include a management fee, Rule 12b-1 fee, and other expenses, such as custodial, accounting, legal, and directors' fees. Account fees can include no-load purchase, redemption, switching, and account maintenance fees. There may also exist costs in the form of open-end mutual funds having some potential tax liabilities precipitated by the selling behavior of fellow fund shareholders.

Mutual funds publicly disclose the fees in the broad categories. Obtaining information on certain fees such as trading costs presents a challenge to most investors.

In the U.S. market, the average front-end load has decreased dramatically since the 1960s. Meanwhile, the incidence and average amount of deferred loads has increased. The trend in operating expenses has been less clear. Calculated as a simple (arithmetic) average, expense ratios are now at approximately their level of 15 years ago. Viewed using an asset-weighted average, expense ratios have declined by about 1 basis point per year since 1993. Expense ratios outside the United States tend to be much higher, sometimes by a factor of 2 or 3.

Passively managed mutual funds have much lower expense ratios than do actively managed funds. International equity mutual funds have the highest expense ratios, followed by U.S. domestic stock funds, bond funds, and mutual funds.

The empirical evidence concerning performance versus fees is both statistically and economically significant. Results from a variety of sources show that front-end loads, deferred loads, high expenses, and high 12b-1 fees fail to produce a performance benefit to the investor sufficient to compensate for the charges. Indeed, many "actively managed" mutual funds charge high fees for portfolio management that has the appearance of being passive, and can be done much more cheaply using no-load index funds.

The strong and consistent evidence about the fee versus performance link leads naturally to a recommendation that mutual fund investors minimize investment fees and expenses. Fortunately, there exist no-load, 12b-1-free, low-expense-ratio, passively managed mutual funds that are suitable to most investors' portfolio objectives, preferred asset classes, and desired investment styles.

REFERENCES

American Mutual Fund. 2009. "Part B: Statement of Additional Information," www. americanfunds.com/pdf/mfgepb-903_amfb.pdf.

Babalos, V., A. Kostakis, and P. Nikolaos. 2009. "Managing Mutual Funds or Managing Expense Ratios? Evidence from the Greek Fund Industry," *Journal of Multinational Financial Management*, in press.

Barber, B., T. Odean, and L. Zheng. 2005. "Out of Sight, Out of Mind: The Effects of Expenses on Mutual Fund Flows," *Journal of Business* 78: 6 (November): 2095–2119.

Bergstresser, D., J. M. R. Chalmers, and P. Tufano. 2009. "Assessing the Costs and Benefits of Brokers in the Mutual Fund Industry," *Review of Financial Studies*, in press.

Birdthistle, W. A. 2006. "Compensating Power: An Analysis of Rents and Rewards in the Mutual Fund Industry," *Tulane Law Review* 80: 4 (March): 1401–1465.

Buffett, Warren E. 2004. "Chairman's Letter to Berkshire Hathaway Shareholders." Downloaded from http://www.berkshirehathaway.com/letters/2004ltr.pdf.

Chance, D., and S. P. Ferris. 1991. "Mutual Fund Distribution Fees: An Empirical Analysis of the Impact of Deregulation," *Journal of Financial Services Research* 5: 1 (March): 25–42.

Chordia, T. 1996. "The Structure of Mutual Fund Charges," *Journal of Financial Economics* 41: 1 (May): 3–39.

Dellva, W., and G. Olson. 1998. "The Relationship Between Mutual Fund Fees and Expenses and Their Effects on Performance," *Financial Review* 33: 1 (February): 85–103.

Elton, E. G., M. Gruber, and C. R. Blake. 2003. "Incentive Fees and Mutual Funds," *Journal of Finance* 58: 2 (April): 779–804.

Ennis, R. M. 2005. "Are Active Management Fees Too High?" *Financial Analysts Journal* 61: 5 (Summer): 44–51.

Freeman, J. P. 2007. "The Mutual Fund Distribution Expense Mess," *Journal of Corporation Law* 32: 4 (Summer): 739–831.

Gao, X., and M. Livingston. 2008. "The Components of Mutual Fund Fees," *Financial Markets, Institutions & Instruments* 17: 3 (August): 197–223.

Haslem, J. A., H. K. Baker, and D. M. Smith. 2007. "Identification and Performance of Equity Mutual Funds with Excessive Management Fees and Expense Ratios," *Journal of Investing* 16: 2 (Summer): 1–20.

Haslem, J. A., H. K. Baker, and D. M. Smith. 2008. "Performance and Characteristics of Actively Managed Retail Equity Mutual Funds with Diverse Expense Ratios," *Financial Services Review* 17: 2 (Summer): 49–68.

Haslem, J. A., H. K. Baker, and D. M. Smith. 2009. "Performance and Characteristics of Actively Managed Institutional Equity Mutual Funds," *Journal of Investing* 18: 1 (Spring): 1–19.

Hill, J. M., and R. K. Cheong. 1996. "Minimizing Cash Drag with S&P 500 Index Tools." Working Paper, Goldman Sachs, New York.

Hooks, J. A. 1996. "The Effects of Loads and Expenses on Open End Mutual Fund Returns," *Journal of Business Research* 36: 2 (June): 199–202.

Houge, T., and J. Wellman. 2007. "The Use and Abuse of Mutual Fund Expenses," *Journal of Business Ethics* 70: 1 (January): 23–32.

Investment Company Institute. 2005. "How Mutual Funds Use 12b-1 Fees," www.ici.org/pdf/fm-v14n2.pdf.

Investment Company Institute. 2007. "The Economics of Providing 401(k) Plans: Services, Fees, and Expenses," www.ici.org/stats/res/fm-v17n5.pdf.

Investment Company Institute. 2008. *Investment Company Fact Book*. Downloaded from www.icifactbook.org.

Karceski, J., M. Livingston, and E. O'Neal. 2004. "Portfolio Transactions Costs at U.S. Equity Mutual Funds." Working Paper, University of Florida.

Khorana, A., H. Servaes, and P. Tufano. 2009. "Mutual Funds Fees around the World," *Review of Financial Studies*, 22: 3 (March): 1279–1310.

Livingston, M., and E. S. O'Neal. 1998. "The Cost of Mutual Fund Distribution Fees," *Journal of Financial Research* 21: 2 (Summer): 205–218.

Livingston, M., and E. S. O'Neal. 1996. "Mutual Fund Brokerage Commissions," *Journal of Financial Research* 19: 2 (Summer): 273–292.

Malhotra, D. K., and R. McLeod. 1997. "An Empirical Analysis of Mutual Fund Expenses," *Journal of Financial Research* 20: 2 (Summer): 175–190.

Miller, R. M. 2007. "Measuring the True Cost of Active Management by Mutual Funds," *Journal of Investment Management* 5: 1 (First Quarter): 29–49.

Morey, M. R. 2003. "Should You Carry the Load? A Comprehensive Analysis of Load and No-Load Mutual Fund Out-of-Sample Performance," *Journal of Banking and Finance* 27: 7 (July): 1245–1271.

Morey, M. R. 2002. "Deferred-Load Mutual Funds: Duds or Divine." Working Paper, Pace University.

Morningstar Principia Pro. January 2008.

Rosella, M. R., and D. Pugliese. 2007. "Rule 12b-1: A Look at the Past, Present and Future," *Journal of Investment Compliance* 8 (2): 9–16.

Russel, P. S., and D. K. Malhotra. 2008. "Unraveling the Closed-End Funds Pricing Puzzle: Some New Evidence." Working Paper, Philadelphia University.

Trzcinka, C., and R. Zweig. 1990. "An Economic Analysis of the Cost and Benefits of SEC Rule 12b-1." Monograph Series in Finance and Economics, Salomon Brothers Center for the Study of Financial Institutions, New York.

Walsh, L. 2004. "The Costs and Benefits to Fund Shareholders of 12b-1 Plans: An Examination of Fund Flows, Expenses, and Returns." Working Paper, Office of Economic Analysis, United States Securities and Exchange Commission.

Wermers, R. 2000. "Mutual Fund Performance: An Empirical Decomposition into Stock-Picking Talent, Style, Transaction Costs and Expenses," *Journal of Finance* 55: 4 (August): 1655–1695.

ABOUT THE AUTHOR

David M. Smith is Associate Professor of Finance and Director of the Center for Institutional Investment Management at the University at Albany, State University of New York. He conducts research on corporate finance and investments and is author of more than 20 published articles. Dr. Smith is Associate Editor (finance and accounting) for the *Journal of Business Research.* He serves on boards or committees for the Index Business Association, CFA Institute, and the Institute of Certified Management Accountants. Dr. Smith is the recipient of several teaching and research recognitions, including the SUNY Chancellor's Award for Teaching Excellence and the Financial Planning Association's Financial Frontiers Award. He holds the Chartered Financial Analyst (CFA), Certified Financial Manager (CFM), and Certified Management Accountant (CMA) designations. Dr. Smith earned bachelor's and doctoral degrees in Finance from Virginia Tech.

PART II

The Realities and Analogies of Investing

CHAPTER 5

How Financial Markets Work

LARRY E. SWEDROE
Principal, Buckingham Asset Management, LLC, St. Louis

D espite its obvious importance to every individual, our education system almost totally ignores the field of finance and investments. This is true unless you go to an undergraduate business school or pursue an M.B.A. in finance. The result is that individuals are making investments without the basic knowledge required to understand the implications of their decisions. It is as if they took a trip to a place they have never been with neither a road map nor directions. Lacking a formal education in finance, most investors make decisions based on the accepted *conventional wisdom*—ideas that have become so ingrained that few individuals question them. Unfortunately, most of the conventional wisdom about investing is not only wrong, but it is illogical.

The goals for this chapter are threefold. The first is to explain how markets really work, doing so in a way that makes it easy to understand even difficult concepts. I hope to accomplish this objective through the use of stories and analogies that present the logic in a paradigm with which you are already familiar, and then relate that logic to the world of investing. If you understand the logic in the story, it should be just as clear when the logic is related to investing—especially when the evidence supports the logic.

If I am successful in meeting the first objective, I will have also achieved the second objective—to forever change the way you think about investing and how markets work. The third objective is to provide you with sufficient knowledge to begin to make more informed and more prudent investment decisions.

We begin with a story related to the betting on sporting events and show how that relates to how the financial markets set prices.

HOW MARKETS SET PRICES

It is not easy to get rich in Las Vegas, at Churchill Downs, or at the local Merrill Lynch office.

—Paul Samuelson

Note: Charter Financial Publishing Network kindly granted permission to include selected material from Larry E. Swedroe, *Wise Investing Made Simple*, 2007. Shrewsbury, NJ: Charter Financial Publishing Network.

On any given Saturday during the college basketball season, there may be 100 games being played. In some of those games, it is easy to identify the better team. For example, Duke is a perennial contender for the national college basketball championship. Duke's illustrious coach, Mike Krzyzewski (Coach K), is a graduate of West Point. Each year he schedules a game with Army as a favor to his alma mater. Though the likelihood of Army winning is about as likely as the sun rising in the west, the game does generate a large amount of revenue for West Point. These types of mismatches are known as cupcake games.

Every major school has a few cupcake games on its schedule, particularly early in the season. Even a fan with limited knowledge would be able to predict the winner of this type of game the majority of the time. A fan who was an "expert" would be able to predict the winner at least 90 percent of the time. The reason is simple. Duke has better shooters, better rebounders, better defenders, quicker athletes who can also jump higher, a better coach, better training facilities, and so on. This makes it easy to identify which team will likely win a game between Army and Duke.

Yet there are many games in which it is more difficult to predict the winner. This is especially true later in the season when conference play begins. A good example of a game that is typically difficult to predict the winner of would be when the Duke Blue Devils play their hated rivals, the Tar Heels of North Carolina. Since a monkey throwing darts would be expected to predict the winner of such games 50 percent of the time, a fan with limited knowledge should be expected to do no worse. A fan with "expert" knowledge should, however, be able to do better than monkeys. Perhaps such an expert might be able to forecast the winner of these types of games with an accuracy of 60 percent.

Most of us know at least a few individuals who think they are experts on sports. Some may even have an account with a local bookie or a Las Vegas book-making firm. As I said earlier, such experts are likely to be able to predict the winners of the cupcake games with 90 percent accuracy and the winners of the remainder of the games with an accuracy of 60 percent. Thus, they might be expected to be able to predict the winner of all games with an accuracy of perhaps 75 percent. But the story gets even better—these experts do not have to bet on all the games. They can avoid betting on the games when it is difficult to predict the winner. They can limit the selection of games on which they place a bet to only those games where they are highly confident they can predict the winner. By so doing they can be confident that they will be successful at least 90 percent of the time. Yet despite the ability to bet only on games where there is a greater than 90 percent chance of being able to predict the winner correctly, it is unlikely that you know even a single person who has become rich betting on sporting events. It is also likely that you do not know anyone who knows anyone who has made a fortune in that way. You might, however know someone who has made a small fortune betting on sporting events by starting out with a large one!

With the odds of success of being able to predict winners so high, why don't we know people who have achieved great wealth by betting on sports? The answer is quite simple: You cannot simply bet on Duke to beat Army. If you want to bet on Duke to beat Army, you might have to provide the counterparty to your bet with a handicap (known as the point spread) of perhaps 40 points. In other words, Duke not only has to beat Army, Duke has to beat Army by more than 40 points for you to win the bet. This point spread is the reason we don't hear about rich gamblers, only rich bookies. And the reason we hear about rich bookies is that gambling involves costs. Consider the next example.

Mark is a Duke fan and bets on the Blue Devils to beat Army by more than 40 points. In betting lingo, Mark "gives" points. Steve is a graduate of West Point and even though he knows Duke is likely to beat Army, he does not think it likely that they will do so by such a large margin. Thus, he "takes" the points and bets on Army. If Mark and Steve are friends and they bet against each other, we have what is known as a zero-sum game. For example, if they bet $10, one would win $10 and the other would lose $10. The net of the two is zero. If they made a bet through a bookie, however, each would have to bet $11 to win just $10. This becomes a negative-sum game for Mark and Steve. The winner of the bet will win $10. The loser, however, is out $11. The difference of $1 is known as the vigorish. It is a profit for the bookie. The game for Mark and Steve has become a negative sum. Note that the bookies win whether you win or lose. They just need you to play in order for them to win. I hope you are beginning to see the analogy to investing—we could compare a stockbroker to a bookie! They win whether you win or lose. They only need you to play for them to win. Perhaps that is why Woody Allen said, "A stockbroker is someone who invests your money until it is all gone." One translation: The objective of stockbrokers is to transfer assets from your account to their accounts. As my good friend, and author of three wonderful books, Bill Bernstein (2002) says: "The stockbroker services his clients in the same way that Bonnie and Clyde serviced banks."

Continuing our story, it is important to understand who sets the point spreads. Most people believe that it is the bookies who determine the spread. Although that is the conventional wisdom, it is incorrect. It is the market that determines the point spread. The bookies only set the *initial* spread. This is an important point to understand. Let us begin with an understanding of whether the bookies want to *make* bets or *take* bets—and there is a difference between the two.

If the bookies were to make bets, they might actually lose money by being on the wrong side of the bet. Again, think of a stockbroker. If you want to buy a stock (making a bet on the company), you have to buy it from someone. A stockbroker is not going to sell that stock to you because he might lose money. Instead, he finds someone that wants to sell the stock and matches the buyer with the seller. He is *taking* bets, not *making* bets. In the process he earns the vigorish (a commission). Like stockbrokers, bookies want to *take* bets, not *make* them. Thus, they set the initial point spread at the price they believe will balance the forces of supply and demand (the point at which an equal amount of money will be bet on Duke and Army). To illustrate how the process works, consider the next example.

What would happen if a bookie made a terrible mistake and posted a point spread of zero in the Duke versus Army game? Obviously, gamblers would rush to bet on Duke. The result would be an imbalance of supply and demand. The bookies would end up making bets—something they are loath to do.

As with any market, an excess of demand leads to an increase in price. The point spread would begin to rise, and it would continue to rise until supply equals demand, and the bookies had an equal amount of money bet on both sides (or at least as close to that as they could manage). At that point they are taking bets, not making them. And the bookies would win no matter the outcome of the game.

In one of my favorite films, *Trading Places*, Eddie Murphy makes a similar observation about the commodity brokerage firm of Duke and Duke. When the Duke brothers explain that they get a commission on every trade, whether the clients make money or not, Murphy exclaims: "Well, it sounds to me like you guys are a couple of bookies."

As you can see, it is the market that determines the point spread (or the price of Duke). In other words, it is a bunch of amateurs like you and me (and I played college basketball), who think they know something about sports, who are setting the spread. And even with a bunch of amateurs setting the spread (not the professional bookies), most of us do not know anyone who has become rich betting on sports. It seems that a bunch of amateurs are setting point spreads at prices that make it extremely difficult for even the most knowledgeable sports fan to exploit any mispricing, after accounting for the expenses of the effort. The important term here is *after expenses*.

Because of the vigorish, it is not enough to be able to win more than 50 percent of the bets. With a vigorish of 10 percent, a bettor (investor) would have to be correct about 53 percent of the time to come out ahead. And that assumes there are no other costs involved (including the value of the time it takes to study the teams, analyze the spread, and make the bet).

In economic terms, a market in which it is difficult to persistently exploit mispricings after the expenses of the effort is called an *efficient market*. Because we do not know of people who have become rich betting on sports, we know intuitively that sports betting markets are efficient. However, intuition is often incorrect. It helps to have evidence supporting your intuition. Before we look at the evidence, however, we need a definition.

Point Spreads and Random Errors

An *unbiased estimator* is a statistic that is *on average* neither too high nor too low. The method of estimation does not always produce estimates that correspond to reality, but errors in either direction are equally likely. It turns out that the point spread is an unbiased estimate of the outcome of sporting events—while it is not expected to be correct in every instance, when it is incorrect the errors are randomly distributed with a zero mean. To make this clear, we return to our Duke-versus-Army example in which Duke was favored by 40 points. Duke does not have to win by *exactly* 40 points for the market in sports betting to be considered efficient. In fact, the likelihood of Duke winning by exactly that amount would be very low. However, that is not relevant to the issue of whether the market for sports betting is efficient. What is relevant is whether you can predict whether Duke will win by more than 40 or less than 40. If half the time it wins by more and half the time it wins by less, and there is no way to know when Duke will be above or below the point spread, the point spread is an unbiased predictor—and the market is efficient. With this understanding, we are ready to examine the evidence.

Examining the Evidence

Research has found that point spreads are accurate in the sense that they are *unbiased predictors*. For example, in a study covering six NBA seasons, Raymond Sauer (1998) found that the average difference between point spreads and actual point differences was less than one-quarter of one point. When you consider that, on average, the market guessed the actual resulting point spread with an error of less than one-quarter of one point, and there is a 10 percent cost of playing, it is easy to understand why we do not know people who have become rich from betting on sports. And it is easy to see that the market in sports betting is what economists call efficient. The important lesson is that while it is often easy to identify the better team (in this case Duke), that is not a *sufficient* condition for exploiting the market. It is only a *necessary* condition. The *sufficient* condition is that you have to be able to exploit any mispricing by the market. For example, if you knew that Duke should be favored by 40 points, but the point spread was only 30 points, and you could consistently identify such opportunities, then the market would be inefficient. This, however, is not the case.

Horse racing presents an even more amazing outcome, especially when you consider this story. My mother loved to go to the track. Like many people, she chose the horses on which she would bet by either the color of the jockey's outfit or the name of the horse. If the jockey wore purple, forget about it. She hated the color purple. And she always bet on the three horse in the first race. Now, there are fans who go to the track and make a "science" of studying each horse's racing history and under what racing conditions the horse did well or poorly. And perhaps these experts even attend workouts to time the horses. So we have these "experts" competing against people like my mother. Yet, the final odds, which reflects the judgment of all bettors, reliably predict the outcome—the favorite wins the most often, the second favorite is the next most likely to win, and so on. It gets even better. Surowiecki (2004) states that a horse with three-to-one odds wins about one-fourth of the time! It seems that the collective wisdom of the crowd is a tough competitor, indeed.

An Efficient Market

An efficient market is one in which trading systems fail to produce excess returns because everything *currently* knowable is already incorporated into prices (Duke is so much better than Army they should be favored by 40 points, but not more). The next piece of available information will be random as to whether it will be better or worse than the market already expects. The only way to beat an efficient market is either to know something that the market does not know—such as the fact that a team's best player is injured and will not be able to play—or to be able to interpret information about the teams better than the market (other gamblers collectively) does. You have to search for a game where the strength of the favorite is underestimated or the weakness of the underdog overestimated; and thus the spread, or the market, is wrong. The spread is really the competition. And the spread is determined by the collective wisdom of the entire market. This is an important point to understand. Let us see why.

Returning to our example of Mark and Steve betting on Duke versus Army, if there were no sports betting market to which Mark and Steve could refer, they would have to set the point spread themselves—instead of the market setting the spread. Now, Mark might be a more knowledgeable fan than Steve, who also happens to be a graduate of West Point. Steve's heart might also influence his thinking. Thus, when Mark offers to give Steve 30 points, Steve jumps at the chance and bets on Army. Mark has just exploited Steve's lack of knowledge. (Mark might still lose the bet, but the odds of winning the bet have increased in his favor.)

The existence of an efficient public market in which the knowledge of all investors is at work in setting prices serves to protect the less informed bettors (investors) from being exploited. The flip side is that the existence of an efficient market prevents the sophisticated and more knowledgeable bettors (investors) from exploiting their less knowledgeable counterparts. And, as we have seen, the spread is an unbiased predictor and the market is efficient. The result is that the *market* is a tough competitor.

There are other important points to understand about sports betting and how it relates to investing. The first is that in the world of sports betting, a bunch of amateurs are setting prices. Even though that is the case, we saw that it is difficult to find pricing errors that could be exploited. In the world of investing, however, professionals are setting prices.

It is estimated that about 80 percent of all trading is done by large institutional traders. In fact, Ellis (1998) states that the most active 50 institutions account for about one-half of all trading on the New York Stock Exchange. Thus, they are the ones setting prices, not amateur individual investors. With professionals (instead of amateurs) dominating the market, the competition is certainly tougher. Every time an individual buys a stock, he should consider that he is competing with these giant institutional investors. The individual investor should also acknowledge that the institutions have more resources, and thus it is more likely that they will succeed.

Another difference between sports betting and investing is best illustrated by returning to our example of Duke versus Army. Imagine that you are best friends with Coach K. As a birthday present, he invites you into the Duke locker room to meet the players and hear the pregame talk. As the players are exiting the locker room to start warming up, Duke's star point guard trips over a water bucket and breaks his ankle. Your mercenary instincts take over and you immediately pull out your cell phone and place a large bet on Army, taking 40 points. You possessed information that others did not have and took advantage of it. And the best part is that there is nothing illegal about that "trade."

Now remember that it is likely that few, if any, of us knows anyone who has become rich betting on sports, despite the existence of rules that allow you to exploit what in the world of investing would be considered inside information. And in the world of investing, it is illegal to trade and profit from inside information, as Martha Stewart found out. Even individuals who have had inside information, such as Pete Rose, and could influence the outcomes of sporting events, do not seem to be able to persistently exploit such information.

The conclusion that we can draw from the evidence is that the markets for betting on sports are highly efficient. This is true despite both the lack of rules against insider trading and the fact that it is a bunch of amateurs who *think they know* something about sports (and often bet on their home team or alma mater with their hearts and not their heads) who are setting prices. In the world of investing, there are specific rules against insider trading and the competition is tougher since it is the professional investors who are setting prices. In addition, as is the case with sports betting, being smarter than the market is not enough because there are costs involved. In sports betting, the cost is the vigorish.

The problem for those investors trying to exploit mispricings in the stock market is that there are also costs involved. As with sports betting, the "bookies" (brokerage firms) have to be paid when active investors place their bets. Trading involves not only commissions but also the spread between the bid (the price dealers are willing to pay) and the offer (the price at which dealers are willing to sell). If you place your assets with a mutual fund, you also have to pay the operating costs of the mutual fund—which generally are higher for actively managed funds than for passively managed ones.

And for institutional investors, costs may also include what are called market-impact costs. Market impact is what occurs when a mutual fund (or other investor) wants to buy or sell a large block of stock. The fund's purchases or sales will cause the stock to move beyond its current bid (lower) or offer (higher) price, increasing the cost of trading. For taxable accounts, there is also the burden of capital gains taxes created by actively trading the portfolio.

I continue with the analogy between sports betting and investing by examining how investors set the prices of individual stocks.

How Stock Prices Are Set

Stock prices are set in a similar manner to how point spreads are established. A good analogy to the point spread setting process is how underwriters set the price of an *initial* public offering (IPO). Just as bookies survey the market to set the initial point spread so that supply will equal demand (so that they can take bets, not make them), underwriters survey potential investors and set the price based on their best estimate of the price needed to sell all the shares. Once the IPO is completed, the shares will trade in what is called the secondary market. Just as with sports betting, in the secondary market, the forces of supply and demand take over. The only difference is that instead of point spreads setting prices, they are determined by the price-to-earnings (P/E) ratio or the book-to-market (BtM) ratio. The P/E and BtM ratios act just like the point spread. The next example will make this clear.

Battle of the Discount Stores

As an investor, you are faced with the decision to purchase the shares of either Wal-Mart or JC Penney. Wal-Mart is generally considered to be one of the top retailers. It has great management, the best store locations, an outstanding inventory management system, a strong balance sheet, and so on. Because of its great prospects, Wal-Mart is considered a growth stock. JC Penney, however, is a weak company. It has had poor management, old stores in bad locations, a balance sheet that has been devastated by weak earnings, and the like. JC Penney is a company that is distressed. Because of its poor prospects, JC Penney is considered a value stock. Just as it was easy to identify the better team in the Duke versus Army example, it is easy to identify the better company when faced with choosing between Wal-Mart and JC Penney. Most individuals faced with having to buy either Wal-Mart or JC Penney would not even have to think about the decision—they would rush to buy Wal-Mart. But is that the right choice?

As we saw in the sports betting story, being able to identify the better team did not help us make the decision as to which one was the better bet. Let us see if the ability to identify the better company helps us make an investment decision. Before reading on, think about which company is Duke and which one is Army.

Imagine that both Wal-Mart and JC Penney have earnings of $1 per share. That is certainly possible even though Wal-Mart generates far more profits.

Wal-Mart might have 1 billion shares outstanding and JC Penney might only have 100 million shares outstanding. Now imagine a world where Wal-Mart and JC Penney both traded at a price of 10. Which stock would you buy in that world? Clearly you would rush to buy Wal-Mart. The problem is that Wal-Mart is like Duke and JC Penney is like Army. And Wal-Mart and JC Penney trading at the same price is analogous to the point spread in the Duke-versus-Army game being set by the bookies at zero. Hell will freeze over before either happens. Just as sports fans would rush in and bet on Duke, driving up the point spread until the odds of winning the bet were equal, investors would drive up the price of Wal-Mart relative to the price of JC Penney until the *risk-adjusted expected returns* from investing in either stock was equal. Let us see how that might look in terms of prices for the shares of Wal-Mart and JC Penney.

As JC Penney is a weak company with relatively poor prospects, investors might be willing to pay just seven times earnings for its stock. Thus, with earnings of $1 per share, the stock would trade at $7. The company might also have a book value of $7 per share. Thus, the BtM would be 1 ($7 book value divided by its $7 market price). Wal-Mart is not only a safer investment due to its stronger balance sheet, but it has outstanding growth prospects. Thus, investors might be willing to pay 30 times earnings for Wal-Mart stock. Thus, with $1 per share in earnings, the stock would trade at $30. The company might also have a book value of just $3 per share. Thus, the BtM would be 0.1 ($3 book value divided by its $30 market price). Wal-Mart is trading at a P/E ratio that is over four times that of the P/E ratio of JC Penney. It is also trading at a BtM that is only one-tenth that of the BtM of JC Penney. Wal-Mart is Duke having to give Army 40 points to make Army an equally good bet.

Financial Equivalent of the Point Spread

The P/E and the BtM ratios act just like point spreads. The only difference is that instead of having to give away a lot of points to bet on a great team to win, you have to pay a higher price relative to earnings and book value for a great glamour company than for a distressed value company. If you bet on the underdog (Army), you get the point spread in your favor. Similarly, if you invest in a distressed value company (JC Penney) you pay a low price relative to earnings and book value. The great sports team (Duke) has to overcome large point spreads to win the bet. The great company (Wal-Mart) has to overcome the high price you pay in order to produce above-market returns. In gambling, the middlemen who always win as long as you play are the bookies. In investing, the middlemen who always win—as long as you try to pick mutual funds or stocks that will outperform—are the active fund managers and the stockbrokers. They win regardless of whether you win or not. They win as long as you agree to play—betting that one fund, or one stock, is going to outperform another.

Let us again consider the analogy between sports betting and investing in stocks via six arguments.

1. In sports betting, sometimes it is easy to identify the better team (Duke versus Army) and sometimes it is more difficult (Duke versus North Carolina). The same is true of stocks. It is easy to identify which company, Wal-Mart or

JC Penney, is the superior one. It is harder when our choices are Wal-Mart and Costco.

2. In sports betting, we do not have to bet on all the games; we can choose to bet only on the games in which we can easily identify the better team. Similarly we do not have to invest in all stocks. We can choose to invest only in the stocks of the superior companies.

3. In sports, the problem with betting on the good teams is that the rest of the market also knows that they are superior and you have to give away lots of points. The point spread eliminates any advantage gained by betting on the superior team. The same is true with investing. The price you have to pay for investing in superior companies is a higher P/E ratio (offsetting the more rapid growth in earnings that are expected) and a lower BtM (offsetting the lesser risk of the greater company). In sports, the pricing mechanism in place would make betting on either team an equally good bet. The same applies for investing: Either stock would make an equally good investment. Thus, while being able to identify the better team (company) is a *necessary* condition of success, it is not a *sufficient* one.

4. When a bet is placed between friends, it is a zero-sum game. However, when the bet is placed with a bookie, the game becomes a negative-sum one because of the costs involved (the bookies win). Since we cannot trade stocks between friends, trading stocks must be a negative-sum game because of the costs involved (the market makers earn the bid–offer spread, the stockbrokers charge commissions, the active managers charge large fees, and Uncle Sam collects taxes).

5. In the world of sports betting, it should be relatively easy to exploit mispricing because it is amateurs that are the competition setting prices. In the world of investing, the competition is tougher since the competition is mostly large institutional investors, not amateurs like you and me.

6. In sports betting, it is legal to trade on inside information. Yet even with such an advantage it is likely that you do not know anyone who has become rich by exploiting this type of knowledge. It is illegal to trade on inside information regarding stocks, however. Thus, it must be even more difficult to win that game.

The evidence from the world of investing supports the logic of these arguments. Study after study demonstrates that the majority of both individual and institutional investors who attempt to beat the market by either picking stocks or timing the market fail miserably, and do so with great persistence. A brief summary of the evidence follows.

Individual Investors

University of California professors Brad Barber and Terrance Odean have produced a series of landmark studies on the performance of individual investors. One Barber and Odean (2000b) study found that the stocks individual investors buy underperform the market after they buy them, and the stocks they sell outperform after they sell them. Barber and Odean (2001) also found that male investors underperform the market by about 3 percent per annum, and women (because they trade less and thus incur less costs) trail the market by about 2 percent per annum. In addition, Barber and Odean (2000b) found that those investors who traded the most trailed the market on a risk-adjusted basis by over 10 percent per annum. And to prove that more heads are not better than one, Barber and Odean (2000a) found that investment clubs trailed the market by almost 4 percent per annum. Because all these figures are on a pretax basis, once taxes are taken into account, the story would become even more dismal. Perhaps it was this evidence that convinced Andrew Tobias (1978), author of *The Only Investment Book You Will Ever Need*, to offer this sage advice: "If you find yourself tempted to ask the question what stock should I buy, resist the temptation. If you do ask, don't listen. And, if you hear an answer, promise yourself that you will ignore it."

Institutional Investors

Institutional investors do not fare much better than individual investors. Mark Carhart's (1997) study, "On Persistence in Mutual Funds," analyzed 1,892 mutual funds for the period 1962 to 1993. Based on the conclusions reached in this landmark study, once one accounts for common risk factors such as size and value, the average equity fund underperformed its appropriate style benchmark by about 1.8 percent per annum on a pretax basis.

In addition, Carhart, now cohead of the quantitative strategies group at Goldman Sachs, found no evidence of any persistence in outperformance beyond the randomly expected. And if there is no persistence in performance, there is no way to identify the few future winners ahead of time. The figures here are all on a pretax basis as well. Thus, the effect of taxes on after-tax returns would make the story even worse.

Moral of the Tale

All good stories have morals. So what is the moral of this tale? The moral is that betting against an efficient market is a loser's game. It does not matter whether the "game" is betting on a sporting event or trying to identify which stocks are going to outperform the market. While it is possible to win betting on sporting events, because the markets are highly efficient, the only likely winners are the bookies. In addition, the more you play the game, the more likely it is you will lose and the bookies will win. The same is true of investing. And the reason is that the securities markets are also highly efficient.

If you are trying to time the market or pick stocks, you are playing a loser's game. Just as it is possible that by betting on sporting events you can win, it is possible that by picking stocks, timing the market, or using active managers to play the game on your behalf, you will win (outperform). However, the odds of winning are poor. And just as with gambling, the more and the longer you play the game, the more likely it is that you will lose (as the costs of playing compound). This makes accepting market returns (passive investing) the winner's game.

By investing in passively managed funds and adopting a simple buy, hold, and rebalance strategy, you are guaranteed to not only earn market rates of returns, but you will do so in a low-cost and relatively tax-efficient manner. You are also virtually guaranteed to outperform the majority of professional and individual investors. Thus, it is the strategy most likely to achieve the best results. The bottom line is that while gamblers make bets (speculate on individual stocks and actively managed funds), investors let the markets work for them, not against them.

Surowiecki's (2004) quote sums up this tale: "Information isn't in the hands of one person. It's dispersed across many people. So relying on only your private information to make a decision guarantees that it will be less informed than it could be."

The next story focuses on debunking one of the greatest investment fables. It does so by explaining how risk and expected return must be related.

GREAT COMPANIES DO NOT MAKE HIGH-RETURN INVESTMENTS

Investors must keep in mind that there's a difference between a good company and a good stock. After all, you can buy a good car but pay too much for it.

—Loren Fox

It is New Year's Day 1964. John Doe is the greatest security analyst in the world. He is able to identify, with uncanny accuracy, the companies that will produce high rates of return on assets over the next 40 years. Unlike real-world analysts and investors, he *never* makes a mistake in forecasting which companies will produce great earnings. In the history of the world there has never been such an analyst. Even Warren Buffett has made mistakes, investing in companies like U.S. Air and Salomon Brothers.

While John cannot see into the future as it pertains to the *stock prices* of those companies, following the *conventional wisdom* of Wall Street, he builds a portfolio of the stocks of these great companies. He does so because he has confidence that since these are going to be great-performing companies, they will make great investments. Relating this to our sports betting story, he has identified the Dukes of the investment world. We can identify these great companies ourselves by the fact that growth companies have high price-to-earnings ratios.

Jane Smith, however, believes that markets are efficient. She bases her strategy on the theory that if the market believes a group of companies will produce superior results, the market must also believe that they are relatively safe investments. With this knowledge, investors (the market) will already have bid up the price of those stocks to reflect those great expectations and the low level of perceived risk. While the *companies* are likely to produce great financial results, the *stocks* of these great companies are likely to produce relatively low returns. Jane, expecting (though not being certain) that the market will reward her for taking risk, instead buys a passively managed portfolio of the stocks of value, or distressed, companies. She even anticipates the likelihood that, on average, these *companies* will continue to be relatively poor performers. Despite this expectation, she does expect the *stocks* to provide superior returns, thereby rewarding her for taking risk. We can identify these companies by their low price-to-earnings ratios.

As you will see, Jane believes that markets work—they are efficient. John does not. Relating this to our sports betting story, John believes that you can bet on Duke and not have to give any points when it plays Army.

Faced with the choice of buying the stocks of "great" companies or buying the stocks of "lousy" companies, most investors would instinctively choose the former. Before looking at the historical evidence, ask yourself: What would you do? Assuming your only objective is to achieve high returns, regardless of the risk entailed, would you buy the stocks of the great companies or the stocks of the lousy companies?

Let us now jump forward to 2006. How did John's and Jane's investment strategies work out? Who was right? In a sense, they were both right. For the 42-year period ending in 2005, the return on assets (ROA) for John's great growth stocks was 9.3 percent per year. This was over twice the 4.0 percent ROA for Jane's lousy-value stocks. The average annual return to investors in Jane's value stocks was, however, 16.1 percent per annum—49 percent greater than the 10.8 percent average annual return to investors in John's great growth stocks.

If the major purpose of investment research is to determine which companies will be the great-performing companies, and when you are correct in your analysis, you produce inferior results, why bother? Why not save the time and the expense and just let the markets reward you for taking risk?

Small Companies versus Large Companies

If the theory that markets provide returns commensurate with the amount of risk taken holds true, one should expect to see similar results if Jane invested in a passively managed portfolio consisting of small companies that are intuitively riskier than large companies. For example, small companies do not have the economies of scale that large companies have, making them generally less efficient. They typically have weaker balance sheets and fewer sources of capital. When there is distress in the capital markets, smaller companies are generally the first ones to be cut off from access to capital, increasing the risk of bankruptcy. They do not have the depth of management that larger companies do. They generally do not have long track records from which investors can make judgments. The cost of trading small stocks is much greater, increasing the risk of investing in them. And so on.

When one compares the performance of the asset class of small companies with the performance of the large-company asset class, one gets the same results produced by the great-company versus value-company comparison. For the same 42-year period ending in 2005, while small companies produced returns on assets almost 40 percent below those of large companies (3.7 percent versus 6.0 percent), the annual average investment return on the stocks of small companies exceeded the return on stocks of large companies by about 36 percent (16.1 percent versus 11.8 percent). What seems to be an anomaly actually makes the point that markets work. The riskier investment in small companies produced higher returns.

Why Great Earnings Do Not Translate into Great Investment Returns

The simple explanation for this anomaly is that investors discount the future expected earnings of value stocks at a higher rate than they discount the future earnings of growth stocks. This more than offsets the faster earnings growth rates of growth companies. The high discount rate results in low current valuations for value stocks and higher expected future returns relative to growth stocks. Why do investors use a higher discount rate for value stocks when calculating the current value? The next example should provide a clear explanation.

Let us consider the case of two identical (except for location) office buildings that are for sale in your town. Property A is in the heart of the most desirable commercial area, while Property B borders the worst slum in the region. Clearly it is easy to identify the more desirable property. (Just as it is easy to identify that Duke is better than Army.) If you could buy either property at $10 million, the obvious choice would be Property A. This world, therefore, could not exist. If it did, investors would bid up the price of Property A relative to Property B.

Now let us imagine a slightly more realistic scenario, one in which Property A is selling at $20 million and Property B at $5 million. Based on the projected rental cash flows, you project that (by coincidence) both properties will provide an expected rate of return of 10 percent—the higher rent tenants pay for the better location is exactly offset by the higher price you have to pay to buy the property. Faced with the choice of which property to buy, the rational choice is still Property A. The reason is that it provides the same expected return as Property B while being a less risky investment. Being able to buy the safer investment at the same expected return as a riskier one would be like being able to bet on Duke to beat Army and not have to give away any points. Thus, this world could not exist either.

In the real world, Property A's price would continue to be bid up relative to Property B's. Perhaps Property A's price might rise to $30 million and Property B's might fall to $4 million. Now Property A's expected rate of return is lower than Property B's. Investors demand a higher expected return for taking more risk. It is important to understand that the fact that Property A provides a lower expected rate of return than Property B does not make it a worse investment choice—just a safer one. The market views it as less risky and thus discounts its future earnings at a lower rate. The result is that the price of Property A is driven up, which in turn lowers its expected return. The price differential between the two will reflect the perceived differences in risk. Risk and *ex-ante* reward must be related. The way to think about this is that the market drives prices until the *risk-adjusted* returns are equal. It is true that Property B has higher expected returns. However, we must adjust those higher expected returns for the greater risk entailed.

Most everyone understands the relationship between risk and expected return in the context of this example. However, it always amazes me that this most basic of principles is almost universally forgotten when thinking about stocks and how they are priced by the market.

With this understanding, we can now complete the picture by considering the case of two similar companies, Wal-Mart and JC Penney. Think of Wal-Mart as Property A and JC Penney as Property B. Most investors would say that Wal-Mart is a better company and a safer investment. Another way to think about the two companies is that Wal-Mart is Duke and JC Penney is Army. If an investor could buy either company at the same market capitalization, say $20 billion, the obvious choice would be Wal-Mart. It would be like betting on Duke and not having to give away any points. Wal-Mart not only has higher current earnings, but it is also expected to produce a faster growth of earnings. If this world existed, investors owning shares in JC Penney would immediately sell those shares in order to be able to buy shares in Wal-Mart. Their actions would drive up the price of Wal-Mart and drive down the price of JC Penney. This would result in lowering the risk premium demanded by investors in Wal-Mart and raising it on JC Penney.

Now let us say that Wal-Mart's price rises relative to JC Penney. Wal-Mart is now selling at $100 billion and JC Penney at $10 billion. At this point the two have the same *expected* (not guaranteed) future rate of return—say 10 percent. Given that Wal-Mart is perceived to be the better company, and therefore a less risky investment, investors should still choose Wal-Mart. The reason is that although we now have equal expected returns, there is less perceived risk in owning Wal-Mart. So our process of investors buying Wal-Mart and selling JC Penney continues.

It does so until the expected return of owning JC Penney is sufficiently greater than the expected return of owning Wal-Mart to entice investors to accept the risk of owning JC Penney instead of owning Wal-Mart—say a price of $200 billion for Wal-Mart and $5 billion for JC Penney. The size of the differential (and thus the difference in future expected returns) between the price of the stocks of Wal-Mart and JC Penney will be directly related to the difference in perceived investment risk. Given that Wal-Mart is perceived to be a much safer investment than JC Penney, the price differential (risk premium) may have to be very large to entice investors to accept the risk of owning JC Penney—just as the point spread between Duke and Army has to be very large in order to entice "investors" to take the risk of betting on Army.

Would these price changes make Wal-Mart "overvalued" or "highly valued" relative to JC Penney? The answer is "highly valued." Just as in the case of Duke being favored by 40 points over Army, Duke is not overvalued—it is highly valued. If investors thought Wal-Mart was overvalued relative to JC Penney, they would sell Wal-Mart and buy JC Penney until equilibrium was reached. Instead, the high relative valuation of Wal-Mart reflects low perceived risk. Wal-Mart's future earnings are being discounted at a low rate, reflecting the low perceived risk. This low discount rate translates into low future expected returns. Risk and reward are directly related, at least in terms of expected future returns—"expected" since we cannot know the future with certainty. JC Penney's future earnings are discounted at a high rate. It, therefore, has a relatively low valuation, reflecting the greater perceived risk. However, it also has high expected future returns.

Just as Property A is not a bad investment (it is a safe one) and Property B is not a good investment (it is a risky one), Wal-Mart is not a bad investment (it is a safe one) and JC Penney is not a good investment (it is a risky one). Once we adjust for risk, the expected returns are the same, and they are equally good (or bad) investments.

Moral of the Tale

There is a simple principle to remember that can help you avoid making poor investment decisions. Risk and *expected* return should be positively related. Value stocks have provided a large and persistent premium over growth stocks for a logical reason: Value stocks are the stocks of risky companies. That is why their stock prices are distressed. Investors refuse to buy them unless the *prices* are driven *low enough* so that they can expect to earn a *rate of return* that is *high enough* to compensate them for investing in risky companies. For similar reasons, small stocks have also provided a risk premium relative to large stocks.

Remember, if prices are high, they reflect low perceived risk, and thus you should expect low future returns; and vice versa. This does not make a highly priced stock a poor investment. It simply makes it an investment that is perceived to have low risk and thus low future returns. Thinking otherwise would be like assuming government bonds are poor investments when the alternative is junk bonds.

The final tale of the chapter explains the important truth that every time someone buys a stock, because he is confident that it will outperform the market, there is a seller who is equally confident it will underperform. Both are confident they are right, yet only one can be correct. It also explains the important difference between what is simply information and what is knowledge that one can use to generate above-market returns.

FOR EVERY BUYER THERE MUST BE A SELLER

The greatest advantage from gambling comes from not playing at all.
—Girolamo Cardano, sixteenth-century physician and mathematician

Sherman and Steve were having lunch one day and the topic turned to the stock market.

Steve: I just bought 1,000 shares of Intel.

Sherman: Why did you buy Intel?

Steve: I became interested when I heard a fund manager on CNBC yesterday recommend the stock. He gave a solid explanation for the purchase. So I went home and did my own research. I don't just rely on the recommendations of others. What I found was that the company has a stream of new products in the pipeline that are expected to drive the growth in earnings to a much higher rate. In addition, they have worked off the excess inventories that had developed. The stock, relative to the market, is also trading at a P/E multiple that is below its historic relationship. And, finally, the company's balance sheet is very strong. This is a great company that had some hard times, but it's poised for a turnaround.

Sherman: Those facts sound like good reasons for buying the stock. However, in the end, the only logical reason for your purchasing that particular stock was that you believed that it would outperform the market. This must be so because owning just that one stock is taking more risk, because of the lack of diversification, than if you had purchased a total stock market index fund. Isn't this correct?

Steve: I guess that is so, if you look at it that way.

Sherman: But that is the only way to look at it. At least the only correct way. Now, Steve, where did you get those shares?

Steve: I bought them through a brokerage firm, of course.

Sherman: That is not what I meant. What I meant was, from where did the shares you purchased come? They did not come out of thin air. Someone had to sell them to you. We can break up the market into two types of investors, individuals like you and me and institutional investors like pension funds, mutual funds, and hedge funds. Do you believe that the seller was more likely to be another individual investor like you? Or was the seller more likely to be one of those institutional investors I mentioned?

Steve: I would guess that the seller was another individual investor.

Sherman: That is incorrect. Since institutional investors do as much as 90 percent of all trading, there is as much as a 90 percent chance that the seller was an institution. Since we now agree that while the underlying reason you bought the stock was that you believed that it would outperform the market, we can also agree that the underlying reason that the institutional investor sold the stock was because it believed it would underperform the market. If this were not the case, the investor would have continued to hold that stock. Correct?

Steve: I guess so.

Sherman: Okay. So you believed it would outperform the market and the institutional investor believed it would underperform. How many of you can be correct?

Steve: Just one.

Sherman: Being perfectly honest with yourself, who do you believe had more knowledge about the company, you or the institutional investor?

Steve: I would have to say it is the institutional investor.

Sherman: I agree. Thus, all the reasons you gave me for buying Intel were also known by the institutional investor. What you thought was *knowledge* was really nothing more than *information* that other, more sophisticated investors also had. Yet they decided to sell the stock. So the logical question is: Why did you buy the stock knowing that there could only be one winner in the trade and you were likely to be the loser?

Steve: I never thought of it that way.

Sherman: Again, that is the only way to think about it. You are playing a game where there can only be one winner and you are playing that game with a competitive disadvantage. The most likely way to avoid losing that type of game is to not play. Consider the following. What I believe is the most interesting part of this game of trying to beat the market lies in the answer to this question: Who is the likely seller when one institutional investor buys? Is it an individual investor or another institution?

Steve: Well, since institutions do as much as 90 percent of the trading, the logical answer must be that when one institution is buying, the seller is likely to be another institutional investor.

Sherman: Correct. One institution bought, say, one of Merrill Lynch's mutual funds, because it thought it would outperform, while the other institution sold, say, one of Morgan Stanley's mutual funds, because it thought Morgan Stanley would underperform. How many of them can be right?

Steve:	Obviously, only one.

Steve: Obviously, only one.

Sherman: Now, how many of them are spending your money, in the form of the operating expense ratio, commissions, and other trading costs in the effort to outperform the market?

Steve: Both of them are.

Sherman: This is why active management is a loser's game. Since outperforming the market must be a zero-sum game *before* the expenses of the effort, in aggregate, *after* expenses, it must be a loser's game for investors. Collectively, active investors must underperform the market by the total of all of their expenses. And since most of the competition is between very sophisticated and knowledgeable investors, it is very hard for these sophisticated institutional investors to find enough victims, meaning people like you and me, to exploit in order for them to overcome the hurdle of their expenses. So, Steve, with your newfound insight, would you still have done that trade?

Steve: I see why it really doesn't make sense. I see that it is likely that I will only "discover" information that these institutional investors already know. Therefore, that information is already built into the current price.

Sherman: Now you see why I never buy any individual stocks. I don't like playing a game where the odds are stacked against me. And, more important, I have far more important things to do with my time than doing research on stocks—like spending time with my family.

Steve: Well, I know my wife would agree with you on that.

Barber and Odean's (2000b) study supports the logic of the above tale. They found that the stocks individual investors buy underperform the market *after* they buy them, and the stocks they sell outperform *after* they sell them. Barber and Odean (2000a) also found the same results when they studied the performance of investment clubs. Since there must be another side to every trade, we can conclude that when individuals and investment clubs trade, institutional investors are exploiting them. Unfortunately for the institutional investors, since they do as much as 90 percent of the trading, there are just not enough Steves to exploit to more than overcome the expenses of their efforts.

Moral of the Tale

The moral of the tale is that individual investors should never make the mistake of confusing information with knowledge. The way to avoid that mistake is to remember this: Every time you hear or read a recommendation on a stock or asset class (technology stocks, small caps, emerging markets, etc.), ask yourself this question: Am I the only one who knows this information? If the answer is no (and of course it is, unless it is inside information on which it is illegal to trade), the market has already incorporated that information into prices—and the information cannot be exploited.

Possession of an insight is not sufficient. You can benefit only if other traders do not have the same insight. Unfortunately, valuable information about a company, asset class, or market has no value since it cannot be exploited, at least legally—as

Martha Stewart learned to her regret. And, finally, perhaps the most amusing thing about the stock market is that for every buyer, there must be a seller and both believe that they are doing the right thing. Each must believe that he is somehow smarter than the other. But the stock market is not Lake Wobegon, where everyone is above average.

REFERENCES

Barber, B. M., and T. Odean. 2000a. "Too Many Cooks Spoil the Profits: Investment Club Performance," *Financial Analysts Journal* 56: 1 (January/February): 26–33.

Barber, B. M., and T. Odean. 2000b. "Trading Is Hazardous to Your Health: The Common Stock Investment Performance of Individual Investors," *Journal of Finance* 55: 2 (April): 773–806.

Barber, B. M., and T. Odean. 2001. "Boys Will Be Boys: Gender, Overconfidence, and Common Stock Investment," *Quarterly Journal of Economics* 116: 1 (February): 261–292.

Bernstein, W. J. 2002. *The Four Pillars of Investing*. New York: McGraw-Hill.

Carhart, M. M. 1997. "On Persistence in Mutual Fund Performance," *Journal of Finance* 52: 1 (March): 57–82.

Ellis, C. D. 1998. "The Investment Setting." In P. L. Bernstein and A. Damodaran, eds., *Investment Management*. New York: John Wiley & Sons.

Sauer, R. D. 1998. "The Economics of Wagering Markets," *Journal of Economic Literature* 36: 4 (December): 2021–2064.

Surowiecki, J. 2004. *The Wisdom of Crowds*. New York: Doubleday.

ABOUT THE AUTHOR

Larry Swedroe is a Principal and Director of Research of BAM Advisor Services—a Turnkey Asset Management Provider serving CPA-based Registered Investment Advisor practices—and a Principal and Director of Research for the Buckingham Family of Financial Services (www.bamservices.com). Previously, Mr. Swedroe was Vice-Chairman of Prudential Home Mortgage, the nation's second-largest home mortgage lender. He has held positions at Citicorp as Senior Vice-President and Regional Treasurer, responsible for treasury, foreign exchange, and investment banking activities, including risk management strategies. Mr. Swedroe has an MBA in Finance and Investment from NYU and a BA in Finance from Baruch College. His well-received book, *The Only Guide to a Winning Investment Strategy You'll Ever Need*, was published in 1998 and revised in 2005 (St. Martin's Press, New York). Other works of his include: *What Wall Street Doesn't Want You to Know: How you can profit from the Indexing Revolution* (2001), *Rational Investing in Irrational Times, How to Avoid the Costly Mistakes Even Smart People Make* (2002), *Today's Successful Investor, 14 Simple Truths You Must Know* (2003), *The Only Guide to a Winning Bond Strategy You'll Ever Need*, co-authored with Joe Hempen (2005), *Wise Investing Made Simple*, (2007) and *The Only Guide to Alternative Investments You'll Ever Need*, co-authored with Jared Kizer (2008). He also has a blog at http://moneywatch.bnet.com.

CHAPTER 6

Active versus Passive Investing

LARRY E. SWEDROE
Principal, Buckingham Asset Management, LLC, St. Louis

T here are two theories about how markets work. The first is that smart people, working diligently, can somehow discover pricing errors that the market makes. In other words, they can discover which stocks are undervalued (GE is trading at 30, but it is really worth 40) and buy them. And they can discover which stocks are overvalued (IBM is trading at 30, but it is really worth 20) and avoid them; or, if they are aggressive they can sell them short (borrow IBM stock, sell it at 30, then buy it back at 20 when the market corrects its error). That is called the art of stock selection.

In addition, these same smart people can also anticipate when the bull is going to enter the arena. They recommend increasing your allocation to stocks ahead of the anticipated rally. They can also anticipate when the bear is going to emerge from its hibernation, and recommend lowering your equity allocation ahead of that event. This is called the art of market timing.

The two strategies, stock selection and market timing, combine to form the art of active management. And active management is the conventional wisdom—ideas that are so accepted by the general public that they go unchallenged.

There is a second theory on how markets work. It is based on over 50 years of academic research. This body of work is known as Modern Portfolio Theory (MPT). A major component of MPT is the efficient market hypothesis (EMH). Simply put, the premise of the EMH is that markets are too *efficient* to allow returns in excess of the market's overall rate of return to be achieved consistently through trading systems. A market can be said to be efficient if investors cannot use trading strategies to increase their expected return without at the same time increasing the risks to which they are exposed. If a market is efficient, active management is likely to prove counterproductive. Thus, the conventional wisdom is wrong. If this is what the evidence demonstrates, why is active management the conventional wisdom? And, why do most people follow active strategies? I believe that there are two explanations for this phenomenon.

Note: Charter Financial Publishing Network kindly granted permission to include selected material from Larry E. Swedroe, *Wise Investing Made Simple*, 2007 (Shrewsbury, NJ: Charter Financial Publishing Network).

The first is that most investors are unaware of the evidence. As we discussed in Chapter 5, our education system has failed the public miserably when it comes to investing. Unless you happen to obtain an MBA in finance, it is unlikely that you have even taken a single course in financial economics. The second explanation is that despite its importance, most people do not take the time to read investment books that are based on academic theory.

The bottom line is that most investors are ignorant of the academic evidence. If investors are unaware of the evidence, where do they get their investment "wisdom"? Unfortunately, they get it mostly from two sources that do not have their interests at heart: Wall Street and the financial media. Despite the overwhelming body of academic evidence that demonstrates that while active management does provide you the hope of outperformance, the far greater likelihood is that you will underperform, both Wall Street and the financial media need you to believe active management is the winning strategy. The reason is that it is the winning strategy for them and not you.

WHOSE INTERESTS DO THEY HAVE AT HEART?

Wall Street firms are like bookies. Bookies just need you to play to win. The more you bet, the more they win. If you invest in individual stocks, the more active you are (the more you trade), the more money Wall Street makes. So they need you to be active, persistently buying and selling. Or, if you use mutual funds, then they need you to pay the high fees that active managers charge. While the average actively managed mutual fund charges about 1.5 percent a year, you can buy index funds (that basically buy and hold a predetermined basket of stocks) at a small fraction of that cost. So Wall Street needs you to believe you are better off paying high fees.

The media also needs you to pay attention. They need you to tune in. That is how CNBC makes its profits—selling airtime. And, financial publications like *Money* make their profits from the sale of subscriptions and advertising. If the media told you that the prudent strategy was to develop a plan and then simply buy and hold, you would not need to either tune in or buy their recommended stocks or funds.

The bottom line is that there is a conflict of interest. Wall Street and the financial media, the source of most investor information, say that active management is the winning strategy for investors. Yet the academic evidence demonstrates that the conventional wisdom is wrong. This chapter focuses on the evidence that clearly demonstrates that while active management does offer the hope of outperformance, the far greater likelihood is that passive investment strategies will provide superior results.

There is an overwhelming body of evidence demonstrating the general failure of active management strategies. This holds true whether we look at the results for individual investors, mutual funds, market-timing newsletters, hedge funds, or venture capital. On average, active strategies underperform risk-adjusted benchmarks, and there is little to no evidence of persistent performance beyond the randomly expected.

Obviously one chapter cannot provide all the evidence. However, I suggest that what follows should be more than sufficient to convince you that passive management is the most prudent approach to investing.

WHEN EVEN THE BEST ARE NOT LIKELY TO WIN THE GAME

I believe the search for top-performing stock funds is an intellectually discredited exercise that will come to be viewed as one of the great financial follies of the late 20th century.
—Jonathan Clements, *Wall Street Journal*

A wizard appears, waves his magic wand, and makes you the eleventh best golfer in the world. Being the eleventh best golfer in the world earns you an invitation to the annual Super Legends of Golf Tournament. That is the good news. The bad news is that the competition is the 10 best players in the world. To even the playing field, you are given a major advantage. The rules of the game are these: Each of the other players will play one hole at a time and then return to the clubhouse and report his score. No player gets to observe the others play. Thus, you cannot gain an advantage by watching the others play. After each of the other players completes the hole, you are provided with these options. Option A is to choose to play the hole and accept whatever score you obtain. Option B is to choose not to play that hole and accept par as your score.

The first hole is a par four. After each of the 10 best players in the world has completed the first hole, you learn that 8 of the 10 took five shots to put the ball in the cup—they shot a bogie. Two players shot birdies, needing only three shots to put the ball in the cup. You now must decide to either accept par or play the hole. What is your decision?

The prudent choice would be to choose not to play, take par, and accept a score of four. The logic is that while it was not impossible to beat par (two players did), the odds of doing so are so low (20 percent) that it would not be prudent to try. And by accepting par, you would have outperformed 80 percent of the best players in the world. In other words, when the best players in the world fail the majority of the time, you recognize that it is not prudent to try to succeed. The exception to this line of thinking would be if you could somehow identify an advantage you might have.

For example, if the 10 best players had played the day before you in a rainstorm, with 50-mile-an-hour winds, and you played the following day when the weather was perfect and the course was dry. Given that situation, you might decide that the advantage was great enough that the odds of your shooting a birdie (a three) were greater than the odds of your shooting a bogie (a five, or perhaps even worse). Without such an advantage, the prudent choice would be to not play if you do not have to.

What does this story have to do with investing? Consider this: It seems logical to believe that if anyone could beat the market, it would be the pension plans of the largest U.S. companies. Why is this a good assumption? It is for five reasons:

1. These pension plans control large sums of money. They have access to the best and brightest portfolio managers, each clamoring to manage the billions of dollars in these plans (and earn large fees). Pension plans can also invest with managers who most individuals do not have access to because they do not have sufficient assets to meet the minimums of these superstar managers.

2. It is not even remotely possible that these pension plans ever hired a manager who did not have a track record of outperforming their benchmarks or at the very least matching them. Certainly they would never hire a manager with a record of underperformance.

3. It is also safe to say that they never hired a manager who did not make a great presentation, explaining why the manager had succeeded and why she would continue to succeed. Surely the case presented was a convincing one.

4. Many, if not the majority, of these pension plans hire professional consultants, such as Frank Russell, SEI, and Goldman Sachs, to help them perform due diligence in interviewing, screening, and, ultimately, selecting the very best of the best. Frank Russell, for example, has boasted that it has over 70 analysts performing over 2,000 interviews a year. You can be sure that these consultants have thought of every conceivable screen to find the best fund managers. Surely they have considered not only performance records, but also such factors as management tenure, depth of staff, consistency of performance (to make sure that a long-term record is not the result of one or two lucky years), performance in bear markets, consistency of implementation of strategy, turnover, costs, and so on. It is unlikely that there is something that you or your financial adviser would think of that they had not already considered.

5. As individuals, it is rare that we would have the luxury of being able to personally interview money managers and perform as thorough a due diligence as do these consultants. And we generally do not have professionals helping us to avoid mistakes in the process. As individuals, we are generally stuck relying on Morningstar's ratings; and despite the tremendous resources that Morningstar employs in the effort to identify future winners, its track record is poor. For example, *Morningstar Fund Investor* (2007) reported that all three of its recommended portfolios (Aggressive Wealth Maker, Wealth Maker, and Wealth Keeper) had underperformed since inception. Why then should individual investors with fewer resources believe they can succeed?

Returning to our golf story, I hope you agree that just as it would be imprudent to try to beat par when 80 percent of the best golfers in the world failed, it would be imprudent for you to try to succeed if institutional investors, with far greater resources than you (or your broker or financial adviser), had also failed about 80 percent of the time. The only exception would be if you could identify a strategic advantage that you had over these institutional players. The questions you might ask yourself are: Do I have more resources than they do? Do I have more time to spend finding future winners than they do? Am I smarter than all of these institutional investors and the advisers they hire? Unless when you look in the mirror you see Warren Buffett staring back at you, it does not seem likely that the answer to any of these questions is yes. At least it will not be yes if you are honest with yourself. So let us now turn to the evidence and see just how these institutional investors fare at beating par.

Evidence

The consulting firm FutureMetrics (2005) studied the performance of 192 major U.S. corporate pension plans for the period 1988 to 2005. Because it is estimated that the average pension plan has an allocation of 60 percent equities and 40 percent fixed income, we can compare, using Dimensional Fund Advisors (DFA) (2006) data, the realized returns of these plans to a benchmark portfolio with an asset allocation of 60 percent Standard & Poor's (S&P) 500 Index and 40 percent Lehman Brothers Intermediate Government/Corporate Bond Index. This passive portfolio could have been implemented by each of the plans as an alternative to active strategies. If the return did not match the return of the indexes (less some low expenses), it must be that the players were trying to shoot birdies while running the risk of shooting bogies—they must have been engaging in active management. Unfortunately, only 28 percent of the pension plans playing the game of attempting to outperform the market succeeded. Each pension plan obviously believed that it was likely to outperform. If this were not the case, why would it have played? Unfortunately, in a colossal triumph of hope over experience (and perhaps the all-too-human trait of overconfidence), 72 percent failed in the attempt to beat par. Seventy-two percent shot bogies.

It is important to understand that by trying to be above average (beat par), 72 percent of the players produced returns that were below their benchmark. It is also important to acknowledge that it is unlikely that the failure occurred because of poor corporate governance.

Based on my experience, it is safe to say that the investment policy committee members considered themselves good stewards. In other words, they were smart people who performed their roles diligently—yet 72 percent of the time they failed. It is unlikely that they failed because of bad luck. If it was not bad luck, and it was not failure of process, what led to such a high failure rate? The answer is that the strategy they used—active management—was a losing strategy. This did not have to be so.

Just as you prudently chose not to play the first hole of the Super Legends of Golf Tournament, they too could have chosen not to play by investing instead in index funds. By doing so, they would have earned par.

The story is actually worse than even these dismal results suggest. Consider that a large number of these pension plans invested at least some small portion of their plans in such riskier asset classes as small-cap and value stocks, junk bonds, venture capital, and emerging market equities. As higher-risk asset classes, they have higher expected returns. Yet despite this advantage, for the time period surveyed, 72 percent of the funds failed to beat par. These pension plans were actually taking more risk and they earned lower, not higher, returns.

Consider also that since the average pension plan has an allocation of 60 percent equities and 40 percent bonds, some surely have a higher allocation. Given that equities outperformed bonds over the period of the study, any plan with an allocation of more than 60 percent stocks would have had an advantage. It would be as if these plans teed off from the yellow tee (the tee from which women hit) while the indexers teed off from the blue tee (the tee from which the highest level of men hit). Yet despite these advantages, just 28 percent succeeded. Again, these plans were taking more risk but were "rewarded" with lower returns.

Let us look at some further evidence on the performance of pension plans. Bauer and Frehen (2008) studied 716 defined benefit plans (1992–2004) and 238 defined contribution plans (1997–2004). The study compared their performance to appropriate risk-adjusted benchmarks, and they found that their returns relative to benchmarks were close to zero. They also found that there was no persistence in pension plan performance. Thus, despite the conventional wisdom, past performance is not a reliable predictor of future performance. Importantly, they also found that fund size, degree of outsourcing, and company stock holdings were not factors driving performance. This finding refutes the claim that large pension plans are handicapped by size. Small plans did no better. Bauer and Frehen concluded that it is the "... [S]triking similarities in net performance patterns, over time, which makes skill differences highly unlikely" (p. 3).

Bauer and Frehen, (2008) also studied the performance of mutual funds. The news, unfortunately for individual investors, is even worse. While pension plans failed to outperform market benchmarks, they underperformed pension plans by about 2 percent per annum on a risk-adjusted basis. The underperformance was attributed to the incremental costs incurred by mutual fund investors. Pension plans are able to use their size (negotiating power) to minimize costs and reduce the risks of any conflicts of interest between the fund managers and the investors.

Lots of Counterproductive Activity

A study by Amit Goyal and Sunil Wahal (2008) provides us with further evidence on the inability of plan sponsors to identify investment management firms that will outperform the market *after* they are hired. They examined the selection and termination of investment management firms by plan sponsors (public and corporate pension plans, unions, foundations, and endowments). They built a data set of the hiring and firing decisions by approximately 3,400 plan sponsors from 1994 to 2003. The data represented the allocation of over $627 billion in mandates to hired investment managers and the withdrawal of $105 billion from fired investment managers. Here is a summary of their findings:

- Plan sponsors hire investment managers with large positive excess returns for up to three years prior to hiring.
- The return-chasing behavior does not deliver positive excess returns thereafter.
- Posthiring excess returns are indistinguishable from zero.
- Plan sponsors terminate investment managers for a variety of reasons, including underperformance. But the excess returns of these managers after being fired are frequently positive.
- If plan sponsors had stayed with the fired investment managers, their returns would have been no different from those actually delivered by the newly hired managers.

It is important to note that these results did not include any of the trading costs that would have accompanied transitioning a portfolio from one manager's holdings to the holdings preferred by the new manager. In other words, all of the activity was counterproductive.

In the face of this evidence, ask yourself what advantage you have that would allow you to have a high degree of confidence that you would be likely to succeed where the investors with the most resources failed 72 percent of the time.

You should also consider this fact. Within the last 15 years, Intel, Exxon Mobil, Philip Morris, and the Washington State Investment Board, with combined assets of about $60 billion, have fired all the active fund managers they had previously hired. Surely it is safe to assume that none of these plans ever hired a manager with a poor performance record. Yet each of them fired all of the managers that they had hired after a thorough due diligence process. Why were the managers all fired? Is it even remotely possible that they were fired because they outperformed? Of course it was not. Thus, we can safely assume that while the active managers were hired with the expectation of outperformance, the reality did not live up to the expectation.

In 1996, Philip Halpern was the chief investment officer of the Washington State Investment Board (a large institutional investor). Halpern, Calkins, and Ruggels (1996) wrote an article in the Financial Analysts Journal on their less-than-satisfactory experience with active management. And they knew from attendance at professional meetings that many of their colleagues shared, and corroborated, their own experience. "Few managers consistently outperform the S&P 500. Thus, in the eyes of the plan sponsor, its plan is paying an excessive amount of the upside to the manager while still bearing substantial risk that its investments will achieve sub-par returns." The article concluded: "Slowly, over time, many large pension funds have shared our experience and have moved toward indexing more domestic equity assets."

Returning again to our golf analogy, we determined that while it might be possible to shoot a birdie, it was not prudent for you to try. The reason is that you could not identify an advantage that would lead you to believe that you would be likely to outperform the best. The risk-to-reward ratio was poor—72 percent failed. We have seen that the same thing is true in investing—72 percent of the very best hit bogies.

Moral of the Tale

Wall Street needs and wants you to play the game of active investing. It needs you to try to beat par. It knows that your odds of success are so low that it is not in your interest to play. But it needs you to play so that *it* (not you) makes the most money. Wall Street makes it by charging high fees for active management that persistently delivers poor performance.

The financial media also want and need you to play so that you tune in. That is how *they* (not you) make money. However, just as you had the choice of not playing in the Super Legends of Golf Tournament, you have the choice of not playing the game of active management. You can simply accept par and earn market (not average) rates of return with low expenses and high tax efficiency. You can do so by investing in passively managed investment vehicles like index funds and passive asset class funds. By doing so, you are virtually guaranteed to outperform the majority of both professionals and individual investors—assuming you have the discipline to stay the course. In other words, you win by not playing. This is why active investing is called the loser's game. It is not that the people playing are losers. And it is not that you cannot win. Instead, it is that the odds of success are so low that it is imprudent to try.

The only logical reason to play the game of active investing is that you place a high entertainment value on the effort. For some people there might even be another reason: They enjoy the bragging rights if they win. Of course you rarely, if ever, hear when they lose.

Yes, active investing is exciting. Investing, however, was never meant to be exciting. Wall Street and the media created that myth. Instead, it is meant to be about providing you with the greatest odds of achieving your financial goals with the least amount of risk. That is what differentiates investing from speculating (gambling).

Many people get excitement from gambling on sporting events, horse races, or at the casino tables in Las Vegas. Prudent individuals, however, get entertainment value from gambling by betting only an infinitesimal fraction of their net worth on sporting events. Similarly, even if you receive entertainment value from the pursuit of the "Holy Grail of Outperformance," you should not gamble more than a tiny fraction of the assets on which you wish to retire (or leave to your children or favorite charity) on active managers being able to overcome such great odds.

An article in the *Educated Investor* (2005) quoted Daniel Kahneman, professor of psychology and public affairs at Princeton University, and serves to provide a fitting conclusion to this story.

What's really quite remarkable in the investment world is that people are playing a game which, in some sense, cannot be played. There are so many people out there in the market; the idea that any single individual without extra information or extra market power can beat the market is extraordinarily unlikely. Yet the market is full of people who think they can do it and full of other people who believe them. This is one of the great mysteries of finance: Why do people believe they can do the impossible? And, why do other people believe them? (p. 5)

You have seen the evidence on just how hard it is to beat the market on a persistent basis. The main reason is that the markets are highly efficient and the competition, in the form of the collective wisdom of crowds, is very tough. However, there are other explanations for why persistent performance is so hard to find.

Why Is Persistent Outperformance So Hard to Find?

The Holy Grail was the dish, plate, or cup with miraculous powers that was used by Jesus at the Last Supper. Legend has it that the Grail was sent to Great Britain, where a line of guardians keeps it safe. The search for the Holy Grail is an important part of the legends of King Arthur and his court.

For many investors, the equivalent of the Holy Grail is finding the mutual (or hedge) fund manager who can exploit market mispricings by buying under-valued stocks and perhaps shorting those that are overvalued. While it is very easy to identify after the fact those with great performance, there is no evidence of the ability to do this before the fact. For example, there are dozens, if not hundreds, of studies confirming that past performance is a poor predictor of the future performance of active managers. That is why the Securities and Exchange Commission requires that familiar disclaimer. These studies find that beyond a year, there is little evidence of performance persistence. The only place we find persistence of performance (beyond that which we would randomly expect) is at the very bottom—poorly performing funds tend to repeat. And the persistence of poor performance is not due to poor stock selection. Instead, it is due to high expenses.

The EMH tells us that the lack of persistence should be expected—it is only by random good luck that a fund is able to persistently outperform after the expenses of its efforts. But there is also a practical reason for the lack of persistence: Successful active management sows the seeds of its own destruction.

Jonathan Berk (2005), a professor at the University of California, Berkeley, suggested this thought process:

> *Who gets money to manage? Well, since investors know who the skilled managers are, money will flow to the best manager first. Eventually, this manager will receive so much money that it will impact his ability to generate superior returns and his expected return will be driven down to the second best manager's expected return. At that point investors will be indifferent to investing with either manager and so funds will flow to both managers until their expected returns are driven down to the third best manager. This process will continue until the expected return of investing with any manager is the benchmark expected return—the return investors can expect to receive by investing in a passive strategy of similar riskiness. At that point investors are indifferent between investing with active managers or just indexing and an equilibrium is achieved. (p. 2)*

Berk (2005) went on to point out that the manager with the most skill ends up with the most money. He then added:

> *When capital is supplied competitively by investors but ability is scarce only participants with the skill in short supply can earn economic rents. Investors who choose to invest with active managers cannot expect to receive positive excess returns on a risk-adjusted basis. If they did, there would be an excess supply of capital to those managers. (p. 3)*

This is an important insight. Just as the EMH explains why investors cannot use publicly available information to beat the market (because all investors have access to that information and it is, therefore, already embedded in prices), the same is true of active managers. Investors should not expect to outperform the market by using publicly available information to select active managers. Any excess return will go to the active manager (in the form of higher expenses).

The process is simple. Investors observe benchmark-beating performance and funds flow into the top performers. The investment inflow eliminates return persistence because fund managers face diminishing returns to scale.

The study by Edelen, Evans, and Kadlec (2007) provides evidence supporting the logic of Berk's (2005) theory. The authors examined the role of trading costs as a source of diseconomies of scale for mutual funds. They studied the annual trading costs for 1,706 U.S. equity funds during the period 1995 to 2005 and found:

- Trading costs for mutual funds are on average even greater in magnitude than the expense ratio.
- The variation in returns is related to fund trade size.
- Annual trading costs bear a statistically significant negative relation to performance.
- Trading has an increasingly detrimental impact on performance as a fund's relative trade size increases.
- Trading fails to recover its costs—$1 in trading costs reduced fund assets by $0.41. However, while trading does not adversely impact performance at

funds with a relatively small average trade size, trading costs *decrease* fund assets by roughly $0.80 for large relative trade size funds.

- Flow-driven trades are shown to be significantly more costly than discretionary trades. This nondiscretionary trade motive partially—but not fully—explains the negative impact of trading on performance.
- Relative trade size subsumes fund size in regressions of fund returns. Thus, trading costs are likely to be the primary source of diseconomies of scale for funds.

Edelen et al. (2007) concluded: ". . . [O]ur evidence directly establishes scale effects in trading as a source of diminishing returns to scale from active management" (p. 2).

There is another reason why successful active management sows the seeds of its own destruction. As a fund's assets increase, either trading costs will rise or the fund will have to diversify across more securities to limit trading costs. However, the more a fund diversifies, the more it looks and performs like its benchmark index. It becomes what is known as a *closet index* fund. If it chooses this alternative, its higher total costs have to be spread across a smaller amount of differentiated holdings, increasing the hurdle of outperformance.

Conclusions

The American Law Institute (1992), in its *Restatement of the Law Second, Trusts,* provided its treatment of the legal doctrine known as the Prudent Investor Rule, which has been modified in light of MPT and contemporary investment practices and techniques. This treatment includes these points:

- Economic evidence shows that the major capital markets of this country are highly efficient, in the sense that available information is rapidly digested and reflected in market prices.
- Fiduciaries and other investors are confronted with potent evidence that the application of expertise, investigation, and diligence in efforts to beat the market ordinarily promises little or no payoff, or even a negative payoff after taking account of research and transaction costs.
- Evidence shows that there is little correlation between fund managers' earlier successes and their ability to produce above-market returns in subsequent periods.

The efficiency of the markets and the evidence on the effects of scale on trading costs explains why persistent outperformance beyond the randomly expected is so hard to find. The search by investors for persistent outperformance has proven about as successful as the search for the Holy Grail.

It is hoped that you are now convinced that passive management is the most prudent strategy. However, I have one more objective—to convince you that all market forecasts should be ignored, no matter how intelligent the person making the forecast and no matter how logical an argument he or she presents. In fact, I hope to convince you that all such forecasts should be treated as what should be called investment graffiti.

INVESTMENT GRAFFITI

It must be apparent to intelligent investors that if anyone possessed the ability to do so [forecast the immediate trend of stock prices] consistently and accurately he would become a billionaire so quickly he would not find it necessary to sell his stock market guesses to the general public.
>   —David L. Babson & Company, Weekly Staff Letter, August 27, 1951,
>   quoted in Charles Ellis, *The Investor's Anthology*

Galileo Galilei was an Italian astronomer who lived in the sixteenth and seventeenth centuries. During his lifetime, there was a battle between two theories of astronomy. The conventional wisdom at the time was that Earth was the center of the universe. Ptolemy, a Greek astronomer, had proposed this theory in the second century. It went unchallenged until 1543, when Copernicus published his major work, *On the Revolution of Celestial Spheres,* which stated that Earth rotated around the Sun rather than the other way around. Unfortunately, Galileo spent the last eight years of his life under house arrest, ordered by the church, for committing the "crime" of believing in and teaching the doctrines of Copernicus. Fortunately for the world, there is no army strong enough to defeat an idea whose time has come.

As we have discussed, we now have two competing theories as to which is the winning investment strategy. The generally accepted wisdom is that there are smart people, working hard, who can identify when the bull is about to enter the investment arena—investors should raise their equity allocation—and when the bear is about to emerge from its hibernation—investors should either get out of the market entirely, or at least lower their equity allocation.

History is filled with people clinging to the infallibility of an idea even when there is an overwhelming body of evidence to suggest that the idea has no basis in reality—particularly when a powerful establishment finds it in its interest to resist change. In Galileo's case, the establishment was the church. In the case of the belief in active management, the establishment is comprised of Wall Street, most of the mutual fund industry, and the publications that cover the financial markets. Each of them would make far less money if investors were fully aware of the failure of efforts to time the market.

Two examples from a body of research that demonstrates that market timing is a loser's game follow. The first, reported in Ellis (2002), is from an unpublished study of 100 large pension funds and their experience with market timing. The study found that while all the plans had engaged in at least some market timing, *not one* had improved its rate of return as a result—and losses averaged 4.5 percent over the five-year period.

The second study, by Mark Hulbert, was reported by *Business Week*'s Laderman (1998). Twenty-five newsletters with 32 portfolios were analyzed. For a 10-year period, the timers' annual average returns ranged between 16.9 percent and 5.84 percent, with an average return of 11.06 percent. During the same period, the S&P 500 Index earned 18.06 percent annually, and the Wilshire 5000 Value-Weighted Total Return Index, a broader measure of market performance, earned 17.57%. *None of the timers beat the market.*

Perhaps it was evidence such as this that led famed investor Warren Buffett (1996) to conclude: "Inactivity strikes us as intelligent behavior." To help you determine if Warren Buffett or the conventional wisdom is correct, we will take a look at some of the more famous forecasts that likely influenced millions of investors, causing them to make painful mistakes. Of course, the next list is a cherry-picked one. By digging hard enough, one can find some forecasts that were fairly accurate. The problem is that without the benefit of a perfectly clear crystal ball, there would have been no way to tell the famous from the infamous!

After reviewing the evidence, it is hoped that you will conclude that you should ignore all market forecasts, no matter how rational and intelligent they sound, whether you hear them on CNBC or read them in bestselling books or in financial publications such as the *Wall Street Journal* or *Business Week*. You should also conclude that there are only three types of market forecasters:

1. Those who do not know where the market is going.
2. Those who do not know they do not know where the market is going.
3. Those who know they do not know where the market is going but get paid a lot of money to pretend that they do.

We begin our journey through the land mines of forecasting with a story that illustrates why Warren Buffett was quoted by Faison (1992) in the *New York Times* as saying: "Our stay-put behavior reflects our view that the stock market serves as a relocation center at which money is moved from the active to the patient" (p. D8).

"The Death of Equities"

This title is that of the cover story in the August 13, 1979, *Business Week*. A summary of the main points follows.

- "At least 7 million shareholders have defected from the stock market since 1970, leaving equities more than ever the province of giant institutional investors."
- "Pension fund money can now go not only into listed stocks and high-grade bonds but also into shares of small companies, real estate, commodity futures and even into gold and diamonds" (p. 54).

These observations led Robert J. Salomon, general partner of Salomon Brothers, to be quoted as saying: "We are running the risk of immobilizing a substantial portion of the world's wealth in someone's stamp collection."

The story in *Business Week* (1979) continued:

- "Before inflation took hold in the late 1960s, the total return on stocks had averaged 9 percent a year for more than 40 years, while AAA bonds—infinitely safer—-rarely paid more than 4 percent. Today the situation has reversed, with bonds yielding up to 11 percent and stocks averaging a return of less than 3 percent throughout the decade."
- "Only the elderly who have not understood the changes in the nation's financial markets, or who are unable to adjust to them, are sticking with stocks."
- "Further, this 'death of equity' can no longer be seen as something a stock market rally—however strong—will check" (p. 54).

So let us go to the videotape to see how accurate was this forecast. In 1979, the S&P 500 Index increased over 18 percent. The next year, it increased a further 32 percent. From 1979 through 1999, the index increased at an annualized rate of almost 18 percent. It certainly was a good thing that the "elderly" investors of 1979 did not understand "the changes in the nation's financial markets."

Not long after *Business Week's* (1979) infamous forecast, there was another forecast of the death of equities. This time the forecaster was Joseph Granville (1985) in his book, *The Warning: The Coming Great Crash in the Stock Market.* At one time, Granville was one of the most influential investors on Wall Street. He was one of the very few people who, when they spoke, could move markets. Our videotape reveals that for the period 1985 to 1999 the S&P 500 Index increased almost 19 percent per annum. As Yogi Berra is supposed to have said: "Forecasting is very difficult, especially if it involves the future."

Let us now look at another bearish forecast.

The Great Depression of 1990

This was the title of a book by Southern Methodist University economics professor Ravi Batra (1987). This bestseller created quite a stir and probably caused many investors to alter their investment plans. Once again, let us go to the videotape. In 1989, the S&P 500 Index rose over 31 percent. In the following decade, for which Batra had forecast a great depression, the S&P 500 Index rose at an annualized rate of over 18 percent.

Unfazed by the failure of his prior attempts at forecasting, Batra's (1999) *Crash of the Millennium: Surviving the Coming Inflationary Depression* was released. As we entered 2007, there certainly had been no depression, and inflation has not exceeded 3.5 percent in any year since. In fact, inflation actually reached a low of 1.6 percent in 2001. In only one year since 1964 has inflation been lower than 1.6 percent (1.1 percent in 1986).

Do many people listen to Professor Batra when the markets and the economy keep ignoring him? If so, the reasons are that his arguments are well reasoned and he is also a gifted writer. Like many other highly intelligent economists and market strategists, his analyses seem perfect, except that they are so often wrong.

The next famous forecast we look at came from Peter Peterson, who had a long and distinguished career. In 1971, he was assistant to the President for International Economic Affairs. In 1972, he was named Secretary of Commerce. From 1973 through 1984, he was chairman of Lehman Brothers. Certainly Peterson had credibility.

A summary of the themes in Peterson's (1993) book, *Facing Up: How to Rescue the Economy from Crushing Debt and Restore the American Dream,* follows:

- The U.S. economy is in serious trouble due to massive deficits.
- The savings rate is too low.
- Capital investment is disappearing.
- Productivity is stagnant.

Peterson's conclusion was that there would be severe consequences unless taxes were raised and spending was sharply curtailed. Let us go to the videotape. Over the rest of the decade of the 1990s, capital spending boomed, productivity soared, the economy grew rapidly, and tax revenues soared, turning deficits into surpluses. And the S&P 500 Index rose 23.6 percent per annum from 1994 through 1999.

One can only imagine how many investors abandoned a long-term, buy-and-hold strategy because they were scared off by forecasts such as those from *Business Week,* Joseph Granville, Ravi Batra, and Peter Peterson.

Dow 36,000

So far we have looked only at bearish forecasts. Of course, bullish forecasts can be just as inaccurate. Perhaps the most infamous of the bullish forecasts was made by syndicated columnist James Glassman and Kevin Hassett (1999), a scholar at the American Enterprise Institute and ex–Federal Reserve economist. Their book, *Dow 36,000: The New Strategy for Profiting from the Coming Rise in the Stock Market,* was published when the Dow Jones Industrial Average (DJIA) was about 10,500. The premise of the book was that stocks had been *undervalued* for decades. In other words, investors had been mispricing stocks forever. Their forecast was that the next few years would see a dramatic one-time upward revaluation in stock prices. Once again we go to the videotape. Shortly after publication, the market began its worst bear market in almost 30 years. Ten years later, the DJIA had not moved much above the level it was at the time of publication.

Value of Stock Market Forecasts

On a daily basis, investors are bombarded by economic and stock market forecasts. Because the advice generally comes from intelligent-sounding sources, with fancy titles, making seemingly compelling arguments, investors are often influenced by them. The question is: Do these forecasts have any value?

While preparing testimony as an expert witness, William Sherden analyzed the track records of inflation projections by different economic forecasting methods. He then compared those forecasts to the "naive" forecast—projecting today's inflation rate into the future—and found that the naive forecast proved, to his surprise (since he was a so-called expert), to be the most accurate. That led him to review economic forecasts made during the period 1970 to 1995. One of his findings was that economists could not predict the important turning points in the economy—of 48 predictions, 46 missed the turning points in the economy. He also found that even economists who directly or indirectly can influence the economy—the Federal Reserve, the Council of Economic Advisors, and the Congressional Budget Office—had forecasting records that were worse than pure chance. He concluded that there are no economic forecasters who consistently lead the pack in forecasting accuracy. Even consensus forecasts did not improve accuracy.

Sherden also studied the performance of seven forecasting professions: investment experts, meteorology, technology assessment, demography, futurology, organizational planning, and economics. He concluded that while none of the experts was very expert, the folks we most often joke about—weathermen—had the best predictive powers. Sherden (1998) used this research to write *The Fortune Sellers.*

Even If Your Crystal Ball Was Clear

Reviewing the results of 2003, the best year for equity investors in the last quarter century, provides a concrete example of why prognostications about the stock market should be treated as investment graffiti. Not since 1975–1976 did investors earn such high returns. U.S. large caps rose in excess of 25 percent. U.S. large-value stocks and real estate investment trusts rose in excess of 30 percent. International large-value stocks rose in excess of 40 percent. U.S. small-cap, international small-cap, and emerging market stocks all rose in excess of 50 percent. And U.S. microcaps and international small-value stocks rose in excess of 60 percent.

Unfortunately, almost no one had forecasted a bull market, let alone the kind of returns that were experienced. Worse, if investors had a clear crystal ball, allowing them to foresee the events that would occur, they almost surely would have forecasted a bear market. Let us review some of the major events that occurred. We had an ongoing war in Iraq, an outbreak of severe acute respiratory syndrome (SARS), major corporate and mutual fund scandals, record trade and budget deficits, a renegade North Korea, escalation of the Palestinian–Israeli conflict, and the threat of deflation and a "jobless" recovery.

As you can see, with a clear crystal ball as to the news, investors almost surely would have missed one of the great bull markets of all time. Only those who remained disciplined buy-and-hold investors, adhering to their well-thought-out plans, benefited from this global bull market.

Conclusions

I hope that the evidence presented has led you to conclude that you should ignore—or at least treat only as entertainment—the market forecasts of Wall Street strategists and economists. In fact, if you listen carefully enough, you will learn that the very people making such forecasts agree that it is a loser's game for those who pay attention to the forecasts. However, the forecasters also recognize that it is a winner's game for them because they make their money either selling the advice or from investors acting on it. Pay careful attention to the next quotations:

- "The problem with macro (economic) forecasting is that no one can do it." This quotation reported by Altany (1992) in *Industry Week* is by Michael Evans, the founder of Chase Econometrics—a firm that makes its living selling macroeconomic forecasts.
- "We will continue to ignore political and economic forecasts, which are an expensive distraction for many investors and businessmen." This quote by Warren Buffett (1994) is from his annual letter to Berkshire Hathaway shareholders. Later in the letter, he added: "We try to price, rather than time, purchases."
- "Today's investors find it inconceivable that life might be better without so much information. Investors find it hard to believe that ignoring the majority of investment noise might actually improve investment performance. The idea sounds too risky because it is so contrary to their accepted and reinforced actions." What makes this a particularly interesting statement is that it came from Richard Bernstein (2001), first vice president and chief

quantitative strategist at Merrill Lynch. His employer is responsible for putting out much of the noise he recommends ignoring.
• And perhaps the most telling is that reported by Hick (1997) in the *St. Louis Post-Dispatch*: "You make more money selling the advice than following it." That quote comes from Steve Forbes, publisher of the magazine that bears his name.

By now you should be convinced that the winner's game in investing is to turn off CNBC (or at least hit the mute button), cancel your subscriptions to publications that purport to know where the market is going, and tune out all forecasts from so-called investment gurus. And, finally, remember that the definition of a market forecaster is someone who will tell you tomorrow why the forecast he made today was wrong.

The chapter concludes with the next story demonstrating that often it is more prudent to not play (be a passive investor and accept market returns) than to play (be an active investor and try and outperform the market).

OUTFOXING THE BOX

The greatest advantage from gambling comes from not playing at all.
—Girolamo Cardano, sixteenth-century physician and mathematician

My friend Bill Schultheis (1998), author of *The Coffeehouse Investor*, devised "Outfox the Box" to help investors understand that the winning investment strategy is to accept market returns. It depicts a game that you can choose to either play or not play.

What follows is my version of the game. You are an investor with a choice to make. Exhibit 6.1 contains nine percentages, each representing a rate of return your financial assets are guaranteed to earn for the rest of your life.

You are told that you have this choice: You can either accept the 10 percent rate of return in the center box or you will be asked to leave the room, the boxes will be shuffled around, and you will have to choose a box, not knowing what return each box holds. You quickly calculate that the average return of the other eight boxes is 10 percent. Thus, if thousands of people played the game and each one chose a box, the expected average return would be the same as if they all chose not to play. Of course, some would earn a return of –3 percent per annum while others would earn 23 percent per annum. This is like the world of investing, where if you chose an actively managed fund and the market returns 10 percent, you might be lucky and earn as much as 23 percent per annum; or you might be unlucky and

Exhibit 6.1 Outfoxing The Box

%	%	%
0	5	23
6	**10**	14
–3	15	20

lose 3 percent per annum. A rational risk-averse investor should logically decide to outfox the box and accept the average (market) return of 10 percent.

In my years as an investment adviser, whenever I present this game to an investor, I have never once had anyone choose to play. Everyone chooses to accept par, or 10 percent. While they might be willing to spend a dollar on a lottery ticket, they become more prudent in their choice when it comes to investing their life's savings.

Now consider this. In the "Outfox the Box" game, the *average* return of all choices was the same 10 percent as the 10 percent that would have been earned by choosing not to play. And 50 percent of those choosing to play would be expected to earn an above-average return and 50 percent a below-average return. As we saw earlier, the real-world study on the returns of pension plans demonstrated that among supposedly sophisticated institutional investors, with access to all the great money managers in the world, 72 percent of the players received a below-market return and thus would have been better off not playing. If you would choose to not play a game when you have a 50 percent chance of success, what logic is there in choosing to play a game where the most sophisticated investors have an 72 percent rate of failure? Yet that is exactly the choice those playing the game of active management are making. They are choosing to play the game of outfoxing the box, even when seven of the nine (78 percent) boxes have below-average returns!

You have seen the evidence on how poor the odds of success are for the professional investors—those big institutional pension plans with all of their resources. In addition to their other advantages, institutional investors have one other major advantage over individual investors: Their returns are not subject to taxes. However, if your equity investments are in a taxable account, the returns you earn are subject to taxes. Let us look then at the odds of success of outperforming par (a simple indexing strategy) for those individuals who invest in actively managed mutual funds.

The study by Arnott, Berkin, and Ye (2000) investigated the likelihood of after-tax outperformance. The benchmark used was Vanguard's S&P 500 Index Fund. For the 20-year period from 1979 to 1998, just 14 percent of the funds outperformed their benchmark on an after-tax basis. And, importantly, the average after-tax outperformance was just 1.3 percent per annum. The average after-tax underperformance by the 86 percent that failed to beat par, however, was 3.2 percent annum. In other words, if you had chosen to play that game, you had a slim chance of winning, and even when you did succeed, you likely would have won only a relatively small amount. However, you faced the high likelihood of failure. And, when you did fail, you underperformed by a large amount.

It would be as if in our golf story instead of 8 of the 10 golfers shooting bogies (fives) they would have shot triple bogies (sevens). Since no one would choose to play the game when 80 percent of the best players shot bogies, the logic of taking par becomes even more powerful if they were to shoot triple bogies. The conclusion of the study was that the high odds of failure with large losses combined with low odds of success with small gains produced risk-adjusted odds against outperformance of *over 15 to 1.*

The story is actually even worse than it appears because the data contain survivorship bias. Thirty-three funds disappeared during the time frame covered by the study. Thus, the risk-adjusted odds of outperformance are even lower than the dismal figure presented.

Moral of the Tale

You do not have to play the game of active investing. You do not have to try to overcome abysmal odds—odds that make the crap tables at Las Vegas seem appealing. Instead, you can outfox the box and accept market returns by investing passively. Charles Ellis (2002), author of *Winning the Loser's Game*, put it this way:

> *Successful investing does not depend on beating the market. Attempting to beat the market—to do better than other investors—will distract you from the fairly simple but interesting and productive task of designing a long-term program of investing that* will *succeed at providing the best feasible results for you.*

One of my favorite expressions is "If you think education is expensive, try ignorance." I hope this chapter has whetted your appetite for a deeper understanding of the issues raised and created a desire to broaden your knowledge.

APPENDIX: INVESTMENT VEHICLE RECOMMENDATIONS

Exhibit 6.2 presents a list of funds recommended for use as the building blocks for a passively managed portfolio. Note that funds with an asterisk (*) are tax managed (TM) and, therefore, are strongly recommended for taxable accounts.

Exhibit 6.2   Recommended Investment Vehicles

Domestic Equities Large Cap	International Equities Large Cap
Bridgeway Blue-Chip 35*	DFA Large Cap International
DFA Large Company	Fidelity Spartan International Index
DFA TM U.S. Equity*	Vanguard Developed Markets Index
Dreyfus Basic S&P 500 Stock Index	Vanguard European Stock Index
Fidelity Spartan 500 Index	Vanguard Pacific Stock Index
SSgA S&P 500 Index	Vanguard TM International*
USAA S&P 500 Index	Vanguard Total International Stock Index
Vanguard 500 Index	iShares MSCI EAFE Index
DFA Enhanced U.S. Large†	iShares S&P Europe 350 Index
iShares S&P 500 Index	iShares S&P TOPIX 150 Index (Japan)
Vanguard Total Stock Market Index	iShares MSCI Pacific ex-Japan Index
Vanguard Total Stock Market ETF	
iShares Russell 1000 Index	
iShares Russell 3000 Index	
iShares Dow Jones Total Market Index	
Fidelity Spartan Total Market Index	
Large-Cap Value	**Large-Cap Value**
DFA U.S. Large Cap Value	DFA International Value
DFA TM U.S. Marketwide Value*	DFA TM International Value*
Vanguard Value Index	iShares EAFE Value Index
iShares Russell 1000 Value Index	

Exhibit 6.2   (*Continued*)

Domestic Equities Large Cap	International Equities Large Cap
Small Cap Bridgeway Ultra-Small Company Market DFA U.S. Small Cap DFA TM U.S. Small Cap* DFA Micro Cap Vanguard Small Cap Index Vanguard TM Small Cap* iShares S&P Small Cap 600 Index iShares Russell Microcap Index	**Small Cap** DFA International Small Company
Small-Cap Value DFA U.S. Small Cap Value DFA TM U.S. Targeted Value* Vanguard Small Cap Value Index iShares S&P 600 Value	**Small-Cap Value** DFA International Small Cap Value
Real Estate[†] DFA Real Estate Securities Vanguard REIT Index iShares Cohen & Steers Realty Majors Index iShares Dow Jones Real Estate Index	**Emerging Markets** DFA Emerging Markets DFA Emerging Markets Small Cap DFA Emerging Markets Value DFA Emerging Markets Core Vanguard Emerging Markets Index iShares Emerging Markets Index
Commodities PIMCO Commodity Real Return[†] iPath Dow Jones-AIG Commodity Index Total Return ETN	
Fixed Income: Taxable DFA 1-Year Global DFA 2-Year Global DFA 5-Year Global DFA 5-Year Government DFA Intermediate Government iShares 1–3 Year Treasury Index iShares 7–10 Year Treasury Index TIAA-CREF Fixed Income Annuities Vanguard Short-Term Treasury Vanguard Short-Term Federal Vanguard Short-Term Bond Index Vanguard Intermediate-Term Index Vanguard Inflation-Protected Securities[†] iShares TIPS[†] I bonds	**Fixed Income: Tax-Exempt** DFA Short-Term Municipal Bond Portfolio Vanguard Short-Term Tax-Free Vanguard Limited-Term Tax-Free Vanguard Intermediate-Term Tax-Free

* Tax-managed (TM) funds that are strongly recommended for taxable accounts.
† The fund is appropriate for only tax-advantaged accounts (e.g., IRAs, 401(k)s, 403(b)s, profit-sharing plans, or nontaxable accounts, such as those of pension plans or nonprofit organizations).

A dagger (†) means that the fund is appropriate for only tax-advantaged accounts (e.g., IRAs, 401(k)s, 403(b)s, profit-sharing plans, or nontaxable accounts, such as those of pension plans or nonprofit organizations).

Investors need to be aware that the DFA funds are available only through approved financial advisers.

REFERENCES

Altany, D. 1992. "New Jobs for the Number Crunchers," *Industry Week*, April 20, p. 76.

American Law Institute. 1992. *Restatement of the Law Second, Trusts (Prudent Investor Rule)*. Philadelphia: American Law Institute.

Arnott, R. D., A. J. Berkin, and J. Ye. 2000. "How Well Have Taxable Investors Been Served in the 1980s and 1990s?" *Journal of Portfolio Management* 26: 4 (Summer): 84–93.

Batra, R. 1987. *The Great Depression of 1990*. New York: Simon & Schuster.

Batra, R. 1999. *The Crash of the Millennium: Surviving the Coming Inflationary Depression*. New York: Harmony Books.

Bauer, R., and R. Frehen. 2008. "The Performance of U.S. Pension Funds: New Insights into the Agency Costs Debate." Working Paper, SSRN, February 27, http://ssrn.com/abstract=965388.

Berk, J. B. 2005. "Five Myths of Active Management," *Journal of Portfolio Management* 31: 3 (Spring): 27–31.

Bernstein, R. 2001. *Navigating the Noise*. New York: John Wiley & Sons.

Buffett, W. 1994. Chairman's Letter to the Shareholders, *Annual Report of Berkshire Hathaway*, Berkshire Hathaway, Inc.

Buffett, W. 1996. Chairman's Letter to the Shareholders, *Annual Report of Berkshire Hathaway*, Berkshire Hathaway, Inc.

"The Death of Equities." 1979. *Business Week*, August 13, pp. 54ff.

Dimensional Fund Advisors. 2006. www.dfaus.com.

Edelen, R. M., R. Evans, and G. B. Kadlec. 2007. "Scale Effects in Mutual Fund Performance: The Role of Trading Costs." Working Paper, SSRN, March 17, http://ssrn.com/abstract=9651367.

Educated Investor. 2005. "Three Strikes, You're Out: Approaches Used to Manage Actively Managed Portfolios," December, 1–6.

Ellis, C. D. 2002. *Winning the Loser's Game*, 4th ed. New York: McGraw-Hill.

Faison, Jr., S. 1992. "Guinness Stake Bought by Berkshire Hathaway," *New York Times*, March 25, p. D8.

FutureMetrics. 2005. www.futuremetrics.net.

Glassman, J., and K. Hassett. 1999. *Dow 36,000: The New Strategy for Profiting from the Coming Rise in the Stock Market*. New York: Times Business/Random House.

Goyal, A., and S. Wahal. 2008. The Selection and Termination of Investment Management Firms by Plan Sponsors. *Journal of Finance* 63: 5 (August), 1805–1847.

Granville, J. 1985. *The Warning: The Coming Great Crash in the Stock Market*. New York: Freundlich Books.

Halpern, P., N. Calkins, and T. Ruggels. 1996. "Does the Emperor Wear Clothes?" *Financial Analysts Journal* 52: 4 (July/August): 9–15.

Hicks, V. B. 1997. "Defying Physics Experts: Economy Will Keep on Rolling," *St. Louis Post-Dispatch*, October 4, p. 33.

Laderman, J. 1998. "Market Timing: A Perilous Ploy," *Business Week*, March 9, pp. 102ff.

Morningstar. 2007. *Morningstar Fund Investor*, February.

Peterson, P. G. 1993. *Facing Up: How to Rescue the Economy from Crushing Debt and Restore the American Dream.* New York: Simon & Schuster.

Schultheis, B. 1998. *The Coffeehouse Investor.* Marietta, GA: Longstreet Press.

Sherden, W. 1998. *The Fortune Sellers.* New York: John Wiley & Sons.

ABOUT THE AUTHOR

Larry Swedroe is a Principal and Director of Research of BAM Advisor Services—a Turnkey Asset Management Provider serving CPA-based Registered Investment Advisor practices—and a Principal and Director of Research for the Buckingham Family of Financial Services (www.bamservices.com). Previously, Mr. Swedroe was Vice-Chairman of Prudential Home Mortgage, the nation's second-largest home mortgage lender. He has held positions at Citicorp as Senior Vice-President and Regional Treasurer, responsible for treasury, foreign exchange, and investment banking activities, including risk management strategies. Mr. Swedroe has an MBA in Finance and Investment from NYU and a BA in Finance from Baruch College. His book, *The Only Guide to a Winning Investment Strategy You'll Ever Need*, was published in 1998 and revised in 2005 (St. Martin's Press, New York). Other works of his include: *What Wall Street Doesn't Want You to Know: How you can profit from the Indexing Revolution* (2001), *Rational Investing in Irrational Times, How to Avoid the Costly Mistakes Even Smart People Make* (2002), *Today's Successful Investor, 14 Simple Truths You Must Know* (2003), *The Only Guide to a Winning Bond Strategy You'll Ever Need*, co-authored with Joe Hempen (2005), *Wise Investing Made Simple*, (2007) and *The Only Guide to Alternative Investments You'll Ever Need*, co-authored with Jared Kizer (2008). He also has a blog at moneywatch.bnet.com.

Fund Types and Comparative Performance, Efficient Markets, Asset Allocation, and Morningstar Analysis

CHAPTER 7

Efficient Markets and Mutual Fund Investing
The Advantages of Index Funds

BURTON G. MALKIEL, Ph.D.
Chemical Bank Chairman's Professor of Economics at Princeton University

T his chapter discusses the strategies for investment in mutual funds that are consistent with a belief that securities markets in the United States and the rest of the developed world are reasonably efficient. We shall see that the optimal strategy in such cases is to concentrate one's portfolio in low-cost indexed mutual funds. Equity index funds simply buy and hold all the stocks in a very broad stock market index and do not trade from security to security in an attempt to achieve returns that exceed those of the market as a whole. Portfolio turnover is required only when new companies are added to the index or existing firms are removed because of merger, bankruptcy, privatization, and the like.

The efficient market hypothesis is often cited as the intellectual justification for indexing. We shall see, however, that markets need not be efficient to justify the use of index funds. Index funds tend to outperform the vast majority of actively managed funds even if markets fail to live up to the requirements of efficiency.

In this chapter, I make the case that index funds should constitute the core of every investment portfolio. I also describe what has come to be known as the core–satellite strategy, where index funds are used as the core of the portfolio and actively managed mutual funds may be used as satellite portfolios. Index funds are suitable not only for stocks of companies domiciled in the United States but also for the equities of foreign companies, including companies in the emerging-market countries of the world. Moreover, index funds are also useful instruments for investments in bonds and in real estate securities.

Not all index funds are created equal, however. We note that a major advantage of index funds involves their very low cost. A high-cost index fund vitiates the advantages of indexing. Index funds should be preferred with annual expense ratios less than 20/100, or $1/5$ of 1 percent of assets.

One type of index fund with particularly low expenses is the exchange-traded fund (ETFs). ETFs are not mutual funds but are index funds that trade like stocks on organized securities exchanges, such as the New York Stock Exchange. Unlike a mutual fund, which accepts new investments and honors withdrawal requests from small investors, individuals buy and sell ETFs on the open market. ETFs can, however, be created and redeemed by large investors so as to ensure that they trade at prices very close to their net asset values. And ETFs have the advantage of having extremely low expense ratios. ETFs of the major stock indexes of United States equities have expense rates below 10 basis points (a basis point is $^1/_{100}$ of 1 percent so 10 basis points represent $^1/_{10}$ of 1 percent). In this chapter, I indicate in what situations ETFs should be used instead of index funds and when mutual funds should be the preferred investment vehicles.

JUSTIFICATION FOR USING INDEX FUNDS

Traditionally, the justification for using index funds has been the argument that our securities markets tend to be reasonably efficient. The efficient market hypothesis (EMH) has been a central proposition of the field of finance for over 40 years. Eugene Fama (1970) in an early survey of EMH defines an efficient market as one in which security prices always fully reflect all available information. When information arises about an individual company or about the stock market as a whole, that information gets reflected in share prices without delay. Thus, even an uninformed investor will find that the current tableau of share prices accurately reflects all the information that is known to the market. In such a situation, it would be fruitless for an active portfolio manager to switch from security to security in a vain attempt to buy "undervalued" securities and sell "overvalued" ones. Such an attempt to gain above-average returns would accomplish nothing but to increase transactions charges as well as the taxes that must be paid by the mutual fund shareowner.

The EMH is associated with the view that stock market price movements approximate those of a random walk. If new information develops randomly, then so will market prices, making the stock market unpredictable apart from its long-run uptrend. Thus, neither technical analysis—an attempt to derive the future movement of stock prices by studying charts depicting the past movements of market prices—nor fundamental analysis—the attempt to predict future stock returns from a "fundamental" analysis of accounting data, future corporate investment strategies, competitive conditions, and the like—will allow professional portfolio managers to achieve abnormal (risk-adjusted) returns.

I have suggested (Malkiel, 1973), largely in jest, that a blindfolded chimpanzee throwing darts at the stock pages could select a portfolio that would do as well as the experts. In fact, the correct analogy is to throw a towel over the stock pages and simply buy an index fund, which buys and holds all the stocks making up a broad stock-market index.

In recent years, many financial economists have come to question the efficient market hypothesis. At least *ex-post*, there seem to be several instances where market prices failed to reflect available information. One celebrated example during the late 1900s is when 3Com spun off 5 percent of the Palm shares it owned. Based on the market price of Palm, the 95 percent of Palm still owned by 3Com was worth more than the total capitalization of the parent company. Moreover, periods of large-scale irrationality, such as the technology-Internet bubble of the late 1990s extending into early 2000, have convinced many analysts, such as Robert Shiller (2000), that the EMH should be rejected. In addition, some financial econometricians have suggested that stock prices are, to a significant extent, predictable from past returns or on the basis of certain valuation metrics, such as dividend yields and price-earning ratios. See, for example, Campbell and Shiller (1988a,b), DeBondt and Thaler (1995), Fama and French (1988), and Lo and MacKinlay (1999).

But indexing can be an optimal strategy even if markets are occasionally or even often inefficient. To understand why this must be so, consider the next logic. All of the securities in any market must be held by someone. These investors as a whole must earn the overall return of the market. If the market produces an overall return of 8 percent in any average year, then investors as a group must earn the same 8 percent before any investment expenses. Of course, there are always some stocks that produce above-average returns, and some investors will earn above-average returns in any particular period. But not everyone can be above average. We cannot live in Garrison Keillor's mythical Lake Wobegon, where all the children are above average. Thus, investing must be a zero-sum game, as is illustrated in Exhibit 7.1.

If some investors are fortunate enough to be holding the best-performing stocks, then some other investors must be holding the poorer-performing ones. All investors as a group hold all the stocks, and it must be the case that they earn the overall market average return before expenses.

But mutual funds charge a variety of expenses. There are, for example, administrative costs of collecting and distributing dividends and preparing reports for the fund's shareowners and for the government. There are also investment management costs for the portfolio managers who perform the research analyses to determine which securities the fund will own. Suppose that these costs amount to $8/10$ of one percentage point per year, or 80 basis points. In that case, the situation will resemble that depicted in Exhibit 7.2.

If in an average year the market produces an 8 percent rate of return, the average investor will earn only 7.2 percent after expenses. Moreover, after expenses, most investors will underperform the overall market average, based on the total capitalization of all the outstanding stocks. After expenses, investing will not be a zero-sum game; investing will be a negative-sum game.

From this analysis, the advantages of indexing can be seen clearly. Since index funds do not hire security analysts to pick what are believed to be the best securities,

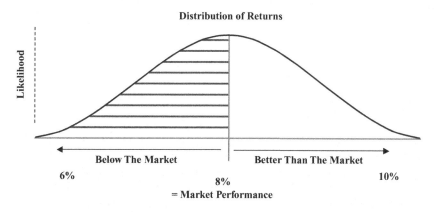

Exhibit 7.1   Case for Indexing: Investment Performance Is a Zero-Sum Game

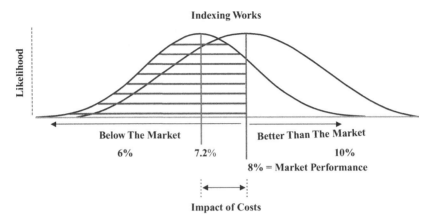

Exhibit 7.2   Case for Indexing: After Costs, Capitalization-Weighted Index Managers Will Outperform Most Active Managers

and since index funds are buy-and-hold investors who generate limited turnover, index funds can be managed at minimal expense. Indeed, low-cost index funds and ETFs can be acquired at expense ratios of 10 basis points or less (i.e., less than $1/10$ of 1 percent). The advantage of indexing is that it allows the investor to achieve the market return at minimal expense.

We can summarize the advantages of index funds in this way. If markets are reasonably efficient and generally reflect whatever information is available, then there will be little scope for professional investors to select portfolios of stocks that outperform the market. Stocks of companies with superior prospects will already have their prices fully reflect those prospects. Therefore, active management is unlikely to find large numbers of mispriced securities that will result in consistent above-average results. But even if markets are often or even usually inefficient, it still must follow that most investment managers will underperform the market. All investors as a group must earn the average market return before expenses. The underperformance of active managers must reflect the additional expenses that they incur in running active portfolios. In the next section, we examine the evidence based on the historical returns of equity mutual funds to test whether indexing is an effective strategy in practice.

EVIDENCE FROM U.S. INDEX FUNDS

Evidence from actively versus passively managed equity mutual funds in the United States strongly supports the efficient market hypothesis. Most investors have been better off investing in index funds. Passive index funds typically provide higher net returns to the investor than actively managed mutual funds. The Standard & Poor's (S&P) 500 Index is the most popular index of large-capitalization (large-cap) stocks in the United States. The index represents about 80 percent of the total capitalization of the U.S. equity market. The most popular index funds in the United States (as well as very popular ETFs) have been indexed to the S&P 500 or to an equivalent 500-stock large-capitalization index (see Exhibit 7.3).

Exhibit 7.3 Percentage of Large-Cap Equity Funds Outperformed by S&P 500 for Periods Ended December 31, 2008

1 Year	3 Years	5 Years	10 Years	20 Years
61%	64%	62%	54%	68%

Source: Lipper and Vanguard.
Past performance is no guarantee of future results.

Exhibit 7.3 shows that over long periods of time, over 60 percent of actively managed large-cap equity mutual funds in the United States have been outperformed by an S&P 500 Index fund (see Exhibit 7.4).

Exhibit 7.4 shows that the average equity mutual fund in the United States (including all categories of funds) has underperformed the index by almost 1 percentage point per year over the 20 years ending December 31, 2008. This difference can be explained by the higher expenses of actively managed funds. The typical active fund carries an expense ratio that is considerably higher than that of a passive index fund. Moreover, active funds have much higher portfolio turnover, leading to higher trading costs (see Exhibit 7.5).

An example of the superiority of index fund investing over the long run is shown in Exhibit 7.5. The exhibit compares the performance of all the U.S. equity funds that existed in 1970 with the return of the S&P 500 stock index. There were 358 equity mutual funds in existence in 1970. Note that only 117 of these funds survived until 2008. The other 241 funds were closed or were merged into other funds. These 241 nonsurvivors were undoubtedly the poorer-performing funds since the more successful funds tend to stay in business. Thus, these data are tainted by "survivorship bias." We can only compare the long-run performance of surviving funds with the S&P 500 stock index. The exhibit shows that most actively managed mutual funds experienced performance that was inferior to the index. Indeed, one can count on the fingers of one's hands the number of equity mutual funds that outperformed the S&P 500 stock index by more than two percentage points or more per year (see Exhibit 7.6).

Exhibit 7.6 documents the lack of persistence in equity fund performance in a rather dramatic way. The exhibit lists the top-performing 19 U.S. equity mutual funds over the period from December 1993 through December 1999. These were the funds that enjoyed average annual returns that were at least twice as large

Exhibit 7.4 Index Funds Have Outperformed: Comparison of Returns—Average Equity Fund* versus Index

20 Years to December 31, 2008	
S&P 500 Index	8.43%
Average Equity Fund	7.50
S&P 500 Advantage (percentage points)	0.93

Sources: Lipper and The Vanguard Group.
*Consists of all Lipper equity categories.
Past performance is no guarantee of future results.

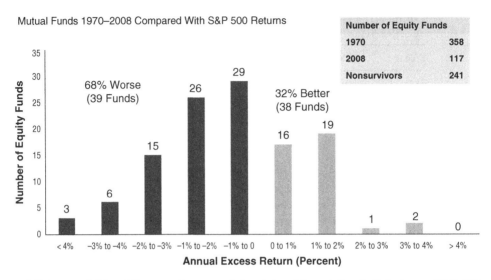

Exhibit 7.5 Odds of Success: Returns of Surviving Mutual Funds Relative to S&P 500 Index, 1970–2008

Sources: Lipper and The Vanguard Group.

Exhibit 7.6   Past Is Not Prologue: The Lack of Persistence of Mutual Fund Performance

	Rank	12/93-12/99 Average Annual Return	Rank	12/99-12/05 Average Annual Return
RS Inv: Emerg GR	1	37.54	410	−9.35
Janus Mercury	2	35.92	397	−8.11
Fidelity New Millennium	3	35.82	229	−0.48
Janus Twenty	4	34.89	394	−7.72
Fidelity Aggr Grow	5	32.70	422	−15.67
Van Kampen Emerg Gro:A	6	31.94	403	−8.47
Janus Enterprise	7	31.15	414	−9.58
Legg Mason Value Tr. Prm	8	31.11	167	2.45
Van Kampen Emerg Gro:B	9	30.90	409	−9.17
TA IDEX: Janus Gro:T	10	30.21	396	−8.00
Janus Venture	11	29.97	387	−7.02
TA IDEX: Janus Gro:A	12	29.85	401	−8.39
Morg Stan Inst:MCG:1	13	29.47	253	−1.22
Putnam OTC Emerg Gro:A	14	29.10	424	−19.25
Phoenix Mid-Cap Gro:A	14	29.10	402	−8.41
Janus Growth & Income	16	28.43	230	−1.13
Harbor:Cap Apprec:Inst	17	28.38	341	−4.28
Fidelity OTC	18	28.16	371	−6.18
USAA Aggr Growth	19	27.84	405	−8.51

Source: Lipper and Bogle Financial Research Center. Rankings are out of 424 finds with at least $100m in assets on December 1995.

as the returns for the stock market as a whole. The portfolio managers of these funds were lionized by the press and treated like rock stars in the popular financial magazines. Their above-average returns were generated, however, by concentrating their portfolios in stocks tied to the Internet. A worldwide bubble in such stocks burst during the first quarter of 2000. The exhibit shows that during the next six-year period, these funds suffered severe losses and significantly underperformed the stock market as a whole.

EVIDENCE IN FAVOR OF PASSIVE MANAGEMENT IN WORLD FINANCIAL MARKETS

Does the evidence in favor of passive management hold outside the United States? The United States has very liquid, transparent, and efficient stock markets. This may not be the case in the rest of the world, particularly in the world's less developed emerging markets. In this section, I examine the case for indexing the markets outside the United States (see Exhibit 7.7).

Turning first to Europe, we can examine the performance of active European portfolio managers. Exhibit 7.7 presents the comparison. We see that over two-thirds of the actively managed large-cap European funds were outperformed by the MSCI Europe index.

Similar results can be shown for global equity managers. Exhibit 7.8 examines the investment returns earned by 414 global equity managers compared with the

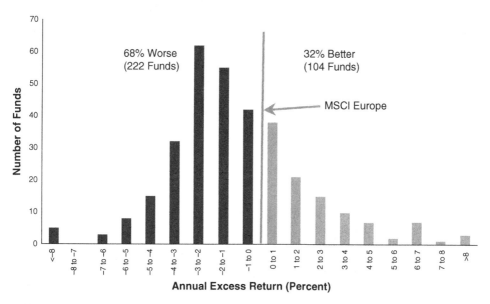

Exhibit 7.7 Returns of Actively Managed European Equity Funds Compared with the MSCI Europe Index, 10 Years Ended December 31, 2008
Source: Lipper, MSCI, and The Vanguard Group.

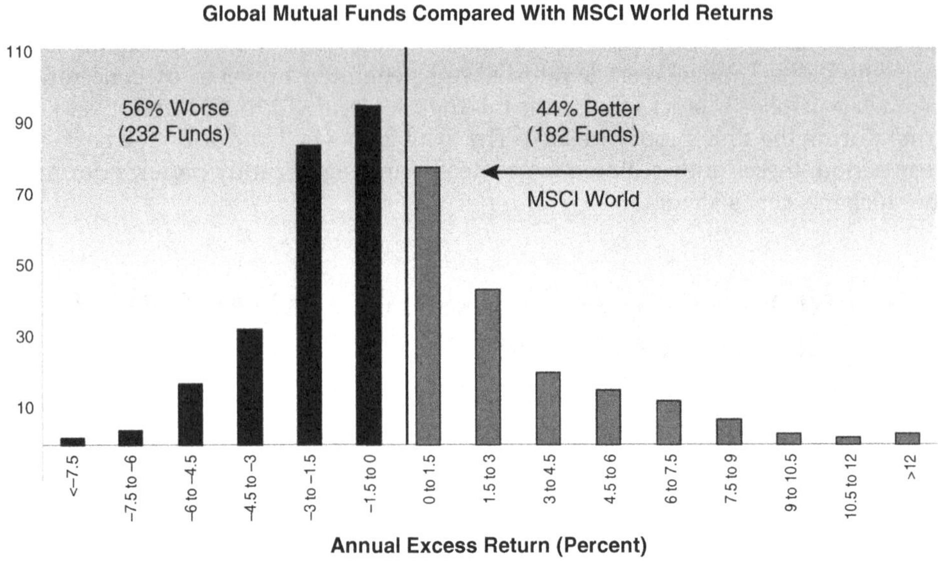

Global Mutual Funds Compared With MSCI World Returns

Exhibit 7.8 Global Equity Managers Outperformed by MSCI World Index, 10 Years Ended December 31, 2007
Source: Lipper, MSCI, and The Vanguard Group.
Universe: Emerging Mkts active equity funds registered in Austria, Belgium, France, Germany, Ireland, Italy, Luxembourg, Portugal, Spain, Switzerland, The Netherlands, UK and Offshore.

MSCI World Index. Well over half of the active managers failed to outperform the passive world index. Even in emerging markets, many of which are far less efficient than markets in the developed countries, passive management appears to be a winning strategy. Exhibit 7.9 indicates that about two-thirds of the active managers of emerging-market funds were outdistanced by the index. Paradoxically, the very inefficiency of the trading markets in many emerging markets, with relatively large bid–ask spreads and a variety of transactions charges (including stamp taxes on security transactions), makes it difficult for active managers to outperform even in less efficient markets.

ACTIVE VERSUS PASSIVE MANAGEMENT IN THE BOND MARKET

Next I examine the efficiency of passive management in the bond markets of the United States and Europe. Exhibit 7.10 presents the results for the United States. It appears that indexing is a particularly effective strategy in the bond markets. Bond funds appear to be commodity-type products. Because passively managed funds charge lower management fees, it turns out that very few active bond portfolio managers are able to achieve net investment returns after expenses that match the net returns of low-cost bond index funds. In Europe, few of the active bond managers were able to outperform their respective benchmarks. Exhibit 7.11 shows the results for the 10-year period ending December 31, 2008.

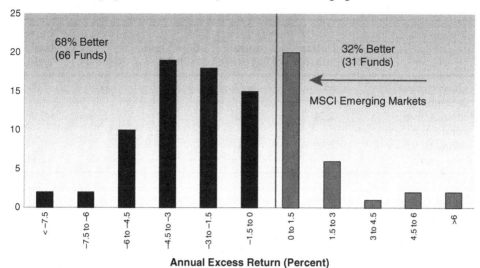

Exhibit 7.9   Emerging Markets Equity Managers Outperformed by MSCI Emerging Markets Index, 10 Years Ended December 31, 2007
Source: Lipper, MSCI, and The Vanguard Group.
Universe: Emerging Mkts active equity funds registered in Austria, Belgium, France, Germany, Ireland, Italy, Luxembourg, Portugal, Spain, Switzerland, The Netherlands, UK and Offshore.

COSTS ARE IMPORTANT DETERMINANTS OF NET RETURNS

Not all index funds investing in U.S. equities are created equal. There are some domestic index funds with annual expense ratios of as much as 100 basis points (one percentage point per year). A high expense ratio destroys a basic advantage of index funds. Every basis point of expenses lowers the net return earned by the investor. Some U.S. index funds and exchange-traded (index) funds are available with an annual expense ratio of 10 basis points ($^1/_{10}$ of 1 percent) per year or less. These are the funds an investor should favor. Index funds with expense ratios greater than 20 basis points per year should be avoided. The industry average expense ratio for actively managed funds is about 100 basis points per year.

Exhibit 7.10   Percentage of Actively Managed U.S. Bond Funds Outperformed by the Benchmark, 10 Years Ended December 31, 2008

	Government	Corporate	Government National Mortgage Association	High-Yield
Short term	98%	99%	95%	67%
Intermediate term	88	73	—	—
Long term	70	57	—	—

Source: Lipper.

Exhibit 7.11   Percentage of European Actively Managed Bond Funds Outperformed by the Benchmark, 10 Years Ended December 31, 2008

	US Dollar Denominated	Euro Diversified	Euro Short Term	Global	Euro High Yield
% Outperformed by Benchmark	88%	99%	99%	71%	71%
Median Active Fund return	2.74	3.26	2.60	2.99	−0.87
Benchmark return	3.90	4.44	3.89	3.47	0.24
Excess return	−1.16	−1.18	−1.29	−0.48	−1.11

Sources: Median active fund returns from Morningstar, Inc. Fixed Income analysis represents 10 years. Benchmark returns provided by Barclays Capital. Data through December 31, 2008.

Foreign index funds and ETFs tend to have higher expense ratios than domestic funds. Low-expense broad international index funds (indexed to the Morgan Stanley Capital International EAFE index of equities in developed foreign markets) might carry an expense ratio of about 25 basis points. (The industry average expense ratio is over 150 basis points for actively managed non-U.S. funds.) EAFE stands for Europe, Australasia and the Far East, and this index contains all the large corporations in the developed nations of the world that are domiciled outside the United States.

Index funds specializing in emerging markets carry even higher expense ratios. Low-cost funds and ETFs may have annual expense ratios between 25 and 50 basis points. In addition, there may be a small purchase charge to defray the fund's costs of buying securities in the less liquid emerging markets. While sales loads (charges of 300 basis points or more) should be avoided by investors, purchase charges of 50 basis points or less for funds that hold illiquid securities are often required. Similarly, index funds holding emerging market or other illiquid securities may impose redemption charges on investors who liquidate their fund shares after a very short holding period. Such charges are meant to discourage short-term trading that would subject the fund to potentially large trading costs, which hurt the long-term owners of the fund's shares.

Costs are just as important for actively managed as they are for passive index funds. A statistical analysis of the net returns from all diversified mutual funds over the 14-year period 1994 through 2008 reveals that the higher the net returns to investors are, the lower the expense ratio of the fund. Moreover, the higher net returns earned by fund investors, the lower is portfolio turnover (i.e., the less the portfolio manager tends to trade). Excessive trading generates transaction charges in addition to the portfolio manager's fees and administrative costs. Portfolio turnover therefore tends to reduce the net returns available to the investor. In addition, trading can often be very tax inefficient. To the extent that high turnover tends to generate realized capital gains (and often short-term capital gains that are taxed at regular income tax rates), portfolio turnover reduces after-tax returns even further. Investors who hold their funds in taxable accounts will want to avoid funds that employ substantial portfolio turnover.

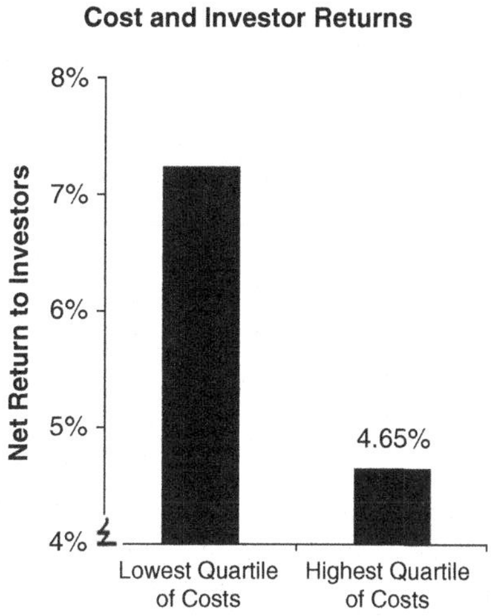

Cost and Investor Returns

Exhibit 7.12   Importance of Costs: Net Returns of Equity Funds after Costs, December 1994–December 2008
Source: Bogle Financial Research Center.

Exhibit 7.12 shows the effect of expenses on net returns. The exhibit compares the net returns of all diversified equity mutual funds that have high versus low expense ratios. The high-expense funds in the exhibit have expense ratios in the top quartile (the top one-quarter) of all funds, while low-expense funds are considered those with bottom-quartile expense ratios. In preparing the exhibit, expenses are calculated by adding the explicit expense ratio of the fund to estimated turnover costs. Every one percentage point of turnover is assumed to increase expenses by one basis point. As the exhibit indicates, the net returns to investors from the funds with the lowest explicit expenses and turnover are more than 200 basis points higher than the returns of the high-expenses funds. In judging the merits of actively managed funds, investors should prefer those with low expenses and low portfolio turnover. Of course, index funds and ETFs, with their rock-bottom expense ratios and very low turnover, are the quintessential funds designed to minimize investment costs.

MUTUAL FUNDS VERSUS ETFs

As indicated, ETFs are index funds that trade like stocks. They can be bought and sold at any time during the trading day, unlike mutual funds, which can be purchased and redeemed only at their net asset value calculated at the end of each trading day. How should an investor decide whether to buy index mutual funds or exchange-traded funds?

ETFs have three important advantages.

1. They tend to carry lower expense ratios than mutual funds.
2. They can, at least in theory, be more tax efficient than mutual funds. If a mutual fund was forced to sell appreciated securities to meet redemptions from the holders of the fund's shares, it could be required to realize capital

gains that must be apportioned to the fund's shareholders. ETFs create and redeem shares only in large blocks and only with large investors and traders. Because the creation and redemption of units of ETFs serve to ensure that the ETF sells at (or very close to) net asset value, any sales of securities to meet redemptions are not considered taxable events.

3. ETFs can be traded during the day, not simply at the closing net asset value at the end of the day. This third advantage should be treated with some skepticism, however. Investors are unlikely to benefit from timing their purchases and sales during the trading day. Indeed, to the extent that investors attempt to "time" the market with ETFs, they are unlikely to improve their return over those earned by the buy-and-hold investor.

ETFs have a disadvantage, however, in that purchases and sales incur brokerage charges. Transactions in (no-load) mutual index funds do not incur transaction charges. Even if a discount broker is used to purchase and sell ETF shares, there are commissions to pay as well as the bid–ask spread. (Purchases are made at the "ask" price while sales are made at the "bid" price, which is lower. Therefore, an investor who purchases at one time and sells at another will incur the cost of the bid–ask spread.)

How should an investor trade off the lower annual costs of many ETFs with the additional transactions charges involved with buying and selling ETFs?

The answer is relatively straightforward. If you will be investing a large sum in an index fund (say $10,000 or more), you are likely to be better off with a low-cost ETF. If, however, you are making periodic contributions (say $100 a month) into an index fund that is part of your retirement portfolio, a mutual fund is far and away the better alternative. The transactions costs of putting small amounts regularly into an ETF are likely to be prohibitive. Similarly, if you are retired and are drawing money out of your retirement nest egg, you will be better off keeping the money you will soon need in mutual funds rather than in ETFs. In any event, there are a wide variety of expense ratios for different mutual funds and ETFs. Some mutual funds have even lower annual expenses than ETFs. Before making any fund investment decision, be sure to check the actual charges associated with any investment you are considering.

STOCK MARKET RETURNS VERSUS INVESTOR RETURNS

It is customary in calculating mutual fund returns (as well as the historical returns from equity investments in general) to measure the returns earned by a buy-and-hold investor who buys at the start of the period being measured and holds the investments until the end of the period. Thus, when Ibbotson Associates (2008) reports that equity returns in the United States have averaged 9.6 percent per annum from 1926 through 2008, those are the returns earned by an investor who buys at the start of 1926 and holds throughout the entire period. The actual returns of investors are determined, however, not only by the average annual returns of the market index, but also by the timing of their purchases and sales in and out of the market. Moreover, individual investors may deliberately move in and out of various market sectors over time. Hence, the actual returns of individual investors may differ substantially both from overall stock market returns and also from the long-run rates of return of the mutual funds they hold.

We can measure the actual returns earned by equity investors by calculating dollar-weighted returns rather than returns to the buy-and-hold investor. A simple numerical example, taken from an article by Ilia Dichev (2007), will illuminate the difference between buy-and-hold returns and investor returns. Suppose an investor buys 100 shares of XYZ Company at $10 per share at the start of period 1. By the end of period 1, the stock doubles to $20 per share, at which time the investor purchases another 100 shares. Then the stock falls back to $10 per share at the end of period 2.

The normal return calculation yields the result of a zero rate of return over the two-year period. (The stock started and ended at $10 per share.) That would be the correct return for the investor who bought at the start of period 1 and sold at the end of period 2. But for our hypothetical investor who bought 100 shares both at $10 and $20 per share and then sold at the end of period 2 at $10, the result was a negative return ($3,000 was invested and then sold at the end of period 2 for $2,000). Indeed, that investor's internal rate of return was −26.8 percent per annum. While the buy-and-hold return gives a reasonable estimate of the return for holding the stock over the entire period, it will be a very poor measure of the actual returns of investors whose capital flows in and out of the market vary over time.

When there are significant correlations between the timing of capital contributions into the equity market and withdrawals from the market, then dollar-weighted returns will tend to differ from buy-and-hold returns. There is considerable evidence that capital flows into the equity market are significantly correlated with past returns.

One of the insights from the field of behavioral finance is that investors are often influenced by herd behavior. They tend to buy stocks when everyone is optimistic and sell stocks during times of ubiquitous pessimism. Specifically, individuals tend to put money into the stock market after the market has experienced relatively high returns and optimism prevails and take money out of the stock market following periods in which the market has declined. See, for example, Ikenberry, Lakonishok, and Vermaelen (1995) and Loughran and Ritter (1995). Because of these correlations, dollar-weighted returns will differ systematically from buy-and-hold returns. Dichev (2007) found that the return differential is substantial. The return differential was 1.3 percentage points for exchange-traded stocks during the period 1926 to 2002. The return differential between dollar-weighted and buy-and-hold returns for Nasdaq stocks was 5.3 percentage points per year from 1973 to 2002. In all cases the dollar-weighted returns are lower than the buy-and-hold returns because individual investors tend to add money to their investments at particularly inopportune times.

The next two exhibits illustrate the problem. Exhibit 7.13 superimposes data on cash flows into equity mutual funds with the behavior of the S&P 500 stock index. The exhibit shows that new cash flows into equity mutual funds are significantly higher following increases in stock prices. Indeed, the largest inflows into equity mutual funds occurred during the last quarter of 1999 and the first quarter of 2000, exactly at the peak of the Internet bubble in the stock market. The exhibit also shows that record withdrawals from equity mutual funds occurred during the

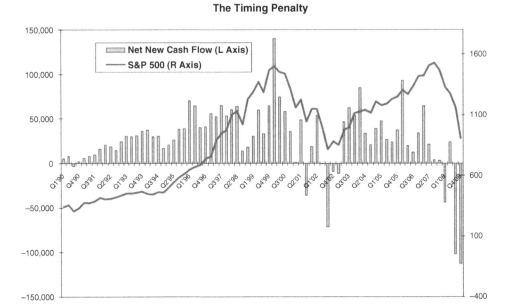

Exhibit 7.13 Timing Penalty: Equity Fund Cash Flow Follows the Stock Market
Source: Investment Company Institute.

third quarter of 2002, just at the bottom of the stock market. Huge withdrawals were also made as the stock market sank in the fourth quarter of 2008.

This tendency of individuals to put their money in the stock market (and take money out) at inopportune times is what I have called the timing penalty. The situation is even worse, however, because investors also suffer from what can be called the selection penalty, shown in Exhibit 7.14. Not only did more money flow into the stock market than ever before during the Internet bubble, but those fund flows were concentrated in high-technology growth mutual funds, precisely the part of the market that turned out to be the most overvalued. Note that during the fourth quarter of 1999 and first quarter of 2000, there were significant outflows from "value" mutual funds, precisely the funds with the most attractive relative valuations. So not only did more money flow into the market at an inopportune time, but investors tended to put their money into exactly the kinds of stocks that were experiencing the biggest recent gains. This tendency of investors to follow what have recently been the attractive sectors in the stock market is another factor responsible for the substantial differential between buy-and-hold returns and dollar-weighted returns. The tendency for investors to alter the composition of their mutual fund portfolios exaggerates the differentials between the overall returns to the stock market and the returns earned by the average investor that result from inopportune market timing.

STYLE OR FACTOR TILTS IN MUTUAL FUNDS

Many mutual funds, whether actively managed or indexed, employ certain style or factor tilts in composing their portfolios. For example, some mutual funds

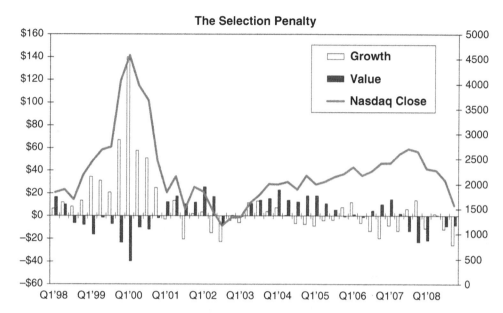

Exhibit 7.14 Selection Penalty: Quarterly Flows into Growth and Value Funds, and the Nasdaq's Close
Source: Strategic Insight.

specialize in smaller companies—those whose market capitalizations are below the average capitalization for traded companies in general. Other funds concentrate on so-called value stocks—those stocks that sell at relatively low multiples of their book values and earnings. Some indexed market mutual funds are broken up into value and growth components or into small-cap and large-cap portfolios. The Morningstar mutual fund service uses nine breakdowns to describe the style focus of the fund. Funds are categorized by a nine-box grid, where funds are categorized on one axis as being invested in small-, medium-, and large-cap stocks, and on the other axis by style (i.e., invested in value or growth stocks or in a blend of the two).

Considerable recent interest had been shown in a new set of indices that are weighted by certain fundamental factors, such as sales, earnings, dividends, or book values, rather than by capitalization. The best known of the new fundamentally weighted indices that claim to improve on cap-weighted indexes is the Research Affiliates Fundamental Index™ (RAFI). The RAFI index contains 1,000 stocks weighted by fundamental measures of book value, earnings, and so on, and has outperformed traditional large-cap indices, such as the S&P 500 Index and the Russell 1000 by margins of over 300 basis points per year during the early 2000s. Such performance has emboldened the proponents of the Fundamental Index™ (FI) to claim that this new method of indexing could replace the old paradigm of capitalization-weighted indexing. See, for example, Arnott, Hsu, and Moore (2005) and Arnott, Hsu, and West (2008).

In my judgment, the reason for the ability of FI portfolios to outperform certain market benchmarks during the period from 2000 through 2006 is that FI relies on the two factor tilts that researchers have understood for years. To the extent that earnings and book values are some of the factors used to weight stocks in the portfolio, FI will systematically overweight value stocks and underweight growth stocks. Moreover, since FI underweights stocks with high market capitalizations relative to fundamental factors, there will be a tendency for an FI portfolio to contain smaller-capitalization stocks than those in a traditional cap-weighted index.

A long literature in empirical finance has isolated a value effect in asset pricing. Studies such as Basu (1983) and Keim (1988) have shown that stocks selling at low prices relative to their earnings (P/E) and book values (P/BV) have generated higher returns for investors. Similar results have been shown for stocks selling at low multiples to their sales. One can interpret such findings as being inconsistent with efficient markets. Portfolios made up of stocks with low P/BV ratios earn excess risk-adjusted returns when risk is measured by beta from the Capital Asset Pricing Model (CAPM). But any test of market efficiency is a joint test of the relationship of return to P/BV and the efficacy of CAPM's beta to fully measure risk. According to Fama and French (1992), the ratio of price to book value itself is a risk measure; therefore, the larger returns generated by low P/BV stocks are simply compensation for risk.

Investigators such as Banz (1981) have also found a strong relationship between company size (measured by total market capitalization) and returns. Smaller firms appear to generate higher returns than large firms. Again, the interpretation of these results is controversial. The excess returns of small firms can be interpreted as an inefficiency. The interpretation of Fama and French, however, is that both P/BV and size are risk factors in addition to beta. Low P/BV stocks are often those in some financial distress, and small stocks may be far more sensitive to economic shocks than are larger firms.

Over the period from 2000 through 2005, there was a particularly strong value effect as well as a small-firm effect. The bursting of the Internet bubble in early 2000 produced extremely poor returns for the overpriced large-cap growth stocks that were the market leaders during the late 1990s. FI portfolios were not alone in performing very well over the early 2000s. Managed as well as index funds focusing on value and small-cap stocks all tended to outperform the broad market indexes.

One direct method of measuring the factor tilts inherent in FI portfolios is to perform a regression analysis of the monthly FI returns in the United States against a Fama-French three-factor model. Fama and French (1993) argue that the CAPM should be augmented by two additional risk factors: company size and the market price to book (M/B) ratio. Thus, risk is captured by CAPM's beta, M/B, and an equity capitalization (size) measure.

If one performs such a regression over the period from January 1979 through December 2008, it is possible to show that the FI return can be fully explained by the three Fama-French risk factors, as has been shown by Jun and Malkiel (2008). The coefficient of determination of a regression of FI returns and the three Fama-French risk factors is 0.96, and all of the coefficients of the factors are highly significant. Moreover, a zero alpha, or excess return, is generated by the FI method of weighting the portfolio. In addition, it is possible to replicate the FI returns with a variety of ETFs that employ similar factor tilts.

We need also to maintain some degree of skepticism concerning the long-term productivity of value and size portfolio tilts. From the mid-1960s to the present,

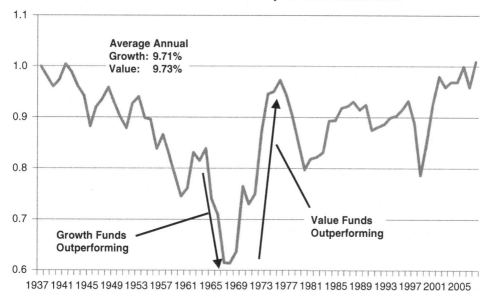

Exhibit 7.15 Reversion to the Mean: Growth Funds versus Value Funds, 1937–2008

value mutual fund managers have usually outperformed growth managers (although not during the late 1990s). Fama and French (1992) come to the same conclusion. In earlier periods, however, from the late 1930s to the mid-1960s, growth stocks appeared to be the persistent winners. There appears to be considerable mean reversion evident in the time series when measured over a very long time period. Indeed, Exhibit 7.15, which measures the relative performance between mutual funds with growth and value mandates, shows that, over more than a 70-year period, the performance of both types of funds was essentially the same. A similar kind of mean reversion can be shown to exist between large- and small-capitalization stocks.

CONCLUSIONS

This chapter has examined the efficiency of equity and bond markets and the efficacy of passive (index fund) compared with active portfolio management. If securities markets were characteristically inefficient, we would expect professional portfolio managers to achieve excess performance over the returns earned by the market as a whole. I interpret the inability of professional portfolio managers to outperform passive capitalization-weighted index funds as powerful evidence that securities markets around the world are generally efficient. To be sure, markets make mistakes—sometimes egregious ones, as during the time of the Internet bubble of late 1999 and early 2000. But there is no evidence that professional investors are able to recognize such mispricing *ex ante* and to adjust their portfolios accordingly.

As a result, many professional portfolio managers have adopted what is called a core–satellite strategy. The core of the portfolio is invested in low-cost index funds. This guarantees broad diversification and no risk that at least a part of the portfolio will underperform a broad market benchmark. Satellite portfolios can employ specialized and undiversified equity managers with far less risk than if the entire portfolio were actively managed.

REFERENCES

Arnott, R. D., J. Hsu, and P. Moore. 2005. "Fundamental Indexation," *Financial Analysts Journal* 61: 2 (March/April): 83–99.

Arnott, R. D, J. C. Hsu, and J. M. West. 2008. *The Fundamental Index: A Better Way to Invest.* New York: Wiley CDA.

Banz, R. 1981. "The Relationship Between Return and Market Value of Common Stocks," *Journal of Financial Economics* 9: 1 (March): 3–18.

Basu, S. 1983. "The Relationship Between Earnings' Yield Market Value and Return for NYSE Common Stocks: Further Evidence," *Journal of Financial Economics* 12: 129–156.

Campbell, J. Y., and R. J. Shiller. 1988a. "The Dividend–Price Ratio and Expectations of Future Dividends and Discount Factors," *Review of Financial Studies* 13: 3 (Fall): 195–228.

Campbell, J. Y., and R. J. Shiller. 1988b. "Stock Prices, Earnings, and Expected Dividends," *Journal of Finance* 43: 3 (July): 661–676.

DeBondt, W. F. M., and R. H. Thaler. 1995. "Financial Decision-Making in Markets and Firms: A Behavioral Perspective." In R. S. Jarrow, V. Maksimovic, and W. T. Ziemba, eds., *Finance, Handbooks in Operations Research and Management Science*, Vol. 9. Amsterdam: North Holland.

Dichev, I. D. 2007. "What Are Stock Investors' Actual Historical Returns? Evidence from Dollar-Weighted Returns," *American Economic Review* 97 (1): 386–400.

Fama, E. 1970. "Efficient Capital Markets: A Review of Theory and Empirical Work," *Journal of Finance* 25 (May): 383-423.

Fama, E., and K. French. 1988. "Permanent and Temporary Components of Stock Prices," *Journal of Political Economy* 96: 2 (April): 246–273.

Fama, E., and K. French. 1992. "The Cross-Section of Expected Stock Returns," *Journal of Finance* 47: 2 (June): 427–465.

Fama, E., and K. French. 1993. "Common Risk Factors in the Returns of Stocks and Bonds," *Journal of Financial Economics* 33: 1 (February): 3–56.

Ibbotson Associates. 2008. *Stocks, Bonds, Bills, and Inflation Yearbook*. Chicago: Ibbotson Associates.

Ikenberry, D., J. Lakonishok, and T. Vermaelen. 1995. "Market Underreaction to Open Market Share Repurchases," *Journal of Financial Economics* 39: 2–3 (October/November): 181–208.

Jun, D., and B. G. Malkiel. 2008. "New Paradigms in Stock Market Indexing," *European Financial Management* 14: 1 (January): 118–126, in press.

Keim, D. B. 1983. "Size Related Anomalies and Stock Return Seasonality: Further Empirical Evidence," *Journal of Financial Economics* 12 (June): 13–32.

Lo, A. W., and A. C. MacKinlay. 1999. *A Non-Random Walk Down Wall Street*. Princeton, NJ: Princeton University Press.

Loughran, T., and J. R. Ritter. 1995. "The New Issues Puzzle," *Journal of Finance* 50: 1 (March): 23–51.

Malkiel, B. G. 1973/2007. *A Random Walk Down Wall Street*. New York: W. W. Norton.

Shiller, R. 2000. *Irrational Exuberance*. Princeton, NJ: Princeton University Press.

ABOUT THE AUTHOR

Burton G. Malkiel has been the Chemical Bank Chairman's Professor of Economics at Princeton since 1988. His research interests center on financial markets, asset pricing, and investment strategies. He is a regular op-ed page writer for the *Wall Street Journal* and serves on the boards of several financial and nonfinancial corporations. He is also the author of the classic investment book, *A Random Walk Down Wall Street*, now in its ninth edition. He received his Ph.D. from Princeton University.

CHAPTER 8

Asset Allocation
Design and Care of Portfolios

WILLIAM J. BERNSTEIN, Ph.D., M.D.
Coprincipal and Cofounder, Efficient Frontier Advisors

Harry Markowitz (1952), in writing in the *Journal of Finance*, fired "the shot heard around the world," a 15-page article unobtrusively titled "Portfolio Selection," in which he suggested that rational investors were concerned not only with maximizing return but also with minimizing volatility. In other words, if there is more than one portfolio that returns 10 percent per year, then the optimal one is that which has the lowest volatility, with variance being his designated proxy for volatility. More obviously, the converse is also true: If there are multiple portfolios with a given volatility, then the one with the highest return is the optimal one. Put another way, the investor should always be willing to trade off some return for a reduction in risk or take additional risk in order to get a larger return. For risk-averse investors, the ratio of incremental required return to risk is large; and for risk-tolerant ones, small.

Much has been made of a landmark trio of papers by Gary Brinson and several colleagues (1986, 1991, 1995) that demonstrated that over 90 percent of the *variance* of portfolio return was explained by the allocation among three different asset classes: stocks, bonds, and cash by pension funds. Later, Jahnke (1997) pointed out that this rather artificial and constrained example overstated the importance of the policy portfolio.

So how important is asset allocation, really? Obviously, stocks and bonds have very different risk and return characteristics, and the overall stock–bond mix is the single most important parameter determining the long-run risk and return of any portfolio.

Allocation within equity categories, however, is another story. There is no reason why long-term equity returns in different national markets or industry sectors, after adjustment for risk, should be different: All compete in a nearly global capital marketplace. Consider, for example, the returns of the Standard & Poor's (S&P) 500 and the EAFE (Europe, Australasia and the Far East) for the 38-year period between 1970, and 2007 which were nearly identical, at 11.07 percent and 11.57 percent annualized, respectively. Exhibit 8.1 plots the returns and risks of varying mixes of these two assets. On the x-axis is plotted the standard deviation (SD), and on the y-axis is plotted the annualized return.

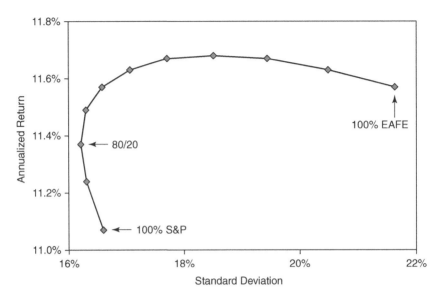

Exhibit 8.1 Return/Risk Characteristics of Annually Rebalanced S&P 500/EAFE Portfolios, 1970–2007
r = .59

First, note how compressed the y-axis is, with the returns of all the portfolios falling within a relatively narrow range. Next, note that although the EAFE was more volatile than the S&P 500, adding in a small amount of the foreign equity index actually *decreased* portfolio volatility. This is one of the basic principles of portfolio theory: A volatile asset class may actually decrease the risk of a portfolio if its correlation to the portfolio is low enough.

In terms of long-term portfolio return, then, the precise mix of foreign and domestic stocks mattered relatively little, since their returns were nearly identical. But in any individual calendar year, the mix mattered a great deal. In 1986, for example, the S&P returned 18.47 percent, while the EAFE returned 69.94 percent, while in 1997, the pattern reversed, with returns of 33.36 percent and 2.06 percent, respectively. So, the answer seems to be, in the very long run, the only truly important dimension of asset allocation is the overall stock–bond mix, whereas in the short term, the precise allocation among equity classes matters a great deal.

Now, let us look at a more complex mix of assets. Exhibit 8.2 plots a large number of randomly constructed portfolios, consisting of random mixtures of one riskless asset (in this case, five-year Treasury notes) and six risky assets. In this case, I have used U.S. large and small stocks, and Japanese, European, Pacific Rim, and precious metals stocks for the seven-year period between 1990 and 1996. However, for the purposes of this discussion, it really does not matter which assets or time period is used.

First, take a look at the vertical line, which is placed at a standard deviation (SD) of 10 percent. (The SD is simply the square root of the variance and is today the more commonly accepted measure of portfolio volatility.) All of the portfolios that lie along this line have an SD near 10 percent. Clearly, the one with the highest return is preferable to all the others.

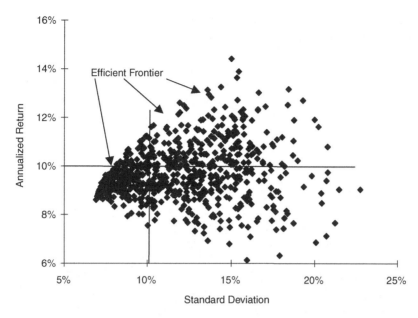

Exhibit 8.2 Risk/Return Characteristics of 800 Randomly Generated Portfolios, 1990–1996

Next, focus on the horizontal line, placed at a return of 10 percent. All of the portfolios along this line have a return near 10 percent. Obviously, the one at the far left—that is, with the lowest SD—is the optimal one. The portfolios along the upper left edge of this cloud form the so-called efficient frontier of optimal asset allocations, which produces the highest return at a given degree of risk, or, conversely stated, the lowest risk at a given degree of return.

In Exhibit 8.3, I have expanded the analysis over a much longer period, from 1970 to 1996. Note how much thinner the cloud is; this is because mean reversion

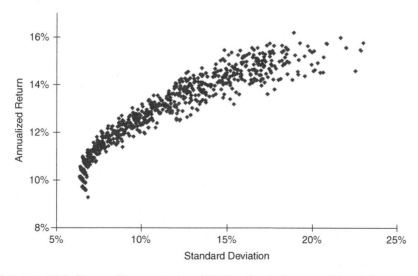

Exhibit 8.3 Risk/Return Characteristics of 800 Randomly Generated Portfolios, 1970–1996

has smoothed out the long-term return differences among the risky asset classes, demonstrating that in the long run, the precise allocation among risky assets matters much less than the overall stock–bond mix.

Which portfolio along the efficient frontier should the investor choose? As a practical matter, most investment policies, from those of the smallest individual portfolios to those of the largest institutions, begin with an estimation of risk tolerance and time horizon. The goal, then, is to seek the highest return at that degree of risk. Markowitz's genius lies first in clearly describing this principle and, second, and more profoundly, in providing an algorithm that allows the investor to calculate the compositions of the efficient frontier portfolios.

This methodology, known as mean-variance analysis, needs only three sets of deceptively simple inputs: the return and variance (or SD) for each asset, and the correlations among them. For the given example of seven asset classes, there are 35 variables: 7 returns, 7 SDs, and 21 correlations.

Calculating the Markowitz efficient frontier for even the simplest combinations of portfolios cannot be accomplished easily by hand. Typically it is performed with a software package known as a mean-variance optimizer, or MVO. What could be simpler? Simply gather up a long list of asset classes, obtain their returns and SDs, calculate a correlation grid among them, and, presto, you now possess a wide range of optimally efficient portfolios.

If this all seems too good to be true, then your instincts are sound. The problem is twofold:

1. An MVO will favor assets with high returns and low correlations, particularly the former. Increase an asset class return by a percent or two, and it will dominate the portfolio—perhaps even constituting all of the allocation to risky assets; decrease it by a percent or two, and it disappears entirely.
2. Over periods of several years, asset class returns have a slight tendency to mean-revert; that is, the best-performing asset class for the past five years will tend to be below average over the next five years, and vice versa.

In the late 1980s, MVOs became all the rage, and investment professionals naively fed historical data into them. Their outputs, and the inevitable results, were predictable: portfolios heavy with the previous winners: foreign equity, particularly Japanese, and U.S. small stocks. (Since at that time small investors could neither afford the software and nor access the necessary data, they avoided this particular train wreck.) For example, Bernstein (2000b) showed that if between 1975 and 1998 one had designed an all-stock portfolio of the six-stock asset classes mentioned earlier (U.S. large and small stocks, and Japanese, European, Pacific Rim, and precious metals stocks) based on optimizations of the trailing five years' performance, the overall annualized return of those portfolios would have been 8.40 percent versus 15.79 percent for a naive strategy consisting of equal amounts of all six asset classes. Practitioners and programmers attempted to compensate for this unfortunate tendency of optimizers (or "error maximizers," as they came to be known in some quarters) by constraining their outputs within "reasonable" bounds. But this begged the question: If one already has an idea of what a reasonable portfolio looks like, of what real use is the optimzer?

An MVO is useful only to the extent that one is able to forecast the returns of securities or asset classes with great accuracy. This, alas, is a fool's errand. And if one *could* accomplish this, the optimizer would still be of little additional use since in that case, one would largely confine one's risky assets to the best performers.

We thus spend the rest of this chapter answering three questions:

1. What does a "reasonable" portfolio look like?
2. How should the practitioner adjust the allocations back to policy over time—that is, rebalance—as allocations change with market prices?
3. How should the practitioner change the policy target allocation, if at all, over time?

POLICY ALLOCATION

If one believes that the global equity markets are efficient, then the obvious starting point for the equity portion of any portfolio is the capitalization-weighted world market portfolio of all investible equities. For example, as of December 31, 2007, the Morgan Stanley Capital Indexes World Index, consisting of the free float, or tradable, shares of world equity, consisted of the allocation shown in Exhibit 8.4.

How should one modify this allocation? Most U.S. investors would find the 50.6 percent foreign weighting excessive and would likely cut it down to less than 25 percent. For starters, foreign stocks are more expensive to trade. Further, investing is simply an operation that defers present consumption for future consumption, and for almost all U.S. investors, most of that consumption will take place in the United States, so it makes good sense to keep more of that investment in dollar-denominated securities.

For the past decade or so, it has been possible to execute such a cap-weighted global equity strategy with the appropriate mix of just two low-cost vehicles: a U.S. S&P 500 or Total Market index fund and an international equity index fund. Retail mutual fund investors can now purchase open-end and exchange-traded mutual funds that accomplish this at a cost as low as 10 to 20 basis points

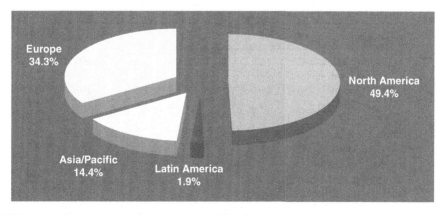

Exhibit 8.4 Composition of the MSCI World Index, December 31, 2007

(0.10 to 0.20 percent) per year; for U.S. government employees, the cost is just 1.5 basis points—0.015 percent.

The final balanced stock–bond investment strategy can be obtained by adding in a bond index fund. Because of its low fee structure and near-total absence of internal transactional costs, such a three-fund Simpleton's portfolio has outperformed the overwhelming majority of active managers over the long term, and should continue to do so.

Does the investor believe that small stocks or value stocks have higher returns than growth stocks? If so, then he or she will deviate away from market-cap weighting in each of the world's regions. Note that this method of allocation is geographic. Some have argued that with the rising correlations of world equity markets, this is obsolete, and that a sector-based strategy is more useful. During the late 1990s, correlations among many industry groups were indeed lower than among nations, but this appeared to be an artifact of the tech-related bubble of that era; more recently, the physical location of where a stock trades has regained its primacy.

This does not, preclude, however, adding sector weightings to a geographic one; because of the low correlations of the next asset classes to other equities, many practitioners add these asset classes futures to primarily geographically based allocations: real estate investment trusts (REITs), both domestic and foreign; precious metals equity; and commodities.

One widely followed and respected allocation that employs a largely, but not exclusively, geographically based value- and small-biased allocation is the Balanced Equity Strategy of Dimensional Fund Advisors (DFA) (2008) shown in Exhibit 8.5.

This does not look anything like the uneven allocations that typify MVO outputs; the numbers are round and quite obviously somewhat arbitrary, but they conform to a basic principle: large allocations to economically broader and less volatile components, and smaller allocations to less conventional and more volatile components. Between 1995 and 2007, this strategy returned 13.04 percent versus 11.27 percent for the S&P 500. Even more impressively, it did so at a lower SD, 13.13 percent, versus 14.21 percent for the S&P (and also was less volatile overall

Exhibit 8.5 Dimensional Fund Advisors' Balanced Equity Strategy

Asset Class	Allocation
U.S. Large Market	20%
U.S. Large Value	20%
U.S. Microcap	10%
U.S. Small Value	10%
REIT	10%
Foreign Large Value	10%
Foreign Small Market	5%
Foreign Small Vale	5%
Emerging Markets Large Market	3%
Emerging Markets Small Market	4%
Emerging Markets Value	3%

than the least volatile component, international small-value stocks, which had an SD of 13.96 percent). Note that many of these asset classes are quite volatile; for example, the SDs of the emerging markets and small-cap portfolios were greater than 20 percent yet added no significant risk to the overall portfolio because of their relatively low correlations to other asset classes.

The performance of this allocation becomes even more impressive when one realizes that this was not a theoretical exercise, conducted inside of a microprocessor, but an allocation designed in the early 1990s and that could be executed almost completely with actual mutual funds that paid management fees and transactional expenses. (The Emerging Markets Small and Value, and International Small portfolios were not available for the first few years after 1995; substituting similar funds would not have affected the results materially.)

There was nothing magic about DFA's strategy; any "reasonable" globally diversified, value- and small-biased allocation that was efficiently and inexpensively executed would have performed similarly. The drivers of this performance—asset class returns, standard deviations, and correlations—simply cannot be known in advance with nearly enough accuracy to reliably improve on allocations that do not stray too much from market-cap weighting (see Exhibits 8.5 and 8.6).

Even the most successful allocations, however, will temporarily underperform. Exhibit 8.6 plots the annual returns of the DFA Balanced Equity strategy versus that of the S&P 500, and Exhibit 8.7 plots the difference between the two. Note how the DFA strategy, even with its superior performance, underperformed the S&P 500 in 6 out of 13 years. Worse, 5 of those years occurred consecutively. Between 1995 and 2000, all three of the "biases" of the DFA strategy relative to the S&P—foreign, small, and value—lost money. Consequently, the DFA strategy yielded a total

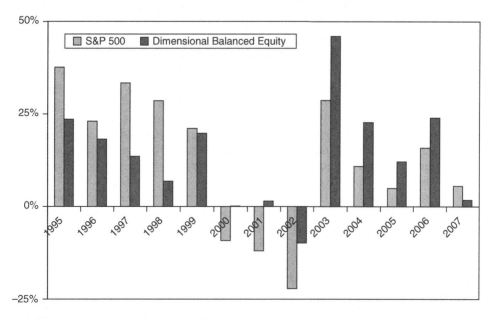

Exhibit 8.6 Annual Performance of the Dimensional Balanced Equity Strategy and S&P 500, 1995–2007

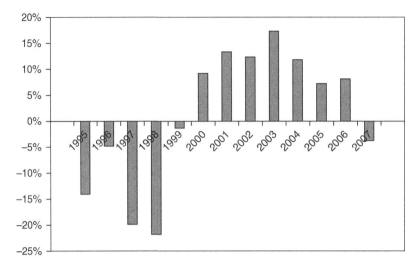

Exhibit 8.7 Difference between the Dimensional Balanced Equity Strategy and S&P 500 Annual Returns (Tracking Error), 1995–2007

return of 112 percent versus a return of 219 percent during the same period for tech-heavy S&P. Between 1995 and 1999, deviating from the S&P 500 (or any other broadly based domestic index, such as the Wilshire 5000) sorely tested the most rational and best-informed investment strategies, and rewarded those who bought into the new-era euphoria of the period. Eventually, the more diversified and historically grounded DFA strategy won out, but many inexperienced investors, and even many seasoned ones, abandoned this efficient strategy before it paid off. The experience of those years underscores what is perhaps the most important principle of investing: Mastering the theory is not nearly so hard as applying it under fire. Talking the talk is easy; walking the walk is another matter.

The temporary underperformance of the DFA strategy is a direct warning to most institutional money managers, very few of whom would survive five such years of subpar results. Even the best managers are likely to suffer long droughts, during which they will likely hemorrhage assets and lose their jobs. Unless one's clients are extremely sophisticated and/or loyal, superior strategies always entail substantial tracking errors and are consequently best left to organizations, such as endowments, pension plans, and individual investors, that do not have to answer to excitable, uninformed investors and committees every quarter.

One size does not fit all. Several factors will influence the policy asset allocation. We have already touched on risk tolerance, which is the primary driver of the overall stock–bond allocation. Another factor that determines the overall stock–bond balance is time horizon; only portfolios designed with a greater than 5- or 10-year horizon should contain appreciable amounts of equity. Obviously, funds designated for a house purchase in one or two years should be invested only in either in a diversified pool of short-term high-quality debt securities or in a U.S. Treasury issue.

Samuelson (1969) states that human capital also needs to be taken into account. Much has been made in recent years about the fact that stocks do not in fact become less risky with time and that this does *not* consequently demand a reduction in equity as the investor ages. However, human capital—the investor's future income stream—does decrease with time. This income stream behaves similarly to a bond. Thus, the young investor, with a small amount of investment capital and a large amount of human capital, can and should invest nearly all of that investment capital in equity; the older investor, with a large amount of investment capital and a small amount of human capital, should hold a substantial amount of his or her investment capital in bonds.

The nature of that human capital also needs to be taken into consideration; if the investor works in a stable, noneconomically sensitive job, such as repossession work or in the government, then a relatively large amount of equity can be held. Contrariwise, the investor who works in the securities industry should be more cautious, since a severe economic downturn might lose him his job as well as his portfolio. (And needless to say, an employee of a publicly traded company should never, ever own stock in his employer's company.) And finally, the nature of the employer should be considered; if it is highly leveraged or distressed, then the employee probably should not pursue a value tilt, since value companies also tend to be both leveraged and distressed.

Does the investor have a pension or significant Social Security income? Then these should likewise be treated as a bond holding of a grade appropriate to the issuer and would mandate that they be balanced by equity holdings in the investible portfolio. Further, Social Security payments are, at least for the moment, indexed not only to inflation but also to wages, which provide even more inflation protection. Most private pensions do not have this feature; this will affect the rate at which the respective payments streams must be discounted by to arrive at the appropriate present value for these "bonds."

REBALANCING

A portfolio resembles nothing so much as a garden in a tropical climate; unless constantly tended, it does not remain in its intended condition for long. Consider, for example, a simple 50/50 mix of the S&P 500 and Barclays Capital U.S. Aggregate Bond Index purchased at the beginning of 1995 and left untended for five years until the end of 1999. During the interval, the very high stock returns would have increased the equity allocation to 71 percent, just in time for the bursting of the bubble. By the end of 2002, the losses in the equity part of the portfolio would have reduced the mix back to 53/47. Overall, the portfolio would have had a creditable annualized return of 9.50 percent, albeit with a very rocky ride toward the end.

Had the investor been wise enough or lucky enough to rebalance the portfolio back to 50/50 on December 21, 1999, the ride down would have been much gentler and the returns even more agreeable: 11.80 percent annualized. Of course, one is only this skilled or lucky in exceptional circumstances. Mechanically rebalancing the portfolio back toward policy at the end of every year would still have improved the portfolio's annualized return to 10.10 percent, as opposed to 9.50 percent for the unrebalanced portfolio.

Bernstein (2000a) and Booth and Fama (1992) have shown a reliable benefit to portfolio rebalancing; in most, but not all, circumstances, regular rebalancing back to policy results in higher returns and lower risk. This, of course, directly violates the efficient market hypothesis, since rebalancing is a bet that the past losers will have above-average returns going forward and that past winners will have below-average returns. If securities returns are truly a random walk, then there should be no rebalancing benefit. What is going on here? Campbell, Lo, and MacKinlay (1997) state that asset classes do *not* obey a random walk: Over periods of less than one year, they exhibit a slight tendency toward momentum—that is, for the best-performing asset classes to continue with above-average returns going forward and the worst-performing ones tending to have below-average future returns.

Over longer periods, however—three to five years—asset classes tend to mean-revert; that is, the past best performers tend to have below-average returns going forward, and vice versa. Such was the case with the S&P 500 between 1995 and 2003: For the first five years, stocks produced high-double-digit returns in each and every calendar year, and for the last three, negative ones. Clearly, it was best not to rebalance too often: If done every year, as already noted, the annualized return of the 50/50 portfolio was 10.10 percent; if rebalanced every other year, 10.41 percent; and if done every four years, 10.78 percent.

Thus, it is best to let asset class momentum work its magic; do not rebalance too often. Once every two to four years is just fine.

Many practitioners, in fact, do not rebalance according to a calendar schedule but rebalance only when asset class allocations exceed a certain threshold. Just as care should be taken not to rebalance too often when using the calendar method, the investor should employ relatively wide thresholds that are custom-designed for each asset class.

Three factors directly affect the amount of excess return generated by rebalancing. The first is the amount of dispersion among asset classes: If one asset class consistently outperforms another by a wide margin, then it may not pay to rebalance at all. For example, in the 10 years between 1990 and 1999, the S&P 500 and Japanese large stocks, as measured by the MSCI Japan Index, returned 18.21 percent and –0.85 percent, respectively. Once-yearly rebalancing a 50/50 portfolio of these two assets resulted in an annualized return of 9.65 percent, whereas *never* rebalancing produced a 12.06 percent return; during this period, Japanese stocks so reliably underperformed U.S. equity that one was simply throwing good money after bad by frequently shifting assets from U.S. to Japanese stocks. Fortunately, such a wide disparity of equity returns for such a long period of time is the exception rather than the rule.

On the other hand, when asset classes are very similar, then a large excess return can be earned. A good example of this is obtained by examining the same two assets—U.S. and Japanese equity, but this time over a much longer period. For the 38 years between 1970 and 2007, a 50/50 portfolio that was rebalanced annually returned 11.84 percent, which was higher than for either asset class alone: 11.07 percent and 10.73 percent for U.S. and Japanese equity, respectively.

The longer the rebalancing period or the wider the threshold, the larger the excess returns earned are likely to be. But this excess return comes at a price; with both longer rebalancing intervals or high thresholds, the portfolios will get farther out of whack before being rebalanced, thus increasing risk. And if the thresholds are set too wide, there is the additional risk of *never* rebalancing. Thus, the rebalancing bonus can be viewed as a sort of risk premium, earned for bearing the additional risk incurred by allowing the portfolios to deviate from policy allocations.

High volatility also increases the benefit of rebalancing. This stands to reason: Crudely put, the excess return of rebalancing comes from buying low and selling high; the more volatile an asset class is, the lower one buys, and the higher one sells. Likewise, low correlation also increases rebalancing benefit; obviously, the highest excess returns are earned when one asset zigs while the other zags. If they move together, then relatively little rebalancing is done.

If the investor is using no-load open-end mutual funds, then she incurs no *direct* costs. Rather, the transactional costs incurred by buying and selling are spread out over all fund shareholders, whether they trade or not. If the investor, however, is investing directly in individual securities, then the commissions and transactional costs incurred by rebalancing are borne directly by him or her—one more reason not to rebalance too often.

Third, rebalancing should be done sparingly, if at all, in taxable accounts. As shown earlier, the rebalancing bonus is usually less than 1 percent per year, which is dwarfed by the much larger capital gains cost of selling a highly appreciated asset. Investors with substantial amounts of both taxable and sheltered assets can avoid this problem by arranging their portfolios so that all of their rebalancing is accomplished in the sheltered account.

STRATEGIC ASSET ALLOCATION

Strategic asset allocation refers to the process of periodically altering asset allocations with the goal of achieving higher returns. Let me first be clear about what I believe to be the only viable strategy for altering policy allocations: relatively small changes in portfolio composition in a direction opposite to large price or valuation movements.

Is this not the same as market timing, demonstrably a fool's errand? Yes and no. Recall that portfolio rebalancing is itself a form of market timing—a bet that asset classes that have outperformed/underperformed will underperform/outperform in the future. If rebalancing increases returns, then purchasing/selling even more to raise/lower the baseline policy allocation can simply be thought of as over-balancing. Further, a belief in market efficiency does not absolve the intelligent investor of the responsibility of estimating asset class returns. I will go one step further: One has no business investing at all if one is unwilling or unable to understand and abide by the principles first described by Irving Fisher (1954) and John Burr Williams (1964) early in the past century. Expected returns generally move in a direction opposite prices: Low prices imply high expected returns, and high prices, low expected returns. Different metrics can be used for different asset classes. For example, Asness (2005) and others have shown a high degree of correlation between the P/E ratio using trailing 10-year earnings and future returns for industrial stocks. For other asset classes, things are even easier. Examination of the National Association of Real Estate Investment Trusts (NAREIT) database shows that the real dividend growth for its equity REIT index is in the range of –1 percent to 0 percent; thus, when the index yields 4 percent, a real return of 3 to 4 percent can be expected; at a yield of 8 percent, a return of 7 to 8 percent can be expected. Both of these extremes have been observed within the last decade, with the predicted subsequent low and high returns, respectively. Similar predictions can be made with most other asset classes.

Like rebalancing, such tilts in allocation are in effect a risk premium. Securities markets are highly noisy; asset classes that are over- or undervalued can become even more so, and such bets are likely to be harmful a significant minority of the time. Thus, the major danger of strategic asset allocation is running out of room: mandating an uncomfortably large allocation to an asset class whose price level has fallen by a very large amount over a long period, or completely eliminating an asset class whose price has risen by a large amount.

Finally, simply adhering to an unchanging, written-in-stone asset allocation is difficult enough, requiring that the investor buy out-of-favor asset classes: One should not invest in emerging stocks at all unless one can hold on when banks are failing in Argentina or consumers are rioting in Indonesia. Similarly, it requires almost as much discipline to sell asset classes whose prices have been buoyed by popular euphoria. Strategic asset allocation requires even larger purchases and sales at such times, and demands more discipline and detachment than many, or even most, investors can manage.

Thus, changes to policy, if they are to be made at all, should be: (1) made only in response to very large changes in valuation and extended return, (2) relatively small, and (3) infrequent, varying overall equity allocation no more than 5 to 10 percent.

Let us now return again to our original question: How important is asset allocation? By now, the answer is clear: Over the very long term, a portfolio's risk/return characteristics are determined largely by its overall stock–bond mix. While, over the very long term, the precise allocation among risky assets is of little importance to overall return, it should be crafted, using historical standard deviation and correlation data, to produce a "sensible" portfolio of relatively low volatility. What is critical is not so much the precise policy allocations, but that they are adhered to, rebalanced to, and changed sparingly, all in accordance with a strict procedural discipline. Ultimately, investment success rests less on brilliance and hard work than on the emotional stamina to stay the plotted course in the face of all adversity.

REFERENCES

Asness, C. S. 2005. "Rubble Logic: What Did We Learn from the Great Stock Market Bubble?" *Financial Analysts Journal* 61: 6 (November/December): 36–54.

Bernstein, W. J. 2000a. "Case Studies in Rebalancing," www.efficientfrontier.com/ef/100/rebal100.htm.

Bernstein, W. J. 2000b. *The Intelligent Asset Allocator*. New York: McGraw-Hill.

Bernstein, W. J., and D. J. Wilkinson. 1997. "Diversification, Rebalancing, and the Geometric Mean Frontier," http://papers.ssrn.com/sol3/papers.cfm?abstract_id=53503.

Booth, D. G., and E. F. Fama. 1992. "Diversification Returns and Asset Contributions," *Financial Analysts Journal* 48: 3 (May/June): 26–32.

Brinson, G. P., L. R. Hood, and G. L. Beebower. 1986. "Determinants of Portfolio Performance," *Financial Analysts Journal* 42: 4 (July/August): 39–44.

Brinson, G. P., L. R. Hood, and G. L. Beebower. 1995. "Determinants of Portfolio Performance," *Financial Analysts Journal* 51: 1 (January/February): 133–138.

Brinson, G. P., B. D. Singer, and C. R. Harvey. 1991. "Determinants of Portfolio Performance II: An Update," *Financial Analysts Journal* 47: 3 (May/June): 40–48.

Campbell, J. Y., A. W. Lo, and C. MacKinlay. 1997. *The Econometrics of Financial Markets.* Princeton, NJ: Princeton University Press.

Dimensional Fund Advisors. 2008. *2007 Matrix Book.* Santa Monica, CA: Author.

Fisher, I. 1954. *The Theory of Interest as Determined by Impatience to Spend Income and Opportunity to Invest It.* New York: Kelly and Millman.

Jahnke, W. 1997. "The Asset Allocation Hoax," *Journal of Financial Planning* 10: 1 (February): 109–113.

Markowitz, H. 1952. "Portfolio Selection," *Journal of Finance* 7: 1 (March): 77–91.

Samuelson, P. A. 1969. "Lifetime Portfolio Selection by Dynamic Stochastic Programming," *Review of Economics and Statistics* 5: 3 (August): 239–256.

Williams, J. B. 1964. *The Theory of Investment Value.* Amsterdam: North Holland.

ABOUT THE AUTHOR

William Bernstein is neurologist, cofounder of Efficient Frontier Advisors, an investment management firm, and has written several titles on finance and economic history. He has produced two finance books, *The Intelligent Asset Allocator* and *The Four Pillars of Investing,* and also two volumes of economic history, *The Birth of Plenty* and *A Splendid Exchange*, the former about the economic growth inflection of the early nineteenth century and the latter a wide-angle look at the history of world trade. He is currently working on a third finance book and exploring the effects of access to technology on human relations and politics.

CHAPTER 9

The Morningstar Approach to Mutual Fund Analysis—Part I

DON PHILLIPS
Managing Director, Corporate Strategy, Research, and Communications, and President, Fund Research, Morningstar, Inc.

PAUL D. KAPLAN, Ph.D., CFA
Vice President, Quantitative Research, Morningstar, Inc.

CYCLE OF FEAR AND GREED

The mutual fund industry has done a remarkable job of creating scores of fine, reasonably priced funds that can meet almost any conceivable investment need. Unfortunately, however, good funds do not always translate into good results for investors. Even when using high-quality investment vehicles, such as low-cost, broad market index funds, investors too often buy high and sell low. The resulting damage from poorly timed buy and sell decisions can sabotage investors' returns and represents what may well be considered the Achilles' heel of investment management.

Both investors and fund companies share part of the blame for investors' suboptimal use of the industry's fund offerings. No one wins when investors are enticed to throw money at an overheated market or are tempted to pull out after a sharp correction, but little has been done to curb the practice. Fund companies do not run ads discouraging investors from buying their hottest funds, nor do they tout the recent losses of their most out-of-favor funds. Instead, the mutual fund marketing machine often amplifies the cycle of investors' fear and greed—promoting aggressive funds at the market's peak and more conservative offerings at its trough.

At Morningstar, we have tried to shine a light on this problem of poor fund usage by publishing a metric that we call Investor Return™. It is a money-weighted performance calculation that weights performance in periods when more money is in a fund more heavily than those periods when less money is invested. It gives an approximate feel for how much money a fund makes (or loses) for investors in the aggregate. This calculation differs from traditional total return, which is a time-weighted calculation that assumes all of an investor's money goes in at the beginning of the evaluation period and remains in place with no additions or withdrawals.

Total return remains the most appropriate way to evaluate a fund manager's prowess, but the Investor Return metric helps show how well the average investor has actually fared in a fund. Sadly, investor returns almost always trail total returns, as investors tend to chase past performance and buy funds only after a good run. Not surprisingly, the gap between investor results and stated fund performance widens as fund volatility increases and investor resolve is tested. For relatively staid investment vehicles such as balanced funds, the gap is typically small, perhaps just 20 basis points (0.20 percent) per year. For domestic equity funds as a whole, the gap was roughly 187 basis points per year over the 10-year period ended December 2007. For higher-volatility funds, such as sector funds or emerging-market stock funds, the gap can often be in excess of 300 basis points per year. For more aggressive investors, this hidden cost can easily dwarf the impact of fund fees in terms of undermining investment success.

Clearly, this behavioral aspect of investing is at least as important as seminal investment considerations such as asset allocation and security/fund selection. It is only when all three aspects of the investment process—asset allocation, security/fund selection, and investor behavior—are working in concert that investors are apt to succeed. By becoming proficient in all three stages, investors and their advisers can moderate the fear-and-greed cycle and make meaningful progress toward their goals.

RISK MANAGEMENT

As Investor Return statistics show, trying to chase after hot funds is a losing game. A more prudent and usually more rewarding strategy is to take a long-range view and focus on balancing return and risk by building a diversified portfolio of securities. Tomes have been written by Nobel Prize winners and other leading scholars on the mathematical justification for risk management and portfolio diversification, but for our purposes here, suffice it to say that risk matters and diversification is critical.

As the academic community has taught us, investment risks come in many shapes and sizes. One type of risk, known as systematic risk, results simply from choosing to invest in a given securities market. Systematic risk is sometimes referred to as market risk or macro risk, and represents the generic risks of investing in a certain asset class or security type. Unsystematic risk, however, is the risk that is specific to an individual security rather than to a whole class of securities. An investor who owns shares in IBM, for example, takes on the systematic risks of the stock market and the technology sector as well as the unsystematic risks associated with IBM—as defined by that company's specific competitive pressures, product line, stock valuation, and so forth.

Anyone who invests is exposed to certain systematic risks that can be managed and mitigated through portfolio construction and diversification. As for unsystematic risk, some investors believe it makes more sense to minimize unsystematic risk and cost by investing in market-mimicking index funds, sometimes referred to as a passive investment strategy. Others believe in a more active strategy, where the investor takes on certain unsystematic risks, picking certain securities over others, in an effort to beat the market. Whichever the strategy, understanding different types of securities, the systematic and unsystematic risks they present, and how the securities work together when combined in a portfolio should be a key priority for any investor.

APPROACHES TO PORTFOLIO CONSTRUCTION

Portfolio assembly is more art than science. There is no one right way to do it, but there are plenty of wrong ways.

The first step to successful portfolio construction is to determine the desired level of complexity. A good portfolio can be as simple as one fund, especially with the recent proliferation of well-constructed target date and target risk funds. Target date funds, which offer a diversified blend of securities that shift appropriately in asset allocation over time, are a great choice for individual investors who are new to investing. Target risk funds maintain a relatively stable asset allocation over time in order to maintain a fairly stable level of risk. Choosing a lower-cost target date or target risk fund from a well-known firm leaves relatively little room for error. The only trick is accurately matching investor time horizon or risk tolerance with that of the fund. As funds increasingly make these criteria explicit in their names, the potential for a mismatch narrows. There are, however, degrees of difference between the approaches taken by major institutions, and at least some due diligence into the chosen fund's investment approach is warranted.

For those investors who want to more finely tune their portfolios, à la carte portfolio construction remains a popular option. This approach is the most widely used among financial planners, who often believe that their knowledge of their clients' financial situation gives them insights into the asset allocation appropriate for each client. Investors or advisers who opt for customized asset allocations then fall into three camps for implementation of their plans. Some opt for the simplicity, low cost, and dependability of index funds. Others try to add value through the selection of active managers. They will most often use actively managed funds, separate accounts, and occasionally hedge funds. Still others forgo outside managers and select at least some portion of the stocks and bonds used in the portfolio themselves. These options require substantially more research effort to ensure that the resulting portfolios are appropriate and stay on track to meet investor goals.

Any of these approaches can succeed if the investor's level of skill, commitment, and resources is appropriate for the level of sophistication selected. The key with any approach is understanding the portfolio implications of individual investment decisions. Whether your portfolio contains 1 fund or 20 funds, your choices will have performance and risk implications that must be understood and managed if you are to stay onboard and successfully meet your goals. In the next section, we describe how to use Morningstar tools as a lens through which to understand and even visualize the portfolio implications of investment selections. Only by knowing where you stand can you determine if you are pointed in the right direction.

TOOLS FOR ANALYZING FUNDS

Understanding investment portfolios starts with understanding the underlying components, whether they are individual securities or funds made up of individual securities. We begin by discussing some key tools for analyzing mutual funds but ultimately come around to how to analyze the nature of the underlying securities in a fund, an essential piece of the fund analysis and portfolio construction process.

Morningstar Category

Morningstar provides a wealth of information and analysis about each mutual fund in its database. In order to use this information effectively, it makes sense to begin with the Morningstar category. Each U.S.-sold fund is placed into 1 of 70 categories, based primarily on the fund's largest systematic risk exposures. We believe that placing a fund into the proper category is one of the most important pieces of analysis that Morningstar performs. The categories enable meaningful comparisons among similar funds and make it easier to assess potential risk, identify the top-performing funds, and build well-diversified portfolios.

Morningstar does not use the investment objective stated in a fund's prospectus to place it in a category because the stated objective may not reflect how the fund actually invests. Rather, the category is assigned based on the underlying securities in each portfolio. Morningstar places a fund in a given category based on its portfolio statistics and compositions over the past three years. If the fund is new and has no portfolio history, Morningstar estimates where it will fall before giving it a more permanent category assignment. When necessary, Morningstar may change a category assignment based on recent changes to the portfolio. Morningstar regularly reviews and updates the list of categories to reflect changes in the fund industry. The categories described in this chapter are based on classifications as of 2007, and please visit www.corporate.morningstar.com/US for the most updated list of categories for U.S.-based mutual funds.

The Morningstar categories are organized into five broad groups:

1. Balanced
2. U.S. stock
3. International stock
4. Taxable bond
5. Municipal bond

Let us consider each group and the categories within each group.

Balanced Funds

An investor who decides to build a portfolio consisting of a single fund would most likely use a balanced fund from one of these categories:

- Conservative allocation
- Moderate allocation
- World allocation
- Target Date 2000–2014
- Target Date 2015–2029
- Target Date 2030+

These funds combine stocks, bonds, and possibly other asset classes to provide a well-diversified portfolio in a single fund. The three allocation categories generally maintain a consistent exposure to stocks, bonds, and interest-bearing cash over time. Conservative- and moderate-allocation funds have more than 60 percent of their assets invested in U.S. securities. The difference is that conservative-allocation funds have 20 to 50 percent of their assets in stocks while moderate-allocation funds devote 50 to 70 percent of assets to stocks. World-allocation funds have at least 40 percent of their assets invested in non-U.S. stocks and bonds, and have a stock allocation between 20 and 70 percent. By selecting one of these funds, you easily maintain diversified exposure to stocks, bonds, and cash. Of course, in order to pick the right one for you, you need to find one that has the combination of asset classes that best meets your needs and goals.

The three target-date categories make up a special class of funds that are specifically designed for retirement savings. Generally, these funds come in sets with each fund specifying a target year for retirement or other savings goal. For example, a fund family may offer five funds with target years 2010, 2015, 2020, 2025, and 2030. As each fund approaches the target year, the stock exposure is reduced and the bond and cash exposures are increased. The path of the changing asset mix over time is known as the glide path. Some glide paths continue past the target date under the theory that investors should continue to become more conservative as they age during retirement.

To use these funds, you would first pick a fund family and then choose the individual fund that has a target year that most closely matches the year of your planned retirement or other goal. Before making a selection, keep in mind that different families can vary widely in their approaches: how much they invest internationally; how much they invest in asset classes beyond stocks, bonds, and cash; their styles of stock investing; their asset mixes; and their glide paths.

U.S.-Stock Funds

U.S. investors who decide to build a portfolio of funds rather than relying on a single balanced fund will most likely hold a significant stake in U.S.-stock funds.

U.S.-stock funds can be used for three purposes in a U.S. investor's portfolio:

1. They can form the core of the equity portion of the portfolio.
2. They can add exposure to particular segments of the U.S. stock market, either for diversification purposes or to enhance return.
3. They can provide an exposure to a manager whom the investor believes has skill in either a broad or narrow segment of the U.S. stock market.

A U.S.-stock fund is defined as one that has at least 70 percent of its assets in U.S. stocks. If the fund is not focused on a particular economic sector, Morningstar places it into one of nine categories based on the market capitalization (cap for short) and the value/growth orientation of the stocks held over the past three years. This is because research over the past few decades has identified market cap and value/growth orientation as two major systematic risk factors of stock markets. *Market cap* refers to the total value of a company's stock and is often used as a proxy for the size of the firm. *Value/growth orientation* refers to investment styles. Value investors focus on stocks that are perceived as undervalued, expecting that these stocks' worth eventually will be recognized by the market. Growth investors, however, seek securities with high rates of revenue or earnings growth. Many

Exhibit 9.1 Morningstar Style-Based U.S. Stock Fund Categories

Large Value	Large Blend	Large Growth
Mid-Cap Value	Mid-Cap Blend	Mid-Cap Growth
Small Value	Small Blend	Small Growth

investors adopt elements from both approaches. Market cap and value/growth orientation are discussed in more detail in Chapter 10.

Reflecting the nine squares of the Morningstar Style Box, these nine categories can be arranged in a grid as shown in Exhibit 9.1.

Investment advisers generally recommend that U.S. investors hold a diversified portfolio of large-cap stocks. Since blend funds hold diversified portfolios of value and growth stocks, you can use large blend funds to form this part of your portfolio. An alternative is using a combination of large-value and large-growth funds.

Many funds that Morningstar categorizes as large cap also hold mid-cap and small-cap stocks. If the mid-cap and small-cap exposures of your large-cap funds are insufficient, however, you can increase your exposure to stocks of smaller companies with funds in the mid-cap and small-cap categories.

Funds from any of the nine style-based categories can be used to tilt your portfolio toward styles that you wish to emphasize. You also may be willing to deviate from your ideal blend of styles and court some extra unsystematic risk in order to gain exposure to one or more managers whom you believe are particularly talented.

Morningstar also includes several other U.S.-stock categories. Funds that invest at least 50 percent of their assets in a single economic sector are placed in one of the specialty categories. These sectors include communications, financial, health care, natural resources, precious metals, real estate, technology, and utilities. Funds that use leverage or take substantial short positions (selling borrowed shares in securities that appear to be unattractive) are placed in special categories including long-short (funds that hold sizable stakes in both long and short positions); leveraged net long (funds that take leveraged long positions in some stocks, short positions in other stocks, but have an overall net exposure similar to traditional long-only funds); and bear market (funds that take only short positions).

International-Stock Funds

Stock funds that have at least 40 percent of their assets in non-U.S. securities fall into the international-stock categories. Funds that have less than 20 percent of their assets in U.S. securities and are geographically diversified in developed economies are classified into five style-based categories, which can be arranged in a grid as shown in Exhibit 9.2.

Exhibit 9.2 Morningstar Style-Based Foreign Stock Fund Categories

Foreign Large Value	Foreign Large Blend	Foreign Large Growth
Foreign Small/Mid Value		Foreign Small/Mid Growth

Funds in these categories can be used in the non-U.S. part of your portfolio in the same ways that funds in the style-based U.S.-stock categories can be used in the U.S. part. You can use either foreign large-blend funds or combinations of foreign large-value and foreign large-growth funds to form the core of the non-U.S. stock part of your portfolio. Funds from any of these categories can be used to bias your non-U.S. stock exposure toward styles that you wish to emphasize. You also may be willing to deviate from your ideal blend of non-U.S. styles in order to gain exposure to one or more managers whom you believe are particularly talented.

In international stock investing, the geographic location of a stock is also viewed as a systematic risk factor. Many international-stock funds specialize in a particular country, a geographic region, or emerging markets. The Morningstar categories for these funds include:

- Europe stock
- Japan stock
- Pacific/Asia ex-Japan stock
- Diversified Pacific/Asia
- Diversified emerging markets
- Latin America stock

There are at least three ways to use funds in these categories:

1. Combine funds from across these categories to build your own geographically diversified non-U.S. stock portfolio (as part of your overall portfolio).
2. Use funds from one or more of these categories to create a geographic bias.
3. Select funds from these categories that have managers whom you believe are particularly talented, possibly introducing biases into your overall portfolio.

One additional international-stock category is the world-stock category. Funds in these categories hold diversified portfolios of stocks in the United States and the developed markets of Europe and Asia, with the U.S. exposure between 20 and 60 percent. These funds provide global diversification in a single fund.

Taxable-Bond Funds

Bond funds can be used to form the fixed-income portion of a diversified portfolio. Like stock funds, bond funds can be used in at least three ways:

1. They can form the core of the fixed-income portion of the portfolio.
2. They can add exposure to particular segments of the bond market for either diversification purposes or to enhance return.
3. They can be used to gain exposure to a manager believed to have skill.

With fixed-income investments, there is the additional twist of tax treatment. The income from municipal bonds (bonds issued by state and local governments) is exempt from federal taxes and also from state taxes if you are a resident of the same state as the issuer. This is why Morningstar divides bond funds into two broad groups: taxable-bond funds (which have no special tax treatment) and municipal-bond funds (which are treated specially for tax purposes). As a general rule, for the taxable portion of your portfolio, you should hold taxable-bond funds if you are in one of the lower tax brackets or municipal-bond funds if you are in one of the higher tax brackets, but not both. To decide which is right for you, it is wise to compare after-tax yields using your marginal tax rate. For the portion of your portfolio that you hold in tax-advantaged accounts, such as individual retirement accounts (IRAs), hold taxable-bond funds.

The most important systematic risk factors for bonds are duration, credit quality, and issuer. The longer out into the future a bond's payments are, the longer its duration and the more sensitive its price to changes in interest rates or yields. A bond's credit quality measures how likely the bond issuer is to make all of its scheduled payments. All other things being equal, the lower a bond's credit rating, the lower its price and the higher its yield. A bond issued by the U.S. government or one of its agencies has the highest credit quality because no one expects the U.S. government to default on its obligations. Bonds issued by corporations that are unlikely to default are investment-grade bonds. Bonds in which the likelihood of default is high are referred to as junk bonds. Because junk bonds have high promised yields, they are also called high-yield bonds.

Morningstar categories for taxable U.S.-bond funds are organized around those factors most related to systematic risk—issuer, duration, and credit quality—as depicted in Exhibit 9.3.

The first row contains categories of funds that focus on U.S. government and agency bonds. The second row contains categories of funds that focus on investment-grade bonds. In the third row, multisector bond funds are those that hold a blend of investment-grade and high-yield bonds. High-yield bond funds, being of the lowest credit quality, appear in the bottom row. The columns are arranged by duration, with the first column containing categories of funds that hold securities with cashlike durations. Ultrashort bond funds hold investment-grade issues with durations that are less than a year, and bank-loan funds invest in risky floating-rate bank loans. The remaining columns represent more rate-sensitive intermediate-term and long-term funds.

This grid can be used much like the stock category grids in Exhibits 9.1 and 9.2. You probably would use intermediate government or intermediate-term bond funds to form the core of the fixed-income portion of your portfolio. If you are willing to take the risk of long-term bonds in the hope of earning higher returns, you should consider long government or long-term bond funds. If you want to take on less risk and are willing to earn lower returns, consider short government or short-term bond funds. For minimal interest-rate sensitivity, but possibly the lowest returns, consider ultrashort bond funds. If you are willing to take some credit risk in the hope of earning additional returns, you can add funds from

Exhibit 9.3 Morningstar Categories for Taxable U.S.-Bond Funds

Ultrashort Bond	Short Government	Intermediate Government	Long Government
	Short-term Bond	Intermediate-term Bond	Long-term Bond
Bank Loan	Multisector Bond		
	High-yield Bond		

multisector and high-yield bonds, but you probably want to do so in a limited way.

One additional U.S. taxable-bond category not captured in the fixed-income grid in Exhibit 9.3 is inflation-protected-bond funds. These funds invest in bonds that adjust their payouts to keep pace with inflation. The largest single issuer of these securities in the United States is the U.S. Treasury, which issues TIPS (Treasury Inflation-Protected Securities). Because the payments made by conventional bonds are fixed, there is risk that future inflation will erode their purchasing power. Inflation-protected-bond funds protect their investors from this risk.

Funds that invest mainly in non-U.S. bonds are classified in one of two categories: world-bond funds and emerging-markets bond funds. World-bond funds invest 40 percent or more of their assets in bonds issued outside the United States, with at least 35 percent of their assets invested in developed countries. Emerging-market bond funds invest more than 65 percent of their assets in emerging-market countries.

Municipal-Bond Funds

As discussed earlier, if you are in a high tax bracket, you should consider municipal-bond funds for the fixed-income portion of your taxable accounts. Since income from municipal bonds issued in your state of residency is exempt from both federal and state income, first consider funds that hold primarily investment-grade municipal bonds in your state. For some of the larger states, there is a large enough choice of state-specific investment-grade funds, so Morningstar created a category for each of them. (Morningstar considers a fund to be state-specific if at least 80 percent of its assets are in municipal bonds issued in a single state.) In the cases of New York and California, the number of funds is large enough to classify them into two categories based on duration. These state-specific categories are:

- Muni California Long
- Muni California Intermediate/Short
- Muni Massachusetts
- Muni Minnesota
- Muni New Jersey
- Muni New York Long
- Muni New York Intermediate/Short
- Muni Ohio
- Muni Pennsylvania

If you do not live in one of the eight states that appear in the list, look for funds that specialize in your state in the single-state categories. Each of these categories contains funds that specialize in the investment-grade municipal bonds issued in one of the 42 other states. They are organized by duration:

- Muni Single-State Long
- Muni Single-State Intermediate
- Muni Single-State Short

Some funds invest in municipal bonds issued in multiple states. Like the single-state funds, Morningstar classifies these national municipal bond funds into one of three categories based on duration:

- Muni National Long
- Muni National Intermediate
- Muni National Short

MUTUAL FUND ANALYSIS TOOLS

Once you have determined which fund categories are most appropriate for your portfolio, you are ready to begin evaluating and selecting individual funds from within these categories. There are numerous fund analysis tools available, many of which can be accessed through either the free or premium areas of www.morningstar.com. Throughout this discussion, we will use online reports and tools from Morningstar.com® to explain and illustrate many of these analytical tools.

Some fund analysis tools are returns-based and focus on each fund's historical performance. Other tools are holdings-based and focus on the contents of each fund's investment portfolio. There are also qualitative tools that address a fund company's culture and stewardship. All of these tools play an important part in the fund analysis process, and each Morningstar fund report begins with the Snapshot™ page summarizing key returns- and holdings-based statistics. Exhibit 9.4 gives two examples of the Performance and Key Stats sections that appear at the top of the Snapshot page.

RETURNS-BASED ANALYSIS

Total Returns

Historical fund performance forms the basis for a number of important risk and reward analysis tools. Before delving into the details of these performance-based tools, let us review the definition and calculation of total return, the fundamental performance measurement for mutual funds.

The price of one share of a mutual fund is referred to as net asset value per share, or NAV. The monthly total return of a fund measures the percentage change in the value of an investment in the fund over the month, assuming purchase on the last day of the previous month and immediate reinvestment of any distributions. For example, suppose that a fund's NAV was $100 on November 30, that it paid a dividend of $1 per share on December 15 when its NAV was $101, and that its NAV on December 31 was $102. A $100 investment on November 30 would purchase a single share. The $1 dividend paid on December 15 would allow for the purchase of 1/101 of a share so that on December 31, we own 1 and 1/101 shares each worth $102 for a total value of $103.01. So the total return for December was 3.01 percent, calculated by dividing the end value of $103.01 by the initial investment of $100.

After monthly total returns have been calculated over a period of time, they can be used to calculate total returns over longer periods, such as quarters, years,

Fund LB1

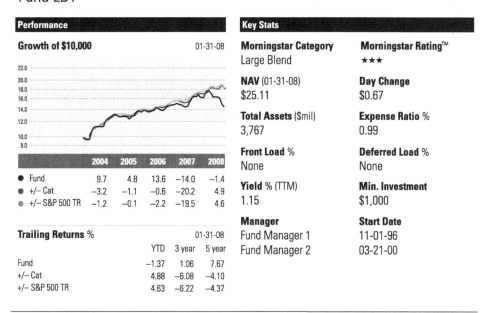

Performance

Growth of $10,000   01-31-08

	2004	2005	2006	2007	2008
● Fund	9.7	4.8	13.6	−14.0	−1.4
● +/− Cat	−3.2	−1.1	−0.6	−20.2	4.9
● +/− S&P 500 TR	−1.2	−0.1	−2.2	−19.5	4.6

Trailing Returns %   01-31-08

	YTD	3 year	5 year
Fund	−1.37	1.06	7.67
+/− Cat	4.88	−6.08	−4.10
+/− S&P 500 TR	4.63	−6.22	−4.37

Key Stats

Morningstar Category	Morningstar Rating™
Large Blend	★★★
NAV (01-31-08)	**Day Change**
$25.11	$0.67
Total Assets ($mil)	**Expense Ratio** %
3,767	0.99
Front Load %	**Deferred Load** %
None	None
Yield % (TTM)	**Min. Investment**
1.15	$1,000
Manager	**Start Date**
Fund Manager 1	11-01-96
Fund Manager 2	03-21-00

Fund LB2

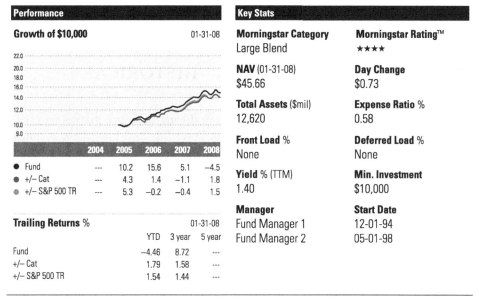

Performance

Growth of $10,000   01-31-08

	2004	2005	2006	2007	2008
● Fund	---	10.2	15.6	5.1	−4.5
● +/− Cat	---	4.3	1.4	−1.1	1.8
● +/− S&P 500 TR	---	5.3	−0.2	−0.4	1.5

Trailing Returns %   01-31-08

	YTD	3 year	5 year
Fund	−4.46	8.72	---
+/− Cat	1.79	1.58	---
+/− S&P 500 TR	1.54	1.44	---

Key Stats

Morningstar Category	Morningstar Rating™
Large Blend	★★★★
NAV (01-31-08)	**Day Change**
$45.66	$0.73
Total Assets ($mil)	**Expense Ratio** %
12,620	0.58
Front Load %	**Deferred Load** %
None	None
Yield % (TTM)	**Min. Investment**
1.40	$10,000
Manager	**Start Date**
Fund Manager 1	12-01-94
Fund Manager 2	05-01-98

Exhibit 9.4   Performance and Key Statistics Snapshots for Two Large Blend Funds

or multiyear periods. When presenting results for multiyear periods, it is common practice to state the total return as a compound annual return, also known as annualized return. For example, if over a three-year period the annual returns on a fund were 10 percent, –5 percent, and 15 percent, a $10,000 initial investment would be worth $12,017.50 at the end of the three years. The end result would have been the same had the annual total return been 6.32 percent in each year, so the compound annual return is 6.32 percent for the entire three-year period.

Now let us turn to the specific returns-based data that Morningstar provides.

Historical Performance

At the top of the Snapshot page for each fund on www.morningstar.com is a chart that shows what would have happened if you had invested $10,000 in the fund five years ago, reinvested all income from the fund, and paid no taxes. These results are derived from the monthly total returns just described. For comparison, the chart also shows the growth of $10,000 in two hypothetical investments, namely, a portfolio of all funds in the same Morningstar category and a benchmark index. See Exhibit 9.4 for an example of this chart.

The purpose of the Growth of $10,000 chart is to show how the fund has performed over the past five years, both in absolute and relative terms. Below the chart, the yearly total returns are presented along with the difference between the returns of the fund, the category average, and the index. The goal is to provide a quick comparison between the fund's performance and alternatives that have similar systematic risks.

SAMPLE FUND COMPARISON—HISTORICAL PERFORMANCE

To illustrate the various analytic tools discussed throughout this chapter, we will use two large-cap blend funds; let us call them Fund LB1 and Fund LB2. A quick look at the calendar-year returns below the graphs in Exhibit 9.4 indicates that Fund LB2 has been the better performer. Most of Fund LB1's underperformance happened in 2007, when the fund returned –14.0%, trailing both the large-blend category average and the S&P 500 Index by about 20 percentage points. Past performance is not necessarily indicative of the future, however, and as a rational investor, you should consider whether Fund LB1's experience in 2007 will likely repeat.

To analyze the longer-term performance history of Fund LB1, go to the Performance charts on the Total Returns page (see Exhibit 9.5). Both the graph and the performance history table show that the fund did well in the recessionary years of the early 2000s. The Trailing Returns section shows that Fund LB1 posted a 10-year annualized return of 10.35 percent, outperforming the S&P 500 Index by 4.44 percentage points and ranking in the top 4 percent of the large-blend category. (Whenever Morningstar shows percentile rank within a category, the highest [or most favorable] percentile rank is 1 and the lowest [or least favorable] percentile rank is 100.)

Fund LB1

Performance

Growth of $10,000

01-31-08

● Fund: Fund LB1 ● Category: Large Blend ● Index: S&P 500

	1997	1998	1999	2000	2001	2002	2003	2004	2005	2006	2007
Total Return %				25.8	26.1	−12.5	29.0	9.7	4.8	13.6	−14.0
+/− Category				32.1	39.6	9.8	2.0	−0.3	−1.0	−0.6	−20.2
+/− Index				34.9	38.0	9.6	0.3	−1.2	−0.1	−2.2	−19.5
% Rank in Category				24	3	48	70	83	60	62	99

Trailing Returns

01-31-08

	Total Return%	+/− S&P 500 TR	+/− Morningstar Large Core TR Index	% Rank in Category
1-Day	2.11	0.35	0.52	6
1-Week	5.69	3.51	4.58	1
1-Month	−4.96	3.37	2.78	2
3-Month	−16.52	−5.17	−7.50	97
Year-to-Date	−5.15	2.55	1.83	3
1-Year	−18.80	−15.83	−19.21	99
3-Year Annualized	0.15	−6.78	−7.50	99
5-Year Annualized	6.64	−4.92	−5.31	98
10-Year Annualized	10.35	4.44	4.13	4

Exhibit 9.5 Total Returns Page for a Large Blend Fund

RISK AND RISK-ADJUSTED PERFORMANCE MEASURES

In addition to reflecting how well a fund has performed over time, total return statistics also form the basis for several key risk analysis tools. The Risk Measures page on www.morningstar.com presents several returns-based measures of risk and performance, the most important of which are discussed here.

Standard Deviation

Standard deviation is a statistical measure of the volatility of a fund's performance. The monthly standard deviation of a fund's total return over a period is the square root of the average of the square of the difference between each month's total return and its average monthly total return over the period. The standard deviation figure shown on the Risk Measures page is calculated from the past 36 months of total returns, but the result is rescaled to be an annual figure by multiplying the monthly standard deviation by the square root of 12 (about 3.464).

Assuming that a fund's total returns fall in a bell-shaped distribution (also known as normal distribution), a fund's total returns are expected to differ from its average total return by no more than ±1 standard deviation approximately 68 percent of the time; a fund's total returns should be within a range of ±2 standard deviations from its average 95 percent of the time. For example, assume that a fund's average total return is 10 percent, and its standard deviation is 8 percent. Hypothetically, this fund's total returns should be between 2 percent and 18 percent approximately 68 percent of the time and between –6 and 26 percent approximately 95 percent of the time.

However, the assumption that total returns follow a bell-shaped distribution is highly disputed. Therefore, some researchers believe that standard deviation or a standard deviation–based statistic such as the Sharpe Ratio (see details in the next section) is of limited use. In any case, the greater the standard deviation of a fund's total returns over a period, the greater is the fund's volatility.

Sharpe Ratio

The purpose of investing in risky securities, such as mutual funds, is to earn a rate of return above that which can be earned from investing in risk-free securities, such as money market funds and U.S. Treasury bills. We can measure how a risky security performed relative to a risk-free alternative by subtracting the risk-free rate of return from the total return on the risky security. This difference is called the excess return on the riskier security.

The Sharpe Ratio, developed by Nobel laureate William Sharpe, is a risk-adjusted performance measure based on excess return and standard deviation. It is the ratio of the average of a fund's excess return over a specified period to the standard deviation of excess return over the same period. The Sharpe Ratio that appears on the Risk Measures page is based on a 36-month period and uses the 90-day U.S. Treasury bill as the risk-free rate when calculating monthly excess return. The average monthly excess return is then annualized and divided by the annualized standard deviation of excess returns to arrive at the annualized Sharpe Ratio reported on the page.

The Sharpe Ratio is useful in that it allows comparisons of funds that operate at different levels of volatility. It represents the average excess return per unit of risk. For example, suppose that fund A had an average annual excess return of 6 percent with a standard deviation of 10 percent, while fund B had an average annual excess return of 10 percent with a standard deviation of 20 percent. Fund B had a higher average excess return but was more volatile. So on a risk-adjusted basis, fund A outperformed fund B because fund A provided an excess return of 0.6 per unit of risk, while fund B provided an excess return of 0.5 per unit of risk. In other words, fund A's Sharpe Ratio of 0.6 was higher than fund B's Sharpe Ratio of 0.5, so fund A was the better performer on a risk-adjusted basis.

MODERN PORTFOLIO THEORY STATISTICS

Note that the Sharpe Ratio makes no distinction between systematic and unsystematic risk. Risk is measured by the standard deviation of excess return regardless

Fund LB1

Volatility Measurements		Trailing 3-Yr through 12-31-07 I *Trailing 5-Yr through 12-31-07	
Standard Deviation	11.07	Sharpe Ratio	−0.26
Mean	1.45	Bear Market Decile Rank*	9

Modern Portfolio Theory Statistics		Trailing 3-Yr through 12-31-07	
		Standard Index S&P 500 TR	Best Fit Index Morningstar Services TR
R-Squared		72	75
Beta		1.21	1.15
Alpha		−8.12	−4.67

Fund LB2

Volatility Measurements		Trailing 3-Yr through 12-31-07 I *Trailing 5-Yr through 12-31-07	
Standard Deviation	7.02	Sharpe Ratio	0.82
Mean	10.43	Bear Market Decile Rank*	---

Modern Portfolio Theory Statistics		Trailing 3-Yr through 12-31-07	
		Standard Index S&P 500 TR	Best Fit Index S&P 500 TR
R-Squared		86	86
Beta		0.84	0.84
Alpha		2.10	2.10

Exhibit 9.6   Risk Measures Page for Two Large Blend Funds

of the sources of volatility. The set of statistics that appear next on the Risk Measures page (see Exhibit 9.6), the Modern Portfolio Theory Statistics, do make this distinction.

Alpha, beta, and R-squared are the components of the Modern Portfolio Theory (MPT) statistics. These measures comprise a standard method for assessing the performance of a fund relative to a benchmark, and they are commonly used by both investment practitioners and academics. (These measures are referred to as Modern Portfolio Theory statistics because they are derived from Harry Markowitz's theory of portfolio construction developed in the 1950s, which is considered modern relative to the approach to portfolio construction that preceded it.)

Morningstar calculates a fund's alpha, beta, and R-squared statistics by running a regression of the fund's excess return over the 90-day U.S. Treasury bill compared with the excess returns of the index that Morningstar has selected as the standard index for the fund's broad category group. The Morningstar standard indexes are as shown in Exhibit 9.7.

The calculations are made using the fund's excess returns over the past 36-month period. The results using the standard index appear on the Risk

Exhibit 9.7 Morningstar Standard Indexes

Broad Category Group	Standard Index
Balanced	Dow Jones Moderate Portfolio
U.S. Stock	S&P 500
International Stock	MSCI Europe Australasia Far East ("EAFE")
Taxable Bond	Barclays Capital U.S. Aggregate Bond
Municipal Bond	Barclays Capital Municipal Bond

Measures page under the column heading "Standard Index." See Exhibit 9.6 for two examples.

Beta

Beta is a measure of the sensitivity of a fund's excess returns to movements in an index's excess returns. By design, the beta of the index is 1.00. A fund with a beta of 1.10 has tended to have an excess return that is 10 percent higher than that of the index in up markets and 10 percent lower in down markets, assuming all other factors remain constant. A beta of 0.85 would indicate that the fund has performed 15 percent worse than the index in up markets and 15 percent better in down markets. A low beta does not imply that the fund has a low level of volatility, though; rather, a low beta means only that the fund's index-related risk is low. A specialty fund that invests primarily in gold, for example, will usually have a low beta (and a low R-squared), as its performance is tied more closely to the price of gold and gold-mining stocks than to the overall stock market. Thus, although the specialty fund might fluctuate wildly because of rapid changes in gold prices, its beta will be low.

Alpha

Alpha measures a fund's performance after adjusting for the fund's systematic risk as measured by the fund's beta. The alpha calculation assumes that an investor could form a passive portfolio with the same beta as that of the fund by investing in the index and either borrowing or lending at the risk-free rate of return to heighten or dampen exposure to that index. Alpha is the difference between the average excess return on the fund and the average excess return on the levered or delevered index portfolio. For example, if the fund had an average excess return of 6 percent per year and its beta with respect to the S&P 500 was 0.8 over a period when the S&P 500's average excess return was 7 percent, its alpha would be $6\% - 0.8 \times 7\% = 0.4\%$.

The aim of alpha is to depict how a fund manager adds or subtracts value relative to a levered or delevered index portfolio, but there are limitations to its accuracy. In some cases, a negative alpha can result from the expenses that are present in the fund returns but are not present in the returns of the comparison index. Also, the usefulness of alpha is completely dependent on the accuracy of beta. If you accept beta as a conclusive definition of risk, a positive alpha would be a conclusive indicator of good fund performance.

R-Squared

R-squared is another statistic that is produced by the regression analysis. R-squared is a number between 0 and 100 percent that measures the strength of the relationship between the excess returns of the fund and those of the index. An R-squared of 0 percent means that there is no relationship between the fund and the index, and an R-squared of 100 percent means that the relationship is perfect. Thus, stock index funds that track the S&P 500 Index will have an R-squared very close to 100 percent. A low R-squared indicates that the fund's movements are not well explained by movements in the index. An R-squared measure of 35 percent, for example, means that only 35 percent of the fund's return movements can be explained by movements in index returns.

R-squared can be used to judge the significance of a particular beta estimate. Generally, a high R-squared will indicate a more reliable beta figure.

Best-Fit Index

Morningstar also shows additional alpha, beta, and R-squared statistics based on a regression against a best-fit index. The best-fit index for each fund is selected based on the highest R-squared result from separate regressions on a number of different indexes. For example, many high-yield funds show low R-squared results and thus a low degree of correlation when regressed against the standard bond index, the Barclays Capital U.S. Aggregate Bond Index. These low R-squared results indicate that the index does not adequately explain the behavior of the returns of most high-yield funds. Many of these funds, however, show significantly higher R-squared results when regressed against the CSFB (Credit Suisse First Boston) High-Yield Bond Index.

Both the standard and best-fit results can be useful measures. The standard index R-squared statistics can help with portfolio diversification. For example, if you already own a fund with a very high correlation (and thus a high R-squared) with the S&P 500 and wish to diversify, you might choose not to buy another fund that correlates closely to that index. In addition, the best-fit index can be used to compare the betas and alphas of similar funds that show the same best-fit index.

SAMPLE FUND COMPARISON—RISK AND RISK-ADJUSTED PERFORMANCE MEASURES

Let us return to our example comparing Fund LB1 and Fund LB2. On the Risk Measures page (see Exhibit 9.6), you can see that Fund LB1's three-year annualized standard deviation is 11.07 percent while Fund LB2's is 7.02 percent. This means that Fund LB1 has been more volatile than Fund LB2, the reasons for which can be explored later during our holdings-based analysis. Earlier in the chapter, we had determined that Fund LB2 had higher total returns overall. Now we also know it had less volatility, so it should not be surprising that Fund LB2's three-year Sharpe Ratio (risk-adjusted performance) of 0.82 is better than Fund LB1's ratio of –0.26.

In addition to evaluating volatility as measured by standard deviation, let us look at the systematic risk of these funds relative to the stock market, as measured by the beta in the Modern Portfolio Theory Statistics section (see Exhibit 9.6). Fund

LB1 shows higher sensitivity to stock market movements with a beta of 1.21 versus Fund LB2's beta of 0.84. This means that, after deducting the risk-free rate from returns, Fund LB1 captures 121 percent of the up-and-down movements of S&P 500 Index's excess return. Fund LB1's alpha is –8.12 percent, a large negative number reflective of its underperformance in 2007. Hypothetically, in a year when the S&P 500 Index has an excess return of 7 percent, Fund LB1 is estimated to post an excess return of 0.35 percent (–8.12% + 1.21 × 7%). Interestingly, Fund LB1's Best Fit Index is Morningstar Services Total Return (TR), another observation worth noting and investigating later when we perform our holdings-based analysis of Fund LB1.

MORNINGSTAR RATING™ FOR FUNDS

The Morningstar Rating™ for funds, often called the star rating, debuted in 1985 and was quickly embraced by investors and advisers. Using a scale of 1 to 5 stars, the original rating allowed investors to easily evaluate a fund's past performance within four broad asset classes. For the first time, it introduced the concept of risk- and cost-adjusted return to the average investor. However, over time, investors moved from owning one or two funds to assembling diversified portfolios of funds. This meant they were more likely to need a specific type of fund, such as mid-cap value or small-cap growth, to complement their other holdings. Morningstar responded to this change in the way that investors use funds, first in 1996 by supplementing star ratings with category ratings, which rated funds within their Morningstar categories, and again in 2002 by making the star rating itself a category-based rating (eliminating the need for two ratings). Therefore, since 2002, Morningstar has assigned star ratings based on how each fund has performed relative only to funds within its category. In this way, there are always 1-, 2-, 3-, 4-, and 5-star funds in every category. As Exhibit 9.8 shows, the top 10 percent of distinct funds receives 5 stars, the next 22.5 percent receives 4 stars, the middle 35 percent receives 3 stars, the next 22.5 percent receives 2 stars, and the bottom 10 percent receives 1 star.

The Morningstar Rating is a *quantitative* assessment of a fund's *past* performance—both return and risk. Since the fund star rating is strictly quantitative, Morningstar fund analysts cannot add stars to funds they like or remove stars from those they do not. Because the star rating captures only a fund's past

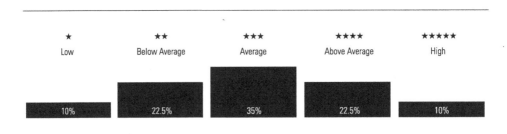

Exhibit 9.8 Distribution of Stars in the Morningstar Rating™ for Funds

risk/reward profile, there will definitely be occasions when a fund with a low star rating has terrific future prospects, and vice versa. For example, in 2007, when American Funds Washington Mutual was a 2-star fund, it was one of the Morningstar Fund Analyst Picks[SM] within the large-value category. (We discuss Morningstar Fund Analyst Picks later.) The fund had been struggling, but our analysts liked its management's consistent approach, which has delivered good results over the life of the fund. More recently, it has been a 3-star fund and remains one of Morningstar Fund Analyst Picks.

Risk- and Cost-Adjusted Performance

The Morningstar approach to adjusting performance for risk differs from the approaches discussed earlier (Sharpe Ratio and alpha). Instead, the star rating is based on a type of economic analysis called expected utility theory, which recognizes that investors are: (1) more concerned about a possible poor outcome than an unexpectedly good outcome; and (2) willing to give up some portion of their expected return in exchange for greater certainty of return. The risk-adjusted return that Morningstar uses for the star rating is effectively the fund's compound annual return less a penalty for its volatility, with monthly returns below the average counting a bit more than monthly returns above the average when measuring volatility.

In addition, Morningstar adjusts performance for the purpose of the star rating to account for any front-end loads, back-end loads, and redemption fees that are charged to investors. Morningstar makes these adjustments so that the rating is based on the performance that investors are likely to experience after paying these costs.

Overall and Period-Specific Ratings

The star rating that appears in the Key Stats section of the Snapshot pages is what we refer to as the fund's overall rating. The overall rating is a weighted average of up to three period-specific ratings: the 3-year rating (based on the past 36 months), the 5-year rating (based on the past 60 months), and the 10-year rating (based on the past 120 months.) These period-specific ratings are also provided on each fund's Morningstar Rating page. See Exhibit 9.9 for an example of this page. For each of the periods shown, Morningstar uses risk- and cost-adjusted performance data to rank all of the funds within each category that have a long enough performance history for the period in question.

In addition to the star ratings, Morningstar also presents ratings on the two components of the star rating—Morningstar Return and Morningstar Risk. Morningstar Return measures the fund's performance after investor costs but makes no adjustment for risk. Morningstar Risk is the risk penalty embedded in the risk- and cost-adjusted return used to assign the star rating. These ratings are distributed among the funds within each category in the same way as the star rating, but rather than being reported as a number between 1 and 5, they are presented as "High," "Above Average," "Average," "Below Average," and "Low."

Fund LB1

Morningstar Rating (Relative to Category)			01-31-08
	Morningstar Return	**Morningstar Risk**	**Morningstar Rating**™
3-Year	Low	Above Average	★
5-Year	Low	Above Average	★
10-Year	High	Above Average	★★★★★
Overall	Average	Above Average	★★★

Morningstar Category: Large Blend

Fund LB2

Morningstar Rating (Relative to Category)			01-31-08
	Morningstar Return	**Morningstar Risk**	**Morningstar Rating**™
3-Year	Above Average	Low	★★★★
5-Year	---	---	Not Rated
10-Year	---	---	Not Rated
Overall	Above Average	Low	★★★★

Morningstar Category: Large Blend

Exhibit 9.9 Morningstar Rating™ for Two Large Blend Funds

How to Use the Star Rating

The fund universe, with more than 17,000 offerings, can be a bit overwhelming at first glance, and that is where the star rating comes in. If you know you want a certain type of fund, you can use the star rating to winnow that group down to a more manageable list of options that deserve further research. In so doing, you can reduce the large-cap growth universe from more than 500 funds to those that fit your criteria and merit further investigation. True, you might miss out on that 1-star fund with bright prospects, but that may be a small price to pay for greatly streamlining the number of funds you have to consider. You can also use the star rating to help monitor your funds' performance. If your former 5-star fund is now sporting a single star, you should research what has driven the downturn. It is possible that the manager's investment style is simply out of favor and will eventually rebound. But a dramatic shift in a fund's star rating could indicate that there is something more substantive going on—perhaps the fund is taking bigger risks than it once did, or perhaps its management team has changed.

How *Not* to Use the Star Rating

Although the star rating can be a handy tool for evaluating and monitoring funds, it should not be viewed as a buy-or-sell signal. Because Morningstar recalculates funds' star ratings every month, funds frequently gain or lose a star, and that action can best be described as noise that should be tuned out. Moreover, a fund is not automatically worth buying just because it earns a 5-star rating. There are 5-star funds in every category, so your first task is determining which categories make sense for you. (A 5-star large-value fund might make sense for a broad swath of investors, but a 5-star precious-metals fund might not.) In addition, a fund's rating may not reflect underlying changes—a manager or strategy change, for example—that make it more or less attractive. Finally, remember that the star rating is just a starting point for your research, not the be-all and end-all for determining its future prospects. Although Morningstar stands by the assertion that 5-star funds are generally a better lot than 1-star offerings, you will need to assess a number of other factors—notably, strategy, costs, and management—to determine whether a given fund makes sense for you.

Sample Fund Comparison—Star Rating

Now that we understand the methodology and the uses of the star rating, let us return to our comparison of Fund LB1 and Fund LB2. Looking at Exhibit 9.9, you can see that Fund LB1's 3-star overall rating is derived from 1-star ratings in the 3- and 5-year periods and a 5-star rating in the 10-year period. Recall from our performance analysis earlier that Fund LB1 took a pretty bad hit in 2007 but performed quite well in the bear market years of the early 2000s. The Morningstar Return column reflects the fund's good long-term and poor short-term performance.

The Morningstar Risk column shows that Fund LB1 has had above-average (meaning higher/worse than average) risk. Combine that with the fund's higher standard deviation of 11 percent and its above-market beta of 1.2, and it is safe to conclude that Fund LB1 has indeed been the riskier of the two funds.

Fund LB2 has a shorter performance history and carries information based only on the past three years. Its above-average Morningstar Return and low Morningstar Risk scores result in a 4-star rating, indicating good risk- and cost-adjusted performance. Summarizing all three risk measures, Fund LB2 has been the more conservative investment for having low Morningstar Risk, a smaller standard deviation of 7 percent, and a below-market beta of 0.8.

CONCLUSIONS

At this point in our analysis, we have a fair amount of detail about *how* these two funds have performed in the past, but we have very little information about *why* they have performed as they have. In order to understand the reasons behind their performance and how they are likely to perform in the future, we need to take the next step and examine the holdings of each fund as well as some other qualitative factors. We discuss analyzing holdings and qualitative factors in detail in Chapter 10.

The authors would like to thank Catherine Sanders and Cindy Sin-Yi Tsai, CFA, CAIA, for their contributions. Credit is also due to Regina Comito and Randal Pawlicki for graphics design.

ABOUT THE AUTHORS

Don Phillips is a managing director of Morningstar, Inc. and is responsible for corporate strategy, research, and corporate communications. He has served on the company's board of directors since August 1999. Mr. Phillips is also president of fund research, which includes research on mutual funds, exchange-traded funds, and alternative investments.

Mr. Phillips joined Morningstar in 1986 as the company's first mutual fund analyst and soon became editor of its flagship publication, *Morningstar*® *Mutual Funds*™, establishing the editorial voice for which the company is best known. Mr. Phillips helped to develop the Morningstar Style Box™, the Morningstar Rating™, and other distinctive proprietary Morningstar innovations that have become industry standards.

Journalists regularly turn to Don Phillips for his insight on industry trends. *Investment Advisor* magazine has named him to its list of the most influential people in the financial planning industry. *Financial Planning* magazine has named him one of the planning industry's "Movers & Shakers." *Registered Rep.* has named him one of the investment industry's 10 key players.

Mr. Phillips holds a bachelor's degree in English from the University of Texas and a master's degree in American literature from the University of Chicago.

Paul D. Kaplan is vice president of quantitative research at Morningstar, Inc., responsible for the quantitative methodologies behind Morningstar's fund analysis, indexes, adviser tools, and other services. Many of Dr. Kaplan's research papers have been published in professional books and publications. He received the 2008 Graham and Dodd Award and was a Graham and Dodd Award of Excellence winner in 2000.

Before joining Morningstar in 1999, he was a vice president of Ibbotson Associates and served as the firm's chief economist and director of research. Prior to that, he served on the economics faculty of Northwestern University where he taught international finance and statistics.

Dr. Kaplan holds a bachelor's degree in mathematics, economics, and computer science from New York University and a master's degree and doctorate in economics from Northwestern University. Dr. Kaplan holds the Chartered Financial Analyst (CFA) designation.

CHAPTER 10

The Morningstar Approach to Mutual Fund Analysis—Part II

DON PHILLIPS
Managing Director, Corporate Strategy, Research, and Communications, and President, Fund Research, Morningstar, Inc.

PAUL D. KAPLAN, Ph.D., CFA
Vice President, Quantitative Research, Morningstar, Inc.

In Chapter 9, "The Morningstar Approach to Mutual Fund Analysis—Part I," we focused primarily on returns-based analysis tools. But equally if not more important are tools that allow you to understand the contents and not just the past behavior of a mutual fund. In this chapter, we focus on holdings-based analysis as well as several important qualitative factors.

HOLDINGS-BASED ANALYSIS

Just as most professional stock pickers agree that it is impossible to pick securities based solely on their past performance patterns, we at Morningstar have long argued that successful fund investing must go beyond checking last year's leaders' lists to incorporate fundamental analysis of funds' holdings. True, looking at returns and volatility for any given time period can provide important clues about certain funds and market trends. That is why Morningstar provides the returns-based analyses we described in Chapter 9. But to truly understand a fund and the role it might play in your overall portfolio, you have to drill down into its holdings, understand the manager's strategy, assess the shareholder-friendliness of the fund company, and evaluate the fund's risk level. Furthermore, funds are not static; styles evolve, portfolio managers come and go. To use a fund wisely in a portfolio, you need to check up on it periodically.

Next we describe various holdings-based analysis tools, which appear mainly on the Snapshot™ and Portfolio pages of a fund's Morningstar.com® report.

Asset Allocation

The most basic thing we can learn from a fund's portfolio is what type of securities it invests in: stocks, bonds, interest-bearing cash, or some other type of security. This

Portfolio Analysis

Morningstar Style Box™

	Large	Average Mkt Cap ($Mil)
	Mid	24,198
	Small	Price/Prospective Earnings
		16.4

Value Blend Growth

Ownership Zone™

	Large	● Fund Centroid represents
	Mid	weighted average of
		domestic stock holdings
	Small	Zone represents
		75% of fund's domestic
		stock holdings

Value Blend Growth

Sector Breakdown (% of stocks)

↻ **Information**		**31.13**
🗓 Software		0.00
🖥 Hardware		8.05
🎙 Media		19.43
☎ Telecommunications		3.66
☞ **Service**		**64.75**
⚕ Healthcare		8.88
🛒 Consumer Services		32.09
🏢 Business Services		6.16
$ Financial Services		17.62
⚒ **Manufacturing**		**4.12**
🛍 Consumer Goods		0.00
⚙ Industrial Materials		4.12
🔋 Energy		0.00
⚡ Utilities		0.00

Asset Allocation %

	% Long	% Short	% Net Assets
Cash	3.3	0.0	3.3
Stocks	95.6	0.0	95.6
Bonds	1.1	0.0	1.1
Other	0.0	0.0	0.0

Annual Turnover %	22
% Assets in Top 10	61.44

Exhibit 10.1 Portfolio Analysis Section of Snapshot Page for a Stock Fund

information is summarized in the Asset Allocation table in the Portfolio Analysis section of each fund's Snapshot page, as shown in Exhibit 10.1. This table provides a percentage breakdown of the fund's portfolio into cash, stocks, bonds, and other assets, indicating at the broadest level if the fund is exposed to the systematic risks of the stock market, the bond market, or some combination of both.

As shown in Exhibit 10.2, the Portfolio page repeats the asset allocation data in table and chart form. In addition, it reveals what percentage of the portfolio is invested in foreign stocks (i.e., stocks outside the United States).

Note that the asset allocation information is broken into three columns: % long, % short, and % net assets. Morningstar introduced this breakdown in 2007 because a growing number of mutual funds had begun using strategies that involve taking short positions, which involves borrowing securities. In a traditional long-only fund, the % short column is all zeroes so that % long is the same as % net assets. In a fund that takes short positions, the numbers in the % short column are netted against the numbers in the % long column to get to % net assets. For example, a 130/30 stock fund takes short positions in stocks worth 30 percent of its assets and uses the proceeds from borrowing those stocks so that its

Fund LB1

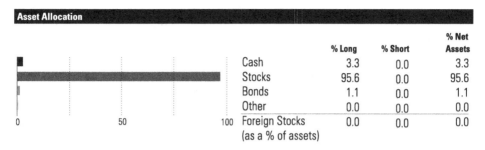

	% Long	% Short	% Net Assets
Cash	3.3	0.0	3.3
Stocks	95.6	0.0	95.6
Bonds	1.1	0.0	1.1
Other	0.0	0.0	0.0
Foreign Stocks (as a % of assets)	0.0	0.0	0.0

Fund LB2

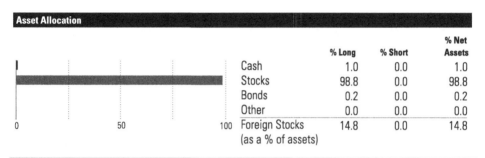

	% Long	% Short	% Net Assets
Cash	1.0	0.0	1.0
Stocks	98.8	0.0	98.8
Bonds	0.2	0.0	0.2
Other	0.0	0.0	0.0
Foreign Stocks (as a % of assets)	14.8	0.0	14.8

Exhibit 10.2   Asset Allocation Section of Portfolio Page for Two Large Blend Funds

total long holdings in stocks amounts to 130 percent of its assets. The stocks row of the asset allocation table of such a fund would show 130 for % long, 30 for % short, and 100 for % net assets.

Let us continue with the example introduced in Chapter 9, where we compare data on two large-cap blend funds: Fund LB1 and Fund LB2. In Exhibit 10.2, you can see that both are long-only funds that have 100 percent of the portfolio in long positions and nothing in short positions. Note also that Fund LB2 has nearly 15 percent in foreign stocks. This is worth noting, as it might create overlap with a dedicated foreign-stock fund when we construct an overall portfolio of funds in Chapter 11.

Stock Portfolio Analysis

Holdings-Based Style Analysis

Investment style is a powerful, fundamental lens for understanding stocks, funds, and portfolios. Style is a means of describing securities in terms of their relative market capitalization (size) and value/growth orientation.

Style has been an extremely relevant measure in explaining many of the performance differences of various segments of the market over the years. For example, growth stocks topped the charts in the late 1990s while value strategies led the way from 2000 to 2006. Then, in 2007, growth stocks again outperformed value stocks. There is no guarantee that style will be as illustrative of market trends in the future as it has in the past, but it is certainly an analysis tool no investor would want to be without.

Morningstar Style Box™ for Stocks

The Morningstar Style Box™ for Stocks, first developed in the early 1990s, is a nine-square grid that provides a graphical representation of the investment style of stocks and mutual funds. It classifies securities according to market capitalization—large, mid, or small (the vertical axis)—and growth and value factors—value, blend, or growth (the horizontal axis). It appears on the Portfolio Analysis section of the Snapshot page for stock funds on www.morningstar.com. See Exhibit 10.1 for an example.

We think of the Style Box as a descriptive tool, not a restrictive one. How lines are drawn among value, blend, and growth is somewhat arbitrary, and it is perfectly acceptable for a fund manager to invest in a range of styles. The Style Box tool provides a context for understanding the holdings, not a constraint. Few funds are a pure play on a single style, but investors who better understand how their fund managers deploy assets are more likely to use their funds wisely in a portfolio.

Determining a fund's placement in the Style Box begins with an analysis of the style of each underlying stock. Morningstar assigns a stock's vertical position in the Style Box based on its market capitalization. The vertical axis is divided into three bands: large-cap, mid-cap, and small-cap. The large-cap band includes the stocks of the largest companies, which, in aggregate, account for 70 percent of the total capitalization of the Morningstar common-stock universe. The mid-cap band includes stocks of the next largest firms, the medium-size firms, which account for the next 20 percent of the universe. Small-cap stocks account for the remaining 10 percent of the market, representing stocks of smaller firms.

Morningstar measures value and growth on the horizontal axis, using five factors for measuring value and five for growth (see Exhibit 10.3). No single factor (such as a price/earnings ratio or a cash-flow growth rate) can fully capture the growth or value orientation of a stock. The Morningstar 10-factor model reflects both historical and projected financial data. A stock proves its worth with its reported numbers, but the market trades on anticipation—on how the stock is expected to perform in the future. It is then possible to determine which orientation is dominant, and to create a "net" value/growth score or classification based on it.

The style and size scores for a fund are asset-weighted averages of the style and size characteristics for each stock in its portfolio. By asset weighting, we place more emphasis on stocks that constitute a larger portion of the fund portfolio than their smaller counterparts. Morningstar receives fund portfolio holdings from fund companies regularly and matches those holdings against the appropriate stock scores as of the date of the portfolio.

Ownership Zone™

In an effort to provide even greater insight into funds' investment styles, Morningstar developed the Ownership Zone™, which shows not only a fund's average style but also the distribution of the fund's holdings across the Style Box. To

Exhibit 10.3 Morningstar Style Box™ Methodology for Stocks

Horizontal Axis: Style	Value Score Components and Weights		Growth Score Components and Weights	
	Forward looking measures ▶ Price-to-projected earnings	50.0%	**Forward looking measures** ▶ Long-term projected earnings growth	50.0%
	Historical based measures	50.0%	**Historical based measures**	50.0%
	▶ Price-to-book	12.5%	▶ Historical earnings growth	12.5%
	▶ Price-to-sales	12.5%	▶ Sales growth	12.5%
	▶ Price-to-cash flow	12.5%	▶ Cash flow growth	12.5%
	▶ Dividend yield	12.5%	▶ Book value growth	12.5%
Vertical Axis: Market Capitalization	Top 70% of the market: large cap Next 20%: mid cap Next 10%: small and micro cap			

form the Ownership Zone, we first plot the weighted average investment style of the securities in the fund (the "centroid"). We then plot each individual holding within the fund along the nine-box grid of the Style Box and draw an ellipse that marks the minimum territory we need to outline around the centroid in order to capture 75 percent of a fund's assets. As shown in Exhibit 10.1, the Ownership Zone tool appears directly below the Style Box in the Portfolio Analysis section of the Snapshot page.

The Ownership Zone tool can help you compare two funds that have similar mandates. Exhibit 10.4 shows the Ownership Zones of two funds that have

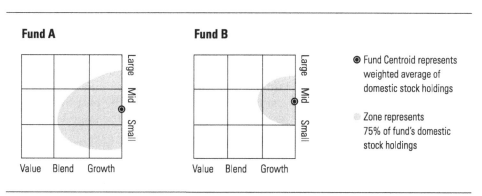

Exhibit 10.4 Ownership Zone™ Comparison of Two Mid-Cap Growth Funds

"mid-cap growth" in their names and are in fact in the mid-cap growth category. A glance at the two Ownership Zone charts of these funds immediately reveals that they have different interpretations of the mid-cap growth style. Fund B sticks tightly to a strict mid-cap strategy, while Fund A explores a range of mid-, small-, and even micro-cap holdings. This has implications for portfolio construction. An investor in Fund B might consider adding a small-cap fund for diversification; however, such a move might only duplicate the style of the existing holdings for the shareholder in Fund A.

Additional information on a fund's style is available on the fund Portfolio pages on www.morningstar.com. Exhibit 10.5 contains information shown on the Portfolio page, but the layout has been modified for easier comparison of two funds. As you can see in the exhibit, the middle part provides a five-way breakdown of market capitalization. In this extended breakdown, stocks that fall into the top band are broken down into giant and large, and stocks that fall into the bottom band are broken down into small and micro. In this breakdown, giant stocks make up the top 40 percent of the Morningstar stock universe and large stocks make up the next 30 percent; together they make up the entire top band of 70 percent. Similarly, micro stocks make up the bottom 3 percent and small stocks make up the 7 percent above them, making up the bottom band of 10 percent. Also shown in Exhibit 10.5, the Valuations and Growth Rates section of the Portfolio page provides values for the 10 value and growth factors, calculated by averaging the factors of the stocks that make up the fund's stock portfolio.

Now that we understand how to use the Ownership Zone and related information to gain insight into a fund's investment style, let us return to the example comparing Fund LB1 and Fund LB2 in Exhibit 10.5. Immediately apparent is that these two funds have different Ownership Zones even though they were chosen from the same category. Fund LB1's centroid is closer to the value side of the large-blend box, and its Ownership Zone reaches a bit farther down in market capitalization. The Market Capitalization breakdown below the chart confirms that more than 30 percent of Fund LB1's assets are in mid-cap stocks. The 10 factors in the Valuation and Growth Rates section also support Fund LB1's stronger value orientation, as the fund's value factors are more similar to the S&P 500 Index and the peers in the large-blend category, while its growth factors are considerably lower.

Fund LB2, however, is a purer large-blend fund. The Ownership Zone is confined primarily to large caps, and its centroid clearly represents a large-blend style. The Market Capitalization breakdown shows that the vast majority of the portfolio is invested in giant and large stocks. Fund LB2's 10 value and growth factors are similar to those of the Standard & Poor's (S&P) 500 Index and the peers in the large-blend category. The Investment Style History over the past three years illustrates that both funds have been consistently occupying the large-blend box in every one of the past three years.

Sector Breakdown

The sector breakdown picks up where a fund's investment Morningstar Style Box leaves off. Eyeballing a fund's sector weightings is an essential step on the road to understanding how a fund will behave and how you might use it (or not use it) to build a diversified portfolio. After all, funds may land in different categories, but

Fund LB1

Style Box Details

Ownership Zone™

◉ Fund Centroid represents weighted average of domestic stock holdings

⬤ Zone represents 75% of fund's domestic stock holdings

Value   Blend   Growth

Investment Style History (as of 12–31)

2007

2006

2005

Size

| Average Mkt Cap $Mil | 24,198 |

Market Capitalization	% of Portfolio
Giant	31.05
Large	37.73
Medium	31.22
Small	0.00
Micro	0.00

Valuations and Growth Rates

	Stock Port	Rel to S&P 500 TR	Rel to Cat
Price/Prospective Earnings	16.4	1.0	1.0
Price/Book	2.0	0.8	0.7
Price/Sales	1.6	1.1	1.1
Price/Cash Flow	7.4	0.7	0.7
Dividend Yield	1.9	1.0	1.1
Long-Term Earnings	11.7	1.1	1.0
Historical Earnings	2.4	0.1	0.1
Sales Growth	5.1	0.5	0.6
Cash-Flow Growth	−3.4	−0.4	−0.4
Book-Value Growth	8.8	0.8	0.8

Fund LB2

Style Box Details

Ownership Zone™

◉ Fund Centroid represents weighted average of domestic stock holdings

⬤ Zone represents 75% of fund's domestic stock holdings

Value   Blend   Growth

Investment Style History (as of 12–31)

2007

2006

2005

Size

| Average Mkt Cap $Mil | 43,695 |

Market Capitalization	% of Portfolio
Giant	50.97
Large	36.20
Medium	12.49
Small	0.00
Micro	0.34

Valuations and Growth Rates

	Stock Port	Rel to S&P 500 TR	Rel to Cat
Price/Prospective Earnings	15.1	1.1	1.0
Price/Book	2.2	0.9	0.8
Price/Sales	1.3	0.9	0.9
Price/Cash Flow	9.5	0.9	0.9
Dividend Yield	1.6	0.8	1.0
Long-Term Earnings	11.8	1.1	1.0
Historical Earnings	19.4	1.2	1.1
Sales Growth	11.4	1.5	1.3
Cash-Flow Growth	9.9	1.2	1.1
Book-Value Growth	13.2	1.7	1.2

Style Box Detail calculations do not include the fund's short positions (if any).

Exhibit 10.5   Stock Style Box™ Details for Two Large Blend Funds

if their sector compositions are similar, it is possible that their performances will be, too.

As shown in Exhibits 10.1 and 10.6, Morningstar divides the stock market into three broad economic spheres—information, service, and manufacturing—each of which contains four specific industry sectors. The Morningstar sectors are based on what companies actually do. That is, unlike some other sector classification systems, sectors are not based on expected behavior of companies over the course of the business cycle.

Knowing which sectors of the economy the fund favors helps gauge how diversified the fund is. A fund that has more than 25 percent of assets concentrated in a single sector is almost certain to carry more risk than a more diversified offering. Knowing the fund's sector breakdown, both the level of the 3 economic spheres and the level of the 12 sectors, can help you maintain a well-diversified portfolio.

In Exhibit 10.6, the economic sphere and sector weightings on the Portfolio page are also shown relative to the funds' standard indices and to the average weightings of all funds in the fund's Morningstar category. Since these two benchmark comparisons are expressed in relative terms, a 1.00 figure would mean that the fund's sector weight is the same as the benchmark's weighting, and a 2.00 figure would imply that the fund's sector weight is twice that of the index's weighting.

A look at the sector weightings of Fund LB1 and Fund LB2, shown in Exhibit 10.6, highlights more differences between these two sample funds. Fund LB1 is clearly willing to take on more sector risk. It has over six times more exposure to the media sector than the S&P 500 Index and the large-blend category average. Similarly, it has more than four times the exposure to consumer services than the two benchmarks. Moreover, Fund LB1 has no exposure to energy, partly explaining the fund's relative underperformance in recent years when that sector has done well.

As mentioned earlier, a fund that has more than 25 percent of assets concentrated in one sector is almost certain to carry more risk than a more diversified offering, and Fund LB1's 32 percent exposure to consumer services certainly fits this profile. This helps explain why we observed a higher level of risk in Fund LB1 than in Fund LB2 in the risk analysis portion of our returns-based analysis. In addition, when studying Fund LB1's Modern Portfolio Theory statistics we noted that the best-fit index is actually the Morningstar Services Index and not the S&P 500 Index. That makes sense, given that nearly 65 percent of Fund LB1's portfolio is in the service sphere consisting of healthcare, consumer services, business services, and financial services.

In contrast, Fund LB2's sector composition in Exhibit 10.6 indicates broader diversification. There is exposure to all sectors except for utilities, which is one of the smallest sectors in the S&P 500 Index. Sector weights deviate from the benchmarks, as one would expect of an actively managed fund. However, in the case of Fund LB2, the maximum deviation of roughly two times the benchmark weighting is within a reasonable range.

Concentration

The Portfolio Analysis section of the Snapshot page (see Exhibit 10.1) lists the percentage of each fund's assets in its 10 largest holdings (% assets in top 10). When this number is relatively high, it means that the fund is making a few

Fund LB1

Sector Weightings

	% of Stocks	Rel to S&P 500 TR	Rel to Category Avg
Information			
Software	0.00	0.00	0.00
Hardware	8.05	0.79	0.78
Media	19.43	6.69	6.17
Telecommunications	3.66	1.01	1.00
Service			
Healthcare	8.88	0.74	0.77
Consumer Services	32.09	4.74	4.24
Business Services	6.16	1.40	1.25
Financial Services	17.62	1.01	0.94
Manufacturing			
Consumer Goods	0.00	0.00	0.00
Industrial Materials	4.12	0.32	0.30
Energy	0.00	0.00	0.00
Utilities	0.00	0.00	0.00

Fund LB2

Sector Weightings

	% of Stocks	Rel to S&P 500 TR	Rel to Category Avg
Information			
Software	2.03	0.49	0.52
Hardware	3.86	0.38	0.38
Media	6.35	2.19	2.02
Telecommunications	1.57	0.43	0.43
Service			
Healthcare	3.55	0.30	0.31
Consumer Services	10.16	1.50	1.34
Business Services	4.61	1.05	0.94
Financial Services	36.95	2.12	1.96
Manufacturing			
Consumer Goods	12.93	1.41	1.41
Industrial Materials	3.53	0.27	0.25
Energy	14.45	1.15	1.38
Utilities	0.00	0.00	0.00

Exhibit 10.6 Stock Sector Weightings Section of Portfolio Page for Two Large Blend Funds

concentrated bets, thereby increasing the level of diversifiable unsystematic risk. Keep in mind that a manager must have skill in order for exposure to unsystematic risk to pay off, so you should hold a highly concentrated fund only if you have a great deal of faith in the manager's stock-picking abilities.

To apply our knowledge of concentration risk, let us return to our example comparing Fund LB1 and Fund LB2. Fund LB1 is very concentrated with almost 60 percent of assets in the top 10 holdings, meaning that 60 percent of the portfolio's performance is driven by 10 stocks. Fund LB2 is more diversified, with 35 percent in its top 10 holdings. This further explains our earlier finding of higher risk scores for Fund LB1.

Turnover

The turnover rate provides a rough measure of the fund's level of trading activity. The annual turnover figure is shown in the Portfolio Analysis section of the Snapshot page in Exhibit 10.1. This publicly reported figure is calculated by the funds in accordance with Securities and Exchange Commission (SEC) regulations, and Morningstar gathers the information from fund shareholder reports. A fund divides the lesser of purchases or sales (expressed in dollars and excluding all securities with maturity of less than one year) by the fund's average monthly assets. The resulting percentage can be loosely interpreted to represent the percentage of the portfolio's holdings that have changed over the past year. The turnover ratio is most accurate, however, when a fund's asset base remains stable.

A low turnover figure (typically less than 30 percent) might indicate that the manager is following a buy-and-hold strategy. High turnover (more than 100 percent) could be an indication of an investment strategy involving considerable buying and selling of securities. To provide some context, the average annual turnover for U.S.-stock funds is about 85 percent.

If a fund has a high turnover rate, make sure the manager has a proven record as a good stock picker; investors will end up the losers if a high-trading manager consistently buys and sells at the wrong time. Also, high turnover drives up a fund's costs because more brokerage commissions are being paid; therefore, high turnover can be a source of performance drag. High-turnover funds also tend to be less tax-efficient, although that is not always the case if the manager is offsetting gains with losses. Still, if a fund has a high turnover rate, check the fund's tax efficiency. (Tax-related topics are covered in more detail in the Tax Analysis section later in this chapter.) Last but not least, watch for significant year-to-year changes in the turnover rate, as it could indicate a new management style or a change in the fund's investment strategy.

Note that turnover is not as meaningful for bond funds, as it can be driven higher by certain cash management strategies.

International Exposure

Whether you are analyzing a foreign-stock fund or a domestic-stock fund that has significant exposure to stock markets outside the United States, you need to know where the fund is investing. As shown in Exhibit 10.7, the International Exposure section of the Portfolio page provides a breakdown of a fund's stock holdings by geographic region. It also lists up to five countries where the fund has the most assets invested.

International Fund 1

International Exposure			
Regional Exposure	**% of Assets**	**Country Exposure**	**% of Assets**
North America	10.5	United Kingdom	13.7
UK/Western Europe	54.5	Switzerland	11.6
Japan	9.9	France	11.2
Latin America	5.7	Japan	9.9
Asia ex-Japan	11.3	Canada	8.1
Other	4.9		
Not Classified	3.2		

International Fund 2

International Exposure			
Regional Exposure	**% of Assets**	**Country Exposure**	**% of Assets**
North America	4.9	Japan	13.3
UK/Western Europe	48.8	United Kingdom	12.1
Japan	13.3	France	11.6
Latin America	7.2	Switzerland	9.2
Asia ex-Japan	17.5	China	7.1
Other	2.0		
Not Classified	6.4		

International Exposure calculations do not include the fund's short positions (if any).

Exhibit 10.7   International Exposure Section of Portfolio Page for Two International Stock Funds

To illustrate international exposure, let us examine International Fund 1 and International Fund 2. Exhibit 10.7 demonstrates that both funds are diversified across regions and have some emerging markets exposure (e.g. Latin America). *Emerging markets* refer to countries that have smaller but faster-growing economies, and investments in emerging markets can be risky but rewarding. Having a small portion of the portfolio in emerging markets can provide diversification, but having too much can lead to high volatility. The Country Exposure section shows the largest country allocations of each fund. It is interesting to note International Fund 2's 7.1 percent weighting in China, which is a sizable allocation given that China's stock market is a small but volatile segment of the overall global stock market.

Bond Portfolio Analysis

Bond-fund portfolio analysis relies on completely different factors from stock-fund analysis. As such, the Portfolio Analysis section of the Snapshot page for a bond fund on www.morningstar.com contains three portfolio analysis tools that are unique to bond funds: Morningstar Style Box™ for Bonds, bond quality breakdown, and sector-weighting breakdown.

Morningstar Style Box for Bonds   The Morningstar Style Box for Bonds focuses on two main systematic factors of bond performance and risk: duration (interest-rate sensitivity) and credit quality. Morningstar splits bond funds into three groups of interest-rate sensitivity as determined by duration (short, intermediate, and long) and three credit-quality groups (high, medium, and low). As you can see in Exhibit 10.8, nine possible combinations exist, ranging from short duration/high quality for the safest funds to long duration/low quality for the most risky funds.

The horizontal axis of the Style Box measures the interest-rate sensitivity of a fund's bond portfolio based on average effective duration, which is calculated by the fund companies. The longer a fund's duration, the more sensitive it is likely to be to changes in interest rates. A fund with a duration of five years would be expected to lose 5 percent of its net asset value (NAV) if interest rates rose by 1 percentage point or gain 5 percent if interest rates fell by 1 percentage point. Effective duration provides a more accurate description of a bond's true interest-rate sensitivity than does maturity because it takes into consideration all mortgage prepayments, puts and call options, and adjustable coupons.

In the Morningstar system, taxable, high-quality bond funds with an average effective duration that is between 25 to 75 percent of the average effective duration of the Morningstar Core Bond Index (MCBI) qualify as short term. Funds with an average effective duration that is between 75 to 125 percent of the average effective duration of the MCBI are classified as intermediate. Funds with an average effective duration of greater than 125 percent of the average effective duration of the MCBI are considered long term. Municipal-bond funds with an average effective duration of less than 4.5 years are short term, between 4.5 and 7 years are intermediate term, and greater than 7 years are long term.

Bond Fund 1

Style Box Details	
Average Eff Duration	4.10 Yrs
Average Eff Maturity	6.60 Yrs
Average Credit Quality	AA

Investment Style History (as of 12–31)
2007
2006
2005

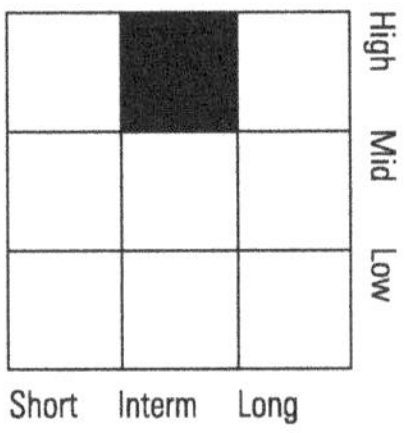

Bond Fund 2

Style Box Details	
Average Eff Duration	5.10 Yrs
Average Eff Maturity	6.00 Yrs
Average Credit Quality	AAA

Investment Style History (as of 12–31)
2007
2006
2005

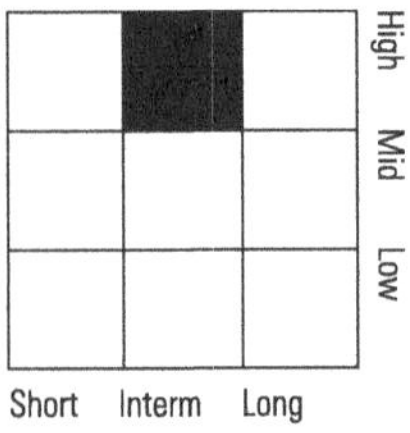

Exhibit 10.8   Style Box Details Section of Portfolio Page for Two Bond Funds

Most managers keep duration either pegged to a benchmark or within a pre-scribed range around a benchmark. For most investors, a fund with a disciplined duration strategy makes the most sense for two reasons.

1. Such an approach confines managers' interest-rate bets. Few managers have proven they can consistently time the short-term direction of interest rates.
2. A fund with a consistent duration strategy may be easier to place in a portfolio. For example, a bond fund whose duration fluctuates dramatically poses asset-allocation problems for investors, as it is difficult to tell how it will react to interest rate changes.

First-time bond-fund buyers, especially those looking to cushion their stock-heavy portfolios, probably should stick with funds in the intermediate-term range (3.5 to 6 years). Historically, intermediate-term bond funds have offered yields and returns similar to long-term bond funds but with less volatility.

Average effective maturity also appears near the Style Box as a supplement to average effective duration. It is a weighted average of all the maturities of the bonds in a portfolio, computed by weighting each bond's effective maturity by the market value of the security. Longer-maturity funds are generally considered more interest-rate sensitive than their shorter counterparts. However, as stated, duration is a better measure of a bond fund's interest-rate sensitivity than maturity.

The vertical axis of the Style Box indicates the average credit-quality rating of a bond portfolio. Credit quality is an important aspect as it measures the creditwor-thiness of the fund's holdings. A fund with an average credit quality of AAA, for example, is less likely to get stung by defaults than a fund with an average credit quality of BBB.

In the Morningstar system, funds that have an average credit rating of AAA or AA are categorized as high quality. Bond portfolios with average ratings of A or BBB are medium quality, and those rated BB and below are categorized as low quality. (For the purposes of Morningstar calculations, U.S. government securities are considered AAA bonds, nonrated municipal bonds generally are classified as BB, and all other nonrated bonds generally are considered B.)

Now that we understand bond style, let us walk through a brief holdings-based analysis on two bond funds: Bond Fund 1 and Bond Fund 2. The Style Box Details section (see Exhibit 10.8) illustrates that both funds are classified as intermediate in duration and high in quality. The average effective duration of Bond Fund 1 is 4.10 years, while that of Bond Fund 2 is 5.10, meaning that Fund 2 is more interest-rate sensitive than Fund 1. The average credit quality of Fund 1 is AA, which is lower than Fund 2's AAA; however, both of these ratings are considered high quality. In the next section, you will gain a better understanding of what drives the average credit quality of each fund.

Bond Quality Breakdown   While average credit quality provides a snapshot of a portfolio's overall credit quality, the bond quality breakdown gives more detail, showing the percentage of fixed-income securities that fall within each credit-quality rating, as assigned by ratings agencies Standard & Poor's or Moody's. The lower a bond's rating, the greater is its default risk and the higher its yield. Bonds rated BBB and above are considered investment-grade issues; those rated BB and

Bond Fund 1		Bond Fund 2	
Bond Quality		**Bond Quality**	
	% of Bond		% of Bond
AAA	61.2	AAA	100.0
AA	5.5	AA	0.0
A	5.8	A	0.0
BBB	11.7	BBB	0.0
BB	5.5	BB	0.0
B	3.5	B	0.0
Below B	2.2	Below B	0.0
Not Rated	4.6	Not Rated	0.0

Exhibit 10.9 Bond Quality Section of Portfolio Page for Two Bond Funds

below are high yield, commonly called junk bonds. Pay particular attention to a fund's weightings in below-B and nonrated bonds. Often these are riskier bonds that are in danger of defaulting or that have already defaulted. They are also typically less liquid than higher-quality bonds, meaning that one may not be able to sell these securities quickly without taking a significant discount in the sale price. Diversify with a good mix of high- and low-quality bond funds (lean more toward the high-quality side), if not with one of the multisector bond funds (which tend to cost more), then with a portfolio of two or three good bond funds.

Exhibit 10.9 displays the Bond Quality section of the Portfolio page. Note that Bond Fund 2 has 100 percent of its assets invested in bonds rated AAA, the safest rating. Bond Fund 1, by contrast, is invested across all quality ratings. It has 61.2 percent invested in bonds rated AAA; another 23 percent in the next three categories, which are also considered investment grade; 11.2 percent in high-yield bonds; and 4.6 percent in bonds that are not rated or where rating information is not available. Depending on your risk tolerance, you might see the 11.2 percent in high yield and the 4.6 percent in nonrated bonds as a diversifier and potential return enhancer, or you could view them as risk you do not wish to take.

Bond Sector Breakdown   The bond sector breakdown helps investors compare and understand the sector exposure of each bond fund. These data are especially useful for comparing two funds that may be in the same category. In the Sector Weightings section of the Portfolio page (see Exhibit 10.10), the sector weightings of the fund are also shown relative to the average weightings of all funds in the same category. These relative weightings provide an indication of how over- or underweighted the fund is in each sector relative to its peers.

As shown in the fund comparison in Exhibit 10.10, Bond Fund 1 is more diversified across sector groups, having 7.38 percent in U.S. government, 46.40 percent in mortgage, 36.02 percent in credit, 0.50 percent in foreign, and the remainder in cash. Bond Fund 2, however, has 4.85 percent in cash and the rest in the mortgage sector. This example illustrates that even though Bond Fund 2 has 100 percent of

Bond Fund 1

Sector Weightings	% of Bonds	Rel to Cat Avg
US Government		
US Treasuries	3.49	0.34
TIPS	0.00	0.00
US Agency	3.89	0.70
Mortgage		
Mortgage Pass-Thru	43.09	2.03
Mortgage CMO	3.31	0.22
Mortgage ARM	0.00	0.00
Credit		
US Corporate	32.08	1.21
Asset-Backed	3.94	0.84
Convertible	0.00	0.00
Municipal	0.00	0.00
Corporate Inflation-Protected	0.00	0.00
Foreign		
Foreign Corp	0.50	0.27
Foreign Govt	0.00	0.00
Cash	**9.72**	**8.77**

Bond Fund 2

Sector Weightings	% of Bonds	Rel to Cat Avg
US Government		
US Treasuries	0.00	0.00
TIPS	0.00	0.00
US Agency	0.32	0.06
Mortgage		
Mortgage Pass-Thru	16.78	0.79
Mortgage CMO	78.05	5.09
Mortgage ARM	0.00	0.00
Credit		
US Corporate	0.00	0.00
Asset-Backed	0.00	0.00
Convertible	0.00	0.00
Municipal	0.00	0.00
Corporate Inflation-Protected	0.00	0.00
Foreign		
Foreign Corp	0.00	0.00
Foreign Govt	0.00	0.00
Cash	**4.85**	**0.38**

Exhibit 10.10   Sector Weightings Section of Portfolio Page for Two Bond Funds

its assets receiving the highest quality rating (see Exhibit 10.9) and appears to be very safe, it actually has sector concentration risk. This example demonstrates the importance of detailed holdings-based analysis.

INCOME, COSTS, AND TAXES

In addition to the returns-based and holdings-based analysis tools that we have discussed so far, Morningstar provides additional data showing how much of a fund's total return comes from income as opposed to capital gains as well as how much return may be lost to various costs or taxes.

Yield

As shown in Exhibit 10.11, yield is one of the figures included in the Key Stats section of the Snapshot page. Yield represents a fund's income return on capital investment for the past 12 months. Income is that portion of a fund's return that comes from dividends paid on stock investments or coupon payments from bond investments, as opposed to the capital gains portion of return that derives from

Fund LB1

Key Stats	
Morningstar Category Large Blend	**Morningstar Rating**™ ★★★
NAV (01-31-08) $25.11	**Day Change** $0.67
Total Assets ($mil) 3,767	**Expense Ratio** % 0.99
Front Load % None	**Deferred Load** % None
Yield % (TTM) 1.15	**Min. Investment** $1,000
Manager Fund Manager 1 Fund Manager 2	**Start Date** 11-01-96 03-21-00

Fund LB2

Key Stats	
Morningstar Category Large Blend	**Morningstar Rating**™ ★★★★
NAV (01-31-08) $45.66	**Day Change** $0.73
Total Assets ($mil) 12,620	**Expense Ratio** % 0.58
Front Load % None	**Deferred Load** % None
Yield % (TTM) 1.40	**Min. Investment** $10,000
Manager Fund Manager 1 Fund Manager 2	**Start Date** 12-01-94 05-01-98

Exhibit 10.11 Key Statistics Section of Snapshot Page for Two Large Blend Funds

changes in the prices of the securities. Morningstar computes yield by dividing the sum of the fund's income distributions for the past 12 months by the previous month's NAV (adjusted upward for any capital gains distributed over the same period), and expressing the result as a percentage.

Yield may provide some instant gratification in the form of regular income payments, but basing your buy decision on a fund's high yield instead of total returns could cost you in the end. To pump up yields, some funds, especially bond funds, use accounting tricks that can erode a fund's NAV over time. In other words, part of the "income" they are distributing to you is a return of your principal. Others invest in lower-quality debt and/or complex derivatives in an effort to enhance yield. Shrinking principal leads to smaller income checks, though, even if the yield percentage stays the same. Imagine a $10,000 investment in a fund carrying an NAV of $10 and yielding 7 percent. One year later, the fund still yields 7 percent, but its NAV has slipped to $9. Income would have dropped to $630 from $700. Be wary if a fund has a high payout relative to its category and an NAV that is eroding, particularly in years when interest rates have declined. That fund may have to fight hard to keep writing big income checks.

Loads

A load is a fund's initial or deferred sales charge. For initial, or front-end, loads, this figure is expressed as a percentage of the initial investment and is incurred upon purchase of fund shares. For deferred sales charges (also known as back-end loads or contingent deferred sales charges), the amount charged is based on the lesser of the initial or final value of the shares sold. In Exhibit 10.11, the Key Stats section of the Snapshot page shows a fund's maximum front load and deferred load.

Loads can have a substantial impact on your bottom line because some of your money is going to the broker or adviser who sold you the fund rather than to the fund company to be invested. For example, if a fund has a front-end load of 4 percent and you put out $2,000 for it, you are actual buying $1,920 worth of shares of the fund.

If you do not want to pay a load, you have three other options.

1. Many funds are no-load funds, meaning they can be purchased directly from the fund companies that offer them without having to pay a sales charge to an intermediary, such as a broker or adviser. Both of the large-blend funds shown in Exhibit 10.11 are examples of no-load funds, as neither charges a front or deferred load.
2. If you are making a large enough investment in a fund, the front-end load may be reduced or eliminated.
3. A fund that generally has a load may be available to you without a load through your employer's retirement savings plan (typically a 401[k] plan).

Expense Ratio

Another important statistic in the Key Stats section of the Snapshot page is the expense ratio (see Exhibit 10.11). The annual expense ratio, taken from the fund's annual report, expresses the percentage of assets deducted each fiscal year for fund expenses: fees to cover distribution and marketing costs (called 12b-1 fees), management fees, administrative fees, operating costs, and all other asset-based costs incurred by the fund. Portfolio transaction fees, or brokerage costs, as well as initial or deferred sales charges are not included in the expense ratio.

The expense ratio tells you how much it costs to own the fund each year. Generally, look for funds with expense ratios lower than 1.25 percent. Many great domestic-stock funds keep expenses below 1 percent, and top-notch bond funds often charge less than 0.75 percent. Raise the bar a little for international funds, because it costs more to do business overseas.

Searching for low-expense funds is especially critical with bond funds. Expenses can quickly eat into total returns, and typically, only a narrow difference separates the returns of the leaders and laggards in a bond-fund category. Also, high-cost bond funds tend to be riskier than low-cost funds. Expenses are deducted from a fund's income payments. To keep yields at high-cost funds competitive, managers often make riskier investments, such as buying longer-duration issues, lower-quality debt, or complex derivatives. Managers with lower expense hurdles can offer the same returns without taking on the extra risk. In general, broker-sold funds cost a bit more than no-load offerings, but you can find many government or corporate high-quality bond funds with expense ratios of 0.75 percent or less. For specialty bond funds, such as high-yield or international-bond funds, you should aim to pay less than 1 percent.

Fund LB1

Tax Analysis			
	3-Yr Avg %	5-Yr Avg %	10-Yr Avg %
Pretax Return	0.79	7.70	10.35
Tax-adjusted Return	−0.82	6.59	9.06
% Rank in Category	99.00	97.00	4.00
Tax-Cost Ratio	1.60	1.03	1.17
Potential Cap Gains Exposure %	16.00		

Fund LB2

Tax Analysis			
	3-Yr Avg %	5-Yr Avg %	10-Yr Avg %
Pretax Return	10.21	—	—
Tax-adjusted Return	9.87	—	—
% Rank in Category	13.00	—	—
Tax-Cost Ratio	0.31	—	—
Potential Cap Gains Exposure %	33.40		

Exhibit 10.12   Tax Analysis Page for Two Large Blend Funds

Tax Analysis

If you are considering holding a fund in the taxable part of your portfolio, you need to consider the tax consequences. The information provided on the Tax Analysis page (see Exhibit 10.12) of www.morningstar.com can be used to evaluate a fund's after-tax returns, measured by the tax-adjusted return figures, and its efficiency in achieving them, as measured by the tax-cost ratio. Additionally, the potential capital gains exposure figure can provide a glimpse at a shareholder's potential exposure to additional taxation. All these figures can help you judge which funds have used tax-friendly strategies. They can also aid in deciding which funds are best suited to tax-deferred accounts and which serve better as taxable investments.

Tax-Adjusted Return
The tax-adjusted return figures are estimates of a fund's annualized after-tax total return for the 3-, 5-, and 10-year periods, excluding any capital gains effects that would result from selling the fund at the end of the period. Consistent with SEC guidance regarding tax-adjusted returns, these figures reflect the maximum load paid by fund shareholders. To determine this figure, all income and short-term (less than one year) capital gains distributions are taxed at the maximum federal rate at the time of distribution. Long-term (more than one year) capital gains are taxed at the capital gains rate. The after-tax portion is then reinvested in the fund. State and local taxes are ignored, and only the capital gains are counted for tax-exempt funds, because the income from these funds is nontaxable.

For domestic-stock funds, which report income that qualifies for a lower tax rate under the dividend tax cut enacted in 2003, Morningstar applies the lower rate consistent with that legislation. In practice, however, most fund companies do not specify if their distributions are eligible for this lower rate. Further, Nasdaq, which supplies the raw daily data feed on distributions and NAVs for mutual funds to Morningstar, currently is not equipped to distinguish between income distributions that are eligible for the lower rate and those that are not. For funds that do not make such a distinction in their direct reports, Morningstar adjusts their after-tax returns using the maximum federal rate. As a result, since most stock dividends qualify for a lower tax rate, some domestic-stock funds with sizable yields may have understated after-tax returns.

The category percentile rank (% rank in category) for each fund's tax-adjusted return is also listed. This ranking helps you compare a fund's estimated after-tax performance with that of other funds in the category. (Recall from Chapter 9 that the highest [or most favorable] percentile rank is 1 and the lowest [or least favorable] percentile rank is 100.)

Tax-Cost Ratio

A fund's tax-cost ratio figures represent the estimated percentage-point reductions in annualized returns that have resulted from income and capital gains taxes over the past 3-, 5-, and 10-year periods. These calculations assume that investors pay the maximum federal rate on capital gains and ordinary income. The tax-cost ratio is usually concentrated in the range of 0 to 5 percent. A ratio of 0 percent indicates that the fund had no taxable distributions, and 5 percent indicates that the fund was less tax-efficient. In our example comparing two large-blend funds, Exhibit 10.12 shows that Fund LB1 has a tax-cost ratio of 1.60 percent over a three-year period. This implies that investors gave up 1.6 percentage points of the fund's value to taxes, driving the tax-adjusted return into the negative territory (−0.82%). Meanwhile, Fund LB2 was significantly more tax-efficient, with a tax-cost ratio of 0.31 percent over the same period.

Potential Capital Gains Exposure

Morningstar calculates a fund's potential capital gains exposure to give investors some idea of the potential tax consequences of their investment in a fund. No one can predict precisely what a fund's taxable distributions might be, but Morningstar offers some clues based on a fund's liquidation liability.

A mutual fund's assets are composed of paid-in (investment) capital, appreciation or depreciation of this capital, and any undistributed net income. Paid-in capital is simply the monies investors have put into the fund (which can decrease should shareholders decide to redeem their shares). Any appreciation of this capital may eventually be taxed. The potential capital gains exposure figure shows what percentage of a fund's total assets represents unrealized (or at least undistributed) capital appreciation.

Capital appreciation can be either unrealized or realized. In the first case, the fund's holdings have increased in value, but the fund has not yet sold these holdings; taxes are not due until the fund does so. Realized net appreciation (commonly called realized gains) represents actual gains achieved by the sale of holdings; taxes must be paid on these realized capital gains, which the fund must distribute each year if it cannot offset them with realized losses. Unrealized appreciation may turn into realized gains at any time, should the fund's management decide to sell the profitable holdings. Thus, the formula Morningstar uses includes unrealized appreciation as part of the potential capital gains exposure.

A negative potential capital gains exposure figure means that the fund has greater net losses than it has gains. This likely indicates that the fund has or will have a tax-loss carryforward, which would mean that some amount of future gains could be offset by past losses. To keep the calculation current, Morningstar updates the information between shareholder reports by accounting for a fund's market losses or gains, the sale or redemption of shares, and the payment of capital gains. This updated figure is not quite as precise as the one stated in the shareholder report, but it is more current and therefore more relevant to the investor.

QUALITATIVE ANALYSIS

As important as all of the previously mentioned statistics are to the fund analysis process, we at Morningstar believe that looking at numbers alone is not enough. As such, we have devised several qualitative tools to help shed light on the real nature of a fund.

Stewardship Grade^{SM}

At Morningstar, we have become increasingly aware of how a fund company's actions define its character. We believe that fund companies define themselves along a spectrum that ranges from salesmanship to stewardship, with most fund companies exhibiting some of both qualities but often leaning toward one. To us, salesmanship is a mind-set that says: If we had a certain type of fund today, would it be easy to sell? A mind-set of stewardship, in contrast, asks: If we sell this certain type of fund today, how will our clients think about us 5, 10, or 15 years from now? Needless to say, we believe that those groups that put investors' interests first, that exhibit greater stewardship, are those that most deserve investor attention.

In 2005, our analysts began scoring fund companies on stewardship by looking at external evidence of a concern for shareholders. The grades consider a fund's regulatory history, board quality, manager incentives, fee levels, and corporate culture. To find the overall grade and its components, go to the Stewardship Grade^{SM} page on www.morningstar.com (see Exhibit 10.13).

Regulatory history is pretty straightforward, as any fund complex's record with regulators is public knowledge. Our analysts sort through the minor technical infractions and those issues that raise real questions about the fiduciary culture at a firm. For board quality, we look at the independence of directors, whether directors invest their own money in the funds they oversee, and their history of acting in investors' best interests. For fees, we look at whether a fund's costs are above or below the median of similar offerings. For manager incentives, we look to see how a manager's incentives are structured and whether the manager invests in the funds he or she oversees.

The most interesting aspect of the grade, however, and the area that receives the biggest weighting, is corporate culture. Fund complexes define themselves by the types of funds they launch and how they promote them. We look to see if an institution has a history of launching ill-conceived offerings, such as Internet funds that prey on investor greed. We also monitor how they promote their offerings and

Fund LB1

| Stewardship Grade^{SM} | | | | | |

Overall Grade	Corporate Culture	Board Quality	Manager Incentives	Fees	Regulatory Issues
B	A	B	A	C	A

Range: A B C D E F

Fund LB2

| Stewardship Grade^{SM} | | | | | |

Overall Grade	Corporate Culture	Board Quality	Manager Incentives	Fees	Regulatory Issues
A	A	A	A	A	A

Range: A B C D E F

Exhibit 10.13   Stewardship Grade^{SM} Page for Two Large Blend Funs

communicate about them. Some firms advertised tech-heavy funds during the Super Bowl at the market peak. Others consistently advocate a more prudent, long-term approach. Finally, we check the tenure of the investment staff and ask whether this shop is a place where investment professionals want to have long careers, or if it is a place that constantly churns through portfolio managers and analysts.

The stewardship information serves as a nice supplement to the performance analysis described previously. It gives some insight into the character of the organization behind the funds. At the end of the day, investment management is a people business, and knowing the type of people to whom one entrusts one's money is paramount. We favor doing business with partners who put their money next to yours and who display a sound commitment to stewardship rather than a mere proficiency at salesmanship.

In the example shown in Exhibit 10.13, Fund LB2 has an overall grade of A, stemming from A grades across all subcategories of stewardship. Fund LB1 has an overall grade of B. It earned a C grade in the fees subcategory, consistent with its higher expense ratio in Exhibit 10.11.

Morningstar Fund Analyst Picks^{SM}

For investors who want help sorting through all of the quantitative and qualitative information on a fund, www.morningstar.com offers Morningstar Fund Analyst Picks^{SM}, a hand-selected group of our favorite funds in each category. While Morningstar Rating™ and other factors play a role in the picks, they do not determine them. Indeed, sometimes a lower-rated fund may be chosen as a pick—if, for example, a new manager brightens the fund's prospects—or a top-rated fund may not be chosen. The picks represent our analysts' exercise of judgment on all of the available data. The main attributes we look for are superior long-term risk-adjusted returns, exceptional management, sound strategies, reasonable costs, and good steward-ship. Generally only a handful of funds are chosen in any category, so focusing on these preferred funds is an effective means of streamlining the investment selection process. Lists of Morningstar Fund Analyst Picks, sorted by category, can be found on www.morningstar.com. On an individual fund basis, you can go to the Premium Features section of the Snapshot page where the Morningstar Analyst Picks and Pans[SM] field indicates the status.

Analyst Research Report

Last but not least, we recommend that you read our fund analysts' research reports, which can be found on the Analyst Research page on www.morningstar.com. There you can find current and past reports. In addition to devoting extensive amounts of time analyzing these funds, our analysts meet with fund managers and in-vestment analysts to develop greater insight into more qualitative considerations. These reports may address concerns that have arisen during your own fund analy-sis process. For example, when we were comparing sector breakdowns of our two bond funds earlier in the chapter, we pointed out that Bond Fund 2 was highly concentrated in the mortgage sector. Your concern about this sector concentration risk might be mitigated somewhat if you read a Morningstar analyst report prais-ing the fund for its expert navigation of the subprime-mortgage meltdown and liquidity crisis of 2007.

CONCLUSIONS

In this chapter, we have discussed numerous qualitative and holdings-based ana-lytic tools. Combined with returns-based analysis presented in Chapter 9, they pro-vide a comprehensive set of tools essential for mutual fund analysis. The next step is to take these analytic principles and apply them more broadly to the portfolio-building process, as we explore in Chapter 11.

The authors would like to thank Catherine Sanders and Cindy Sin-Yi Tsai, CFA, CAIA, for their contributions. Credit is also due to Regina Comito and Randal Pawlicki for graphics design.

ABOUT THE AUTHORS

Don Phillips is a managing director of Morningstar, Inc. and is responsible for corporate strategy, research, and corporate communications. He has served on the company's board of directors since August 1999. Mr. Phillips is also president of fund research, which includes research on mutual funds, exchange-traded funds, and alternative investments.

Mr. Phillips joined Morningstar in 1986 as the company's first mutual fund analyst and soon became editor of its flagship publication, *Morningstar® Mutual Funds™*, establishing the editorial voice for which the company is best known. Mr. Phillips helped to develop the Morningstar Style Box™, the Morningstar Rating™, and other distinctive proprietary Morningstar innovations that have become industry standards.

Journalists regularly turn to Don Phillips for his insight on industry trends. *Investment Advisor* magazine has named him to its list of the most influential people in the financial planning industry. *Financial Planning* magazine has named him one of the planning industry's "Movers & Shakers." *Registered Rep.* has named him one of the investment industry's 10 key players.

Mr. Phillips holds a bachelor's degree in English from the University of Texas and a master's degree in American literature from the University of Chicago.

Paul D. Kaplan is vice president of quantitative research at Morningstar, Inc., responsible for the quantitative methodologies behind Morningstar's fund analysis, indexes, adviser tools, and other services. Many of Dr. Kaplan's research papers have been published in professional books and publications. He received the 2008 Graham and Dodd Award and was a Graham and Dodd Award of Excellence winner in 2000.

Before joining Morningstar in 1999, he was a vice president of Ibbotson Associates and served as the firm's chief economist and director of research. Prior to that, he served on the economics faculty of Northwestern University where he taught international finance and statistics.

Dr. Kaplan holds a bachelor's degree in mathematics, economics, and computer science from New York University and a master's degree and doctorate in economics from Northwestern University. Dr. Kaplan holds the Chartered Financial Analyst (CFA) designation.

CHAPTER 11

Building a Portfolio of Mutual Funds
A Morningstar Approach

DON PHILLIPS
Managing Director, Corporate Strategy, Research, and Communications, and President, Fund Research, Morningstar, Inc.

PAUL D. KAPLAN, Ph.D., CFA
Viceo President, Quantitative Research, Morningstar, Inc.

I n Chapters 9 and 10, we discussed in detail many of the tools that can be used to analyze and compare mutual funds. In this chapter, we address how you can apply similar principles to the portfolio construction process so you will not end up with a basket of funds that look good in isolation but may not be as attractive when combined together in a portfolio.

APPROACHES TO PORTFOLIO CONSTRUCTION

As mentioned earlier, we believe that portfolio assembly is more art than science and that much of its success depends on selecting the proper level of complexity. Investors desiring maximum simplicity might choose a target-date fund, where asset allocation, fund selection, and rebalancing are all handled for them. Investors wanting more customization or control can construct portfolios with index (passively managed) mutual funds, actively managed mutual funds, and/or individual stocks and bonds.

If you decide that you are most interested in selecting a suite of actively managed funds to meet your desired asset allocation, there are several ways to go about it. One common approach is to combine top-down asset allocation and bottom-up fund selection. The top-down process of determining an asset allocation to match your investment goals and risk tolerance is beyond the scope of this discussion, but it essentially involves deciding how much of your portfolio to assign to stocks, bonds, cash and possibly other types of investments. (See Chapter 8 for a discussion on asset allocation.) For the stock portion of the portfolio, you would likely further divide assets based on geographic region (domestic versus foreign), market cap (size of company), and investment style (value versus growth). For the bond portion of the portfolio, you would need to make some decisions about duration (interest-rate sensitivity), credit quality, issuer, and tax status. This top-down asset-allocation process would divide your portfolio into segments that would essentially mirror the Morningstar categories described in Chapter 9. For the bottom-up fund-selection process, you would pick one or more funds from each category to fill each segment of your portfolio. For example, if you determined that you should have 25 percent of your overall $100,000 portfolio in large-cap blend funds, you would purchase $25,000 worth of your favorite fund in the large-blend category.

This top-down/bottom-up approach has benefits and limitations. It is relatively straightforward and intuitive. However, recall from the discussion of Morningstar Style Box™ and Morningstar Ownership Zone™ in Chapter 10 that few funds are pure plays on a single style, and even funds that have similar mandates and belong to the same category can have very different characteristics. For example, one mid-cap fund may invest strictly in mid-cap stocks while another may invest in a range of mid-, small-, and even micro-cap holdings. If you own the second fund, combining it with a small-cap fund could result in over allocation to the small-cap asset class, unintentionally increasing the risk profile of your overall portfolio. Similarly, if your domestic-stock funds already have significant exposure to foreign stocks, you may not want to assign as much money to a designated foreign-stock fund. You can compensate for this kind of portfolio overlap by carefully studying and regularly monitoring the Morningstar Category, Style Box, Ownership Zone, and other portfolio statistics of the funds you select.

FUND SELECTION

Let us assume that you have evaluated your investment goals and risk tolerance and settled on this following asset allocation: 30 percent domestic large-cap stocks, 15 percent domestic small/mid-cap stocks, 15 percent foreign stocks, and 40 percent domestic bonds. The next step is selecting individual funds to fill those allocations.

As discussed in earlier chapters, there are many factors to consider when selecting a fund. To briefly review, there are returns-based considerations such as performance relative to a benchmark, risk, risk-adjusted returns, Modern Portfolio Theory statistics, and Morningstar Rating™. You must also carefully analyze holdings-based information to understand the fund's exposure to asset classes, overseas markets, market caps, investment styles, sectors, interest-rate sensitivity, and credit risk, to name a few of the factors. Combined with portfolio turnover and concentration, these holdings-based factors drive a fund's risk and return profile. Costs and taxes matter, too, as they reduce your take-home return. Meanwhile, stewardship information can help you determine whether a fund company's fiduciary culture is shareholder-friendly.

Trying to perform comprehensive returns- and holdings-based analysis on a large quantity of funds can be impractical for many investors. Some of the Morningstar tools can help winnow the list of funds meriting further investigation. The Morningstar Rating, often called the star rating, ranks funds from 1 to 5 stars based on risk- and cost-adjusted performance over the past 3, 5, and 10 years. Beginning your search with higher-rated funds can help streamline the process. Another potential time saver is checking out the Morningstar Fund Analyst Picks℠—a handful of funds from each category that meet our analysts' rigorous due diligence criteria. But even if you confine your universe to our analyst picks or highly rated funds, there is still work to be done in understanding the characteristics of individual funds and how they work when combined with other funds. Unfortunately, it is quite possible to put together a lousy portfolio of good funds.

To help illustrate how you can not only identify good funds but also combine them in a way that results in a good portfolio, we will walk through a hypothetical portfolio-building exercise. We first analyze two sample funds from Morningstar Fund Analyst Picks for each of the prescribed asset classes, pointing out various strengths, weaknesses, similarities, and differences. We then use these funds to build two hypothetical portfolios. All of the sample funds presented are decent choices on their own, but we build one portfolio that is well diversified and one that, while featuring solid funds, is not as well designed.

Domestic Large-Cap Stocks

To fill our hypothetical portfolio's 30 percent allocation to domestic large-cap stocks, we consider the two funds that we analyzed in detail in Chapters 9 and 10: Fund LB1 and Fund LB2. Let us summarize our previous findings. Fund LB1 has been a good long-term performer, but it has also been the more volatile of the two funds, owing in part to big bets on its top 10 holdings and dramatic sector concentrations. Its Ownership Zone™ indicates that the fund has a value tilt and significant exposure to mid-cap stocks, something to keep in mind when considering another fund to fill the smaller-cap portion of your asset allocation. Fund LB1 may be a good choice if you have a relatively long time horizon and do not mind some bumps along the way.

Fund LB2 may be a better option for the domestic large-cap portion of a portfolio. It is diversified enough to reduce risks yet sufficiently concentrated to add value through active portfolio management. It has a good risk-return profile and has been tax- and cost-efficient as well as shareholder-friendly. The fund's holdings are primarily large caps and are not likely to overlap with other smaller-cap funds. Do note, however, that a portion of the portfolio is invested in foreign companies, which may overlap with your foreign-stock fund allocation.

Domestic Small/Mid-Cap Stocks

In the small-cap arena, we assume you would like to combine a growth fund and a value fund rather than choosing a single blend fund. As such, we evaluate two small-value funds as well as two small-growth funds. In the small-value category, both Fund SV1 and Fund SV2 rate 5 stars, implying good historic risk- and cost-adjusted performance relative to their peers. Note, however, that Fund SV1 has a shorter track record of four years, and while returns have been high, so has the level of risk. SV1 has an attractive expense ratio of just 0.88 percent, along with moderate turnover and decent tax efficiency. Its holdings have mid-cap and growth tilts, requiring some attention if we want to incorporate this fund into an overall portfolio that already has mid-cap exposure.

Analysis of Fund SV2 presents a different picture. The fund has a longer track record of outperforming its category average. Compared with Fund SV1, the fund has higher concentration in its top 10 holdings and higher sector concentrations.

However, the fund's historic volatility has actually been rather low. Its Ownership Zone covers the small-cap value and mid-cap value boxes, and the centroid is positioned right at the center of these two boxes.

In the small-growth category, we have Fund SG1 and Fund SG2, both with 3-star ratings. SG1's Ownership Zone primarily covers the small- and mid-cap growth areas, and its portfolio is overweight in the energy and utilities sectors relative to its peers. Fund SG2's Ownership Zone spans over the small-cap growth and small-cap blend areas of the Style Box, with the centroid landing right in the center of the small-growth box. About 11 percent of the portfolio is in micro-cap stocks, a moderate amount that can help enhance return and diversify risk. SG2's holdings are well diversified across sectors.

Foreign Stocks

For the foreign-stock portion of the portfolio, we consider two funds from the Foreign Large Blend category. Both have 5-star ratings, implying good historic risk- and cost-adjusted performance relative to their peers. Both have had similar levels of risk and return, and both provide exposure to developed and emerging markets. International Fund 1 is a purer large-cap fund, while International Fund 2 has a significant stake in stocks of smaller companies. International Fund 1 has had better tax efficiency. But if tax is a secondary concern and exposure to smaller stocks attracts you, International Fund 2 might be the better choice. This is especially true given that International Fund 2 has a reasonable expense ratio of 1.06 percent despite the often-high costs of investing in smaller foreign companies.

Domestic Bonds

The first question when choosing bond funds should be taxable or tax-free. If you are in a high tax bracket, you definitely want to consider tax-free municipal bonds, but for this example, we evaluate taxable offerings. We also assume you want the moderate interest-rate sensitivity of intermediate-term bonds and the credit quality of investment-grade rather than junk bonds. In selecting a bond fund, you would also need to choose between funds that invest strictly in U.S. government and agency bonds versus funds that have a broader mandate of adding investment-grade corporate bonds and mortgage-backed securities. The choice is based on personal preference, but for the purpose of this example, we use the more broadly defined intermediate-term bond category.

We return to Bond Fund 1 and Bond Fund 2, which we analyzed in Chapter 10. Both funds have had good risk- and cost-adjusted performance, with Bond Fund 1 earning 4 stars and Bond Fund 2 boasting a 5-star rating. Both have posted annualized 10-year returns exceeding 6 percent, giving them very high percentile rankings compared with their category peers. In terms of risk, Bond Fund 1 has a slightly lower standard deviation of 1.97 percent, compared with 2.47 percent for Bond Fund 2. Note that both the differential and the magnitude of the standard deviation statistics for bond funds are lower than those observed when comparing stock funds.

Although these two funds have similar volatility statistics, recall from our earlier holdings-based analysis that their risks come from different places. Bond Fund 1 has less interest-rate risk, lower but diversified credit quality, and broad sector diversification. Bond Fund 2 has more interest-rate risk, higher credit quality, and greater sector concentration. Some might favor Bond Fund 1 for its diversification, an important consideration for the anchor of the bond portion of your overall portfolio. Others might prefer Bond Fund 2's expertise in its chosen area of concentration.

Construction of the Overall Portfolio

Now that we have briefly reviewed the 10 funds under consideration, we can start the portfolio assembly process. Recall that the asset allocation for this example calls for 30 percent domestic large-cap stocks, 15 percent domestic small/mid-cap stocks, 15 percent foreign stocks, and 40 percent domestic bonds.

Let us begin by selecting the broadly diversified Bond Fund 1 to anchor the portfolio. Assuming that you have $100,000 to invest, you would purchase $40,000, representing 40 percent of assets.

Next, we map out two different paths to building the equity portion of the portfolio. The first path leads to a less well-diversified overall portfolio, while the second path results in a more balanced solution.

PORTFOLIO 1: A LESS DIVERSIFIED APPROACH

For this first portfolio's large-cap stock segment, let us assume you choose Fund LB1, a large-blend fund with mid-cap value slant. For the small/mid-cap area, we assume that you select Fund SV1 as the value fund and Fund SG1 as the growth fund. Unfortunately, however, these two small-cap funds overweight some of the same sectors: energy and utilities. In addition, Fund SG1's Ownership Zone tilts toward mid-cap and growth, areas that Fund SV1 also occupies.

PORTFOLIO 2: A WELL-BALANCED APPROACH

Next, we construct a better-balanced portfolio. For the domestic large-cap portion of the portfolio, Fund LB2 is a better core holding. It is well-diversified and does not have strong sector biases. Because the fund consists primarily of large caps and does not have a strong style tilt, it is less likely to overlap with our smaller-cap choices. However, we mentioned earlier that this fund has a 15 percent stake in foreign stocks. This means that if we allocate the target weight of 30 percent for domestic large-cap stocks to Fund LB2, we would be underweight in domestic stocks and overweight in foreign stocks. Therefore, the correct amount to allocate to Fund LB2 is actually 35 percent, calculated as the target asset class weight of 30 percent divided by 0.85, representing the 85 percent of Fund LB2 that is actually invested in domestic stocks.

For the foreign portion of the portfolio, let us select International Fund 1, which is more focused on foreign large caps than International Fund 2. Keep in mind that we have increased the investment in Fund LB2 to 35 percent of the overall portfolio due to its partial exposure to foreign stocks, so we will reduce International Fund 1's weighting accordingly to 10 percent in order to meet the 15 percent target allocation to foreign stocks.

For the small/mid-cap portion, we explained that combining Fund SV1 and Fund SG1 gives the small-cap segment a growth bent and some sector biases. The other alternatives are combining Fund SV1 with Fund SG2, Fund SV2 with Fund

Exhibit 11.1 Portfolio 1

Portfolio Allocation (%)	Fund	Exposure to Domestic Large-Cap Stocks (%)	Exposure to Domestic Small/Mid-Cap Stocks (%)	Exposure to Foreign Stocks (%)	Exposure to Domestic Bonds (%)
30	Fund LB1	30			
7.5	Fund SV1		7.5		
7.5	Fund SG1		7.5		
15	International Fund 1			15	
40	Bond Fund 1				40
	Total Portfolio	**30**	**15**	**15**	**40**

SG1, and Fund SV2 with Fund SG2, and we will examine the effect of each of these three combinations. Blending Fund SV1 with Fund SG2 creates a growth tilt in both small-cap and mid-cap areas, and the growth bias is especially pronounced in the mid-cap area because of SV1's exposure to mid-cap growth stocks. Combining Fund SV2 with Fund SG1 would lead to a better balance of growth and value in the small-cap area because SV2 does not have growth exposure, and it softens but does not eliminate the growth bias in the mid-cap space. Pairing Fund SV2 with Fund SG2 produces the best balance of growth and value in both small-cap and mid-cap areas.

See Exhibits 11.1 and 11.2 for the summary construction of Portfolio 1 and Portfolio 2.

ANALYSIS OF THE PORTFOLIOS

To analyze the characteristics of the two portfolios, we can use the Instant X-Ray® tool on Morningstar.com. This tool aggregates funds into a single portfolio based on the weightings you assign and then calculates portfolio statistics on the total portfolio. Essentially, most of the analytic data provided for individual mutual funds are calculated for the overall portfolio of funds.

Exhibit 11.2 Portfolio 2

Portfolio Allocation (%)	Fund	Exposure to Domestic Large-Cap Stocks (%)	Exposure to Domestic Small/Mid-Cap Stocks (%)	Exposure to Foreign Stocks (%)	Exposure to Domestic Bonds (%)
35	Fund LB2	30		5	
7.5	Fund SV2		7.5		
7.5	Fund SG2		7.5		
10	International Fund 1			10	
40	Bond Fund 1				40
	Total Portfolio	**30**	**15**	**15**	**40**

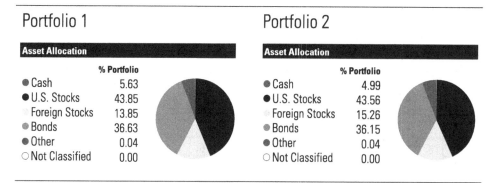

Portfolio 1		Portfolio 2	
Asset Allocation		**Asset Allocation**	
	% Portfolio		% Portfolio
● Cash	5.63	● Cash	4.99
● U.S. Stocks	43.85	● U.S. Stocks	43.56
Foreign Stocks	13.85	Foreign Stocks	15.26
● Bonds	36.63	● Bonds	36.15
● Other	0.04	● Other	0.04
○ Not Classified	0.00	○ Not Classified	0.00

Exhibit 11.3 Asset Allocation Section of Morningstar Instant X-Ray for Two Portfolios

Asset Allocation

Asset allocation statistics for the two portfolios are shown in Exhibit 11.3. It is not unusual for mutual funds to hold some cash to facilitate transactions, and indeed both of our portfolios have 5 to 6 percent in cash. There are a couple of ways to account for this.

1. You could add it to the bond stake, since cash is essentially defined as fixed-income securities with maturities of less than one year.
2. You could recalculate the percentages in the other asset classes by dividing each percentage by 95 percent, the portion of the portfolio not in cash.

With either approach, the resulting asset allocation is fairly close to the target allocation of 45 percent domestic stocks, 15 percent foreign stocks, and 40 percent bonds.

In the case of Portfolio 1, the asset allocation is on target because the funds chosen were fairly pure plays. None of the domestic-stock funds chosen invests in foreign stocks, and the foreign-stock fund holds no domestic stocks. Similarly, our stock funds do not invest in bonds, or vice versa. With Portfolio 2, we see that the adjustments we made to account for the foreign stake in Fund LB2 were successful.

Style Diversification

Exhibit 11.4 contains Morningstar Style Box for the stock and bond portions of the aggregate portfolios. The blackened squares represent the areas of greatest concentration for each portfolio, while the numbers in each square indicate the portfolios' allocations to each area of the box.

Both bond portfolios are firmly rooted in the prescribed intermediate-term high-quality arena. The stock portfolios, however, show more variation. In Portfolio 2, our well-balanced example, the focus is in the large-core area. (When discussing style of individual stocks rather than funds, we use the term *core* in place of *blend*.) Portfolio 2 has 67 percent of the stock portfolio in large caps and a fairly even

Portfolio 1

Stock Diversification

Valuation

Value	Core	Growth		Size
8	20	26	Large
14	8	8	Med
2	6	8	Small

Interest Rate Sensitivity

Short	Interm	Long		Credit Quality
0	100	0	High
0	0	0	Med
0	0	0	Low

Not Classified 0.00%   Not Classified 0.00%

Portfolio 2

Stock Diversification

Valuation

Value	Core	Growth		Size
23	26	18	Large
5	7	5	Med
5	5	6	Small

Interest Rate Sensitivity

Short	Interm	Long		Credit Quality
0	100	0	High
0	0	0	Med
0	0	0	Low

Not Classified 0.00%   Not Classified 0.00%

Exhibit 11.4 Style Diversification Section of Morningstar Instant X-Ray for Two Portfolios

distribution across the growth/value spectrum for large, medium, and small caps. This is consistent with our original goal of having two-thirds of the stock portfolio in large caps and one-third in small/mid-caps. Portfolio 1, however, is slanted toward growth stocks and has 46 percent in small- and mid-cap stocks, giving the portfolio more risk than intended. (For more detail on how the individual fund choices affect the aggregate style distribution, see the Portfolio Style Detail in Exhibit 11.5.)

Portfolio 1

Stock Style Detail

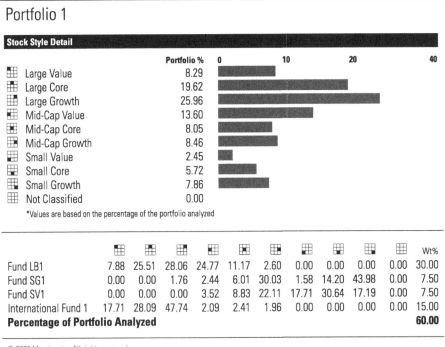

	Portfolio %
Large Value	8.29
Large Core	19.62
Large Growth	25.96
Mid-Cap Value	13.60
Mid-Cap Core	8.05
Mid-Cap Growth	8.46
Small Value	2.45
Small Core	5.72
Small Growth	7.86
Not Classified	0.00

*Values are based on the percentage of the portfolio analyzed

											Wt%
Fund LB1	7.88	25.51	28.06	24.77	11.17	2.60	0.00	0.00	0.00	0.00	30.00
Fund SG1	0.00	0.00	1.76	2.44	6.01	30.03	1.58	14.20	43.98	0.00	7.50
Fund SV1	0.00	0.00	0.00	3.52	8.83	22.11	17.71	30.64	17.19	0.00	7.50
International Fund 1	17.71	28.09	47.74	2.09	2.41	1.96	0.00	0.00	0.00	0.00	15.00
Percentage of Portfolio Analyzed											**60.00**

Exhibit 11.5 Stock Style Detail Section of Morningstar Instant X-Ray for Two Portfolios

In summary, Portfolio 2 has broader style diversification, which should help give it a smoother ride as the various investment style areas swing in and out of favor with investors. It also has a mix of large cap versus small/mid cap that is consistent with the policy asset allocation weightings.

Stock Sector

The stock sector breakdown for both portfolios can be found in Exhibit 11.6. Listed next to each portfolio's sector weightings are the corresponding sector weights for the Standard & Poor's (S&P) 500 Index, which helps identify where the portfolios deviate from market norms. Portfolio 1 shows overweightings in media and consumer services and underweightings in financial services and energy. Portfolio 2 has its own biases, though not as pronounced. Basically, it is important to check your portfolio's aggregate sector exposure periodically to make sure your managers are not placing large sector bets that put you outside your comfort level.

Regional breakdowns are presented in Exhibit 11.7. Both portfolios have similar breakdowns, and both appear adequately diversified. As with sector weightings, regional breakdowns help you understand a fund's investment style and/or explain recent performance patterns. At the aggregate portfolio level, you should

Portfolio 1

Stock Sector	Portfolio % of Stocks	S&P 500 %
☁ **Information**	**26.29**	**20.99**
🔲 Software	1.28	3.62
🖥 Hardware	7.81	10.44
🎙 Media	13.01	3.17
📱 Telecommunications	4.19	3.76
☲ **Service**	**48.29**	**42.50**
🩺 Healthcare	9.65	11.69
🛒 Consumer Services	18.86	7.23
📋 Business Services	8.33	3.89
💲 Financial Services	11.45	19.69
⌐ **Manufacturing**	**25.43**	**36.53**
🚗 Consumer Goods	6.66	8.69
⚙ Industrial Materials	12.08	12.81
🔥 Energy	5.54	11.54
💡 Utilities	1.14	3.49
▬ Not Classified	0.00	0.00

Portfolio 2

Stock Sector	Portfolio % of Stocks	S&P 500 %
☁ **Information**	**15.63**	**20.99**
🔲 Software	2.92	3.62
🖥 Hardware	3.33	10.44
🎙 Media	5.17	3.17
📱 Telecommunications	4.21	3.76
☲ **Service**	**53.10**	**42.50**
🩺 Healthcare	6.73	11.69
🛒 Consumer Services	12.54	7.23
📋 Business Services	5.70	3.89
💲 Financial Services	28.13	19.69
⌐ **Manufacturing**	**31.27**	**36.53**
🚗 Consumer Goods	11.92	8.69
⚙ Industrial Materials	7.49	12.81
🔥 Energy	11.38	11.54
💡 Utilities	0.48	3.49
▬ Not Classified	0.00	0.00

Exhibit 11.6   Stock Sector Section of Morningstar Instant X-Ray for Two Portfolios

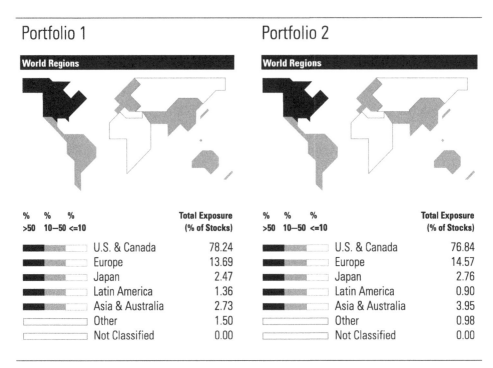

%	%	%	Total Exposure	%	%	%	Total Exposure
>50	10–50	<=10	(% of Stocks)	>50	10–50	<=10	(% of Stocks)

Portfolio 1

World Regions

	Total Exposure (% of Stocks)
U.S. & Canada	78.24
Europe	13.69
Japan	2.47
Latin America	1.36
Asia & Australia	2.73
Other	1.50
Not Classified	0.00

Portfolio 2

World Regions

	Total Exposure (% of Stocks)
U.S. & Canada	76.84
Europe	14.57
Japan	2.76
Latin America	0.90
Asia & Australia	3.95
Other	0.98
Not Classified	0.00

Exhibit 11.7 World Regions Section of Morningstar Instant X-Ray for Two Portfolios

make sure that unexpected or undesired imbalances are not created when combining multiple funds.

Stock Stats

Additional stock-portfolio statistics are shown in Exhibit 11.8. Numbers are compared to the S&P 500 Index in relative terms. So, for example, Portfolio 1's price/prospective earnings ratio of 16.32 is 1.04 times that of the S&P 500 Index. With the exception of average market cap, most of the numbers in this exhibit are fairly similar to the index, so there are no major concerns. The lower average market-cap statistics are understandable, given that the S&P 500 is made up of the market's largest companies while both of our sample portfolios include stakes in small- and mid-cap stocks. Not surprisingly, Portfolio 1, with its larger percentage of smaller stocks, has a lower average market cap than Portfolio 2.

Fees and Expenses

Exhibit 11.9 shows aggregate fee information. In our example, the average expense ratios for the two portfolios are similar at 0.81 and 0.68 percent. To gauge whether these figures are reasonable, you can compare them to the expense ratio of a similarly weighted hypothetical portfolio, which is listed underneath the portfolio's expense data. This benchmark expense ratio is calculated using the relevant

Portfolio 1

Stock Stats		
	Your Portfolio	Relative to S&P 500
Price/Prospective Earnings	16.32	1.04
Price/Book Ratio	2.25	0.84
Return on Assets (ROA)	7.93	0.96
Return on Equity (ROE)	22.09	1.00
Projected EPS Growth–5Yr%	13.25	1.25
Yield %	2.45	1.25
Average Market Cap $mil	14,525.84	0.25

Portfolio 2

Stock Stats		
	Your Portfolio	Relative to S&P 500
Price/Prospective Earnings	15.16	1.06
Price/Book Ratio	2.23	0.92
Return on Assets (ROA)	6.76	0.79
Return on Equity (ROE)	18.49	0.83
Projected EPS Growth–5Yr%	12.53	1.14
Yield %	2.70	1.33
Average Market Cap $mil	20,605.95	0.37

Exhibit 11.8   Stock Stats Section of Morningstar Instant X-Ray for Two Portfolios

category average expense ratios. In this example, it is good to see both portfolios coming in significantly below the 1.2 percent average.

Conclusions
Overall, while both hypothetical portfolios are viable options, Portfolio 2 is better diversified and does the best job of meeting our target asset allocation.

ONGOING MAINTENANCE

Assuming you are satisfied with the results of the Instant X-Ray analysis, you would take the next step and purchase the funds in the specified quantities. Then to monitor the portfolio, you would ideally rerun the Instant X-Ray tool periodically. As market prices fluctuate and portfolio managers trade securities, the composition of your portfolio will change. Your 60/40 stock/bond split could easily become a

Portfolio 1

Fees & Expenses	
Average Mutual Fund Expense Ratio (%)	0.81
Expense Ratio of Similarly Weighted Hypothetical Portfolio (%)	1.22
Estimated Mutual Fund Expenses ($)	0.81
Total Sales Charges Paid ($)	0.00

Portfolio 2

Fees & Expenses	
Average Mutual Fund Expense Ratio (%)	0.68
Expense Ratio of Similarly Weighted Hypothetical Portfolio (%)	1.20
Estimated Mutual Fund Expenses ($)	0.68
Total Sales Charges Paid ($)	0.00

Exhibit 11.9   Fees and Expenses Section of Morningstar Instant X-Ray for Two Portfolios

70/30 split if stocks are outperforming bonds. To keep your portfolio in line with your targets, you will most likely need to rebalance it from time to time by adding to some holdings and trimming others. You may even decide to eliminate a fund completely if it undergoes major changes or fails to perform as expected over time.

CONCLUSIONS

We began our discussion by saying that the process of building a portfolio is more art than science and that there are many possible paths. The key is not trying to discover the magic answer but being willing to delve in and ask the right questions. It is our hope that these chapters have shed some light on what questions you should ask and where you can find the answers.

ABOUT THE AUTHORS

Don Phillips is a managing director of Morningstar, Inc. and is responsible for corporate strategy, research, and corporate communications. He has served on the company's board of directors since August 1999. Mr. Phillips is also president of fund research, which includes research on mutual funds, exchange-traded funds, and alternative investments.

Mr. Phillips joined Morningstar in 1986 as the company's first mutual fund analyst and soon became editor of its flagship publication, *Morningstar*® *Mutual Funds*™, establishing the editorial voice for which the company is best known. Mr. Phillips helped to develop the Morningstar Style Box™, the Morningstar Rating™, and other distinctive proprietary Morningstar innovations that have become industry standards.

Journalists regularly turn to Don Phillips for his insight on industry trends. *Investment Advisor* magazine has named him to its list of the most influential people in the financial planning industry. *Financial Planning* magazine has named him one of the planning industry's "Movers & Shakers." *Registered Rep.* has named him one of the investment industry's 10 key players.

Mr. Phillips holds a bachelor's degree in English from the University of Texas and a master's degree in American literature from the University of Chicago.

Paul D. Kaplan is vice president of quantitative research at Morningstar, Inc., responsible for the quantitative methodologies behind Morningstar's fund analysis, indexes, adviser tools, and other services. Many of Dr. Kaplan's research papers have been published in professional books and publications. He received the 2008 Graham and Dodd Award and was a Graham and Dodd Award of Excellence winner in 2000.

Before joining Morningstar in 1999, he was a vice president of Ibbotson Associates and served as the firm's chief economist and director of research. Prior to that, he served on the economics faculty of Northwestern University where he taught international finance and statistics.

Dr. Kaplan holds a bachelor's degree in mathematics, economics, and computer science from New York University and a master's degree and doctorate in economics from Northwestern University. Dr. Kaplan holds the Chartered Financial Analyst (CFA) designation.

CHAPTER 12

Performance of Actively Managed versus Index Funds

The Vanguard Case

EDWARD TOWER, Ph.D.
Professor of Economics, Duke University
Visiting Professor, Chulalongkorn University

Paul Merriman: How does Vanguard justify with this great family of index funds also having all of these actively managed funds?

John C. Bogle: Well, I don't run Vanguard any longer, but I will take plenty of responsibility for having those active funds in all of the years I ran it. And the answer to that is really a couple of things. One, a lot of investors, no matter how persuasive the case for indexing is, and it's overpoweringly persuasive, just don't quite get it. They want a little more activity. They want something to watch. Index funds, as you all know, are roughly as exciting as watching paint dry or maybe watching the grass grow. They create great returns but they're not that exciting. So what we tried to do and what I tried to do personally was pick good managers, and that's very, very hard to do. I want to be clear on that, and I have some hits and some runs and some errors in that category, have funds with multiple managers, so you get a much broader diversification, which is not unlike an index fund....[For example, take] our Windsor II fund. It's a large cap value fund. And it has five different managers. I think that's the number now. And so you are going to tend to have a value average return for that fund. And then, actually, make sure you have the other two big advantages of indexing, or three really, no sales commissions, very low expense ratios, because I negotiated with all those advisers and got those fees as low as I could possibly get them, and hire advisers with low portfolio turnover. An article was done by some professors at Duke University about a year ago and they showed that our active managers in the life of the index fund actually did a hair better than the index fund [Reinker and Tower (2005)]. On the other hand if we had started the comparison a little bit later, the active managers would have done a little bit worse. But I think it's a valid strategy. What can I do and tell you? I'm still 80% indexed.

—Paul Merriman, 2006 interview with John Bogle

This chapter builds on the work of Rodriguez and Tower (2008). It uses more recent data and more funds, with some modifications to the methodology, tests new hypotheses, and focuses on a longer time period. Thanks go to Michael Connolly, Paul Holden, Susan Iddings, Ken Reinker, Allan Sleeman, Phil Steinmeyer, and Dan Wiener for help with the chapter. Their approval is not implied.

A s if by reply, Dan Wiener, editor of the *FFSA Independent Guide to the Vanguard Funds*, writes (2007, p. 1):

Vanguard wants you to "believe" in indexing. Your faith in indexing is the cornerstone of their business. But it's a lie. And your trust could cost you . . . plenty! . . . Indexing doesn't work for you. It works for them. The big famous Index funds at Vanguard have chronically underperformed over the last few years, exposing conservative investors to the worst risks of bear markets. But Vanguard knows investors who plunk money into an index become "passive." Their money goes "dead." And Vanguard never has to worry about these clients getting antsy. Indexing is a great business—but it's a lousy investment!

INTRODUCTION

Is John Bogle correct that Vanguard's index and managed equity funds are comparable, and should investors follow his example and hold a mix of both? Is Wiener correct that Vanguard's index funds, especially the big index funds, underperform? How should Vanguard investors choose between Vanguard's index funds and its managed funds?

This study asks:

- Did Vanguard's managed funds outperform their indexed counterparts?
- Were the managers of Vanguard's active funds wise stock pickers and style pickers?
- Did the degree of outperformance of a managed mutual fund predict the degree of future outperformance?
- Has the degree of outperformance of Vanguard's managed funds been rising, falling, or staying the same?
- Which predicted outperformance best: past outperformance, the number of Morningstar stars awarded to funds for past performance, or Wiener's (2003) sell, hold, or buy recommendations?
- What was the best combination of these predictors?

METHODOLOGY

This chapter defines the tracking index fund basket (for short, the tracking index) of a managed fund as that collection of indexed funds whose monthly returns most closely track the returns of the managed fund. Each Vanguard managed fund can be matched to a tracking basket of Vanguard index funds that produces the same return plus a differential. If the average differential, alpha, is positive, the return of the managed fund is superior to that of the tracking index. This chapter uses the geometric alpha. This is the amount by which the geometric average return of a mutual fund exceeds the geometric average return of its tracking index. The geometric alpha is more useful than the standard arithmetic alpha, for it measures how much the mutual fund outreturns its tracking index over the period analyzed rather than the average annual excess return, measured by the arithmetic alpha. Two funds that have the same tracking index and total return over a time period, but different standard deviations of return, will have different arithmetic alphas but the same geometric alphas.

Wiener (2006, p. 186) provides correlations of returns between different Vanguard equity funds to help investors reduce risk. Morningstar's (2009) portfolio instant X-Ray is also useful. It describes the composition of each managed fund as a combination of the nine style groups (from large-cap value, through mid-cap blend, and small-cap growth), and it distinguishes between domestic and foreign equity.

A complementary tool is the one provided here, the tracking index. Investors who find that one of their managed funds substantially duplicates one of their index funds may wish to lighten their holdings of one or the other in order to maintain portfolio diversification.

The chapter ignores taxes. Thus, the analysis applies to mutual funds in a tax-sheltered account. Taxes are ignored, because mutual funds are less appealing as a saving vehicle in a taxable account, where one can hold individual stocks, selling off losers for capital losses when need be and postponing taxable sales or else passing them onto heirs tax-free. The variability of individual stock returns facilitates tax loss harvesting in a non–tax-sheltered account.

The first step is to describe each of Vanguard's managed funds in terms of its index funds. The index funds used are the 12 diversified equity funds available over the 10-year period July 1, 1998, to June 31, 2008. These along with their symbols are:

1. VFINX   500 Index
2. VEIEX   Emerging Market Stock Index
3. VEURX   European Stock Index
4. VEXMX   Extended Market Index
5. VIGRX   Growth Index
6. VIMSX   Mid-Cap Index
7. VPACX   Pacific Stock Index
8. NAESX   Small-Cap Index
9. VISGX   Small-Cap Growth Index
10. VISVX   Small-Cap Value Index
11. VTSMX   Total Stock Market Index
12. VIVAX   Value Index

The inception date of the Large-Cap Index, VLACX, is January 2004. It is used as part of the tracking index for funds born after that date.

Each index fund represents an investment in a patch of the stock market (i.e., a particular style of investment). This list has gaps in coverage. No Vanguard indexes correspond to international growth, international value, or international small. The Vanguard index funds for Mid-Cap Growth and Mid-Cap Value have inception dates of 2006, too late for inclusion in this study. If such funds had existed for the entire period, it would have been possible to find tracking indexes that were closer trackers of the managed funds.

Three of the index funds were established only in May 1998. The need to use as many index funds as possible for as many years as possible restricted the study to the 10-year period July 1998 through June 2008.

Here is the list of the 18 Vanguard managed funds that have operated for this whole 10-year period and met our criteria for inclusion in the study:

1. VHCOX   Capital Opportunity
2. VDIGX   Dividend Growth (formerly Utilities Income)
3. VEIPX   Equity Income
4. VEXPX   Explorer
5. VXGEX   Global Equity
6. VQNPX   Growth and Income
7. VGEQX   Growth Equity
8. VINEX   International Explorer
9. VWIGX   International Growth
10. VTRIX   International Value
11. VMGRX   Mid-Cap Growth
12. VMRGX   Morgan Growth
13. VCMPX   PRIMECAP
14. VASVX   Selected Value
15. VSEQX   Strategic Equity
16. VWUSX   U.S. Growth
17. VWNDX   Windsor
18. VWNFX   Windsor II

The study also considers 10 recent additions listed with the first full month of observations for returns from Morningstar (2008):

1. VFTSX   06/2000   FTSE Social Index investor class
2. VUVLX   07/2000   U.S. Value
3. VCLVX   01/2002   Capital Value
4. VDEQX   07/2005   Diversified Equity
5. VSLVX   01/2006   Structured Large-Cap Value Institutional Plus
6. VSGPX   02/2006   Structured Large-Cap Growth Institutional Plus
7. VDAIX   05/2006   Dividend Appreciation
8. VSTCX   05/2006   Strategic Small-Cap Equity
9. VSLIX   06/2006   Structured Large-Cap Equity Institutional
10. VSBMX   12/2006   Structured Broad Market Institutional

Eighteen managed funds have existed for the whole period (the old funds) and 10 additional funds have existed for shorter periods (the young funds). These are Vanguard's diversified funds whose median proportion of assets invested in cash and bonds was less than 9 percent at the annual reporting times indicated on Morningstar Principia (2008). The young funds consist of seven managed funds, an index fund that uses social screening criteria (FTSE Soc); a fund of funds (Diversified Equity) that is permitted to vary its mix of funds; and Dividend Appreciation, which as Chapter 13 discusses is an enhanced index fund.

The structured funds, all of which are in the young collection, are institutional or institutional plus funds, and they do not have other share class counterparts. These are share classes like the investor or Admiral share classes and are not limited to institutions. They simply have the "institutional" share class name. They have high minimum investment levels ($5 million and $200 million, respectively). While not many investors will be able to invest in them, it is worthwhile to see whether they beat the index funds and whether less wealthy investors should lobby to have them made available, perhaps with higher fees attached for smaller accounts.

The Investor share class carries higher expenses than the Admiral share class. But some funds do not have Admiral shares, so to keep the sample size large and for the sake of uniformity, the study works with Investor shares.

Investors are concerned with real returns, so we adjust nominal returns by the Consumer Price Index provided in Morningstar (2008) to get real returns. Henceforth, "return" unless accompanied by "nominal" indicates real return. The formula used for the conversion is

$$1 + R = [1 + N]/[1 + I] \qquad (12.1)$$

where

R = real rate of return
N = nominal rate of return
I = rate of inflation in the consumer price index, with all expressed as a proportion per month

To describe the return of a managed fund (say, PRIMECAP) in terms of the index fund returns, the monthly return of PRIMECAP is regressed on the monthly returns of all of the indexes, while constraining all of the coefficients of the index funds to be nonnegative and to sum to one. The result is:

$$\begin{aligned} R_{\text{PRIMECAP}} = &+ 4.33/12 + 0.18\ R_{\text{S\&P500}} + 0.04\ R_{\text{European}} + 0.41\ R_{\text{Growth}} \\ &+ 0.03\ R_{\text{Mid-Cap}} + 0.16\ R_{\text{Small-Cap Growth}} + 0.18\ R_{\text{Small-Cap}} \\ &+ 0.01\ R_{\text{Total Stock Market}} \end{aligned} \qquad (12.2)$$

where

R = monthly (real) return in percentage points per year

Henceforth except where confusion might result, all returns and return differences are simply % per month or year. This regression says that PRIMECAP is an asset whose return is best described as the return of a basket of index funds consisting of 18 percent invested in the 500 Index fund, 4 percent in European Stock Index, 41 percent in Growth Index, 3 percent in Mid-Cap Index, 16 percent in Small-Cap Growth Index, and 1 percent in Total Stock Market Index, with an additional return of 4.33/12 percent per month, and a random term, where the index basket is rebalanced at the beginning of each month. This index basket is defined as the tracking index. (Rounding error causes the coefficients to sum to 101 percent.) Here the managed fund outperforms the tracking index by 4.33/12 percent per month, or 4.33 percent per year, the arithmetic α. This composition of the tracking index is recorded in Exhibit 12.1. This methodology of style analysis was developed by Sharpe (1992) and is explained there and by Bodie, Kane, and Marcus

Exhibit 12.1   Tracking Indexes for the Old Funds (July 1998–June 2008 Inclusive, %)

Mgd funds	Index funds	500 x VFINX	Emerging Mkt x VEIEX	Eur Stk x VEURX	Ext Mkt x VEXMX	Growth x VIGRX	Mid Cap x VIMSX	Pacific Stk x VPACX	SG x VISGX	S x NAESX	S Value x VISVX	Total Stk x VTSMX	Value x VIVAX	Sum or avg
1 VHCOX	Cap Opp	0	0	0	28	37	0	0	13	22	0	0	0	100
2 VDIGX	Dividend G	0	0	9	0	2	0	7	0	0	5	0	77	100
3 VEIPX	E-Income	0	0	0	0	0	0	2	0	0	0	0	98	100
4 VEXPX	Explorer	0	0	0	29	0	0	0	34	37	0	0	0	100
5 VHGEX	Global E	0	11	19	0	0	0	21	0	0	18	0	32	100
6 VQNPX	G & Income	86	0	0	2	4	0	2	0	0	4	0	2	100
7 VGEQX	Growth E	0	0	0	56	44	0	0	0	0	0	0	0	100
8 VINEX	Intl Explorer	0	7	35	24	0	0	25	0	10	0	0	0	100
9 VWIGX	Intl Growth	0	8	69	0	0	0	15	0	9	0	0	0	100
10 VTRIX	Intl Value	0	12	41	0	0	0	25	0	0	5	0	16	100
11 VMGRX	Mid Cap G	0	0	0	81	0	0	0	19	0	0	0	0	100
12 VMRGX	Morgan G	0	3	0	27	53	8	0	2	0	0	0	7	100
13 VPMCX	PRIMECAP	18	0	4	0	41	3	0	16	18	0	1	0	100
14 VASVX	Selected V	0	0	0	0	0	0	0	0	0	39	0	61	100
15 VSEQX	Strategic E	0	0	0	0	0	28	8	16	0	22	0	27	100
16 VWUSX	U.S. Growth	0	0	0	16	84	0	0	0	0	0	0	0	100
17 VWNDX	Windsor	0	1	0	0	0	1	0	0	0	12	0	86	100
18 VWNFX	Windsor II	0	0	0	0	0	0	0	0	0	4	0	96	100
	Average	6	2	10	15	15	2	6	6	5	6	0	28	100
avg real rtn 1st half (%/yr)		−0.40	0.11	−0.72	−0.24	−0.56	0.46	−0.44	0.03	−0.10	0.14	−0.36	−0.31	−0.2
avg real rtn 2nd half (%/yr)		0.38	2.23	1.24	0.80	0.41	0.88	1.13	0.85	0.75	0.64	0.48	0.48	0.86
avg real rtn overall (%/yr)		−0.01	1.17	0.26	0.28	−0.08	0.67	0.34	0.44	0.33	0.39	0.06	0.08	0.34

Note: E = Equity. G = Growth. S = Small. V = Value. x = index.

Conclude : Aside from the emerging markets, Europe and Pacific no Vanguard index fund returned more than 1% real per year in either period or overall.

All index funds had slightly higher returns in the second half of the period.

For comparison over the 10-year period, the real continuously compounded returns were: Vanguard short-term Treasury, VFISX, 1.89%/year; Vanguard intermediate-term Treasury, VFITX, 3.03%/year; Vanguard long-term bond index, VBLTX, 3.18%/year, considerably higher than the comparable figures in the table for equities.

(2008, pp. 875–879). Sharpe writes (1992) "style analysis provides measures that reflect how returns act, rather than a simplistic concept of what the portfolios include" (p. 13). His paper is online, clear, displays helpful graphs, and is easy to read.

In the tables and figures, all returns and return differentials are real and are continuously compounded. Continuously compounded returns are easy to work with because the average return over a number of periods is just the average single-period return: A security that returns continuously compounded geometric rates of return of 2 percent in one year and 4 percent in the following year returns a continuously compounded geometric rate of return of 3 percent over the two-year period.

The solver feature of Microsoft Excel is used to perform all of the calculations, as in Tower and Yang (2008). Next the regression coefficients are used to calculate the tracking index and its return over the period. The geometric alpha is calculated as the geometric average annual return of the managed fund minus that of the index basket, where both are continuously compounded. For PRIMECAP, the geometric alpha is 4.03 percent per year. It is smaller than the arithmetic alpha of 4.33 percent per year (the constant in the regression), and it is recorded in Exhibit 12.2.

The use of the tracking basket is an attempt to deal with Kizer's (2005) point that in assessing managed funds versus index funds, one must compare managed performance with index performance of comparable style.

Returns are not risk-adjusted. Instead, the tables simply report the standard deviations of monthly returns of the fund and the tracking index. Given alpha, the risk-averse investor will prefer the fund with the lower standard deviation.

One could follow Reinker and Tower (2004) and calculate a risk-adjusted alpha by combining a low-risk asset (such as an inflation-protected security) with the security (the managed fund or the tracking basket) that has the higher standard deviation of return, until the standard deviation of return for the combined portfolio fell to that of the lower standard-deviation-of-return security. The return of the combination minus that of the lower standard-deviation-of return security is the risk-adjusted return differential. But the result depends on the low-risk asset chosen. Moreover, the analysis may be misleading. Suppose fund A returns more each period than does fund B, but fund B has a lower standard deviation of return. Then risk-adjusting fund A (using a low-return, low-risk asset) may bring its return below that of fund B, yet no investor would choose fund B over fund A. It is easy to see that this paradox occurs if B is almost riskless and the low-risk asset has a low return.

IN DEFENSE OF GEOMETRIC ALPHA

Let R_1 and R_2 be successive monthly returns, expressed as proportions. The average arithmetic return is $(R_1 + R_2) / 2$, the average return each period. The average geometric return is $(1 + R_1) \times (1 + R_2)]^{.5} - 1$, the common return each period that would generate the observed return over the entire time span.

The expected one-period return exceeds the expected long-period return if future returns are drawn evenly from past returns without replacement. For example, if the past annual returns were 0 percent and 300 percent, the expected one-year return is the average of 0 percent and 300 percent = 150 percent. This is the past arithmetic rate of return. This is also the expected annual return over any number of years if we expect that the return in all future periods will be drawn

Exhibit 12.2 Prowess of Style and Equity Choice for the Old Funds

Mgd funds	R²	PSE α	t_α	Risk of fund	PSE1 α_W1	PSE2 α_W2	PE1 α_H1	PE2 α_H2	PS avg(PSE) −avg(PE)	# of M* stars	Dan Wiener rating
1	2	3	4	5	6	7	8	9	10	11	12
1 Cap Opp	85	6.7	2.4	1.2	10.9	2.6	11.0	2.5	-0.1	5	1
2 Dividend G	59	-1.6	-0.5	0.8	-2.6	-0.5	-2.8	1.2	-0.8	4	1
3 E-Income	87	0.2	0.1	0.8	1.2	-0.7	1.2	-0.6	-0.1	4	0
4 Explorer	98	-1.3	-1.1	1.1	0.5	-3.1	0.6	-3.4	0.1	3	0
5 Global E	92	1.9	1.4	1.0	3.4	0.4	3.4	-1.6	1.0	4	1
6 G & Income	98	-1.4	-2.0	1.0	-2.0	-0.9	-1.9	-1.1	0.1	3	1
7 Growth E	91	-5.2	-2.0	1.3	-7.9	-2.4	-8.1	-3.1	0.4	3	-1
8 Intl Explorer	73	4.1	1.3	1.2	5.4	2.7	5.5	0.9	0.9	3	1
9 Intl Growth	96	-0.2	-0.2	1.0	-0.2	-0.3	0.1	-0.6	0.0	4	1
10 Intl Value	91	-0.2	-0.1	1.1	-0.1	0.1	-1.7	-0.3	1.0	4	0
11 Mid Cap G	90	2.4	0.8	1.3	5.8	-1.1	6.1	-1.3	0.0	3	0
12 Morgan G	97	-0.6	-0.5	1.1	-0.6	-0.5	-0.1	-0.5	-0.3	4	0
13 PRIMECAP	89	4.0	2.1	1.1	5.0	3.0	5.0	3.3	-0.2	5	1
14 Selected V	75	1.2	0.4	1.1	1.1	1.2	1.1	0.6	0.3	2	1
15 Strategic E	93	0.9	0.7	1.0	2.4	-0.6	3.6	-1.4	-0.2	3	1
16 U.S. Growth	91	-5.9	-2.5	1.3	-10.0	-1.8	-10.1	-2.4	0.3	2	-1
17 Windsor	92	-0.2	-0.1	1.1	2.0	-2.3	2.3	-3.3	0.3	3	0
18 Windsor II	91	0.4	0.2	0.9	0.9	-0.1	0.5	-0.3	0.3	3	1
Average	88	0.3	0.0	1.1	0.8	-0.2	0.9	-0.6	0.2	3.4	0.4
t		0.4	0.1		0.8	-0.6	0.8	-1.5	1.8		

Numbers in columns 2 to 9 are expressed in % pts/year.

R^2 is closeness of fit to tracking index.

PSE is prowess of style and equity choice over whole period. It is measured by α.

Risk of fund is measured as the standard deviation of monthly real return for the fund divided by that of the tracking index. Fund beats if less than one.

PSE_i is prowess of style and equity choice in half i, where i = 1 or 2, denoting first or second half of period. It is measured by $\alpha_{W,i}$, where W stands for whole and means that the tracking index used for comparison is that for the entire period.

PE_i denotes prowess of equity choice for period i. It is measured by $\alpha_{H,i}$, where H stands for half and means that the tracking index used for comparison is that of period i.

PS denotes prowess of style choice. It is measured by average α_W minus average α_H.

randomly from past returns with replacement. To see this, recognize that in that case, after two years we expect to have returned sequences of 0 percent then 300 percent, 0 percent then 0 percent, 300 percent then 0 percent, and 300 percent then 300 percent, each with probabilities of 0.25 percent. After two years, $1 becomes an expected $6.25 = (2.5)^2$, for an expected annual return of 150 percent. However, the expected annual return over a two-year span, when returns are drawn evenly from past returns, is $[(1 + 0)(1 + 3)]^{.5} - 1 = 100\%$. This is the past geometric rate of return. It is also the expected return over many periods when future returns are drawn evenly without replacement from past returns. The reason it is lower than the expected return when expected returns are calculated from past returns with replacement is that in the replacement case, the biggest returns occasionally are married with the biggest returns, so the magic of compounding raises the expected return beyond the geometric average return. To some extent, equity prices are characterized by regression to the mean (i.e., big returns are likely to be married with small returns in the future). If this is the case, the sensible policy is to report only geometric average returns and use them to calculate geometric alpha, and we follow it here. But the standard procedure in the literature is to use the arithmetic alpha. Kritzman (2002, chapter 4) addresses this issue, and the discussion here is based on his discussion.

The higher the standard deviation of return, the more the arithmetic average return exceeds the geometric average return; because of this fact, using arithmetic alphas instead of geometric averages as the performance criterion makes a fund that is more risky relative to its tracking index look more appealing relative to a fund that is less risky relative to its tracking index.

TRACKING INDEXES FOR THE OLD FUNDS

Exhibit 12.1 presents the tracking indexes for each of the 20 old funds. Windsor and Windsor II mimic a combination of lots of the Value Index Fund and a little of the Small-Cap Value Index Fund. The Growth and Income Fund mostly tracks the Standard & Poor's (S&P) 500 Index Fund. Reassuringly, the international managed funds have tracking baskets consisting mostly of the international index funds. The returns of all of the index funds have been quite similar over the 10-year period. Their 10-year real geometric average returns ranged from 1.17 percent per year to −0.08 percent per year, with an average of 0.34 percent. All of them performed less well than the three Vanguard bond funds discussed at the bottom of the table.

Using only the S&P 500 Index as a benchmark for managed funds is a misguided strategy. Exhibits 12.1 and 12.4, for the old and young funds, respectively, show that all tracking baskets require at least two different index funds, and no single index fund (neither the S&P 500 Index Fund nor any other) is used consistently across all managed funds. However, one index fund, Total Stock Market Index Fund, adds little explanatory power.

Most of the results from the linear regression are not surprising. For example, the Growth Equity Fund invests heavily in equities highly correlated with the Growth Index Fund. However, some striking patterns arise, illuminating the management style of funds. For example, Exhibit 12.1 shows that Windsor has historically invested 86 percent of its funds in equities linked to the Value Index Fund, although Morningstar (2008) lists it as a large blend fund. Similarly, the

Mid-Cap Growth Fund held 81 percent of its assets in securities linked to the Extended Market Index Fund, while Morningstar describes it as a midcap growth stock. The Growth Equity Fund is described by Morningstar as a large value fund, while it held 56 percent of its portfolio in assets linked to the Extended Market Index Fund. The Dividend Growth Fund is described in Morningstar as large blend, but 77 percent of its securities were linked over the period to the value index. Exhibit 12.1 clearly shows that caveat emptor is necessary in a world of style drift and misleading fund labels.

PROWESS OF STYLE JUMPING AND EQUITY CHOICE FOR THE OLD FUNDS

Exhibit 12.2 records some important results from the analysis. The R^2 measures the closeness of fit of the managed fund to its tracking index. It is the correlation squared of the monthly continuously compounded geometric real returns of the managed fund with its tracking index. The prowess of style jumping and equity choice over the entire period (abbreviated PSE) is alpha. A positive alpha may reflect wise stock picking within a style class, or it may reflect wise style jumping, moving into styles just before they appreciate. It does not reflect the wisdom of the average style choice, for that is controlled for by the selection of the index basket.

The average return differential is a positive 0.30 percent per year. On average, the managed funds were 5 percent riskier than the tracking indexes, with the ratio of the managed standard deviation of monthly return to that of the tracking basket being 1.05. Hence, managed funds are more risky.

This is surprising in view of the fact that managed funds tend to be less fully invested in equity than the index funds. Perhaps managed funds tend to be more risky, because they are less diversified. Referring back to the quote from John Bogle (Merriman, 2006), Windsor II, which strives to improve diversification by hiring more managers, is one of the few funds that have a lower risk than their tracking baskets, and it has the third lowest risk relative to its tracking basket of any managed fund in the collection. This is diversification by spreading mismanagement risk.

Exhibit 12.2 shows that, over the entire period, nine funds have a negative alpha and nine have a positive alpha. Capital Opportunity and PRIMECAP are the only two with a t statistic for alpha, t_α, greater than 2, and U.S. Growth is the only one with a t_α more negative than –2. These alphas are significantly different from zero at better than the 5 percent level.

Breaking up the period into two equal halves generates further insights. α_{W1} and α_{W2} are the alphas calculated for the first and second five-year halves, with the performance of the whole 10-year period tracking index as the benchmark. These alphas reflect the ability of the managed funds to beat the index basket that reflects average style choice over the whole 10-year period. Since they reflect prowess in both style jumping and equity choice in the two half periods, they are denoted by PSE1 and PSE2, respectively.

α_{H1} and α_{H2} are the alphas calculated for the first and second five-year halves of the period, with the performance of the corresponding half-period tracking index as the benchmark. These alphas reflect the ability of the managed funds to beat the index basket that reflects the average style choice over the half period. The alphas with the half-period tracking benchmarks reflect the prowess of equity choice, because style jumping from the first half of the period to the second, if any, is reflected in the change in the index basket. Hence we label them prowess of equity choice, PE1 and PE2. Both the PE's and PSE's indicate management prowess net of any additional cost imposed by the higher expenses of managed funds and the additional costs associated with the excess turnover of managed funds. In the first half, both average PSE1 and average PE1 are positive, and in the second half, they are both negative. Thus there is positive prowess of combined style jumping and equity choice in the first half and negative prowess in the second. The same is true of the prowess of equity choice: positive in the first half and negative in the second half. The use of only two subperiods is arbitrary, and this approach does not reflect style jumping within subperiods. That would emerge in the calculations as stock selection prowess.

The average of PSE1 and PSE2 is +0.30, the same as PSE, meaning that over the whole period, the prowess of style jumping and equity choice swamps transaction costs and expenses. The average of the PEs is +0.125 percent per year, implying that equity selection prowess swamps costs and expenses.

Dividing the whole period in two for calculating the short-period tracking benchmarks is arbitrary. It could be divided into as many as 10 parts, one for each year. If managers are consistently wise style jumpers, finer divisions should generate the same average values for the PSEs and lower values for the PEs.

Exhibit 12.2 includes the Dan Wiener's sell (–1), hold (0), and buy (1) ratings and the number of Morningstar (2003) stars for each managed fund, both for July 2003 (the middle of the entire period). Their predictive power is examined in a later section.

PRESCIENT STYLE JUMPING?

If managers are successful style jumpers, the half-period tracking indexes will perform better than the whole-period one. So if managers are wise style jumpers, the average alpha calculated for the half-period tracking indexes will be lower than the average alpha calculated for the whole-period tracking index. PS is the prowess of style jumping over the entire period. We measure it by the average of the whole alphas (α_{W1} and α_{W2}) minus the average of the half alphas (α_{H1} and α_{H2}). We find that PS is positive. Prescient style jumping has yielded a positive return of 0.175 percent per year. This prowess figure is the difference between two average alphas, both of which reflect the additional expenses and transaction costs of managed funds. Consequently, these additional expenses and transaction costs cancel out in taking the difference, so PS does not reflect them.

Thus, on average, fund managers made prescient style choices. Individuals may wish to adjust their styles in accordance with anticipated differential returns to different styles if they are able to correctly predict differential style returns. A wide range of style predictions used to be provided on the GMO Web site (2009), which were evaluated in *Marketview* (2008) and by Tower (2008), but the range of styles that GMO attempts to predict was narrowed in December 2008.

ALPHA FELL

Barras, Scaillet, and Wermers (2008) argue that conventional analysis finds that more managers are able to outperform the market than is truly the case, because these studies do not correct for luck. They aggregate different share classes of the same mutual fund by assets under management. By correcting for luck, they discover that the number of managers who beat the market net of expenses has dramatically fallen over time, so virtually none existed by 2006: 0.6 percent of fund managers, although on a gross return basis 9.6 percent of mutual fund managers display market-beating ability. They:

> *find a significant proportion of skilled (positive alpha) funds prior to 1995, but almost none by 2006, accompanied by a large increase in unskilled (negative alpha) fund managers due to both a large reduction in the proportion of fund managers with stockpicking skills and to a persistent level of expenses that exceed the value generated by these managers. (p. 1)*

Does the BSW regularity that alpha is falling hold for Vanguard's managed funds? (See Exhibit 12.3.)

The first columns of Exhibit 12.3 provide the t values for the alphas of Exhibit 12.2. The R^2s are indicated for the two half-periods for the alphas that use the whole-period tracking index as benchmark.

Each year's alpha (with the long tracking index as the benchmark) for each mutual fund was regressed on time, measured in years. The coefficients on time are indicated as the Annual PSEG. The average rate of growth of alpha, PSEG, is –0.28 percent per year. Thus alpha declined by over .25 percent per year.

Subsequent columns compare first and second half figures. The average jump from the first half to the second in prowess of style and equity selection is –1.08 percentage points per year. The average jump from the first half to the second in prowess of equity selection is –1.51 percentage points per year. The average style-jumping prowess rose from –.03 percentage points per year in the first half to 0.38 percentage points in the second half, for an increase from the first half to the second of 0.42 percentage point. Thus the prowess of style jumping improved, but the improvement is not enough to offset the decline in the prowess of equity choice, so total management prowess declined between the two halves.

How much of the differential performance was accounted for by cash drag? On average, mutual funds held 4 percent of their portfolios as cash during the whole period. Using the 500 Index Fund to get the equity benchmark real return (–0.4 percentage points per year) and Vanguard's short-term Treasury fund to get the money market return (+3.92 percentage points per year), the cash boost was 4% × (+0.0040 + 0.0392) = 0.17 percentage points per year during the first five years as managers got out of negative real return stocks into positive real return short-term bonds. In the second half, the cash drag was 0.02 percentage points per year as managers got out of positive real return stocks into negative real return short-term

Exhibit 12.3 Deterioration of Prowess in Style and Equity Choice for the Old Funds

	$t_{\alpha 1W}$	$t_{\alpha 2W}$	$t_{\alpha 1H}$	$t_{\alpha 2H}$	R^2_{1W}	R^2_{2W}	Annual PSEG α_W growth rate	PSEG $\alpha_{2W} - \alpha_{1W}$	PEG $\alpha_{2H} - \alpha_{1H}$	PS1 $\alpha_{1W} - \alpha_{1H}$	PS2 $\alpha_{2W} - \alpha_{2H}$	PSG PS2 − PS1
Mgd funds												
1 Cap Opp	2.16	1.20	2.21	1.23	85	89	−2.57	−8.32	−8.48	−0.14	0.02	0.16
2 Dividend Gro	−0.44	−0.32	−0.48	1.02	50	94	0.53	2.11	4.05	0.22	−1.72	−1.94
3 Equity-Income	1.21	−0.73	1.20	−0.55	85	96	0.09	−1.95	−1.75	0.01	−0.18	−0.19
4 Explorer	0.51	−3.07	0.62	−3.41	98	99	−0.90	−3.58	−4.03	−0.11	0.34	0.45
5 Global Equity	2.24	0.98	1.25	−3.63	92	97	−0.22	−3.03	−5.07	0.02	2.05	2.04
6 Gro & Income	−1.63	−1.12	−1.61	−1.49	98	97	0.14	1.08	0.75	−0.07	0.26	0.33
7 Growth Equity	−1.66	−1.13	−1.70	−1.82	92	92	0.48	5.50	4.99	0.12	0.63	0.51
8 Intl Explorer	0.93	1.09	0.95	0.40	69	85	−1.42	−2.75	−4.60	−0.06	1.78	1.84
9 Intl Growth	−0.09	−0.24	0.08	−0.86	96	98	0.00	−0.10	−0.75	−0.29	0.36	0.65
10 Intl Value	−0.72	1.08	−0.68	−0.27	89	97	0.33	0.23	1.46	1.59	0.36	−1.23
11 Mid Cap Gro	1.00	−0.50	1.67	−0.76	91	93	−1.78	−6.89	−7.44	−0.26	0.29	0.55
12 Morgan Gro	−0.33	−0.58	−0.07	−0.68	97	98	0.04	0.12	−0.33	−0.05	−0.05	0.45
13 PRIMECAP	1.40	2.01	1.42	2.42	89	92	−0.73	−1.97	−1.69	−0.02	−0.30	−0.29
14 Selected Valu	0.22	0.63	0.21	0.34	72	86	0.55	0.09	−0.47	0.05	0.61	0.55
15 Strategic Equity	1.04	−0.41	1.63	−1.46	93	97	−0.23	−3.03	−4.95	−1.16	0.76	1.91
16 U.S. Growth	−2.26	−1.28	−0.01	−1.84	91	94	0.92	8.20	7.61	0.03	0.61	0.59
17 Windsor	0.69	−1.55	1.67	−2.62	92	94	−0.49	−4.31	−5.54	−0.27	0.96	0.24
18 Windsor II	0.27	−0.05	1.67	−0.30	87	94	0.19	−0.92	−0.88	0.31	0.27	−0.04
Average	0.25	−0.22	0.56	−0.79	78	90	−0.28	−1.08	−1.51	−0.03	0.39	0.42
t for average	0.92	−0.83	2.21	−2.32			−1.43	−1.27	−1.61	−0.27	2.24	1.93

Annual PSEG is the growth rate of α (% pts/year). It is calculated as the coefficient of annual α_W regressed on year.

PSEG is growth in prowess of style & equity choice between the two periods. It is calculated as $\alpha_{W2} - \alpha_{W1}$.

PEG is growth in prowess of equity choice, measured as $\alpha_{H2} - \alpha_{H1}$.

PSi is prowess of style choice in period i, measured as $\alpha_{Wi} - \alpha_{Hi}$.

PSG growth in prowess of style choice, measured as PS2 − PS1.

Conclude:

α_W has been declining at 0.28% pts/year each year.

Prowess of style and equity choice combined declined between the two periods by 1.08 percentage points.

Prowess of equity choice declined between the periods by 1.51 percentage points.

Prowess of style choice rose from −.03%/year first period to 0.39%/year in the second, for a gain of 0.42%/year.

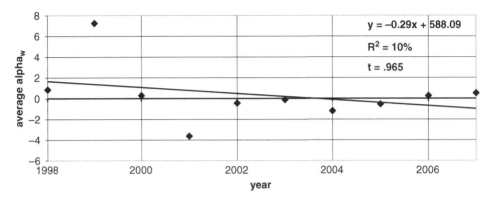

Exhibit 12.4   Average Annual Alpha$_W$ Fell

bonds. Thus we would have expected managers to return 0.19 percentage points per year less in the second half. In fact, the reduction is 1.08 percentage points, so cash drag explains only 18 percent of the reduction in alpha. (See Exhibit 12.4.)

Exhibit 12.4 shows how the average annual alpha (whole) has fallen. Exhibit 12.5 shows the same thing for the median average annual alpha (whole).

The largest outliers are for the period July 1999 to June 2001. From July 1999 through June 2000, the managed funds outperformed their index baskets by an average of over 7 percentage points; from July 2000 through June 2001, the median outperformance is over 2.5 percent. A puzzle is why managed funds performed so well in this period where the tech bubble topped out. Were it not for that one period, managed funds would have underperformed on average in both halves of the period. A small part of the answer may be market timing. The average Vanguard managed fund's holding of cash was 5.1 percent at the end of 1999, 5.2 percent at the end of 2000, and 3.8 percent on average from 2002 to 2006.

The old managed funds on average have expense ratios and turnover that are greater than the index funds. The average expense ratios and average turnover fell for both the old managed and index funds. Tower and Zheng (2008) find that a 100-percentage-point increase in turnover reduces return by 0.83 percentage points

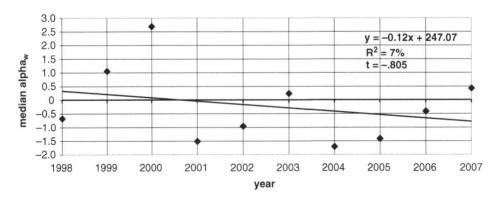

Exhibit 12.5   Median Annual Alpha$_W$ Fell

per year. Using this calculation, the underperformance of managed funds would be expected to fall from 0.66 percentage points per year in the first half of the period to 0.54 percentage points per year in the second half of the period for an increase in alpha of 0.12 points per year. Thus the increasing disadvantage of managed funds swims against the tide of a reduced disadvantage on the basis of differential expense ratios and turnover.

HOW HAVE THE YOUNG FUNDS PERFORMED?

Exhibit 12.6 shows the tracking index and performance of each of Vanguard's young funds.

On average, the young funds underperformed their corresponding index baskets by 1.90 percentage points per year. Their risk was one percent higher. Of particular interest is Vanguard's FTSE social index fund. It underperformed its tracking index by 2.98 percentage points per year and was 12 percent riskier. The two institutional funds, Structured Large Cap Equity I and Structured Broad Market I, underperformed their index baskets by an average of 0.68 percentage points per year; the two institutional plus funds, Structured Large Value IP and Structured Large growth IP, underperformed by an average of 4.22 percent per year. So investors who are unable to commit the $5 million minimum investment for the former or the $200 million minimum investment for the latter should not feel deprived. One should not put much faith in these numbers for the young funds, because the inception of half of them is after the start of 2006. Still, averaging the underperformance of these 8 young funds over the whole period with the average outperformance of the 18 old funds over the entire period, the managed funds now outperform by $(0.42 \times 18 - 1.90 \times 11) / 29\% = -0.46\%$ per year. So by this criterion, managed funds underperformed their tracking indexes.

The Total Stock Market Index fund plays no role in any of the tracking indexes shown in Exhibits 12.1 and 12.6, except for a 1 percent role for Capital Opportunity. Why? My conjecture is that fund managers rebalance frequently, which means that the components of that index show up in the tracking indexes but not the Total Stock Market Index itself.

DID R^2 PREDICT PERFORMANCE (INCLUDING YOUNG FUNDS)?

Some funds have tracking indexes that closely track them. Some funds do not. The latter are funds that do not have indexes that capture performance well. For example, Dividend Growth has an R^2 of only 59 percent. All of the other R^2s are at least 73 percent. Is there any relationship between the closeness of fit of the tracking index and outperformance? We see from Exhibit 12.7's graph of alpha versus R^2 that 8 out of 9 of the managed funds that most closely track their tracking index underperformed their tracking index, while 11 out of the 19 managed funds that more loosely track their tracking indexes outperformed their tracking index. The relationship is a weak one, especially because of the weak performance of the Dividend Growth Fund.

Exhibit 12.6 Tracking Indexes and Performance for the Young Funds (inception–June 2008 inclusive)

	Name	Ticker	Inception	500 Idx VFINX	Emerg x VEIEX	Europe Stk x VEURX	Ext Mkt x VEXMX	Growth x VIGRX	Mid Cap x VIMSX	Pacific Stk x VPACX	S Growth x VISGX	Small Cap x NAESX	S V x VISVX	Total Stk x VTSMX	Value x VIVAX	Large Cap x VLACX	R^2	PSE α	t_α	Risk of fund
1	FTSE Social x	VGTSX	6/00	63	0	0	14	24	0	0	0	0	0	0	0	0	97	−3.0	−2.7	1.12
2	U.S. Value	VUVLX	7/00	4	0	0	0	0	18	1	0	0	15	0	62	0	90	1.1	0.7	0.91
3	Capital Value	VCVLX	1/02	0	0	0	12	13	14	0	0	0	0	0	61	0	89	−4.1	−1.8	1.23
4	Diversified Equity	VDEQX	7/05	58	1	0	0	6	23	5	7	0	0	0	0	0	99	−2.0	−3.1	1.04
5	Structured L V IP	VSLVX	1/06	54	0	0	0	0	0	0	0	0	0	0	46	0	87	−8.7	−3.3	0.92
6	Structured L G IP	VSGPX	2/06	23	0	0	0	66	0	0	11	0	0	0	0	0	99	0.2	0.3	1.03
7	Dividend Apprec'n	VDAIX	5/06	79	0	0	0	0	0	0	0	0	0	0	21	0	91	1.2	0.5	0.83
8	Strategic S Equity	VSTCX	5/06	0	0	0	47	0	0	0	14	0	39	0	0	0	97	−2.4	−1.5	1.03
9	Struct'd L Equity I	VSLIX	6/06	82	0	5	0	0	0	0	0	0	7	0	6	0	100	−0.6	−1.5	1.02
10	Struct'd Broad Mkt I	VSBMX	12/06	0	0	0	5	29	7	0	8	0	0	0	50	2	93	−0.8	−2.2	1.00
	Average			36	0	1	8	14	6	1	4	0	6	0	25	0	94	−1.9	−1.5	−1.01
	t																	−2.2	−3.5	

Note: I = institutional. L = large cap. IP = institutional plus. IP funds have minimum investment of $5 million and expense ratios of between 0.14% and 0.14%. For each fund, the index shares sum to 100%.

I funds have minimum investment of $5 million and an expense ratio of 0.25%.

IP funds have minimum investment of between $20 million and $5 million and lower expense ratios of between 0.14% and 0.15%. IP expenses are lower: between 0.14% and 0.11%.

VLACX did not exist during the whole period, so it appears only in this table.

Inception is first complete month of operation.

R^2 is fit of fund to tracking index in %.

PSE is prowess of style and equity choice over whole period, measured as α (% pts/year).

Risk of fund is measured as SD of fund / SD of tracking index. Fund beats if < 1.

226

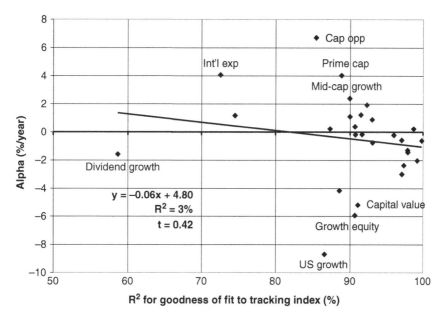

Exhibit 12.7   Does R^2 Predict Performance? Young Funds Included

The regression line crosses the R^2 axis at 82 percent. Thus, investors would have been well advised to buy index funds instead of managed funds that closely tracked them. However, managed funds whose performance is not well explained by a tracking index are more likely to beat the tracking index. Why? Perhaps only competent managers dare to deviate from the indexes. Perhaps risk-averse executives at Vanguard are willing to give fund managers their heads to deviate from the indexes only when they have a lot of confidence in the fund managers or the fund uses a style not captured by Vanguard's index funds, and this confidence turns out to be well placed. It could be argued that when we compare low-R^2 funds to their tracking indexes, we are making an apples-to-oranges comparison and should disregard these results, because there is no good tracking index. A more compelling argument is that it is still worthwhile to discover whether the markets colonized by such managed funds beat the closest available index basket.

IS THE PAST PROLOGUE? DID PAST PERFORMANCE PREDICT FUTURE PERFORMANCE?

It would make no sense to examine alphas for managed funds if alphas have no predictive power. To explore this, we look at Exhibit 12.8. This figure shows that there is a positive relationship between α_W in the first half and α_W in the second half. Each 1-percentage point increase in α_{W1} predicts a 0.23 percentage point increase in α_{W2}. The relationship is similar for the alternative way of calculating α depicted in Exhibit 12.9. Here α_{H1} predicts α_{H2}, with each 1 percentage point increase in α_1 predicting a 0. 19 percent increase in α_2. The R^2s are reasonably high, 41 percent and 26 percent respectively. Thus the α's did predict.

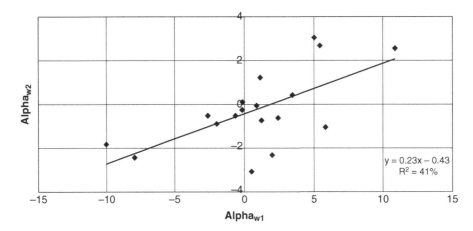

Exhibit 12.8 Predicting Alpha$_{W2}$ with Alpha$_{W1}$

Is this view supported by regressions using annual data? The time-series and cross-section data for the old funds are pooled to explain each fund's annual alpha as a function of the previous year's annual alpha:

$$\alpha_{AW,\,t} = +\,0.252\,\alpha_{AW,\,t-1} + 0.232 \quad (t = 3.41, \; P = 0.08\%) \tag{12.3}$$

where

$$R^2 = 6.8\%$$
$$\text{adjusted } R^2 = 6.2\%$$
$$\text{observations} = 162$$

$\quad\quad\quad\quad\quad$ F = significant at the 0.08% probability level
$\quad\quad\quad\quad\quad$ P = significance level on a two-tailed test

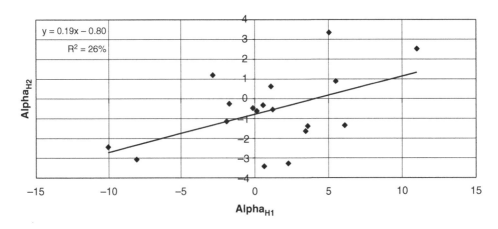

Exhibit 12.9 Predicting Alpha$_{H2}$ with Alpha$_{H1}$

Several regressions were also run on the same data with longer lags. One useful one is

$$\alpha_{AW, t} = +0.018\, \alpha_{AW, t-1} + 0.080\, \alpha_{AW, t-2} + 0.086\, \alpha_{AW, t-3} + 0.099\, \alpha_{AW, t-4} - 0.054$$

$$(12.4)$$

where

$$R^2 = 10.7\%$$
adjusted $R^2 = 7.2\%$
observations $= 108$
$F =$ significant at the 2% probability level

In equation 12.4, the coefficients of past alphas sum to 0.282.

Thus the figures and the regressions support the idea that alpha is predictable. The size and significance of the degree of predictability in equations 12.3 and 12.4 are high enough to make one wonder what mechanisms are at work.

DID A COMBINATION OF R^2 AND PAST ALPHA PREDICT PERFORMANCE?

Since R^2 and alpha independently predict performance, it is natural to ask whether the two combined predict performance. The answer is:

$$\alpha_{AW, t} = -0.107\, R^2 + 0.173\, \alpha_{AW\ t-1} + 8.03$$
$$[(\text{For}\ R^2, t = -1.5,\ P = 0.15)\ (\text{For}\ \alpha_{AW\ t-1}\ t = 1.2, P = 0.24)] \qquad (12.5)$$

where

$$R^2 = 21.4\%$$
adjusted $R^2 = 10.9\%$
observations $= 108$
$F =$ significant at the 16% probability level

Thus, both variables predict in the direction anticipated and have some predictive power.

This predictability might be due to autocorrelation in expense ratios, turnover, the share of assets held out of the stock market, stock-picking genius of managers, or persistent returns of the style of the mutual fund, not captured by the styles of the indexes. As examples of the last point, Vanguard has no international value index, international growth index, or international mid- or small-cap index. Bogle (2007) writes: "Fund investors are confident that they can easily select superior fund managers. They are wrong" (p. xvii). This regression is weak evidence that R^2 and past alpha predict future alpha.

DID MORNINGSTAR STARS PREDICT?

Morningstar rates the past performance of each mutual fund relative to other funds in the same style category, by granting it between one and five stars. Is there any

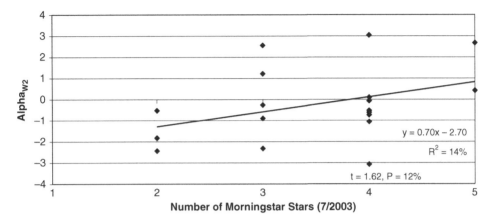

Exhibit 12.10 Predicting Performance with Morningstar Stars

relationship between the Morningstar stars and the alphas? Exhibit 12.10 shows the regression of α_{W2} (July 2003–June 2008) on the number of Morningstar stars as published in Morningstar (2003) and based on performance through June 2003. Each Morningstar star is found to be worth 0.70 percentage points per year of excess return. The R^2 is 14 percent. Thus the Morningstar stars in this case did predict the alphas.

DID DAN WIENER'S RATINGS PREDICT?

Each month Dan Wiener publishes an edition of *The Independent Advisor for Vanguard Investors*. In it he rates Vanguard mutual funds as sell, hold, or buy. What is the relationship between his recommendations and the alphas? Exhibit 12.11 explores this. On the horizontal axis is Wiener's July 2003 recommendation, constructed at the midpoint of our data. A sell is represented as –1, a hold is represented as 0, and a buy is represented as +1. On the vertical axis is α_{W2}. The graph shows that each unit increase in Wiener's recommendation represents a

Exhibit 12.11 Predicting Five-Year Performance with Dan Wiener's Ratings

1.63-percentage-point increase in α_{W2}, the second-half five-year performance. The R^2 is 44 percent. Variations on both the Morningstar and Wiener regressions were carried out with the stars or ratings associated with the tracking index added. The added variables were expected to have negative signs, because if the index funds were top performers, the managed funds they mimic would be more likely to have negative alphas. But in both cases they had the unexpected (positive) sign.

On the basis of R^2s, Wiener beat the Morningstar stars or past alphas in predicting performance of the Vanguard managed funds.

BEST PREDICTION EQUATION

To find the best predictor, a series of regressions were run to predict α_{W2}. The predictors used were α_{W1}, the number of Morningstar (2003) stars for the mutual fund, the number of Morningstar stars for the tracking index, Wiener's rating for the mutual fund, and Wiener's rating for the tracking index. The expected sign pattern is $(+, +, -, +, -)$. Variables with coefficients that had the "wrong" signs were successively eliminated. Those with the ts that had the highest absolute values were eliminated first.

This process of distillation generated

$$\alpha_{W2} = 1.06 \text{ DW Rating} + 0.133\ \alpha_{W1} \quad - 0.82$$
$$\text{(For DW Rating, } t = 1.91,\ P = 7.6\%)$$
$$\text{(For } \alpha_{W1},\ t = 1.63,\ P = 12\%) \tag{12.6}$$

where

$$R^2 = 52\%$$
$$\text{adjusted } R^2 = 46\%$$
$$\text{observations} = 18$$
F is significant at the 0.4% probability level

Thus, even in combination with the number of Morningstar (2003) stars and past performance, Dan Wiener's (2003) recommendation is still the most powerful predictor. We have considered only one observation period and one prediction period, so these qualitative results might not be repeated. The relationship between the prediction and the predictor is shown in Exhibit 12.12.

IS WIENER RIGHT THAT VANGUARD'S MANAGED FUNDS ARE BETTER THAN ITS INDEX FUNDS?

Wiener (2007), in the quote at the beginning of this chapter, denigrates the idea of investing in broad-based index funds. If Wiener is right that the big, famous index funds at Vanguard are particularly poor choices for investors, the managed funds that have big weights for the 500 index fund should outperform it. Lumping together all the managed funds (old and young alike) and excluding the FTSE Social Index Fund, we find that the managed funds underperform the tracking basket on average by 0.44 percent per year. For the funds that have at least a 58 percent weight on the S&P 500 Index Fund, the underperformance is 1.99 percent

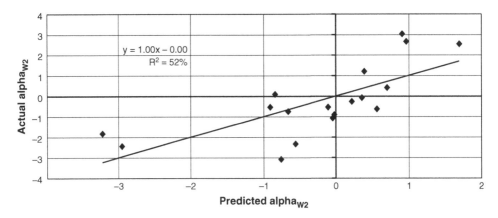

Exhibit 12.12 Predicting Second-Half Performance with Dan Wiener's Recommendation and First-Half Performance

per year. Thus, funds that track the S&P 500 closely considerably underperformed their tracking indexes, making Wiener's assertion suspect. Dan Wiener has written to me that this test is an unfair characterization of his recommendations. He writes that one must evaluate managed funds on a case-by-case basis. For example, his newsletter has consistently recommended against holding Growth Equity.

But Wiener's quote begs investigation of whether some patches of the equities market are better managed than indexed. Bogle (2002) asks whether managed funds beat the index for various styles. Let us ask the same question, using our model.

For the collection of old funds, alpha is regressed on all of the coefficients that determine the tracking index while the constant is suppressed. Exhibit 12.13

Exhibit 12.13 Which Index Styles Do Managed Funds Beat?

Index	Alpha Components	Standard Error	t Stat	P-Value
500 Index	−0.02	0.04	−0.35	0.73
Em Mkt Idx	0.34	0.59	0.57	0.59
Eur Stk Idx	−0.07	0.09	−0.81	0.45
ExtMktIdx	0.07	0.06	1.04	0.34
Gr Idx	−0.08	0.05	−1.73	0.14
Mid Cap Idx	0.18	0.22	0.83	0.44
Pac Stk Idx	−0.14	0.28	−0.15	0.89
SmCp Gr Idx	−0.29	0.28	−1.03	0.34
SmCp Idx	0.28	0.22	1.28	0.25
SmCp Vl Idx	0.03	0.10	0.26	0.80
Tot Stk	7.58	4.93	1.54	0.17
Val Idx	0.00	0.02	−0.15	0.89
Observations = 18. R square = 50%. Adjusted R square = −58%. F. Significance = 0.85%.				

The coefficients indicate the amount by which the managed funds do better than the indexes. Thus an index with a negative coefficient outperforms the managed fund that it mimics. No coefficients are significantly different from zero at the 10% level. The equation is not significant. So the conclusion is that we have not discovered a style where managed funds differ significantly from index funds.

presents the results. The regression coefficients are labeled the alpha components. Alpha for each managed fund is explained as the sum of the alpha components, each multiplied by the corresponding tracking coefficient from Exhibit 12.1. A positive alpha component for an index fund means that the parts of managed funds that are mimicked by that index fund outperform it. So, for example, a managed fund that is mimicked by an equal combination of the Vanguard 500 Index Fund and the Vanguard Small-Cap Index Fund is expected to outperform it by $(-02 + .28) / 2\% = 0.13\%$ per year.

None of the coefficients is significantly different from zero at the 10 percent level. And the equation itself is not significant. Thus we find no style where Vanguard managed funds differ from the funds that make up their tracking indexes.

The alpha component for the 500 Index Fund is slightly negative, so contrary to Wiener's conjecture, it outperforms the managed funds based on it. The four small-cap indexes (including the Extended Market Index) have three positive and one relatively large negative coefficient, so we cannot say that indexing works less well for small caps. Similarly, the international indexes have one positive and two negative signs. The large positive coefficient for the Total Stock Market Index reflects that it plays no role in any tracking index for any managed fund, except for a tiny role in Capital Opportunity, with its large alpha.

Both Bogle (2007) and Swensen (2005) advocate investing in broad-based indexes. Swensen refers to optimum indexing as the selection of index funds that are broadly enough based to minimize transaction costs and provide diversification. It is important to remember the proposition that if markets are efficient, investors should hold all equities in proportion to their market capitalization, which is another rationale for broad-based indexing. Bogle (2007) suggests owning just a few broad-based index funds and pithily summarizes (2009): "Owning the market remains the strategy of choice." William Bernstein, in personal correspondence, believes that a modest excess long-term return can be obtained by making small and infrequent adjustments in asset allocation opposite large changes in asset class valuation. From Exhibits 12.4 and 12.5, managed funds have underperformed their indexed counterparts over the last five out of seven years, whether one looks at average return differentials or median return differentials. Thus, while July 1998 through June 2001 supports Wiener's denigration of indexing in general, recent history does not bear out his view. Wiener responded (April 2009) to an earlier draft of this paper that his position is that "it may be that individual investors can choose active managers presciently."

Wiener's (2007) belief that offering index funds is more profitable than offering managed funds, quoted at the beginning of the chapter, recalls an analogous argument employed by Paul Krugman (1998). Krugman says that when he drives from Boston to New York and faces a headwind, he does not drive more slowly. He compensates by depressing the accelerator further and maintaining his speed. Likewise, he argues, imports from abroad do not cause unemployment. This economic headwind signals the Federal Reserve to sop up the incipient unemployment by depressing the interest rate accelerator, which stimulates investment and leaves employment where it was before. Similarly, when investors invest in a low-cost, low-turnover, broad-based Vanguard index fund, Vanguard is able to sop up the incipient profits by depressing the expense ratio it charges. That Vanguard is unusual in doing this is the thrust of many of John Bogle's speeches and much of his writing. Bogle (2003) also advocates laws that require mutual funds to be run in the interest of the investor and regulations that require mutual funds to present management fees and transaction costs more transparently, which would ensure that investors reap more of the benefits of potential cost savings throughout the industry.

It may be that individual investors can pick styles presciently. If so, that argues for slice-and-dice indexing combined with managed funds for parts of the market not covered by index funds rather than exclusive use of managed funds.

CONCLUSIONS

Did Vanguard's managed funds outperform their indexed counterparts?
Answer: Over the study's 10-year period, the average Vanguard managed fund outperformed at first and subsequently underperformed. Over the entire period, the average managed fund outperformed its index basket counterpart, but the median fund underperformed. When we include the more recently introduced funds, the average active managed fund underperformed.

Were the managers of Vanguard's active funds wise stock pickers and style jumpers?
Answer: Over the past 10 years, for closely tracked funds, no; and for loosely tracked funds, with large variability, yes.

Did the degree of outperformance of a managed mutual fund predict the degree of future outperformance?
Answer: Yes, to some degree.

Did the alphas for Vanguard's managed funds rise, fall, or stay the same?
Answer: Over our 10-year period, they have been falling. This reflects substantial outperformance during the height of the tech bubble and its deflation between July 1999 and June 2001.

Did the sell, hold, or buy recommendations of Dan Wiener's (2003) *FFSA Independent Guide to the Vanguard Funds* predict outperformance?
Answer: Yes, and they performed better than past performance or the number of Morningstar stars awarded to funds for past performance.

The study found that Vanguard's index and managed equity funds are comparable.

There seems to be little reason to build a portfolio solely out of one or the other if one wishes to overweight some style categories, especially since Vanguard's managed equity funds are able to overweight patches of the market not overweighted by its index funds. For example, there are no Vanguard international value, international growth, and international small index funds, although Vanguard's new Mid-Cap Growth Index and Mid-Cap Value Index funds and its brand new International Small-Cap Index Fund capture three more parts of the market for its index funds.

However, the study does find support for the finding of Barras, Scaillet, and Wermers (2008) that the advantage of managed funds has declined. In the first 3 years of our 10-year period, Vanguard's managed funds on average outperformed their tracking index fund basket. In the subsequent 7-year period, they underperformed. Similarly, in the first half, most of Vanguard's managed funds outperformed, and in the second half, most underperformed. Specifically, the average alpha in the first half was 0.86 percent per year; in the second half, it was –0.43 percent per year. In the first half, 27 out of 36 alphas were positive; in the second half, 11 out of 36 alphas were positive.

The study was completed at a bad time, because it misses all the volatility of late 2008 and early 2009. It will be fruitful to see whether the regularities found here continue to hold.

REFERENCES

Barras, L, O. Scaillet, and R. R. Wermers. 2008. *False Discoveries in Mutual Fund Performance: Measuring Luck in Estimated Alphas.* College Park, MD: University of Maryland, R. H. Smith Research Paper Series, 06-043.

Bodie Z., A. Kane, and A. J. Marcus. 2008. *Essentials of Investments.* New York: McGraw-Hill.

Bogle, J. C. 2002. "An Index Fund Fundamentalist," *Journal of Portfolio Management* 28: 3 (Spring): 31–38.

Bogle, J. C. 2003. Statement of John C. Bogle Before the U.S. House of Representatives, Sub-Committee on Capital Markets, Insurance and Government Sponsored Enterprises of the Committee on Financial Services. Washington, DC: GPO (June 18), http://financialservices.house.gov/media/pdf/061803jb.pdf.

Bogle, J. C. 2007. *The Little Book of Common Sense Investing.* Hoboken, NJ: John Wiley & Sons.

Bogle, J. C. 2009. "Six Lessons for Investors." *Wall Street Journal,* January 8, p. A15.

GMO. 2009. www.gmo.com.

Kizer, J. 2005. "Index Fundamentalism Revisited: Redux," *Journal of Portfolio Management* 31: 2 (Winter): 112–119.

Kritzman, M. P. 2002. *Puzzles of Finance.* Hoboken, NJ: John Wiley & Sons.

Krugman, P. 1998. *The Accidental Theorist and Other Dispatches from the Dismal Science.* New York: W. W. Norton.

"Marketview: The Long and Short of It," *Economist,* 2008, August 3, www.economist.com/finance/displaystory.cfm?story_id=11870287.

Merriman, P. 2006. Interview with John Bogle on Sound Investing, August 4, www.fund-advice.com.

Morningstar. 2003. *Morningstar Principia,* July (CD).

Morningstar. 2008. *Morningstar Principia,* July (CD).

Morningstar. 2009. Morningstar Instant X-Ray, http://portfolio.morningstar.com/NewPort/Free/InstantXRayDEntry.aspx?dt=0.7055475.

Reinker, K. S., and E. Tower. 2004. "Index Fundamentalism Revisited," *Journal of Portfolio Management* 13: 2 (Summer): 37–50.

Reinker, K. S., and E. Tower. 2005. "Are Vanguard's Managers Good Stock-Pickers or Style-Pickers?" *Journal of Portfolio Management* 30: 4 (Spring): 109–111.

Rodriguez, A., and E. Tower. 2008. "Do Vanguard's Managed Funds Beat Its Index Funds? Looking for Prescient Stock and Style Selection," *Journal of Indexes* 11: 2 (March/April): 26–35.

Sharpe, W. F. 1992. "Asset Allocation: Management Style and Performance Measurement," *Journal of Portfolio Management* 18: 2 (Winter): 7–19.

Swensen, D. 2005. *Unconventional Success: A Fundamental Approach to Personal Investment.* New York: Simon and Schuster.

Tower, E. 2008. "Are GMO's Predictions Prescient?" Working Paper, Duke University, Department of Economics, www.econ.duke.edu/Papers/PDF/GMO_Predictions1.pdf.

Tower, E., and C.-Y. Yang. 2008. "DFA versus Vanguard: Has DFA Outperformed Vanguard by Enough to Justify Its Advisor Fees?" *Journal of Investing* 17: 4 (Winter): 71–82.

Tower, E., and W. Zheng. 2008. "Ranking Mutual Fund Families: Minimum Expenses and Maximum Loads as Markers for Moral Turpitude," *International Review of Economics* 55: 4 (December): 315–350.

Wiener, D. 2003. *The Independent Advisor for Vanguard Investors* (July) Issues from 2006 on are archived at www.adviseronline.com.

Wiener, D. 2006. *2006 FFSA Independent Guide to the Vanguard Funds*. Potomac, MD: Fund Family Shareholder Association.

Wiener, D. 2007. *Action Plan for Vanguard Investors: A Publication of the Independent Advisor for Vanguard Investors*. Potomac, MD: Fund Family Shareholder Association.

ABOUT THE AUTHOR

Edward Tower has taught economics at Duke University since 1974. He received his Ph.D. in Economics from Harvard in 1971. He has held appointments at the Australian National University, the University of Auckland, Chulalongkorn University, the Fletcher School of Law and Diplomacy at Tufts University, the Helsinki School of Economics and Business Administration, Nanjing University, Simon Fraser University, and the University of Zagreb. He has also consulted on economic development problems with the World Bank, the U.S. Agency for International Development, and the Harvard Institute for International Development in Indonesia, Kenya, Malawi, Sudan, and Washington, D.C. He writes on financial, international, and development economics. He has served on 11 editorial boards, written or coauthored 3 books and monographs and 133 articles, and has compiled 115 books on the teaching of economics.

CHAPTER 13

Classic and Enhanced Index Funds
Performance and Issues

EDWARD TOWER, Ph.D.
Professor of Economics, Duke University
Visiting Professor, Chulalongkorn University

T his chapter discusses the construction of classic index funds and compares this approach with two applications of enhanced indexing. Fundamental indexation weights stocks in a portfolio by something other than market capitalization, such as dividends or earnings. Vanguard's index funds generally use classic indexing, which weights equity shares in a portfolio according to market capitalization. Dimensional Fund Advisors (DFA) uses a combination of classic and fundamental indexation, and WisdomTree (WT) uses fundamental indexation. Following the discussion, the chapter compares the performance of equity portfolios from the three companies, using a modified system of style analysis developed by Sharpe (1992).

With classic capitalization-weighted indexing, fluctuations in stock prices do not require the index fund to buy or sell stocks. This reduces transaction costs. But transaction costs are incurred as a stock migrates between styles indexed by different funds. For example, a stock may grow from mid cap to large cap. As its price falls or its fundamentals improve, it may migrate from growth to value. However, Vanguard manages index funds that colonize different styles, so as a stock migrates between styles, Vanguard ought to be able to move it between its index funds at low cost. The transaction costs should occur mainly as investors rebalance.

WT and some DFA funds use fundamental indexation. Arnott, Hsu, and West (2008) describe the fundamental index as a scheme in which the share of equities in a portfolio depends on fundamentals. WT uses fundamentals rather than capitalization weighting to devise its indexes. An investor can construct a portfolio out of these indexes.

DFA has two mechanisms to devise indexes. One is to determine what goes into each index using stock screens, such as the price-to-earnings ratio, or

Thanks go to Ben Branch, Mel Lindauer, Phil Steinmeyer, and Dan Wiener for their suggestions, but without implying their approval of the chapter.

price-to-book value, or the dividend yield. After screening, stocks are typically capitalization weighted. The second mechanism applies to the construction of DFA's core portfolios. Here the portfolio weights depend on fundamentals and capitalization rather than capitalization alone. Investors who wish to use simple strategies can construct portfolios out of these core index funds.

Asness (2006) asks whether the concept of fundamental indexing "is really new or just a cleverly repackaged version of the discipline known as value investing" (p. 95). He continues:

> *at current price I remain a fan of value indexing. . . . In addition, at the right investment management fee and given more information about the details, I am a fan of fundamentally constructed portfolios. But this is no more than I would say about any other form of value investing with the devil being in the details. (p. 99)*

This chapter tries to answer Asness's question by providing details. The chapter asks how the enhanced indexers, DFA and WisdomTree, perform relative to the portfolio of Vanguard classic index funds that has the same mix of styles.

VANGUARD

In 1976, Vanguard established the 500 Index Fund, which tracks the Standard & Poor's (S&P) 500 Index. Since then, it and other companies have established other index funds, such as Vanguard's Total Stock Market Index Fund, which tracks a broader range of U.S. stocks and also a range of index funds that colonize different parts of the market. The approach of these index funds is to track indexes that comprise stocks with certain characteristics, such as domestic, foreign, or a particular sector; or stocks in a particular category, such as large cap, mid cap, or small cap; or stocks with a value, blend, or growth orientation. In each of these indexes, the stocks are then weighted in proportion to their capitalization.

Recently, Vanguard has introduced the High Dividend Yield Index Fund and the Dividend Appreciation Index Fund. The former is based on the FTSE High Dividend Yield Index. According to FTSE (2009), it attaches "lower weightings to companies that have high yields because of low or falling share prices."

As discussed in Mergent (2006), the "DividendAppreciation Index Fund will track the performance of the Dividend Achievers Select Index,[TM] an index created exclusively for Vanguard by Mergent." It uses "a modified capitalization weighting methodology" and "additional proprietary methodology." Almost all Vanguard's index funds are capitalization weighted with a transparent methodology. In these two cases, however, the distinction is blurred. Thus even Vanguard weights some of its indexes partially on fundamentals.

DIMENSIONAL FUND ADVISORS

DFA's home page, www.dfa.com, is an information-rich and easy-to-use guide to DFA strategy and funds. The page provides the material for much of this chapter's description of DFA. The firm initially constructed stock indexes designed to take advantage of research that showed the better performance of small-cap stocks. DFA constructs indexes strongly based on academic research. A number of academic leaders, including E. F. Fama, K. R. French, R. G. Ibbotson, R. C. Merton, and M. S. Scholes, continue to work with the firm. DFA believes that the higher returns for small-cap and value stocks compensate for risk rather than market imperfections, and it weights its indexes toward these characteristics. DFA measures value by the ratio of book value to market price (BtM).

DFA's Feeder and Master Funds

DFA has two different structures for its funds: the feeder and master structure and the core structure. For example, the Global Equity Portfolio, like DFA's other feeder portfolios, is a fund of funds. The portfolio is made up of master funds that hold individual securities. Master funds use a screen to pick the eligible patch of the market from which they select stocks. In some cases, funds of funds purchase other funds of funds. The master fund uses a market capitalization weighting system or some other method of diversification.

DFA's Core Portfolios

The Core Equity Portfolios, which are described in DFA (2009), invest directly in stocks. The quotations in this and the next two DFA sections are drawn from those descriptions.

> The applied core strategies alter the weighting of stocks by considering both a company's market cap and its book-to-market (BtM) ratio. As a result, exposure to the riskier small and value shares that research shows offer higher expected return is increased. To balance out the greater small and value exposure and still include every stock in the market, the weight of large cap and growth stocks is reduced. . . .
>
> In assessing growth and value, the fund may consider additional factors such as price-to-cash-flow or price-to-earnings ratios as well as economic conditions and developments in the issuer's industry. . . .
>
> Often when using traditional index funds in a portfolio, overlapping areas and gaps can occur, since attempts to achieve diversification and risk factor exposure result in redundant or inefficient allocations. . . .
>
> Core Equity maintains factor exposure without redundancy via an integrated structure and broad diversification. Each security is held once, efficiently weighted.

Thus, DFA's Core Portfolios use a multidimensional fundamental weighting scheme in the sense that the weight attached to each stock in a Core Portfolio depends on its market cap as well as the extent to which it is a value stock. The weight is proportional to market cap with that proportion an increasing function of smallness and value.

DFA: Other Aspects

> A "buffer" range allows small-cap strategies to hold securities that grow out of the buy range, in order to minimize transaction costs and keep portfolio turnover low.

DFA uses larger buffer ranges than classic index funds generally do. This allows funds to hold more securities that have grown out of their buy range in order to minimize turnover and transaction costs.

Additional screening criteria are employed to eliminate securities that do not display the common qualities of the asset class or that lack sufficient liquidity for cost-effective trading, such as OTC stocks with fewer than four market makers and those not included on the Nasdaq Global Market System. . . .

Each portfolio is authorized to lend securities to qualified brokers, dealers, banks and other financial institutions for the purpose of earning added income.

Thus, any outperformance of DFA may not be due just to its indexing techniques.

In emerging markets, Dimensional also applies subject requirements, including fair treatment of foreign investors, well developed property rights and a commitment to free markets.

Excluded are Argentina (from new purchases), Peru, the former Soviet Union, and all of Africa except for South Africa. Consequently, DFA's emerging market universe differs from Vanguard's, which holds both Russian and Egyptian equities. DFA's Global Portfolios target risk factors that have historically delivered increased return, including financial strength.

In summary, DFA practices enhanced indexation by using some indexation based on multidimensional fundamentals and also using a more extensive screening system than classical indexing does.

WISDOMTREE'S APPROACH TO FUNDAMENTAL INDEXATION

Arnott et al. (2008) present the logic behind fundamental indexation, and the WisdomTree Web site, www.wisdomtree.com/home.asp, explains how fundamental indexation has been implemented by WT. This section briefly summarizes some of the material drawn from the Web site. WT believes that weighting the share of equities in a portfolio by indicators such as dividends and earnings, not stock price alone, generates portfolios with higher returns and less risk.

Here are some examples. The WisdomTree LargeCap Growth Fund weights growth stocks by earnings. Companies in the index on which it is based must have cumulative positive earnings in the prior four fiscal quarters and pass WisdomTree's market capitalization and liquidity requirements. The WisdomTree LargeCap Dividend Index is made up of the 300 largest companies by market capitalization, weighted by the share of dividends each component company is projected to pay in the coming year. The WisdomTree Equity Income Index consists of the 30 percent of companies that have the highest dividend yield, and it weights by actual dividends paid. WisdomTree structures its funds in the form of exchange traded funds (ETFs), unlike DFA, which issues ordinary mutual funds. Full descriptions are provided on the Web site.

Most of the WT funds have been established recently, so to assess what their performance would have been historically, one needs to evaluate the monthly performance data for the indexes on which they are based, on the WT Web site, and then subtract the gap by which WT funds are expected to underperform the indexes.

SOME EVALUATIONS OF FUNDAMENTAL INDEXATION

The case for DFA is elegantly presented in Hebner (2007), and the case for WT is thoroughly presented in Arnott et al. (2008). Several authors have criticized the fundamental approach, and others have evaluated the performance. In response to Siegel's (2006) apology for fundamental indexation, Bogle and Malkiel (2006) argue that fundamental indexing is unlikely to be as productive as classic indexing, because of reversion to the mean. They show that from 1937 to 1997 and from 1997 to 2006, value and growth returns have been virtually identical. They also note the less favorable tax consequences, higher transaction costs, and higher expenses of owning fundamental stock index funds.

Blitz and Swinkels (2008) argue that

> *because fundamental indices are primarily designed for simplicity and appeal, they are unlikely to be the most efficient way of benefiting from the value premium. Compared to more sophisticated, multi-factor quantitative strategies, fundamental indexation is likely to be an even more inferior proposition. (p. 1)*

This argument suggests that DFA is superior to WT.

Tower and Yang (2008) used data for the eight-year period from the beginning of 1999 through the end of 2006. They found that the DFA portfolio of domestic funds, with asset weights adjusted each month, beat the style-adjusted portfolio of Vanguard domestic funds by 2.61 percent per year continuously compounded. The corresponding differential for the international funds was 3.59 percent per year. This chapter updates those estimates by using data through the first half of 2008 and uses daily data rather than monthly data.

Bernstein (2006) uses data from 1962 through 2004 to assess the performance, corrected for style, of the composite Research Affiliates Fundamental Index (RAFI) used in Arnott et al. (2008). He finds the combination of the Fama-French Large Value Index and Large Growth indexes (French, 2009) that has the same value load as the RAFI would have underperformed the RAFI by 0.14 percent per year. Thus, the style-adjusted outperformance of the RAFI index is 0.14 percent per year. He concludes:

> *Fundamental indexing is a promising technique, but its advantage over more conventional cap-weighted value-oriented schemes, to the extent that it exists at all, is relatively small.... Differences in the expenses, fees, and transactional costs incurred in the design and execution of real-world portfolios can easily overwhelm the relatively small marginal benefits of any one value-oriented approach.*

This chapter examines the performance of a range of fundamentally weighted indexes and funds that WT has created based on them.

Arnott et al. (2008, p. 208), using data from 1962 through June 2007, find the stock selection component of the outperformance of the RAFI U.S. Large index over the S&P 500 index is 0.26 percent per year. This is after adjusting for size, value, and sector exposure, so it is the contribution of fundamental indexation per se, and is close to the Bernstein figure.

Estrada (2008), using data from 1974 to 2005 inclusive, finds that a dividend-weighted fundamental index using benchmarks from 16 countries outperforms a cap-weighted index by 1.90 percent per year, and that is outperformed by 1.70 percent per year by a strategy of weighting the same country benchmarks by dividend yield, a strategy with an even more pronounced value tilt. This totals to an advantage of fundamental weighting using dividend yield over cap weighting of 3.6 percent per year.

Branch and Cai (2008) find that a cash flow–weighted index beat a sales-weighted index, and a gross profit margin–weighted index beat value weighting. They find a dividend-weighted index had a still higher return, but it was accompanied by higher risk.

STYLE ANALYSIS TO COMPARE VANGUARD AND DFA

In order to assess the choice between passive and enhanced indexation, this chapter asks two questions.

1. Which is better, Vanguard or DFA?
2. Which is better, Vanguard or WisdomTree?

We use two ways to answer each question: a comparison with a tracking index that holds Vanguard index funds in long positions only and one that is permitted to hold some of the funds in short positions, abbreviated as " LONG" and "SHORT." This section explains the LONG simulations. This chapter uses a technique called "style analysis," developed by Sharpe (1992), to explore whether a mutual fund outreturns a basket of indexes with the same style. Chapter 12, which explores the choice between Vanguard index and managed funds, also uses Sharpe's style analysis. One difference from the Sharpe analysis is that the Chapter 12 and 13 comparisons of mutual fund performance are with Vanguard index funds rather than with the indexes used by Sharpe. Using this technique, the return of the DFA fund or portfolio of funds is described as the return of a basket of Vanguard index funds plus a constant term plus a random term. Confusingly, DFA (2009) refers to its funds as "portfolios." The size and sign of the constant term reflects the prowess of DFA's indexing technique relative to Vanguard's. The basket chosen is that which gives the lowest mean square sum of the random terms. Intuitively, it is the basket that tracks the return of the DFA portfolio the best. Specifically, in combination with the constant term that helps the fit the most, it is the basket that predicts most accurately.

This basket is labeled the tracking index for the portfolio. If the DFA portfolio is largely composed of stocks in Vanguard's value and small index funds, then the composition of the tracking index will be largely Vanguard's value and small index funds, because the returns of a combination of these funds will best explain the returns of the DFA portfolio. Thus, the composition of the DFA portfolio can be inferred by examining the composition of the tracking index. The size of the constant term will depend positively on Vanguard's expenses and turnover relative to DFA's and positively on DFA's prowess of stock selection relative to Vanguard's. One appeal of Sharpe's (1992) methodology is that if different degrees of smallness size or valueness have different patterns of return, the Sharpe methodology captures those; simply characterizing the value or size dimension of a portfolio by one number, as Fama-French (1993) loads do, does not capture these different patterns of return. For example, return may be a nonlinear function of size and value. In such cases, characterizing fund performance as a function of Fama-French loads may hide information that emerges from a Sharpe style-analysis approach.

The calculation is performed using Microsoft Excel's solver utility, just as is done in Chapter 12.[1] Solver is instructed to find the weighted sum of the returns of the Vanguard indexes and the constant term that minimizes the mean square error of prediction, subject to the constraints that all the coefficients are positive and add to 1. Requiring all coefficients to be positive means conceptually that no index funds are sold short. Requiring the coefficients to add to 1 means conceptually that the portfolio shares sum to 1.

The figures used in the calculations for DFA are daily returns of both the DFA funds and the Vanguard index funds. These returns are provided in the Center for Research in Securities Prices (CRSP) database. Since daily returns are used, the DFA return is being compared with the return of a Vanguard tracking basket that is rebalanced daily. Such rebalancing would be impossible without incurring transaction cost. Still, the analysis uses daily rather than monthly data to find the tracking index that most closely tracks the DFA portfolio over short periods as well as longer ones. Assuming daily rebalancing is unlikely to introduce a bias, because both the DFA fund and the tracking fund are similarly affected by it. For example, if positive momentum exists in equity returns, frequent rebalancing should boost the performance of both Vanguard and DFA funds by the same amount, leaving no bias in the calculation of the differential return between the two.

The criterion used for outperformance of the DFA portfolio is the geometric alpha, just as in Chapter 12. This criterion is the continuously compounded geometric return of the DFA portfolio minus that of the Vanguard tracking index over the time span. Geometric average returns measure the average return over a span of time, but arithmetic average returns do not. If two funds have the same average return over the time span, the more volatile fund will have a higher average arithmetic return, but by definition the two funds will have the same geometric return. Also, if one believes that anomalous returns in one direction are likely to be followed by anomalous returns in the other direction, so average geometric returns are more likely to be replicated than average arithmetic returns, the geometric average return is superior to the arithmetic average return for predicting multiperiod returns. This argument is more fully developed with a numerical example in Chapter 12.

---

[1]The Excel program used in Chapters 12 and 13 is available from the author at tower@econ.duke.edu. Readers can use it to ask other questions as new statistics become available.

Continuous compounding in measuring average returns is also likely to generate a more stable alpha. If the only reason an alpha is negative is that the expense ratio is higher for DFA than for Vanguard, then if we use differential annual rates of return to measure alpha, alpha will be less negative in falling markets than in rising markets, because of the confusion of compounding. When markets are rising, a small difference in alpha will result in a large difference in return over the year. But, with continuous compounding, constant expense ratios will lead to constant alphas.

Recent Performance of DFA Funds

The methodology of style analysis just described is applied in Exhibit 13.1. It is used in this section to assess the recent performance of DFA domestic funds relative to Vanguard funds. The data series of returns on Vanguard index funds and DFA enhanced index funds start on November 17, 2006, the inception date for Vanguard's High Dividend Yield Index Fund. Including that fund is important, because dividend yield is a measure of value, and it is desirable to have a comparison of enhanced indexing with full range of Vanguard's current index funds. The data series finish on June 30, 2008, the most recent date available for daily returns on the CRSP database, so the period is extremely short. A more recent close date could have been chosen if we were to use the daily return data on Yahoo. But Yahoo's reporting of dividends for some funds is irregular. Yahoo does not always alert the user to missing dividend data, and Yahoo sometimes reports dividends as being paid on the wrong date. DFA does post monthly returns of its funds with almost no lag, but daily data provide more information and lead to more trustworthy tracking indexes. The study focuses on diversified equity funds, ignoring tax managed funds, real estate funds, social funds, and sustainability funds.

For now, let us focus on the top line for each fund. It presents the results of the calculations just described, which constrain the tracking index to contain no Vanguard funds short. "Max short" is the maximum percent of the tracking index that can be held short, so it equals zero for these simulations. Alpha is the outperformance of the DFA fund in percentage points per year (henceforth, simply % per year): DFVEX, DFA's U.S. Vector Equity I Portfolio, underperforms its tracking index by 1.87 percent per year. Alpha's t value is –1.52. The P tells us that alpha is significant on a one-tailed test at the 5.7 percent level. The mean square error of the daily predictions is 0.09 percent. The ratio of the standard deviation of the DFA fund to that of the tracking index is V, which stands for relative volatility. It is 0.998, which means that the DFA fund was slightly less volatile. The correlation squared between the DFA daily return and the tracking index return is 99.4 percent. The interpretation of P is that if the sample of daily returns is selected randomly from an infinitely large population of returns, P is the probability that the signs of the means of the population and the sample differ, or simply that the calculated alpha has the wrong sign. P and the t that supports it are calculated by the t test (paired sample for means) using Excel.

Two funds were added to the DFA collection after the start of the series on November 17, 2006, a social fund and a sustainability fund. These two funds are ignored throughout the chapter. The alpha for the equally weighted portfolio

Exhibit 13.1 Performance of DFA's Domestic Funds (November 17, 2006–June 30, 2008)

	Ticker Name	Max Short	α %	t	P %	mse %	V	R^2 %	Short %
1	DFVEX US Vector	0	−1.87	−1.52	5.7	0.09	0.998	99.4	0
	Equity I	200	−1.52	−1.31	7.4	0.09	0.997	99.4	116
2	DFQTX US Core	0	−1.21	−1.36	8.7	0.07	0.997	99.6	0
	Equity 2 I	200	−1.06	−1.21	11.4	0.07	0.996	99.6	42
3	DFEOX US Core	0	−0.81	−1.20	11.6	0.05	0.995	99.8	0
	Equity 1 I	200	−0.80	−1.19	11.7	0.05	0.996	99.8	31
4	DFSCX US Micro	0	−6.50	−2.22	1.3	0.23	0.998	96.6	0
	Cap I	200	−6.50	−2.95	0.2	0.18	0.999	98.1	200
5	DFFVX US Targeted	0	−3.28	−1.87	3.1	0.14	0.994	98.8	0
	Value I	200	−2.88	−1.68	4.7	0.14	0.996	98.8	163
6	DFELX Enhanced US	0	−0.97	−0.39	34.9	0.2	0.996	96.7	0
	Large Co	200	−0.86	−0.35	36.3	0.19	1.006	96.7	43
7	DFLCX US Large Co	0	−0.03	−0.21	41.9	0.01	0.999	100.0	0
		200	0.02	0.17	43.2	0.01	1.000	100.0	6
8	DFSVX US Small	0	−4.23	−1.66	4.9	0.2	1.049	97.9	0
	Cap Value	200	−3.53	−1.61	5.4	0.17	1.007	98.3	200
9	DFLVX US Large	0	−1.35	−0.49	31.4	0.22	1.045	96.6	0
	Cap Value I	200	−0.53	−0.20	42.1	0.21	1.015	96.9	154
10	DFSTX US Small Cap	0	−3.73	−1.77	3.9	0.17	1.019	98.3	0
		200	−3.33	−2.17	1.5	0.12	1.005	99.1	200
11	DFCVX US Large	0	−1.26	−0.46	32.4	0.22	1.046	96.7	0
	Cap Value II	200	−0.34	−0.13	44.9	0.21	1.014	97.0	153
12	DFUVX US Large	0	−1.16	−0.42	33.9	0.22	1.046	96.6	0
	Cap Value III	200	−0.24	−0.09	46.4	0.21	1.015	96.9	136
13	DFUSX US Large Co.	0	0.14	0.30	38.1	0.04	1.000	99.9	0
	Inst. Index	200	0.17	0.38	35.2	0.04	1.000	99.9	152
14	DFBMX DFA US	0	−1.47	−0.53	29.7	0.22	1.045	96.7	0
	High Book-to-Market	200	−0.64	−0.24	40.4	0.21	1.014	96.9	139
15	Equally weighted	0	−1.80	−1.70	4.5	0.08	1.002	99.5	0
	portfolio of all 14 funds	200	−1.40	−1.34	9.0	0.08	0.998	99.5	81
16	Average of 14 funds	0	−1.98	−0.98	20.1	0.15	1.016	98.1	0
		200	−1.57	−0.90	23.6	0.14	1.004	98.4	124

The 14 funds are those DFA funds that have existed for the whole period since Vanguard's High Yield Dividend Index Fund has been extant (11/17/2006). Throughout the chapter, alpha is expressed as percentage points/year, P is the significance level on a one-tailed test (%). It is the probability that the true alpha has a different sign from that calculated. Mse is the mean standard error between the return of the fund and the tracking index augmented by the constant term (%). V is relative volatility of the DFA fund. It is the standard deviation of the DFA fund divided by that of the tracking index. R is the correlation between monthly return of the mutual fund and the tracking index (%). Max short is the maximum % of the tracking index that is permitted to be short, and Short is the percent of the tracking index that is short.

is −1.80 percent per year, with a P of 4.5 percent. So in this instance, DFA has underperformed Vanguard.

Tracking Portfolio with Long and Short Positions in Tracking Index

Now let us focus on the second line for each fund. DFA focuses on both small funds and value funds. Suppose that all of Vanguard's index funds are less oriented toward value and smallness than a particular DFA fund or DFA portfolio. If so, the way to replicate DFA's style in a comparison portfolio is to construct a Vanguard portfolio that holds some of Vanguard's growth and large-company indexes short. To implement this, Excel is instructed that the sum of the index components must be 1, as before, except Excel is no longer instructed to make all coefficients in the tracking portfolio nonnegative. To limit the magnitude of short selling for any one fund, the short value of any Vanguard index fund in the tracking index is restricted not to exceed 100 percent of the portfolio's value. This is implemented by constraining the coefficient for each fund to be no less than −1. Furthermore, the aggregate short position, "max short," is restricted not to exceed 200 percent of the portfolio. This is implemented by constraining the minimum sum of the negative coefficients to be no less than −2. The advent of exchange traded funds has made short sales possible, so this approach has a relevance that did not exist prior to the introduction of ETFs. In the tables and figures we label the tracking portfolio with all positive quantities the LONG portfolio and the one described in this paragraph the SHORT portfolio.

There is another way to think about this approach. Suppose I hold a wide variety of Vanguard index funds. I can replicate its style by buying a DFA fund and selling the SHORT tracking index. So, for example, if my SHORT tracking index is 150 percent Vanguard Small-Cap Index Fund and −50 percent Vanguard 500 Index Fund, and I buy $100 of the DFA portfolio, I would replicate my initial position by simultaneously selling $150 of the Vanguard Small-Cap and buying $50 of the Vanguard 500 Index Fund.

In Exhibit 13.1, let us revisit fund #1, DFVEX, the fund considered previously. When we allow a short position of 200 percent, the actual aggregate short position is 116 percent. The alpha is −1.52 percent per year. P is 7.4 percent. The mean square error falls (as it must with additional degrees of freedom) to 0.09 percent per day (although table rounding hides the fall). Only two funds have any positive alphas, and the equally weighted portfolio has alphas of −1.80 percent per year and −1.40 percent per year. The method of calculation means that these alphas do not reflect the differential performance of different styles, unless the DFA style is not replicated in the tracking index. Rather, the alphas reflect the differential performance of DFA relative to Vanguard after correcting for style. For the equally weighted portfolio, the SHORT alpha is closer to zero than the LONG alpha. The lower absolute value for the SHORT alpha is expected, since the SHORT alpha has more freedom to approximate the style of the DFA portfolio. Throughout the chapter, the SHORT alpha is generally closer to zero. The difference between the two alphas is smaller for the equally weighted DFA portfolio (0.40 percent) than for the individual funds on average (0.41 percent). The individual funds exhibit

Exhibit 13.2 Tracking Indexes for DFA Equal-Weight Domestic Portfolios

Vanguard Index Funds Inception Date	Whole Period 9/98−6/08		11/17/2006 to 6/30/2008	
	Long	Short	Long	Short
VFINX 500	0	13	34	86
VEXMX Extended Market	0	−4	3	17
VTXMX Total Stock Market	0	−19	2	39
VIVAX Value	46	46	14	−8
VIGRX Growth	8	10	0	−31
NAESX Small-Cap	12	19	28	17
VISVX Small-Cap Value	27	24	16	15
VISGX Small-Cap Growth	2	2	0	−2
VIMSX Mid-Cap	5	8	0	4
VLACX Large-Cap 2/2/2004		non-	0	−23
VDAIX Dividend Appreciation 4/28/2006		existent	0	1
VMVIX Mid-Cap Value 8/25/2007		for	3	0
VMGIX Mid-Cap Growth 8/25/2006		part of	0	−5
VHDYX High Dividend Yield 11/17/2006		period	0	−12
% short	0	23	0	81
α % pts/year	1.05	0.96	−1.80	1.40

Dates are inception of funds. Nondated funds existed for the entire period.

more extreme styles than the equally weighted portfolio does, so the sign of the difference is expected, but the smallness of the difference is a surprise.

Exhibit 13.2 tells the rest of the story of the simulations. The right-hand columns show the tracking indexes for the LONG and SHORT portfolios. For example, the LONG portfolio includes 34 percent of the Vanguard 500 Index Fund and 28% percent the Vanguard Small-Cap Index Fund. The SHORT portfolios involve selling short both the Vanguard Growth Index Fund and the Vanguard Large-Cap Index Fund. Given DFA's focus on small and value styles, this is expected.

Exhibit 13.3 graphs the LONG alphas versus the SHORT alphas for the funds and time periods of Exhibit 13.1. All but two of the points are in the northeast or southwest quadrants on a line through the origin that is at least as steep as the principal diagonal. This indicates, again, that the alphas for the SHORT portfolios are closer to zero than those of the LONG portfolios.

The predominately negative alphas show that for this recent 19.5-month period DFA domestic funds were inferior to the corresponding Vanguard ones. Thus DFA has not always beaten Vanguard.

The middle columns of Exhibit 13.2 show the tracking indexes for the entire period covered by CRSP: September 1, 1998, to June 30, 2008. The next section discusses these simulations.

Domestic DFA over the Entire CRSP Horizon

Exhibit 13.4 shows the performance of the DFA equal-weight domestic portfolio over the period covered by CRSP.

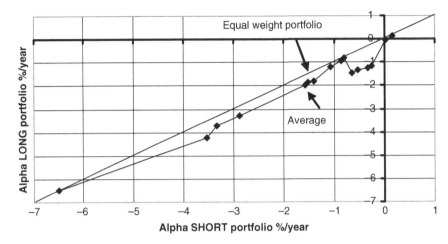

Exhibit 13.3 Alphas for DFA Domestic Mutual Funds (November 17, 2006–June 30, 2008)

It presents the alphas calculated for individual years and parts of years, allowing the tracking index to vary from year to year and recognizing that simulations for recent years have more Vanguard index funds to choose from in selecting the tracking index. Using daily data instead of monthly data allows us to have more faith in the alphas calculated for short periods. The data include for 1998 only the last third of the year and for 2008 only the first half. The alphas average +1.15 percent per year for the LONG tracking index and +1.12 percent

Exhibit 13.4 Performance of the DFA Equal-Weight Domestic Portfolio
(September 1, 1998–June 30, 2008)

	Long					Short					Short %
	α	t	P	mse	R^2	α	t	P	mse	R^2	
9/1998–6/2008	1.05	1.08	14.05	0.19	97	0.96	0.99	16.09	0.19	97	23
2008	−0.72	−2.25	1.26	0.09	100	−0.40	−2.25	1.26	0.09	100	158
2007	−2.92	−2.25	1.26	0.08	99	−2.50	−2.00	2.33	0.08	99	100
2006	2.21	0.69	24.66	0.20	94	1.74	1.60	5.51	0.07	99	48
2005	0.77	0.59	27.79	0.08	99	1.33	1.05	14.70	0.08	99	200
2004	1.33	0.88	18.89	0.09	99	1.15	0.81	21.01	0.09	99	200
2003	2.83	1.73	4.28	0.10	99	2.69	1.66	4.92	0.10	99	74
2002	3.18	1.10	13.59	0.18	99	2.92	1.03	15.26	0.18	99	125
2001	8.24	1.99	2.37	0.26	96	6.07	1.57	5.89	0.24	96	187
2000	−3.38	−0.75	22.83	0.28	95	−2.26	−0.51	30.53	0.28	95	93
1999	2.37	0.66	25.53	0.22	93	2.86	0.82	20.74	0.22	93	196
1998	−8.94	−1.55	6.19	0.21	98	−8.22	−1.55	6.19	0.21	98	26
Annual Average	0.45	0.08	13.51	0.16	97	0.49	0.20	11.67	0.15	98	128

1998 data are for last third of year. 2008 data are for first half of year, so average is weighted.

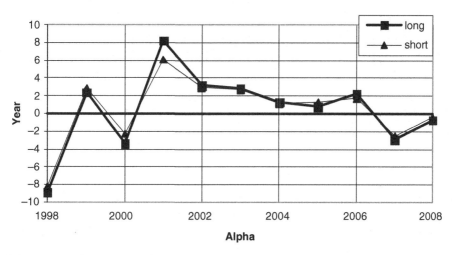

Exhibit 13.5 Alpha for Equal-Weight DFA Domestic Portfolio

per year for the SHORT (with smaller weights for the two partial years). These alphas are remarkably similar. Using the same tracking index throughout the entire period, the alphas are 1.05 percent and 0.96 percent for LONG and SHORT. According to these simulations, and if returns continue to be drawn from the same population, Vanguard will beat DFA with a probability of 14.05 percent and 16.09 percent for LONG and SHORT, respectively (see Exhibit 13.5.).

Exhibit 13.5 graphs the annual alphas for the DFA equally weighted domestic portfolio, both LONG and SHORT. Again the short alphas tend to be closer to zero, and DFA has not done well relative to Vanguard over 2007 and the first half of 2008, with extraordinarily good performance of DFA occurring in 2001 and extraordinarily bad performance occurring in the last quarter of 1998. In these periods, DFA did not closely track its tracking index (see Exhibit 13.6.).

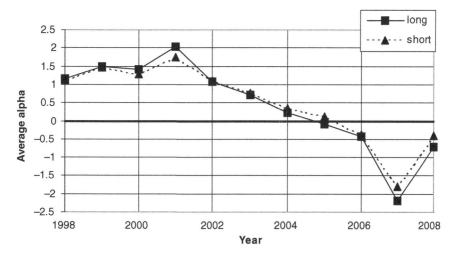

Exhibit 13.6 Average Alpha for Equal-Weight DFA Domestic Portfolio

Exhibit 13.6 graphs the average performance of the DFA equally weighted portfolio from the year indicated through the middle of 2008. DFA has roughly the same performance as Vanguard from January 2005 to the middle of 2008, and outperforms only if one goes back to a start date before 2005.

International DFA over the Entire CRSP Horizon

Exhibit 13.7 shows the tracking index for the equally weighted DFA international funds.

The tracking index is made up solely of Vanguard's international funds. Vanguard has no international small or value or growth index funds. So the international tracking index includes Vanguard funds that are not truly index funds: International Explorer (a small- and mid-cap fund), International Growth, and International Value. However, as John Bogle (2006) has argued, Vanguard's managed funds mimic Vanguard's index funds in the sense of having low expenses and turnover. Moreover, the issue is whether investors should forsake Vanguard's international funds for DFA's international funds. Both the LONG and SHORT tracking indexes have large positive weights for International Explorer and International Value, which is expected.

Exhibit 13.8 presents the performance differentials for the equally weighted portfolio of 18 international funds. Only those funds with an inception date of 2008 are left out on purpose, and the LWAS/DFA International High Book-to-Market Fund was left out inadvertently. The funds are listed on the DFA Web site. The alphas using a constant tracking index are 0.84 percent and 0.29 percent per year for LONG and SHORT, respectively. The average alphas, allowing the tracking indexes to vary annually (with smaller weights for the two partial years), are larger: 2.08 percent and 1.59 percent per year for LONG and SHORT, respectively. It is a puzzle why the latter two exceed the former two, just as was the case for the domestic funds, although the P's are relatively big, which means that the tracking indexes hover less closely around the DFA international portfolio than around the DFA domestic one.

Exhibits 13.9 and 13.10 do the same thing that Exhibits 13.5 and 13.6 do, but they apply it to the DFA equally weighted international portfolio. Again the SHORT alphas are closer to zero than the LONG alphas. Over the entire period, the international DFA portfolio with the tracking index changed each year outperforms

Exhibit 13.7 Tracking Indexes for DFA Equal-Weight International Portfolio for the Entire Period (September 1998–June 2008)

Vanguard Index Fund	Long	Short
VTRIX International Value	35	53
VINEX International Explorer	43	46
VEIEX Emerging Mkt Stock	14	14
VPACX Pacific	8	4
VWIGX International Growth	0	−8
VEURX European Stock	0	−9
Sum	100	100

Exhibit 13.8   Performance of the DFA Equal-Weight International Portfolio

| | Long | | | | | Short | | | | | short |
	α	t	P	mse	R^2	α	t	P	mse	R^2	%
9/1998– 6/2008	0.84	0.46	32.4	0.37	84	0.29	0.16	43.5	0.36	92	17
2008	0.08	0.01	49.4	0.23	97	0.22	0.04	48.3	0.23	99	11
2007	5.14	1.03	15.2	0.31	92	5.09	1.03	15.3	0.31	96	22
2006	0.24	0.06	47.4	0.24	94	0.00	0.00	50.0	0.24	97	26
2005	−1.79	−0.44	33.1	0.26	81	−1.83	−0.45	32.8	0.26	90	7
2004	1.21	0.25	40.3	0.31	84	−0.71	−0.15	44.0	0.30	92	6
2003	0.43	0.11	45.5	0.25	87	0.48	0.12	45.1	0.24	93	12
2002	10.37	1.34	9.1	0.49	66	10.03	1.32	9.4	0.47	82	8
2001	13.24	2.26	1.2	0.37	89	11.90	2.07	2.0	0.36	94	16
2000	0.38	0.07	47.2	0.35	82	−0.32	−0.06	47.5	0.33	91	21
1999	−9.55	−1.92	2.8	0.32	80	−9.62	−1.94	2.7	0.32	89	2
1998	1.85	0.22	41.4	0.31	91	1.95	0.23	40.9	0.31	95	4
Annual Average	1.87	0.29	30.41	0.32	86	1.46	0.20	31.78	0.31	93	13

1998 data are for last third of year. 2008 data are for first half of year.

by more than the domestic DFA fund. But using the constant tracking indexes the ranking is reversed.

DFA's Core Portfolios

DFA has constructed core portfolios that combine stocks based on fundamentals into portfolios for investors who want a simple solution to asset allocation.

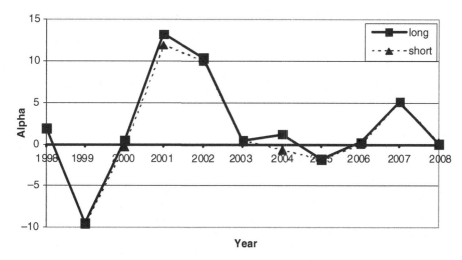

Exhibit 13.9   Alpha for Equal-Weight DFA International Portfolio

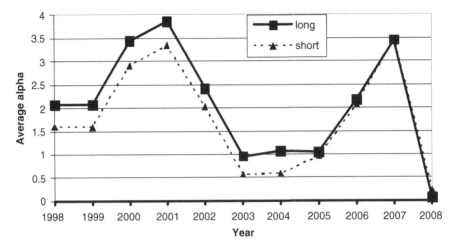

Exhibit 13.10   Average Alpha for Equal-Weight DFA International Portfolio

Investors can combine the core portfolios to create their entire portfolios. Exhibit 13.11 evaluates the DFA core portfolios and the DFA global equity fund, which is constructed on the same principle. These are all the core funds established before August 2006. Recently, Social Core Equity portfolios and Sustainability Core portfolios have been established, which include only those companies that pass social or environmental screens.

Exhibit 13.11   Performance of DFA's Diversified Portfolios since Inception

	Ticker Name Inception	Max Short	α	t	P	mse	V	R^2	Short
1	DFVEX US Vector	0	−0.63	−0.63	27	0.100	1.00	99.2	0
	Equity 1/3/2006	200	−0.07	−0.08	47	0.098	1.00	99.2	64
2	DFQTX US Core	0	−0.60	−0.93	18	0.068	1.00	99.5	0
	Equity 2I 9/16/2005	200	−0.49	0.81	21	0.067	1.00	99.6	36
3.	DFQTX US Core	0	−0.56	−1.10	14	0.054	0.99	99.7	0
	Equity 1I 9/16/2005	200	−0.56	−1.10	14	0.054	0.99	99.7	13
4	DFIEX International	0	−0.51	−0.19	42	0.003	0.97	92.3	0
	Core Equity 9/16/2005	200	−0.45	−0.17	43	0.003	0.97	92.2	9
5	DGEIX Global	0	0.22	0.31	38	0.095	1.00	98.8	0
	Equity I 2/26/2003	200	0.17	0.24	40	0.094	1.00	98.8	16
6	DFCEX Emerging Mkts Core Equity 4/8/2005	0	−1.96	−0.76	22	0.003	0.94	95.0	0

For fund # 6 Vanguard Emg Mkts Stock Idx Fund is the tracking index, so no short simulation exists. For US funds, tracking index is Vanguard US index funds. For International Core Equity, it is Vanguard international except emerging markets. For Global, it is all Vanguard funds with domestic share constrained to lie between the historical limits of the fund reported by Morningstar: 46.6% and 70.5%.

Exhibit 13.11 presents alphas and accompanying data for the extent to which these funds outperform their Vanguard tracking indexes. For the U.S. core funds, tracking indexes of Vanguard U.S. equity index funds are used. For the international core, the five Vanguard international funds are used, excluding Vanguard's Emerging Markets Stock Index Fund. For the Emerging Markets Core, just the Vanguard Emerging Markets Stock Index Fund is used. For the DFA Global Equity Portfolio, all Vanguard index funds, including the three international funds that are not index funds, are used. In devising the tracking index, the share of the U.S. funds is constrained to lie within the historical range of the portfolio reported by Morningstar (2008), which is between 46.6 and 70.5 percent. It is notable for understanding DFA's strategy that DFA has chosen to vary the share of domestic assets in its Global Equity Portfolio so substantially.

The results are that only the DFA Global Equity Portfolio has a positive alpha. The alphas in Exhibit 13.11 for DFA's six diversified funds, five of which are core funds, range from +0.22 percent per year to –1.96 percent per year. This makes DFA look inferior to Vanguard, especially since an investor must incur additional transaction costs and adviser fees to invest with DFA. However, the significance levels are huge. The probabilities that the sign of the population alpha differs from the sign of the sample alpha in all of the simulations of Exhibit 13.11 lie between 47 and 14 percent.

Additional DFA Costs

DFA funds may be purchased only through an adviser. Tower and Yang (2008) explored adviser fees and transaction costs for DFA funds, which are not levied on investors in Vanguard funds. However, some Vanguard international funds have charges on purchases and sales that are paid into the funds; we have not dealt with them here. Tower and Yang estimate that an investor with DFA and a $10 million portfolio would pay an additional 0.0156 to 0.504 percent per year to invest with DFA and that an investor with a $100,000 portfolio could pay as little as 1.665 percent per year additional. Part of these figures should be subtracted from the performance of DFA, to obtain comparability. Smaller proportions should be subtracted to the extent that the adviser provides valuable services, in addition to access to DFA funds; and larger proportions should be subtracted if the comparison is with the less expensive Vanguard Admiral funds, which require larger investments than Vanguard Investor funds do. For example, the expense ratio of the Admiral shares of the Vanguard 500 Index Fund is 0.09 percent per year lower than that of the investor shares, used in this chapter.

DFA Summary

The SHORT alphas are closer to zero than the LONG ones, which implies that the capture of style is better with the SHORT simulations than with the LONG ones. The constant-weight tracking index simulations have alphas closer to zero than the varying-weight ones. Focusing on the SHORT constant tracking indexes since the fourth quarter of 1998 for the equal-weight domestic portfolio, DFA beats Vanguard by 0.96 percent per year, with a P of 16 percent (top line of Exhibit 13.4). For the international portfolio, the corresponding figure is 0.29 percent per year with a P of 44 percent (top line of Exhibit 13.8). The large Ps indicate limited confidence that the sign of the differential will be replicated in the future. Focusing on the SHORT variable tracking indexes, the figures are 1.12 percent for the domestic portfolio (bottom line of Exhibit 13.4) and 1.15 percent for the international (bottom line of Exhibit 13.8). However, the DFA domestic portfolio has underperformed since the beginning of 2006. Strikingly, none of the core portfolios or the global portfolio has outperformed Vanguard by more than 0.22 percent per year (Exhibit 13.11). The median alpha for these portfolios is –0.51 percent per year (Exhibit 13.11). For net returns, one must subtract from these figures the transaction costs and adviser fees associated with DFA. However, these funds have been established recently, so the observation period is short. Perhaps the appropriate lesson is that we are unable to rank with confidence the two fund companies and hence the approaches to indexation they provide. Perhaps this is what we should have expected. Some advisers use both Vanguard and DFA funds. This should happen only if the two are comparable.

How Do These Alphas Differ from Tower and Yang Alphas?

The alphas estimated here are considerably less than those of Tower and Yang (2008). Comparing the constant tracking indexes, the Tower-Yang alpha for domestic funds is 2.61 percent per year as compared with the LONG and SHORT tracking indexes of 1.05 and 0.96 percent per year, respectively. For the international funds, the alpha falls from Tower and Yang's 3.59 percent per year to the LONG and SHORT alphas of 0.84 and 0.29 percent per year, respectively. The differences in approach from the previous study are that the current study (1) includes the last third of 1998 in addition to 2007 through the first half of 2008, (2) equally weights the DFA funds rather than weighting them by assets under management, and (3) uses daily rather than monthly observations.

WISDOMTREE VERSUS VANGUARD: WHICH IS BETTER?

The WisdomTree Web Site, www.wisdomtree.com, presents monthly return data for each WT fund and the index on which it is based. The starting dates for these data are January 1964 for the domestic dividend indexes; April 1990 for the Large Cap Growth Index; January 1996 for India, emerging markets, Global, and international indexes; March 2002 for domestic earnings; and June 2005 for the Middle East Dividend Index. The funds themselves were created between June 2006 and July 2008. CRSP data for WT funds are currently unavailable after December 2007, and, as mentioned, Yahoo's data on dividends are unreliable. Consequently data from WT are used to assess the performance of each WT fund and index. Only monthly data are available, so the analysis compares WisdomTree with Vanguard funds, with both rebalanced monthly.

Vanguard's High Dividend Yield Index Fund was established in November 2006. In order to include it in the performance comparison, we perform the Sharpe style comparison analysis already described, using data from December 2006 to November 2008 inclusive. This analysis is described in Exhibit 13.12. The tracking indexes for WT's domestic funds are calculated from Vanguard's domestic index funds, and the tracking indexes for WT's international funds are calculated from Vanguard's international funds.

Exhibit 13.12 Performance of Individual WisdomTree Indexes (December 2006–November 2008 inclusive)

	Ticker for Fund and Fund Name	α Index Long	α Index Short	Gap	Derived α Fund Long	Derived α Fund Short
1	EXT Total Earnings	0.97	2.30	0.37	0.60	1.93
2	EPS Earnings 500	1.34	2.60	0.55	0.79	2.05
3	EZM MidCap Earnings	1.63	2.98	−0.36	1.99	3.34
4	EES SmallCap Earnings	−4.44	−6.55	−0.67	−3.77	−5.89
5	EEZ Earnings Top 100	−3.08	4.96	0.51	−3.59	4.45
6	EZY Low P/E	−2.77	5.70	0.44	−3.21	5.26
	Domestic earnings average	**−1.06**	**2.00**	**0.14**	**−1.20**	**1.86**
	Domestic earnings median	**−0.90**	**2.79**	**0.40**	**−1.30**	**2.70**
7	DTD Total Dividend	−0.72	1.67	1.01	−1.73	0.66
8	DLN LargeCap Dividend	−0.48	2.10	0.56	−1.05	1.54
9	DON MidCap Dividend	−1.46	1.17	−0.32	−1.13	1.49
10	DES SmallCap Dividend	−3.24	−2.05	0.02	−3.26	−2.07
11	DHS Equity Income	−6.73	0.28	0.69	−7.42	−0.41
12	DTN Dividend Top 100	−1.76	4.12	0.72	−2.49	3.39
	Domestic dividend average	**−2.40**	**1.21**	**0.45**	**−2.85**	**0.77**
	Domestic dividend median	**−1.61**	**1.42**	**0.63**	**−2.11**	**1.07**
13	DOL International LargeCap Dividend	2.86	2.06	0.29	2.57	1.76
14	DIM International MidCap Dividend	2.47	2.38	−0.59	3.06	2.97
15	DLS Intl SmallCap Dividend	−0.09	1.91	0.00	−0.09	1.91
16	DOO Intl Dividend Top 100	−0.80	−0.68	−0.28	−0.52	−0.40
17	DEB Europe Total Dividend	1.51	1.44	1.34	0.16	0.10
18	DFE Europe SmallCap Dividend	−9.91	−6.99	0.70	−10.61	−7.70
19	DEW Europe Equity Income	−1.47	−2.26	1.30	−2.78	−3.57
20	DND Pacific ex-Japan Total Dividend	6.03	5.83	0.66	5.37	5.17
21	DNH Pacific ex-Japan Equity Income	2.64	4.07	0.96	1.68	3.11
22	DXJ Japan Total Dividend	2.64	4.07	−0.47	3.11	4.54
23	DNL Japan Equity Income	8.35	10.69	−0.14	8.49	10.83
24	DFJ Japan SmallCap Dividend	5.61	9.56	−0.15	5.77	9.72
25	EPI India Earnings Fund	1.64	−2.00	0.62	1.02	−2.62
26	DWM DEFA Index	2.29	2.04	2.33	−0.04	−0.28
27	DTH DEFA Equity Income	1.53	0.71	1.08	0.44	−0.37
28	DEM Emerging Markets Equity Income	6.29	6.55	0.51	5.78	6.04
29	DGS Emerging Markets SmallCap Div	6.29	6.55	0.30	5.99	6.26
	International average	**2.23**	**2.70**	**0.50**	**1.73**	**2.20**
	International median	**2.47**	**2.06**	**0.51**	**1.68**	**1.91**
30	IGHIXGlobal High Yielding Equity	−0.27	−0.08			
31	ROI Large Cap Growth	2.96	2.84			
32	GULF Middle East	19.01	10.97			

Index refers to the index on which each WT fund is based. Gap is the underperformance of the ETF below the index on which it is based over the year ending 9/31/2008. It is calculated as the return of the index minus the return of the ETF that is based on it. All figures are % per year. Returns are continuously compounded. Start date is chosen so Vanguard's High Dividend Yield Index Fund can be included in the comparison set. LONG refers to the tracking index that holds no short Vanguard positions. SHORT is the tracking index that can hold up to 200% of the Vanguard portfolio short.

Conclude: Average and median alphas, both LONG and SHORT for the international funds are positive, indicating that they outperformed the corresponding Vanguard tracking indexes. Average and median alphas LONG are negative for the domestic earnings and dividend funds, but the corresponding SHORT ones are positive. Thus international funds outperformed their Vanguard counterparts. The domestic funds underperformed their LONG Vanguard tracking indexes, but outperformed their SHORT Vanguard tracking indexes.

There are six domestic funds and indexes based on weighting earnings and six domestic funds and indexes based on weighting dividends. The construction of these alphas has already been described. The averages and medians for these indexes have negative alphas using the LONG portfolios and positive alphas using the SHORT portfolios. For the WT indexes, the SHORT average and median alphas are over 3 percent per year greater than the LONG ones. As argued earlier, the SHORT alphas do a better job of eliminating style differences.

There are 17 international funds (including emerging markets) that have been in existence for at least a year. Their average and median alphas for both LONG and SHORT range between 2 percent and 3 percent.

What explains a negative alpha for the comparison of WT with the LONG tracking index and a positive one for the comparison with the SHORT tracking index? One possibility is that the WT fund is more value oriented than the Vanguard value fund, so to make the Vanguard tracking index equally value oriented, you would need to sell Vanguard growth short and buy more of the value fund with the proceeds. Now, if the Vanguard growth fund has a higher return than the Vanguard value fund, then selling it short would have been a bad idea that resulted in a higher alpha for the comparison of WT to the SHORT tracking index.

The return of each WT fund differs from the return of the index on which it is based by management fees and costs. To find out how large they are, the return of each WT fund is subtracted from the return of the corresponding WT index over the year ending September 31, 2008, provided by WT. This difference is labeled Gap (% per year). Returns are continuously compounded in this calculation as throughout the chapter.

The WT funds are ETFs. The returns of the ETFs (market returns) differ from the returns on the assets that they hold (net asset value returns), because the arbitrage that keeps the two prices in line is not perfect. The calculations of gap use net asset value (NAV) returns.

For the domestic funds, the expense ratios are 0.28 percent and 0.38 percent. For the international ones, they range from 0.48 percent to 0.88 percent. Gap was expected to be bigger than these figures by the transaction costs. Some of the gaps are negative, reflecting differences between the composition of the indexes and the composition of the funds, perhaps reflecting large buffer ranges designed to keep transaction costs low. For each group, the median gap is larger than the average gap. The alpha for each fund is derived as the alpha for the corresponding index minus the gap. The average and median fund alphas have the same signs as the corresponding index alphas.

The relevant comparison group for Vanguard with WT is the set of WT funds, not the indexes, but since alphas are initially calculated for the indexes, we need to subtract gap. To mitigate the influence of outliers, we focus on median rather than average gaps. The median gaps vary between 0.40 and 0.63 percent. In our comparisons of Vanguard and WT funds, we use a gap of 0.60, at the high end of the range, so if anything this comparison is biased against WT, although using Vanguard's Investor shares rather than its Admiral shares biases the calculations against Vanguard for investors with large portfolios.

Exhibit 13.13 calculates alphas for WT's world portfolios over the period March 2002 to November 2008 inclusive. The start date is constrained by the start date of the series for the domestic earnings index. Calculations are presented both for the

Exhibit 13.13 Performance of WisdomTree World Portfolio Indexes (March 2002–November 2008 inclusive)

Performance % per Year	Asset Weighted		Equal Weighted	
	Long	Short	Long	Short
a % per year	3.55	3.38	3.16	2.78
t for index	3.05	3.86	3.01	3.73
P for index	0.15	0.01	0.17	0.02
mean square error % per mo	0.85	0.64	0.77	0.54
R(fund, track indx, %)	98	99	99	99
α 2008	0.17	−1.74	−0.35	−1.81
α 2007	4.46	5.35	3.36	3.85
α 2006	4.26	3.46	3.61	2.96
α 2005	−1.14	0.53	−0.70	0.38
α 2004	3.38	2.96	3.29	2.69
α 2003	4.11	5.63	2.74	4.47
α 2002	10.49	7.76	11.25	7.26
volatility ratio	0.97	1.01	0.96	1.01
t for fund: gap of 0.6%	2.54	3.17	2.44	2.92
P for fund: gap of 0.6%	0.66	0.11	0.84	0.22
Tracking Index %				
VFINX	6.48	111.31	13.97	110.82
NAESX	0.00	−59.82	0.00	−64.31
VEXMX	0.00	32.83	0.00	41.14
VIGRX	0.00	−58.29	0.00	−63.59
VI VAX	19.31	−43.52	13.90	−44.13
VTSMX	0.00	16.12	0.00	15.64
VIMSX	0.00	−14.72	0.00	−4.57
VISGX	0.00	7.58	0.00	8.51
VISVX	7.43	41.76	15.13	43.50
VEIEX	9.08	19.70	5.66	15.97
VEURX	22.46	29.79	15.42	25.95
VINEX	15.43	20.75	15.61	16.76
VPACX	19.81	15.70	20.32	15.73
VTRIX	0.00	−19.17	0.00	−17.41
VWIGX	0.00	−4.48	0.00	−5.98
short part of portfolio %	0.00	−200	0.00	−200

The alphas for the funds are the alphas for the WT indexes minus the gap from Exhibit 13.12. The volatility ratio is the standard deviation of daily returns of the WisdomTree fund/that of the Tracking index basket. The asset weights are those for 9/31/2008 from the WT Web site.

Conclude: All whole-period alphas are positive and exceed Exhibit 13.12's gap. Average alphas are positive for the last two years. As expected, the alphas for the asset-weight portfolio, using recent weights, exceed those for the equal-weight portfolio.

asset-weighted WT portfolio and the equally weighted WT portfolio, where the asset weights are drawn from the WT Web site and dated September 31, 2008.

Since assets in funds that have done relatively well grow relatively fast due to both valuation and the attraction of additional investor funds, it is expected that asset-weighted performance using recent weights will exceed that using earlier weights and consequently overestimate the returns that a typical investor would have received. This effect should operate on both the WT portfolio and its tracking index, mitigating its effect in determining alpha. To assess this possible bias and to test the robustness of the calculations, Exhibit 13.13 presents calculations both for the asset-weighted and the equally weighted WT world portfolios, using all the indexes from Exhibit 13.12, except GULF with an inception date of July 2008.

In constructing the tracking indexes, we constrain the share of Vanguard domestic index funds to be the same as the share of the WT domestic index funds in the portfolio (43 percent for equally weighted and 33 percent for asset weighted).

As expected, the asset-weighted alphas exceed the equally weighted alphas. The alphas range from 2.78 to 3.55 percent per year. The probability that the sign is incorrect is less than 0.2 percent in each case. As before, the SHORT alphas are closer to zero than the LONG alphas, indicating that the short simulations have captured style better than the long ones.

The alphas for each year are calculated using the tracking-index weights calculated for the entire period, because there are not enough degrees of freedom to do otherwise. The volatility ratio is the standard deviation of monthly return of the WT portfolio divided by that of the Vanguard tracking index. The LONG comparison shows WT to be slightly less risky, but the SHORT comparison shows it to be slightly more risky. Using a gap of 0.6 percent to determine alphas for the WT fund portfolios, the alphas range from 2.18 to 2.95 percent, with Ps always less than 0.9 percent.

What happens when the performance of WT is broken down into categories? Exhibit 13.14 does this. Again, the SHORT alphas are closer to zero than the LONG alphas, except for domestic growth. The composition of the tracking index shows a bias toward value except for domestic growth, which, predictably, has a growth bias. Using our gap of 0.6 percent and focusing on fund SHORT performance, WT earnings under returns Vanguard by a tiny .07 percent per year, with a P value of 47 percent. Domestic growth underperforms Vanguard by 0.23 percent per year, with a P of 46 percent. Domestic dividends outperform Vanguard by 0.78 percent per year. International outperforms Vanguard by a remarkable 3.61 percent, with a tiny P of 0.29 percent.

Exhibit 13.15 performs the same analysis for the recent period December 2006 to November 2008, which permits use of all Vanguard funds. Naturally, the results are similar to those in Exhibit 13.12, which calculated alphas for WT's individual indexes and funds. The SHORT portfolios have alphas averaging 0.2 percent per year closer to zero. Recent inception dates force use of the WT indexes rather than the funds. The alphas of all the fund SHORT portfolios (.6% less than the index portfolio alphas) are positive and exceed 1.2 percent per year. Paradoxically, R^2, the correlation squared between the returns of the WT portfolios and the tracking indexes, does not rise as we move from LONG to SHORT for domestic growth and international dividend. This is possible because the algorithm minimizes mean square error and does not maximize R^2.

Phil Steinmeyer has suggested to me that there is an issue of data snooping bias in using the WT indexes prior to inception of the WT funds. "Presumably, when the folks behind WT were setting things up prior to the inception of their funds, they performed similar backtests" for many different rules, and "the success

Exhibit 13.14 Performance of WisdomTree Equal-Weight Portfolios

Performance %/year	Domestic Earnings		Domestic Dividends		Domestic Growth		International Dividend		Average
	Long	Short	Long	Short	Long	Short	Long	Short	
	3/2002–11/2008				1/1999–11/2008				
α % per year	1.08	0.53	2.16	1.38	0.35	0.37	4.80	4.21	1.86
t for α	1.00	0.63	1.02	0.83	0.15	0.17	1.86	1.75	0.93
Prob t>T (one tailed test %)	16.12	26.57	15.60	20.29	43.97	43.23	3.28	4.15	21.65
mean square error %/mo	0.80	0.61	1.89	1.46	2.05	1.94	1.25	1.15	1.39
R(fund,track indx, %)	98.6	99.0	95.4	95.9	91.6	91.7	96.5	96.7	95.7
α 2008	−2.80	−2.90	0.74	−2.95	−1.72	−1.74	0.95	−5.80	−2.03
α 2007	1.59	2.45	−1.58	1.68	5.62	7.14	1.80	1.15	2.48
α 2006	0.35	−0.70	−0.31	−1.67	2.79	2.51	4.18	6.06	1.65
α 2005	0.95	1.22	−2.28	−0.69	2.35	1.98	−1.52	−0.69	0.16
α 2004	0.11	−0.42	0.50	−0.62	3.61	3.06	7.11	8.63	2.75
α 2003	−0.03	0.94	−1.93	1.81	−3.41	−2.91	5.26	7.69	0.93
α 2002	8.29	3.27	13.80	10.34	8.23	5.61	13.55	10.70	9.22
α 2001			15.41	8.04	−5.68	−3.51	12.82	8.33	5.90
α 2000			11.26	1.81	−12.28	−12.18	8.47	8.72	0.83
α 1999			−14.12	−4.32	3.78	3.54	−4.92	−3.51	−3.26
volatility ratio	0.95	0.99	0.89	0.88	1.07	1.04	0.95	1.04	0.83
α for fund	0.48	−0.07	1.56	0.78	−0.25	−0.23	4.20	3.61	1.26
t for fund: gap of 0.6%	0.44	−0.09	0.78	0.53	−0.11	−0.11	3.04	2.81	0.91
P for fund: gap of 0.6%	33	−47	22	30	−46	−46	0.15	0.29	−6.60
Tracking Index %									
VFINX	0	0	0	−41	0	54	0	0	2
NAESX	0	−88	0	−16	0	−66	0	0	−21
VEXMX	0	22	0	−74	16	82	0	0	6
VIGRX	0	−85	0	−65	58	67	0	0	−3
VIVAX	34	−27	71	5	6	17	0	0	13
VTSMX	9	180	0	217	0	−100	0	0	38
VIMSX	24	14	0	19	9	−7	0	0	7
VISGX	0	27	0	−4	0	11	0	0	4
VISVX	32	56	29	59	11	41	0	0	29
VEIEX	0	0	0	0	0	0	1	0	1
VEURX	0	0	0	0	0	0	9	11	3
VINEX	0	0	0	0	0	0	10	9	2
VPACX	0	0	0	0	0	0	19	15	4
VTRIX	0	0	0	0	0	0	61	55	15
VWIGX	0	0	0	0	0	0	0	−12	−2
short part of portfolio %	0	200	0	200	0	173	0	−200	

Conclude: All whole-period alphas are positive. For the last three years, average alphas averages are negative for domestic earnings and dividends; the averages are positive for other funds.

Exhibit 13.15 Performance of Equal-Weight WisdomTree Index Portfolios with New Vanguard Indexes (December 2006–November 2008 inclusive)

	Domestic Earnings		Domestic Dividends		Domestic Growth		International Dividend	
	Long	Short	Long	Short	Long	Short	Long	Short
Performance								
α per year	−0.85	1.96	−2.69	1.81	2.95	2.90	3.42	2.43
t for α	−0.62	2.10	−0.96	1.41	1.33	1.69	1.78	1.34
P	27.15	2.35	17.39	8.53	9.75	5.25	4.40	9.65
mean square error %/mo	0.53	0.37	1.07	0.49	0.85	0.67	0.75	0.71
R(WT fund,track indx, %)	99.50	99.80	97.90	99.60	98.90	91.20	99.30	97.00
volatility ratio	1.02	1.00	1.05	1.01	0.99	0.98	0.99	1.01
Tracking Index								
VFINX	0	4	0	−17	13	−66	0	0
NAESX	54	86	0	−27	0	0	0	0
VEXMX	0	−98	0	68	0	−48	0	0
VIGRX	0	0	0	45	8	44	0	0
VIVAX	0	−62	0	4	0	49	0	0
VTSMX	31	11	0	−1	0	73	0	0
VIMSX	0	0	0	−7	0	42	0	0
VISGX	0	−25	0	−65	0	16	0	0
VISVX	15	31	41	54	0	−17	0	0
VLACX	0	−16	0	0	29	72	0	0
VDAIX	0	7	0	−79	6	0	0	0
VMGIX	0	0	0	−6	45	−12	0	0
VMVIX	0	0	0	10	0	3	0	0
VHDYX	0	0	59	120	0	−58	0	0
VEIEX	0	0	0	0	0	0	0	1
VEURX	0	0	0	0	0	0	5	−3
VINEX	0	0	0	0	0	0	27	29
VPACX	0	0	0	0	0	0	0	−13
VTRIX	0	0	0	0	0	0	68	87
VWIGX	0	0	0	0	0	0	0	−4
short part of portfolio	0	150	0	200	0	200	0	21

Conclude: For domestic dividend and earnings long portfolios, alphas are negative.
For all others, alphas are positive.

of those backtests probably helped lead to WT's formation. They may not have fine tuned their methodology using backtests, but even if they did not, I doubt that they would have started WT had their brainstorm (fundamental indexation) turned out, upon backtesting, to produce little or no benefit." Thus the post-inception tests are better tests for they are free of data snooping bias.

Exhibits 13.16 and 13.17 assess WT performance for various asset categories through time, based on Exhibit 13.14. Exhibit 13.16 presents the average alphas for

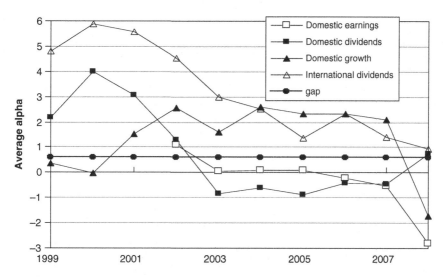

Exhibit 13.16 WisdomTree Average Alphas Long

the LONG simulations. Exhibit 13.17 presents the average alphas for the SHORT simulations. These averages are from the beginning of data in each year through November 2008. They adjust the average returns to recognize that our 2008 data are only 11 months and that for WT domestic earnings, the data start only in March 2002. We include a marker for the level of the gap (0.6 percent). Index average alphas are the levels indicated on the chart. Fund average alphas are the difference

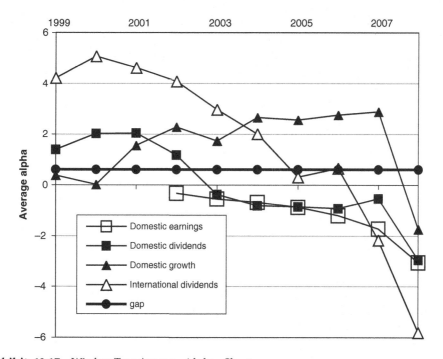

Exhibit 13.17 WisdomTree Average Alphas Short

between the height of the chart and the level of gap. Over the entire period, the WT domestic growth fund underperformed Vanguard in both simulations and domestic earnings underperformed in the SHORT simulation. All the others outperformed. Exhibits 13.16 and 13.17 show the LONG and SHORT simulations respectively. They both show that from the beginning of 2003 through November 2008, two WT fund portfolios underperformed and two outperformed. The two figures also show, from the beginning of 1999 through November 2008, that one WT portfolio underperformed and two outperformed.

WisdomTree Summary

It may be frustrating for the reader that the analysis shows that we cannot confidently rank Vanguard relative to WisdomTree. However, as argued in the context of Vanguard versus DFA, in a competitive market, we would expect that both firms exist precisely because there is no clear-cut preference for one or the other. One cannot conclude that WT beats Vanguard or the opposite. All one can say is that, over a particular period, one firm beat the other for a particular simulation and for a particular asset class.

Some conclusions that do emerge are:

- Exhibits 13.16 and 13.17 tell that except for domestic growth, WT's advantage through mid-2008 has been declining since the beginning of 1999. Barras, Scaillet, and Wermers (2008) find "a significant proportion of skilled (positive alpha) funds prior to 1996, but almost none by 2006." The negatively sloped curves in Exhibits 13.16 and 13.17 could indicate that this downward trend applies to the screens and weighting used by WT as well.
- For periods up to November 2008 and reaching back to 2003 and before, the outperformance of the WT international portfolio is striking and greater than the outperformance of the other portfolios. This is one reason why the launch of Vanguard's international small-cap ETF on April 6, 2009 is welcome.

CONCLUSIONS

Roughly 10 years of historical performance have been examined. Conflicting evidence makes it impossible to rank the three companies with confidence. Different DFA and WisdomTree portfolios perform differently with respect to their Vanguard counterparts, and the differential performance depends on the period over which they are evaluated. The chapter provides two tools, the LONG and SHORT simulations using tracking indexes, to help investors develop informed predictions and decisions. This analysis, by correcting for style, illuminates the role of the way different firms construct portfolios more brightly than just comparing the performance of individual funds.

Analyses like this, which appropriately correct for style, may be useful to encourage fund families to keep costs low and to use efficient screens to colonize productive parts of the equity universe. Perhaps the uncertainty was to be expected. In a competitive market with sophisticated investors or sophisticated advisers, the coexistence of several players is explained by the inability to rank their performance conclusively.

REFERENCES

Arnott, R. D., J. C. Hsu, and J. M. West. 2008. *The Fundamental Index: A Better Way to Invest.* New York: John Wiley & Sons.

Asness, C. 2006. "The Value of Fundamental Indexing," *Institutional Investor* 40: 10 (October): 95–99.

Barras, L., O. Scaillet, and R. R. Wermers. 2008. *False Discoveries in Mutual Fund Performance: Measuring Luck in Estimated Alphas.* College Park: University of Maryland, Smith School Research Paper Series, RHS 06-043.

Bernstein, W. J. 2006. "Fundamental Indexing and the Three-Factor Model," *Efficient Frontier: An Online Journal of Practical Asset Allocation*, www.efficientfrontier.com/ref/Oadhoc/fi.htm.

Blitz, D., and L. Swinkels. 2008. *Fundamental Indexation: An Active Value Strategy in Disguise.* Rotterdam, NL: Robeco Asset Management. SSRN: http://ssrn.com/abstract=1184848.

Bogle, J. C. 2006. Interview with Paul Merriman on Sound Investing, August 4, www.fundadvice.com.

Bogle, J. C., and B. G. Malkiel. 2006. "Turn On a Paradigm," *Wall Street Journal*, June 27, p. A14.

Branch, B., and L. Cai. 2008. "Fundamental Indexing." Working Paper: University of Massachusetts, Amherst, School of Management.

DFA Capital Management. 2009. www.dfa.com.

Estrada, J. 2008. "Fundamental Indexation and International Diversification," *Journal of Portfolio Management* 34: 3 (Spring): 93–109.

Fama, E. F., and K. R. French. 1993. "Common Risk Factors in the Returns on Stocks and Bonds," *Journal of Financial Economics* 33: 1 (January): 3–56.

French, K. R. 2009. Data Library, http://mba.tuck.dartmouth.edu/pages/faculty/ken.french/data_library.html.

FTSE: The Index Company. 2009. High Dividend Yield Index, www.ftse.com/Indices/FTSE_High_Dividend_Yield_Index/index.jsp.

Heber, M. T. 2007. *Index Funds: The 12 Step Program for Active Investors.* Irvine, CA: IFA Publishing.

Mergent. 2006. "Mergent's Dividend Achievers Index Serves as Benchmark for New Vanguard Fund," May 4, www.mergent.com/news-2006-10.html.

Morningstar. 2008. *Morningstar Principia*, February 1 (CD).

Sharpe, W. F. 1992. "Asset Allocation: Management Style and Performance Measurement," *Journal of Portfolio Management* 18: 2 (Winter): 7–19.

Siegel, J. J. 2006. "The 'Noisy Market' Hypothesis," *Wall Street Journal*, June 14, p. A14.

Tower, E., and C.-Y. Yang. 2008. "DFA Versus Vanguard: Has DFA Outperformed Vanguard by Enough to Justify Its Advisor Fees?" *Journal of Investing* 17: 4 (Winter): 71–82.

WisdomTree. 2009. www.wisdomtree.com.

ABOUT THE AUTHOR

Edward Tower has taught economics at Duke University since 1974. He received his Ph.D. in Economics from Harvard in 1971. He has held appointments at the Australian National University, the University of Auckland, Chulalongkorn University, the Fletcher School of Law and Diplomacy at Tufts University, the Helsinki School of Economics and Business Administration, Nanjing University, Simon Fraser University, and the University of Zagreb. He has also consulted on economic development problems with the World Bank, the U.S. Agency for International Development, and the Harvard Institute for International Development in Indonesia, Kenya, Malawi, Sudan, and Washington, D.C. He writes on financial, international and development economics. He has served on 11 editorial boards, written or coauthored 3 books and monographs and 133 articles, and has compiled 115 books on the teaching of economics.

CHAPTER 14

Mutual Funds versus Exchange-Traded Funds

GARY L. GASTINEAU
Managing Member, ETF Consultants LLC and Managed ETFs LLC

T he phenomenal growth of exchange-traded funds (ETFs) is a frequent topic
in the financial press. Most of the press coverage has correctly noted some
of the major advantages of ETFs: lower costs than mutual funds, intraday
trading without material premiums or discounts to the funds' intraday net asset
value (NAV), and high tax efficiency. However, there is a fair degree of misunder-
standing about how ETFs work, why the expense ratios of most ETFs tend to be
low, and how most ETFs manage to avoid significant capital gains distributions.
This chapter attempts to answer these and other questions frequently asked about
ETFs. We also suggest that the ETF investment company structure should replace
the conventional mutual fund structure for most new fund investments by U.S.
investors in the years ahead. Much of the material in this chapter is drawn from
the author's earlier writings, especially Gastineau (2001, 2002b, 2005) and Broms
and Gastineau (2007).

A BRIEF HISTORY OF ETFs

Exchange-traded funds, referred to by friends and foes alike as ETFs, are outstanding examples of the evolution of new financial products. We begin by tracing the
history of ETF antecedents—the proto-products that led to the current generation
of exchange-traded funds—and set the stage for products yet to come.

Portfolio Trading and Stock Index Future Contracts

The basic idea of trading an entire portfolio in a single transaction did not
originate with the Toronto Stock Exchange Index Participations (TIPs) or Standard
& Poor's Depository Receipts (SPDRs), which are the earliest examples of the
modern portfolio-traded-as-a-share structure. It originated with what has come
to be known as portfolio trading or program trading. From the late 1970s through
the early 1980s, program trading was the then-revolutionary ability to trade an
entire portfolio, often a portfolio consisting of all the S&P 500 stocks, with a single
order placed at a major brokerage firm. Some modest advances in electronic order

entry technology and the availability of large order desks at some major investment banking firms made these early portfolio or program trades possible.

At about the same time, the introduction of S&P 500 index futures contracts by the Chicago Mercantile Exchange provided an arbitrage link between these new futures contracts and portfolios of stocks. It even became possible, in a trade called an exchange of futures for physicals (EFP), to exchange a stock portfolio position, long or short, for a stock index futures position, long or short. The effect of these developments was to make portfolio trading either in cash or futures markets an attractive activity for many trading desks and for many institutional investors.

As a logical consequence of these developments affecting large investors, there arose interest—one might even say demand—for a readily tradable portfolio or basket product for smaller institutions and for individual investors. The early futures contracts were relatively large in notional size, and the variation margin requirements for carrying these futures contracts were cumbersome and relatively expensive for a small investor. The need for a low price point security (a Securities and Exchange Commission [SEC]–regulated portfolio product) that could be used by individual investors was increasingly apparent. One of the first such products was Index Participation Shares, known as IPS.

Index Participation Shares

The Index Participation Shares were a relatively simple, totally synthetic, proxy for the S&P 500 Index. While other indexes were also available, S&P 500 IPS began trading on the American Stock Exchange and the Philadelphia Stock Exchange in 1989. A federal court in Chicago found that the IPS were futures contracts and had to be traded on a futures exchange, if they were traded at all. The stock exchanges had to close down IPS trading.

While a number of efforts to find a replacement product for IPS that would pass muster as a security were under way in the United States, Toronto Stock Exchange (TSE) Index Participations were introduced in Canada.

Toronto Stock Exchange Index Participations

TIPs were a warehouse receipt-based instrument designed to track the TSE-35 index and, later, the TSE-100 index as well. TIPs traded actively and attracted substantial investment from Canadians and from international indexing investors. The ability of the trustee to loan out the stocks in the TIPs portfolios led to a negative expense ratio at times. However, the TIPs proved costly for the TSE and for some of its members, who were unable to recover their costs from investors. Early in 2000, the Toronto Stock Exchange decided to get out of the portfolio share business. TIPs positions were liquidated or, at the option of the TIPs holder, rolled into a fund now known as the iShares CDN LargeCap 60. This fund had assets over C$9 billion at the end of 2007.

Meanwhile, two other portfolio share products were under development in the United States: Supershares and SPDRs.

Supershares

Supershares were a complex product using both a trust and a mutual fund structure, one inside the other. Supershares were a high-cost product, particularly after a substantial fee was extracted to compensate their creators and sponsors. The complexity of the product, which permitted division of the Supershares into a variety of components, some with option and optionlike characteristics, made sales presentations long and confusing for many customers. The Supershares never traded actively and the trust was eventually liquidated.

Standard & Poor's Depository Receipts

SPDRS (spiders) were developed by the American Stock Exchange (Amex) in approximate parallel with Supershares. The original SPDRs are a unit trust with an S&P 500 portfolio that, unlike the portfolios of most U.S. unit trusts, can be changed as the index composition changes.

The reason for using the unit trust structure was the Amex's concern for costs. A mutual fund must pay the costs of a board of directors, even if the fund is very small. The Amex was uncertain of the demand for SPDRs and did not want to build a more costly infrastructure than was necessary. SPDRs traded reasonably well on the Amex in their earlier years, but only in the late 1990s did their asset growth take off, as investors began to look past the somewhat esoteric in-kind share creation and redemption process and focus on the investment characteristics and tax efficiency of the SPDRS themselves.

Only a few other ETFs (e.g., Midcap SPDRs, the Nasdaq 100, and the DIAMONDS based on the Dow Jones Industrial Average) still use the unit trust structure. Most ETFs introduced since 2000 use a modified version of the mutual fund investment company structure. Nonetheless, the S&P 500 SPDR remains the largest ETF in the United States and the world, with assets of nearly $102 billion at the end of 2007. Total ETF assets at the end of 2007 were $628 billion.

World Equity Benchmark Shares (Renamed iShares MSCI Series) and Other Products Called ETFs

The World Equity Benchmark Shares (WEBS) are important for two reasons:

1. They are foreign index funds—that is, funds holding stocks issued by non–U.S.-based firms.
2. They are one of the earliest exchange-traded index products to use an investment company (mutual fund) structure as opposed to a unit trust structure. If you are going to create a large number of similar products, the mutual fund structure can be less costly than a separate unit trust for each product.

Another family of foreign index funds designed to compete with the WEBS was introduced on the New York Stock Exchange at about the same time WEBS appeared on the Amex. For a variety of reasons, the most important of which were

Exhibit 14.1 Brands for ETFs and Similar Products

Ameristock	HOLDRs	StateStreet SPDRs
BLDRs	MacroShares	StreetTracks
Claymore	PowerShares	TDAX
Fidelity	ProShares	VanEck
First Trust	Realty Funds	Vanguard
FocusShares	Rydex	Victoria Bay
HealthShares	SPA	WisdomTree

structural flaws in the product, these "Country Baskets" failed, and the trust was liquidated.

The Select Sector SPDRs were the first ETFs with domestic stock portfolios in a mutual fund structure similar to the WEBS. They were introduced in late 1998.

Other brands for ETFs and similarly traded products are listed in Exhibit 14.1. A new "brand" is added almost monthly.

The label *exchange-traded fund* (*ETF*) is applied to a number of financial instruments, some of which are neither funds nor unit trusts like the original SPDR. The fact that investors can trade most of the products called ETFs throughout the day at market-determined prices that are very close to the intraday value of an underlying portfolio or index is one common feature of most of these securities. The ETF label has been attached to:

- Closed-end funds (Nuveen)
- Grantor Trust products based on fixed portfolios (HOLDRS)
- Grantor Trust products based on holdings of a single commodity (Gold and Silver Trusts)
- Currency "money market" Grantor Trusts (Euro Currency Trust)
- Commodity Indexed Trusts (iShares Goldman Sachs Commodity Index Trust)
- "Open-End" Structured Notes (iPath GSCI Total Return Index Notes)
- Mutual fund exchange-traded share classes (Vanguard "ETFs")
- SPDR-style portfolios (SPDRs, QQQs, WEBS, iShares, etc.)

Our focus here is on the last group, which includes the largest number of products and competes head to head with conventional mutual funds.

HOW OPEN-END PORTFOLIO ETFs WORK

The open-end ETFs based on the SPDR model have a number of specific features that will be fundamental characteristics of this new generation of funds. These open-end ETFs do not have shareholder accounting expenses at the fund level, and they have few embedded marketing expenses. These expense-reducing features and the fact that the fund shares are traded like stocks rather than like mutual funds often make ETFs more costly to buy and sell but nearly always less costly to hold than comparable mutual funds. Some early investors in ETFs were attracted by the fact that the ETFs were low-cost index funds. However, today's index funds—ETFs and mutual funds—are not always the low-cost portfolios their owners expect.

Day 1   **Day 2**   **Day 3**

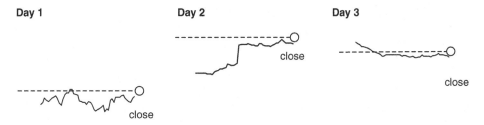

Exhibit 14.2 Since 1968: Buying and Selling Mutual Fund Shares at the Net Asset Value Next Determined

It is useful to focus on two important characteristics of the SPDR-style ETF that were, in some respects, serendipitous. Because these characteristics have helped attract investors, they have been important in the early success of ETFs. These characteristics also provide a basis for growth in the SPDR-style ETF model well beyond its impressive beginnings. Not everyone attaches as much significance as I do to these two features, but I am convinced that they hold the key to the development of better funds. The two key features of most existing SPDR-style ETFs are shareholder protection and tax efficiency.

Shareholder Protection

The material described in this and the next few paragraphs is widely known but not frequently discussed. Swenson (2005) provides a recent comprehensive description of mutual fund pricing over the years.

In 1968, the SEC implemented Rule 22(c)(1), which required mutual fund share transactions to be priced at the NAV next determined by the fund. This meant that anyone entering an order after the close of business on Day 1 would purchase or sell fund shares at the NAV determined at the close on Day 2. Correspondingly, someone entering an order to purchase or sell shares after the close on Day 2 would be accommodated at the NAV determined at the close on Day 3. This process is illustrated in Exhibit 14.2.

There is a transaction fairness problem for fund investors with Rule 22(c)1 in place. That problem is illustrated in Exhibit 14.3.

By pricing all transactions in the mutual fund's shares *at the net asset value next determined*, as required by Rule 22(c)1, the fund provides free liquidity to investors entering and leaving the fund. All the shareholders in the fund pay the cost of providing this liquidity. As Exhibit 14.3 illustrates, anyone purchasing mutual fund

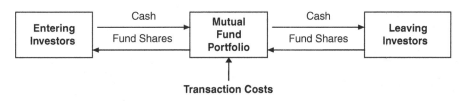

Exhibit 14.3 Cash Moves In and Out of a Mutual Fund: Fund Trades Securities to Invest Incoming Cash or to Raise Cash for Redemptions

shares for cash gets a share of the securities positions already held by the fund and priced at NAV. The new investor typically pays no transaction costs at the time of the share purchase. Furthermore, all the shareholders of the fund share the transaction costs associated with investing the new investor's cash in portfolio securities. Similarly, when an investor departs the mutual fund, that investor receives cash equal to the NAV of the shares when the NAV is next calculated. All the shareholders in the fund bear the cost of selling portfolio securities to provide this liquidity. To the entering or leaving shareholder, liquidity is essentially free. To the ongoing shareholders of the fund, the liquidity given to transacting shareholders is costly. Over time, the cost of providing this free liquidity to entering and leaving shareholders is a perennial drag on a mutual fund's performance.

Exhibit 14.4 shows that exchange-traded funds handle the costs of accommodating entering and leaving shareholders differently from mutual funds. For ETFs, creations and redemptions of shares are typically made *in kind.* Baskets of portfolio securities are deposited with the fund in exchange for fund shares in a creation. To redeem fund shares, shares are turned into the fund in exchange for a basket of portfolio securities. The creating or redeeming investor—in most cases, a market maker in the ETF shares—is responsible for the costs of investing in the portfolio securities for deposit and the cost of disposing of portfolio securities received in the redemption of outstanding fund shares. The market makers even pay a modest creation or redemption fee to cover the fund's administrative expenses.

The market maker expects to pass these transaction costs on to investors when he or she trades fund shares on the exchange. The cost of entering and leaving a fund varies, depending on the level of fund share trading activity and the nature of the securities in the fund's portfolio. For example, the cost of trading in small-cap stocks can be much greater than the cost of trading in large-cap stocks.

ETFs are different from mutual funds in the way they accommodate shareholder entry and exit in at least two important ways. The trading costs associated with ETF shareholder entries and exits are ultimately borne by the entering and exiting investors, not by the fund. Furthermore, unlike a mutual fund, an exchange-traded fund does not have to hold cash balances to provide for cash redemptions. An ETF can stay fully invested at all times. As a result of these differences, the

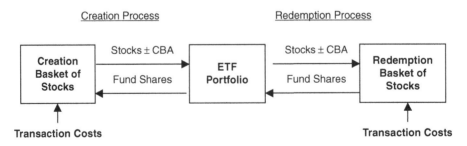

Exhibit 14.4 ETF Creation and Redemption Is In Kind: Transaction Costs Are Paid by Entering and Leaving Investors

All securities transfers are priced at net asset value.
CBA = Cash Balancing Amount

performance experienced by ongoing shareholders in an ETF should, over time, handily surpass the performance experienced by ongoing shareholders of a conventional mutual fund using the same investment process. Ironically, even though the ETF was designed to be traded throughout the trading day on an exchange, it is a much better product than a conventional fund for the shareholder *who does not want to trade.*

As any mutual fund market timer will tell you, a mutual fund is a better product to trade than an ETF because the mutual fund pays the timer's trading costs. Any reader interested in more detailed information on the ETF creation and redemption process should read a fund's prospectus or statement of additional information for a more complete description of the process. I particularly recommend the prospectus for the original SPDR for its clarity and comprehensiveness.

The mutual fund structure that provides free liquidity to investors who enter and leave the fund is responsible for the problems of late trading and market timing that provoked the mutual fund scandals of 2003 and 2004. The SEC has spent a great deal of time and effort trying to deal with the problem of market-timing trades in mutual funds without eliminating the free liquidity that ongoing shareholders in mutual funds give entering and leaving shareholders. This effort has not been successful. Some fund companies have made a variety of operational patches as they attempt to restrict market-timing trades.

The SEC now requires a complex and costly fund share transaction reporting structure with nearly mandatory redemption fees on mutual fund purchases that are closed out within a week. In the final analysis, the elimination of free liquidity—most easily through the ETF in-kind creation and redemption process—is the only way to eliminate market timing without imposing unnecessary costs on all fund investors. Even if there is no such thing as a market timer in the future, long-term investors will fare better in funds that protect them from the costs of other investors entering and leaving the fund.

Tax Efficiency

One of the most frequently discussed advantages of exchange-traded funds is tax efficiency. Tax efficiency benefits some taxable investors profoundly, but it has value to tax-exempt investors as well. The tax efficiency of ETFs is essentially tax-deferral until the investor chooses to sell fund shares. This deferral is a natural result of Subchapter M of the Internal Revenue Code, which permits fund share redemptions in kind (delivering portfolio securities to departing fund shareholders) without tax impact inside the fund. An ETF or mutual fund share redemption in kind does not give rise to a capital gain that is distributable to shareholders of the fund. Gastineau (2005) provides more details on ETF tax efficiency.

This kind of tax efficiency benefits tax-exempt investors in the fund because it prevents the buildup of unrealized gains inside an ETF portfolio. The buildup of unrealized gains in a mutual fund portfolio can lead to portfolio management decisions that adversely affect tax-exempt shareholders. When the choice facing a portfolio manager is (1) to realize gains on appreciated portfolio securities and distribute taxable capital gains to the fund's shareholders or (2) to hold overvalued securities and avoid realizing capital gains, the portfolio manager faces a conflict between the interests of tax-exempt and taxable investors.

The back story on the October 31, 2005, manager change at Fidelity's Magellan Fund and the results of that change illustrates the problems a mutual fund can have in dealing with the conflicting interests of tax-exempt and taxable investors. The Magellan manager change led to the realization of substantial embedded capital gains that had given the fund a very large capital gains "overhang" prior to the beginning of the 2006 tax year. The new Magellan manager realized capital gains, dramatically changed the composition of the portfolio, achieved good near-term performance—and distributed a mammoth capital gain that was taxable to Magellan's taxable shareholders in 2006. The Halloween date of the change in Magellan's manager was no coincidence. The manager change announcement made it clear that portfolio changes were coming. Under mutual fund tax rules, gains realized in the last two months of the calendar year do not affect investors' tax returns for that year. Rather than wait until the end of 2006, Magellan distributed capital gains equal to about 19 percent of the fund's assets to its shareholders in May. While this policy change was certainly the best choice open to the new manager of Magellan, the situation illustrates the inherent portfolio management conflict between taxable and tax-exempt investors in mutual funds.

Magellan had performed poorly for a number of years before 2005, partly because its managers had been reluctant to sell low-cost portfolio securities. Portfolio managers of conventional mutual funds often defer transactions that would improve pretax performance because they do not want to trigger the distribution of taxable capital gains. The conflict of interest between taxable and tax-exempt investors—inevitable in a conventional mutual fund—disappears in an ETF.

With exchange-traded funds, the decision to change the portfolio can be based solely on investment considerations, not on the tax basis of portfolio securities. Any conflict between taxable and tax-exempt shareholders disappears because the achievement of tax efficiency in ETFs is largely a matter of careful designation of tax lots so that the lowest-cost lots of a security are distributed in kind in redemptions and high-cost lots are sold to realize losses in the fund when a sale is necessary or appropriate.

Exchange-traded funds grow by exchanging new fund shares for portfolio securities deposited with the fund. Redemptions are also largely in kind. Investors sell their fund shares on the exchange rather than redeeming them directly with the fund. Dealers buy the fund shares and turn them in to the fund in exchange for portfolio securities. This process serendipitously lets ETF managers take full advantage of the redemption in-kind provision of the Internal Revenue Code. The early developers of ETFs were aware of this tax treatment, but the tax deferral it gives holders was by no means a significant objective in the early development of ETFs. It is largely serendipitous that most well-managed ETFs will never distribute taxable capital gains to their shareholders. Creation and redemption in kind not only transfers the cost of entering and leaving the fund to the entering and leaving shareholders; it also defers capital gains taxes until a shareholder chooses to sell the fund shares.

Interestingly, tax efficiency helps encourage "shareholder loyalty" to an ETF. Investors in a mutual fund usually receive taxable gains distributions that increase their basis as the value of their fund shares increases over time. When they sell the mutual fund shares, the higher basis reduces the capital gains tax on the sale. Investors in most ETFs should never get a capital gains distribution. Consequently, the basis of the fund shares will stay at investors' original cost. The tax due on sale of the ETF shares will tend to be relatively greater than the tax due on an otherwise comparable mutual fund position. Investors with both mutual funds and ETFs will reduce current tax payments by selling the mutual fund shares first when they need money for living expenses. ETF shareholders will be more loyal simply because they want to minimize tax payments and continue to defer their tax liability.

The in-kind creation and redemption of exchange-traded fund shares is a simple, nondiscriminatory way to allocate the costs of entry and exit of fund shareholders appropriately and to solve the portfolio manager's conflict of interest between taxable and tax-exempt shareholders. This in-kind ETF creation/redemption process is an efficient, even elegant, solution to several of the obvious problems that continue to plague the mutual fund industry. A growing number of fund industry experts believe that the ETF structure should replace conventional mutual funds. To make that happen, however, the serendipity of early ETF development needs to be harnessed through creative financial engineering to overcome weaknesses in the index ETF structure and extend the best ETF features to a wider range of portfolios.

IMPROVING ETFs

To understand how effective and efficient ETFs can be, we need to examine a few features of an improved ETF model that builds on the strengths and overcomes the weaknesses of today's ETFs. ETF weaknesses are less egregious and more easily overcome than some of the weaknesses of today's mutual funds. ETF weaknesses are weaknesses we can eliminate. With SEC approval of a few modifications, a new breed of ETF can deliver marked improvements over the current model—and even more dramatic improvements over mutual funds. The 2003–2004 mutual fund market timing scandals mandate that all fund share transactions be consistent with the ETF model, wherein entering and departing shareholders pay the costs of their entry and exit. The great shareholder protection advantage ETFs have over conventional mutual funds can provide more robust shareholder protection than is possible with the mutual fund model after any possible mutual fund reform.

It is time to look at some new ETF features that will improve performance. If any fund is going to serve the interests of its shareholders, the portfolio manager needs to implement portfolio changes without revealing the fund's ongoing trading plans. Whether a fund is attempting to replicate an index or to follow an active portfolio selection or allocation process, portfolio composition changes cannot be made efficiently if the market knows what changes a fund will make in its portfolio before the fund completes its trades. A number of recent studies have highlighted an index composition change problem that many strong supporters of indexing have been aware of for some time: Benchmark indexes like the S&P 500 and the Russell 2000 do not make efficient portfolio templates. Investors in index funds based on any transparent index are disadvantaged by the fact that anyone who cares will know what changes the fund must make before the fund's portfolio manager can make them. Chen, Noronha, and Singal (2006) and Gastineau (2002a, 2002b, 2002c, 2005) discuss this problem at length. When transparency means that someone can earn an arbitrage profit by front-running a fund's trades, transparency is not desirable or acceptable. Gastineau (2008) discusses the cost of trading transparency, a problem for all index funds.

The cost to ongoing shareholders in index ETFs of preannounced portfolio composition changes must be eliminated. The best way to improve index fund performance is to use silent indexes, indexes that keep portfolio composition changes confidential until after the fund has traded. Doing this requires radically new procedures for the management of indexes and of some index funds. A similar procedure will be used for actively managed ETFs. Everyone seems to agree that actively managed funds require confidential treatment of portfolio composition changes until after the fund has traded. Only recently have investors begun to understand the added transaction costs that index transparency imposes on index fund investors. Making portfolio changes confidential and efficient requires changes in the ETF structure and the portfolio trading process.

Intraday trading in ETFs is useful to many investors. However, market makers and other large traders may have an intraday trading advantage over individual investors who are less able to monitor market activity and intraday fund price and value relationships. To state this problem in another way, there is asymmetry in the amount and kind of information available to large traders on one hand and small investors on the other hand.

Many individual investors have a stake in being able to make small, periodic purchases or sales in their fund share accounts. The prototypical investor of this type is the 401(k) investor who invests a small amount in a defined contribution retirement plan every payroll period. The mutual fund industry has developed an elaborate system that permits small orders for a large number of investors to be aggregated and for cash to enter or leave a fund to accommodate a large number of small investors at NAV. There are ways to modify ETF procedures so that these investors, while paying a little more than they have paid in the past to cover the transaction costs of their entry and exit, will still be accommodated in ETFs at low cost. The snowballing rush to *greater transparency in the economics of defined contribution accounts* like 401(k) plans will make fund cost and performance comparisons easier—to the advantage of ETFs.

ETF AND MUTUAL FUND COMPARATIVE ECONOMICS

Exhibit 14.5 provides an economic comparison of ETFs and mutual funds with the advantages of the ETF cost structure measured in terms of improved investment performance for fund shareholders. In the first column, the particular ETF advantage is shown first. The information in parentheses in that column is an estimate of the range of improved annual investment performance a long-term shareholder who uses an ETF rather than a mutual fund will enjoy. As these numbers indicate, the advantage of an ETF over a comparable mutual fund can vary over a wide range in some instances.

The second column lists some possible problems with today's ETF structure under some circumstances. The third column lists solutions for implementation in a new generation of ETFs. In a few cases (such as the need for more efficient indexes), the silent index solution is equally applicable to conventional mutual

Exhibit 14.5 Using ETFs to Deliver Better Investor Performance

ETF Advantages	Possible ETF Problems	Solutions
Shareholder protection (<0.1%–>5.0%)	Uncertain transaction costs Fairness of execution	New trading process improves on basic ETF shareholder protection
Lower operating costs/cost transparency (0%–0.35%)	Under the Alternative Minimum Tax (AMT) embedded costs cover fees	New fund delivery structures
Capital gains tax efficiency (0 to 2.5%)	None	None needed
Taxable/Tax-exempt conflict (0 to 1.0%)	None	None needed
Indexing (Equal)	Inefficient indexes: The more popular the index, the greater the performance drag from index transparency	Silent indexes as portfolio templates
Active management (Equal)	Confidentiality in portfolio changes is essential	Same portfolio disclosure as mutual funds

funds that follow an indexing strategy. It is not in any fund investor's interest to pay significant index change transaction costs that the fund incurs because its index is totally transparent. Each of the features proposed for new ETFs merits at least a brief discussion.

The first ETF advantage reflects the value of shareholder protection from the cost of investors entering and leaving a fund as discussed in connection with Exhibits 14.3 and 14.4. The return comparison in parentheses reflects the allocation of all entry and exit costs to entering and leaving shareholders. In an ETF transaction, shareholders pay only the cost of their own entry to and exit from the fund. Mutual fund shareholders pay a pro rata share of the entry and exit costs of all fund buyers and sellers for as long as they own the fund.

There have been only two appropriately designed studies of the shareholder performance cost of the flow of investor cash into and out of mutual funds. In the first study, Roger Edelen (1999), then a professor at Wharton, measured the cost of flow for a sample of 166 equity and hybrid mutual funds using data from 1985 through 1990. See Gastineau (2004) for a more detailed discussion of this paper.

Edelen calculated the cost of flow in terms of its adverse effect on fund shareholder performance at 143 basis points per year in the average fund in his sample. In a more recent study, Edelen, Evans, and Kadlec (2007) found the average annual cost of flow in a much larger sample of funds to be 75 basis points. The shareholder turnover in all of the sample funds in both studies was low enough that it is clear that market timing and late trading were not significant factors in the cost of flow to these funds' shareholders. Furthermore, shareholder flow into and out of most large mutual funds is lower today than it was in the period covered by Edelen's (1999) original sample, and some of the transaction costs associated with accommodating flow are probably lower today. If the cost of flow for the average mutual fund investor (not the average mutual fund) is as low as 50 basis points per year, the cost to all fund investors is still $25 billion per year. This cost, reflected in lost performance, dwarfs the shareholder costs attributable to mutual fund market timing on any reasonable assumption.

Note the wide range we use for the cost of flow (less than 0.1 percent to more than 5.0 percent per year) in Exhibit 14.5. The less than $1/10$ of 1 percent number is representative of some very large mutual funds with very low shareholder turnover. The more than 5 percent annual cost figure applies to some small-cap funds with high shareholder turnover. Clearly, the cost of accommodating market timers and late traders in some funds implicated in the 2003–2004 scandals was well in excess of 5 percent per year. There is some cost disadvantage to a mutual fund's ongoing shareholders relative to an ETF when there is *any* flow.

The only "problem" that limits the ability of ETFs to deliver this degree of shareholder protection is that the true transaction costs associated with buying and selling shares of an ETF can be difficult for an investor to determine in advance of trading. The information available to investors on intraday values of an ETF is not as good or as readily available as it could be. Calculations of intraday fund portfolio values are made and disseminated, but many investors—including some institutional and semi-institutional investors—do not have easy access to the every-15-second NAV proxy calculations for existing ETFs. Furthermore, these NAV proxy calculations, particularly those for funds that hold a significant number of illiquid or foreign securities, do not always give a meaningful intraday value for the fund. While the ETF structure eliminates the need for fair value pricing, the limited availability and methodology for calculating intraday NAV proxy values can make ETF execution costs uncertain and, in some instances, increase these costs.

The solution to this problem is a trading process that increases the transparency of ETF transaction costs and, consequently, improves the ETF structural shareholder protection without compromising the ETF "gold" standard whereby investors entering and leaving the fund pay the costs of their entry and exit.

The second advantage of ETFs on the list is that they frequently offer lower operating costs and greater cost transparency than conventional mutual funds. Some of the reduction in operating costs and increase in cost transparency is associated with the elimination of costs associated with shareholder accounting at the fund level. Some of these shareholder accounting costs still have to be borne by someone. The financial intermediary that provides fund share transaction and custody services may charge the costs to investors. In addition, sales and advisory charges are paid outside the fund by ETF investors who use those services.

Unbundling costs can create a problem for taxable investors subject to the Alternative Minimum Tax (AMT). The embedded costs of mutual funds are deducted from the income that taxable investors receive. A separately billed advisory fee is usually not fully deductible and may not be deductible at all to an investor who falls under the AMT regime. There can be significant advantages for many taxable investors from embedding advisory and administrative costs and sales charges in the financial instrument rather than having them billed as separate fees. The solution is a variety of new fund delivery structures that provide tax efficiency by re-embedding some of the costs that have been taken out of exchange-traded funds.

Capital gains tax deferral and taxable/tax-exempt conflict of interest elimination are unmitigated gains for all ETF investors. There are no problems in realizing these advantages, so no solution is necessary. These important gains flow to ETF investors almost automatically.

With respect to the last two issues listed in Exhibit 14.5, performance penalties associated with trading transparency in indexing and the need for confidentiality of an active manager's trading activity, the solutions for the two fund structures are essentially identical: Eliminate portfolio trading transparency. All index funds should be based on efficient indexes. There are some very efficient published indexes available today. An outstanding example of an efficient broad-market index is the Dow Jones Wilshire 5000. Gastineau (2006) discusses these issues in additional detail.

Some inherently inefficient indexes are used for such a small asset pool that scalpers who know what the ETF has to do to match the published composition changes in its index are not likely to increase the fund's transaction costs materially by front-running the fund's portfolio manager. If one of these funds grows in response to a spate of fortuitous index changes, however, the manager may face the same front-running problems that S&P 500 and Russell 2000 index fund managers experience regularly. There is no reason why the index templates for all index funds should not be silent indexes. In any event, all investors should have the opportunity to buy index funds based on silent indexes to protect themselves from the cost of index composition front-running trades. Gastineau (2008) discusses these issues in greater detail.

In most discussions of actively managed ETFs, there has been appropriate concern expressed for the cost of achieving enough portfolio transparency to facilitate trading in ETFs without subjecting the fund's trades to the front-running risk that all of today's index funds experience when the index composition changes. The U.S. SEC's Concept Release (2001) on actively managed ETFs stresses the importance of finding a solution to this problem.

In fact, managers of an actively managed ETF need to offer no more information on their portfolio composition and portfolio change than managers of a conventional mutual fund must publish today. Funds that do not require the full measure of confidentiality available under today's rules for fund asset disclosure can reduce transaction costs for their entering and leaving shareholders and market makers by providing more frequent disclosure. Many funds already publish their portfolios more frequently and/or with a shorter lag than required by the SEC. But more frequent disclosure is not essential. An investment process that requires the maximum permitted portfolio confidentiality can work well inside an actively managed ETF with the right fund structure and an improved trading mechanism.

CONCLUSIONS

Fund issuers can build on the compelling advantages of exchange-traded funds to offer better and more varied portfolios. New actively managed and silent index funds can offer shareholder protection from the cost of entry and exit by other fund shareholders and the tax efficiency that is inherent in the initial generation of SPDR-style exchange-traded funds. Investors need new ETF structures and improved trading opportunities when they buy and sell ETF shares. The new ETFs will offer alternative fund delivery structures and systems. Transparent index funds will be challenged by silent index funds that will provide improved performance as a result of lower transaction costs in the fund. Actively managed ETFs will feature flexibility in portfolio disclosure to permit the fund manager to determine the degree of portfolio transparency that is appropriate for the shareholders of a specific fund.

REFERENCES

Broms, T. J., and G. L. Gastineau. 2007. "The Development of Improved Exchange-Traded Funds (ETFs) in the United States," in Y. Fuchita and R. E. Litan, eds., *New Financial Instruments and Institutions*. Washington, DC: The Brookings Institution, pp. 193–209.

Chen, H., G. Noronha, and V. Singal. 2006. "Index Changes and Losses to Index Fund Investors," *Financial Analysts Journal* (July/August): 31–47.

Edelen, R. M. 1999. "Investor Flows and the Assessed Performance of Open-End Mutual Funds," *Journal of Financial Economics* 53: 3 (September): 439–466.

Edelen, R. M., R. Evans, and G. B. Kadlec. 2007. "Scale Effects in Mutual Fund Performance: The Role of Trading Costs." Working Paper, March 17.

Gastineau, G. L. 2001. "ETFs: An Introduction," *Journal of Portfolio Management* (Spring): 88–96.

Gastineau, G. L. 2002a. "Equity Index Funds Have Lost Their Way," *Journal of Portfolio Management* (Winter): 55–64.

Gastineau, G. L. 2002b. *The Exchange-Traded Funds Manual*. Hoboken, NJ: John Wiley & Sons, pp. 31–54.

Gastineau, G. L. 2002c. "Silence Is Golden," *Journal of Indexes* (Second Quarter): 8–13.

Gastineau, G. L. 2004. "Protecting Fund Shareholders from Costly Share Trading," *Financial Analysts Journal* 60: 3 (May/June): 22–32.

Gastineau, G. L. 2005. *Someone Will Make Money on Your Funds, Why Not You? A Better Way to Select Mutual and Exchange-Traded Funds*. Hoboken, NJ: John Wiley & Sons, pp. 39–66.

Gastineau, G. L. 2006. "The Best Index for the Thoughtful Indexer," in Brian Bruce, ed., *A Guide to Exchange-Traded Funds and Indexing Innovations*, 5th ed. New York: Institutional Investor, December, pp. 99–104.

Gastineau, G. L. 2008. "The Cost of Trading Transparency: What We Know, What We Don't Know and How We Will Know," *Journal of Portfolio Management* (Fall 2008): 72–81.

Swenson, D. F. 2005. *Unconventional Success: A Fundamental Approach to Personal Investment*. New York: Free Press, pp. 270–294.

United States Securities and Exchange Commission. 2001. *Actively Managed Exchange-Traded Funds Concept Release*, Release No. IC-25258, File No. S7-20-01, November 8, www.sec.gov/rules/concept/ic-25258.htm.

ABOUT THE AUTHOR

Gary Gastineau is a Cofounder and Managing Member of Managed ETFs LLC, a firm that has filed an application with the Securities and Exchange Commission for permission to launch actively managed and improved index exchange-traded funds. He is Managing Director of ETF Consultants LLC, a firm that provides specialized exchange-traded fund consulting services to ETF issuers, exchanges and other markets, market makers, research organizations, and investors. He is also a Director of Skyhawk Management LLC, an investment management firm that uses ETFs in its investment strategies. His ETF books, *The Exchange-Traded Funds Manual* and *Someone Will Make Money on Your Funds—Why Not You?* were published by John Wiley & Sons. Mr. Gastineau serves on the editorial boards of the *Journal of Portfolio Management, Journal of Derivatives,* and *Journal of Indexes.* He is a member of a number of advisory boards, including the Review Board for the Research Foundation of the CFA Institute. He is an honors graduate of both Harvard College and Harvard Business School.

PART IV

Mutual Funds at the Crossroads

CHAPTER 15

The Challenge to Mutual Fund Stewardship

JOHN C. BOGLE
Founder, The Vanguard Group, Inc., and President, The Bogle Financial Markets Research Center

E ver since the first of the mutual fund scandals came to light shortly after Labor Day 2003, the circle of fund organizations involved continued to grow. Ultimately, more than a score of firms have been implicated in some form of illegal late trading or unethical international time-zone trading in mutual fund shares. The charges brought by former New York Attorney General Eliot Spitzer, Massachusetts Secretary William Galvin, and the Securities and Exchange Commission (SEC) have been settled. The settlements resulted in substantial and well-deserved financial penalties imposed on the managers.

Make no mistake about it. Most of the firms involved in the scandals are major industry participants. Their aggregate fund assets of nearly $1.2 trillion represented nearly 20 percent of the industry's then-$7.2 trillion total in long-term assets. As the scandals unfolded, investor reaction turned from incredulity to revulsion, and then to self-defense, with rising share liquidations at the firms that were affected. Even the firms that have so far received only subpoenas for information seem cautious about declaring their innocence, for it turns out that virtually all 401(k) transactions take place long after each day's 4 P.M. cut-off time for executing orders. What is more, one of the two prime clearinghouses for these transactions has been forced out of business.

The public judgment that these firms have betrayed the trust of their investors is correct. There is no reason why the public reaction should not be harsh. What is really the point of investors keeping their money with a firm that has betrayed their trust? Even the new chief executive officer of one of the largest firms involved seems to agree, as quoted in Strauss (2003). "There were individuals here," he said, "who had a lapse of judgment and who put their interests first ahead of shareholders . . .

Adapted from J. C. Bogle, 2003, "'It's an Ill Wind that Blows No Good': How the Mutual Fund Scandals Will Serve Fund Owners," Keynote Speech, Personal Finance Workshop, Society of American Business Editors and Writers, Denver, October 27, and from J. C. Bogle, 2004, "Has Your Fund Manager Betrayed Your Trust? Consider the 'Stewardship Quotient,'" Keynote Speech, Personal Financial Planning Conference, American Institute of Certified Public Accountants, Las Vegas, January 5.

I believe that was the wrong judgment. When an investment professional violates a fiduciary trust, you don't get a second chance. And, I don't think there's a statute of limitations."

CHALLENGE TO STEWARDSHIP

Let us consider some ideas on how to evaluate whether the managers of the funds you own are truly acting as trustees of other people's money. You should evaluate the funds you own in terms of the extent to which they appropriately balance the conflicts that inevitably exist between business and profession. The scandals have given you the opportunity to address that balance in a new light, for these scandals have arisen when fund managers have clearly put their own interest in business building, asset gathering, and the maximization of fee revenues ahead of the interest of their fund shareholders in financial integrity, fair treatment, honest disclosure, and optimal investment returns.

But the bane of the scandals, truth told, is a blessing in disguise. For they awaken us not only to the shoddy illegal and unethical practices of various extreme forms of market timing but to the damage done by the equally pernicious but far more subtle forms of mutual fund market timing—in which all-too-many fund investors engage, and which the fund industry has aided and abetted—and the organization and operation of funds designed more to enrich the coffers of the managers than the coffers of the fund shareholders. Symptoms of the problem include the creation of style-box funds and sector funds, bought today to be sold on some date near or far, rather than truly diversified equity funds bought to be held, well, forever.

We have come a long, long way from the standards under which the mutual fund industry operated when I joined it in 1951. At that time, the field was composed primarily of funds whose returns would more or less track the stock market itself. These were funds with low costs and low portfolio turnover, funds designed for long-term investors. And funds whose managers measured up to this standard: *We sell what we make.*

What a difference a half century makes. Today, the vast majority of funds that our industry offers to investors are relatively undiversified, most with high costs and high portfolio turnover. These are funds designed for market traders and short-term speculators, with managers that follow a debased new standard: *We make what will sell.*

Happily, there are still funds and fund managers who have tried to hold the fort against the industry's new paradigm in which marketing has superseded management. When you decide you have had enough of the sharp practices and misbehavior that have characterized the scandal-ridden firms and decide to move assets to another fund or organization, it is these firms that you should consider.

If you share these views, where should you turn to replace those funds that have failed to measure up to the trust that you have placed in them? You should select funds from those organizations that have strived to strike a proper balance between the interests of fund shareholders and those of fund managers. These firms place a heavier weight on stewardship than on salesmanship, and have done their best to put service to shareholders above service to themselves.

But do not be naive about this subject. Every profession has elements of a business. Indeed, no organization in which expenses consistently exceed revenues will long exist. But when we look at some of our nation's proudest professions—medicine, law, accounting, journalism, architecture, and, of course, trusteeship—there is evidence that the traditional balance has been gradually shifting away from that of trusted profession and toward that of commercial enterprise. Writing in 2003, Roger Lowenstein bemoaned the loss of the "Calvinist rectitude" that had its roots in "the very Old World notions of integrity, ethics, and unyielding loyalty to the customer." "America's professions," he wrote, "have become crassly commercial...with accounting firms sponsoring golf tournaments." (And, he might have added, mutual fund managers not only doing the same thing, but also buying naming rights to stadiums.) "The battle for independence," Lowenstein concluded, "is never won" (p. 44). And so it is in the field of investment management.

The mutual fund scandals offer substantial evidence that, far too often, the spirit of trusteeship, professional competence and discipline, and a focus on the long term have been losing their role as the driving force and, in the long run, the life-force of this industry. If you doubt that, consider these three trends:

1. The industry's traditional focus on trusteeship—on management—which implies that we place the interest of fund shareholders as our highest priority and charge a reasonable price for our services, has been supplanted by a focus on asset-gathering—on marketing—as it worships at the shrine of the great god market share, the exorbitant cost of which is borne by fund shareholders.
2. The traditional focus on professional competence, discipline, and research and security analysis has moved from long-term investment to what is really speculation, with rapid turnover in industry investment portfolios averaging almost 100 percent per year. Most funds concentrate on ever-narrowing segments of the stock market, and far too many are run by "gunslinger" portfolio managers.
3. The traditional focus on the eminent suitability of mutual funds for long-term investors has morphed into an industry focus on offering fund portfolios with little correlation to the total stock market and thus designed for the short-term investor (or speculator) and, even worse, a focus on enticing fund shareholders to use mutual funds as vehicles for rapid switching, either for the purpose of market timing or of jumping on the bandwagon of the latest "hot fund" (which is yet another kind of speculation).

What we now know is that the consequences of these three industry trends have come home to roost in damage done to the pocketbooks of the shareholders who placed their trust in mutual funds.

The recent market timing scandals, however, are but one manifestation of the problem. The industry's response can be best characterized by a classic line spoken by the police chief in the film *Casablanca*, played by Claude Rains: "I am shocked, shocked to find gambling [timing] going on here." We have been told that these breaches of fiduciary duty are attributable to only to a few bad apples, but this is far from the truth.

Yet there is some good that has come of the scandals. Without the spotlight that has been shined on specific cases (such as Enron, WorldCom, and Tyco) that brought notoriety to corporate America's bad apples, all the nibbling around the edges of proper and ethical conduct that existed without challenge in the conduct of business today could have persisted for another decade or more. Similarly, the spotlight on fund bad apples has illuminated the frequent willingness and eagerness of fund managers to build their own profits at the expense of fund owners.

"It's an ill wind that blows no good." By illuminating the inherent conflict of interest between fund managers and fund investors, these scandals will ultimately prove a blessing for fund owners. This conflict is hardly a secret. As stated in Bogle (1999), the industry should move to a system in which

> *the focus of mutual fund governance and control is shifted . . . to the directors and share-holders of the mutual funds themselves, and away from the executives and owners of mutual fund management companies (where it almost universally reposes today), who seek good fund performance to be sure, but also seek enormous personal gain. (p. 332)*

If such a shift of control and governance had taken place, the market-timing scandals detailed in the Spitzer-Canary (hedge fund) settlement may well never have occurred. The former Attorney General's seemingly airtight case was built on covert practices and open motivations—in a word, payola—in the form of side banking deals, such as lending money to the hedge fund at above-market interest rates and requiring large investments in other funds on which the manager earns high fees ("sticky assets").

One fund manager's e-mail could hardly have made the motivation clearer. This message, from the State of New York's (2003) complaint against Canary Capital Partners, reads: "I have no interest in building a business around market timers, but at the same time I do not want to turn away $10–$20m[illion]." The writer understood that allowing the timing trades would be adverse to the fund shareholders but served the manager's "best interests." Lest his colleagues fail to get the point, he explained in a parenthetical aside what that meant: "increased profitability to the firm." Another e-mail also told the truth: "Market timers are a big problem . . . it's very disruptive to the operation of the funds. [But,] obviously, your call from the sales side" (p. 36–37).

INDUSTRY STRUCTURE AND SCANDALS

It can be little surprise that the mutual fund industry has not escaped the same kinds of scandals that have faced Wall Street and corporate America. In no other line of business endeavor is the conflict between owner's capitalism and manager's capitalism more institutionalized, and therefore more widely accepted. Yet by its very structure, this industry, for all its protestations about its dedication to Main Street investors, seems almost preordained to give fund managers total control over the assets entrusted to them by fund shareowners.

Consider how the typical fund organization operates. Even when their assets are valued in the scores of billions of dollars, fund complexes do not manage themselves. They hire an external management company, with its own separate set of shareholders, to manage their affairs. The management company runs the fund's operations, distributes its shares, and supervises and directs its investment portfolio. It decides when to create new funds, and it decides what kinds of funds they will be. When the funds are badly run, the company replaces the portfolio manager with another one of its own employees. When a fund fails to grow to profitability or outlives its usefulness, the management company persuades the fund's directors either to liquidate it or to merge it into another of the manager's more successful funds.

What is more, this typical management company graciously provides the fund's officers, who are employees of the company, not the fund. While the executives of the manager usually have a minuscule—if any—investment in the funds they run, they select themselves for the fund board and, until recent years, also selected most of the funds' "independent" directors, who by law must now compose at least a majority of the board. In the typical case, the chairman of the board of the management company also serves as the chairman of the board of the mutual fund.

Given the Gordian knot on the rope that binds the fund and the manager together, it is impossible to imagine that at one of the fund's (typically) four annual board meetings, the majority—the less-well-informed independent directors—can stand up to the minority—the management directors who are steeped in the knowledge of how the business works.

But the ability of management company executives and owners to ignore this reality of the fund industry's existence can be traced back to Descartes in 1650: "A man is incapable of comprehending any argument that interferes with his revenue." And, even 2000 years before *that*, in 350 B.C., hear Demosthenes: "Nothing is easier than self-deceit. For what each man wishes, that he also believes to be true."

The fund industry, in the vernacular of the day, "just doesn't get it." You should not be persuaded by the self-aggrandizing comments offered by the Investment Company Institute's (ICI) (2003) president at the annual general membership meeting: "Your unshakable commitment to putting mutual fund shareholder interests first has served our shareholders and our companies well. In a nutshell, we have succeeded because the interests of those who manage funds are well aligned with the interests of those who invest in mutual funds."

MISALIGNED INTERESTS

That is just not so. The interests are *not* well aligned. To deny the obvious and profound conflicts that are manifest in this industry is hardly the beginning of wisdom. The fact is that whatever alignments of interest may exist are far outweighed by misalignments. Consider just four of the major areas in which what is good for the managers is bad for the shareholders:

1. Market timing, which brings in temporary assets that provide higher fees to managers, but only at the cost of dilution in the returns for fund owners.
2. Management fees, which are inversely related to fund performance. As a broad generalization, the higher a fund's management fees and expenses, the lower the returns earned by its shareowners.
3. Growth in a fund's assets to elephantine size, which enriches managers but destroys the fund's ability to repeat the performance success that engendered that very growth. The bigger the fund, the bigger the fee, and the more

likely the fund's reversion to the mean return delivered by the stock market (minus, of course, the management fees and portfolio turnover costs).

4. The industry's marketing focus, which seems inevitably to demand the creation of new and often highly specialized funds to meet the heated investment passions of the day, creating huge capital inflows and huge fees for managers, but ultimately, very often, also creating huge losses to investors.

Market Timing

The market timing issue is the first obvious conflict of interest, and the added conflict in the late-trading scandal truly astonishes. But late trading is only the small tip of a big iceberg. "Time-zone trading" is likely even larger in its negative impact on fund shareholders. The shocking thing about time-zone trading is that traders usually take advantage of (free) arbitrage between an international fund net asset value calculated at 4 P.M. in New York and closing prices across the Pacific 14 hours earlier. This is no secret, and it has been going on for so long, without significant defenses being erected by managers. Academics have been publishing papers about it at least since the late 1990s.

A prescient article by Boudoukh, Richardson, Subrahmanyam, and Whitelaw (2002) carefully described the time-zone trading strategy, quantified its effectiveness, and showed, with specific examples, how easy it was to make money by gaming the system. It also berated the industry for its benign neglect of the market-timing issue: "When the gains from these strategies are matched by offsetting losses incurred by buy-and-hold investors in these funds...why haven't more funds taken stronger actions to restrict short term trading?" (p. 70).

What is more, the authors cite fully 20 other academic studies on the same point. The Canary hedge-fund settlement noted that 30 hedge funds had blatantly listed their investment strategy as "mutual fund timing." If industry participants were asleep before, that article sounded the alarm and answered the question: "What did we know and when did we know it?" Fund shareholders, if not fund managers, owe these academics a major debt of gratitude.

Yet the sole published response to these authors' revelation was from a representative of the manager whose funds were mentioned in the article. Molitor (2002) berated the AIMR Board of Governors: "Publishing such a piece in a publication that is aimed solely at financial professionals is a bad idea in the best of times, but is abhorrent when investor confidence is already shaken by corporate greed" (p. 17). Nonetheless, nine months later, this very firm initiated a 2 percent redemption fee on its international funds.

Market Timing Broadly Accepted
But the overall level of market timing—not illegal late trading or unethical time-zone trading—suggests that investors are doing too much short-term speculation in mutual funds. There is a lot of money sloshing around the fund system. How much market timing is there? We do not know exactly, but we do know a great deal about what is going on.

First, there is much more timing activity than the industry has acknowledged. By failing to acknowledge that "exchanges out" of one fund to another within the same family are actually redemptions, the ICI has substantially understated fund redemption rates. Such intrafamily redemptions are the clearest, but not only, example of a market timing strategy. While the ICI *reported* an equity fund redemption rate equal to 28 percent of assets in 2002, the actual rate, including exchanges out, was 41 percent, half again higher. Subsequently, the ICI changed its policy and now reports fund exchanges out.

Next, the true redemption rate has soared—from 5 percent to 15 percent in the 1950s through the mid-1970s, to the 30 percent to 35 percent range into the late 1990s (excepting a 60 percent rate in the turbulence of 1987), and to the 40 percent to 50 percent range thereafter. The average fund investor, who not long ago held fund shares for an average of more than 10 years (10 percent redemption rate), now holds shares for less than two and one-half years (41 percent redemption rate).

Investor Trading

Interestingly, industry studies of investor behavior show that the typical fund investor does not do much trading. According to an ICI (2001) survey, in 1988, fully 82 percent of equity fund owners did not make a single redemption. Even if that figure holds, consider this: The 41 percent *total* redemption rate, spread over only the remaining 18 percent of investors, indicates that this small segment of investors has an average holding period of just 160 days. If we assume that one-half of these investors maintained a 10-year holding period, the remaining half would have an average holding period of about 90 days (redemption rate of 446 percent).

When we look at fund objectives, it is easy to see what is going on. International funds win the prize, with an average redemption rate rising from 94 percent a year in 2000 to 97 percent in 2002. During the same period, sector fund redemptions averaged 57 percent and aggressive growth funds, 51 percent.

What is more, the annual report of each mutual fund is required to report total redemptions. It is a revelation to examine some of the funds involved in one aspect or another of the recent timing scandals, where the numbers approach the brazen. The Alger equity funds, with total assets averaging $2 billion in 2002, reported redemptions for the year totaling $9 *billion,* a 440 percent redemption rate. Bank of America's Emerging Markets Fund had a 295 percent annual redemption rate, and Janus Adviser International Growth fund had a 372 percent redemption rate.

The dollar amount of redemptions (but not the turnover rate) is clearly set out in each fund's financial statement without comment and sent to shareholders. This redemption activity, then, is not only going on with the tacit knowledge of the managers, directors, and regulators but is fully disclosed for anyone interested enough to look. Yet never has it been questioned or challenged.

The solution to the problems of excessive market timing by fund traders is straightforward:

1. Close the funds' transaction window at 2:30 P.M. instead of 4:00 P.M. for *everybody.* If the assets for 401(k) plans cannot meet the deadline, they will just have to execute the orders on the *next* day.
2. Impose a redemption fee of 2 percent for shares held for less than, say, 30 days.

But with the fierce competition to attract assets, few firms will have the courage to take these two steps on their own because it would cost them business. We need to urge the Securities and Exchange Commission to impose these standards on this reluctant industry. Also, we need to urge a firm such as Morningstar to report on the redemption rates of individual funds. As it almost invariably does, the sunlight of disclosure would quickly modify the behavior of both fund managers and traders in fund shares.

Conflict of Interest in Fund Fees

There is no disagreement that both fund directors and management companies share a common interest in providing good returns to the fund shareholders. But, when it comes to *how* good, their interests diverge. Why? Because the higher the management fees and other fund expenses, the lower the fund's return.

Sometimes this relationship exists on a virtual dollar-for-dollar basis. For example, the correlation between the yields money market funds deliver to their shareholders and the expense ratios of these funds is –0.98. When money market yields are 3 percent, for example, a high-cost fund will deliver as little as 1 3/4 percent to its owners, but a low-cost fund will deliver as much as 2 3/4 percent, more than 50 percent of additional annual income for the investor. Indeed, whenever fund gross returns are commodity-like (e.g., stock and bond index funds in addition to money market funds), the same kind of locked-in relationship of returns to costs prevails.

But even in actively managed funds, costs clearly differentiate the superior performers from the inferior performers over the long run. Consider a recent study prepared quantifying the relationship between the *total* costs of equity funds and their returns. Using all 803 diversified U.S. equity funds in the Morningstar database in existence over the full 10-year period ended August 30, 2003, we compared each fund's investment returns with its costs. The average expense ratio for these funds was 1.3 percent, and their average portfolio transaction costs were estimated at 0.7 percent, for a total of 2.0 percent. Transaction costs were conservatively assumed to total 1.0 percent of turnover, which is equal to 0.50 percent on each side of the trade.

The high-cost quartile of funds, with all-in expenses of 3.4 percent, provided an average annual return of 6.8 percent. But the impact of initial sales charges was omitted, and expense ratios were significantly below the norm because few funds had 12b-1 fees at the start of the period. Further, because no adjustment was made for survivor bias, the average return was also overstated. The low-cost quartile, with all-in expenses of 1.0 percent, provided an average annual return of 10.2 percent, earning an advantage of 3.4 percentage points per year. On a fund-by-fund basis, the inverse correlation between cost and return was –0.60 (–1.0 is perfect negative correlation).

What is more, the funds with the highest costs also assumed the highest risks, with a standard deviation—a measure of volatility—averaging some 30 percent higher than the lowest-cost funds. High-cost funds also generated the highest turnover (160 percent versus 22 percent) and produced the poorest tax-efficiency. As a result, the low-cost group had an even greater advantage (3.8 percent per year) in risk-adjusted return and an advantage of 4.0 percent per year in after-tax return. Compounded over the decade, $10,000 invested in the average high-cost fund grew to $19,300; the same investment in the average low-cost fund grew to $26,400. It is hard to imagine a more persuasive case regarding the relationship between fund costs and fund returns.

But there *is* an even more persuasive case. For when we sort the funds into their nine Morningstar "style boxes," the consistency of the performance margin (without risk and tax adjustments) was little short of astonishing. The low-cost quartile provided a consistent edge in the remarkably narrow range of 2.3 percent to 2.7 percent per year among the nearly 500 large-cap funds and in two of the three mid-cap styles. In the remaining smaller and less statistically reliable styles (the small-cap value group had 28 funds), the excess returns achieved by the low-cost funds were even higher, averaging 5.6 percent per year.

The establishment of a fair cost structure that includes management fees, portfolio turnover expenses, operational expenditures, and sales loads must be the categorical imperative of the fund board. Given the circumstances of fund governance, however, the directors affiliated with a management company have a compelling interest in the reverse. They seek the highest fees that traffic will bear and public opinion will tolerate. Managers not only place a high priority on their own profitability, but they arguably have a fiduciary duty to their own shareholders to do exactly that. Further, independent directors seem reluctant to challenge that interest. Warren Buffett (1985) states: "When the managers care about fees and the directors don't, guess who wins? Negotiating with oneself seldom produces a barroom brawl." Fee negotiation is a myth, and the fund shareholders suffer not only measurably but substantially.

Asset Growth

It must be obvious that as the assets of actively managed funds grow, the challenges of implementing their investment strategies increase. When the assets grow exponentially, so too do the challenges.

1. The number of stocks available for the portfolio manager to choose from shrinks.
2. Portfolio transaction activity tends to either become more expensive, as average trade size increases or, for better or worse, to diminish.
3. As the fund grows, investment returns have a powerful tendency to revert to the market mean.

These are three major negatives for investors who chose the fund because of the superior returns it previously generated. Contrarily, exceptional returns generate exceptional asset growth, and so fund managers are enriched accordingly.

The pressures to let funds grow beyond their ability to be effectively managed are powerful, and only in rare cases do managers summon the courage to close funds to new investments. Fund closings are the exception that proves the rule: Only 10 of the 3,363 domestic equity mutual funds in existence in 2003 had completely closed, although another 127 were closed to new investors. In an industry where average assets of the 50 largest equity funds have burgeoned from $4.6 billion to $23.3 billion in a decade, why have closings been so rare? It seems reasonable to assume that it is because of the manager's interest in ever-higher fees, which outweighs the shareholder's interest in sustaining superior returns.

Let us consider a single (extreme) example of how the interaction of these trends works in practice. I will call it Fund X, but the actual name is well known.

During its early years, it turned in an astonishingly successful record, outpacing the Standard & Poor's (S&P) 500 Index by an *average* of 26 percentage points per year from 1978 through 1983. With such success, its assets burgeoned from a mere $22 million to $1.6 billion during that period. While its performance then reverted *toward* the mean, its excess return from 1984 through 1993 remained a healthy 4 percentage points per year. By then its assets had grown to a staggering $31 billion, and the excess returns came to an abrupt halt. Four years of losing to the S&P followed, and then three small gains and two small losses. From 1993 through 2006, it has fallen an average of almost 2 percentage points per year behind the 500 index. This is a far cry from its success in earlier years.

With soaring management fees leading the way, the expenses borne by the shareholders of Fund X kept growing and growing. From $400,000 in 1978 to $17 million in 1984, to $166 million in 1991, and $500 million in 1996, expenses peaked at $763 million in 2001. At the outset of the period, there were small fees for large returns. At the period's conclusion, there were awesome fees for mediocre returns. Obviously, the fund's asset growth was wonderful for its managers, but the exact opposite was true for its owners.

Further, of course, the larger the fund grew, the more it became like an index fund. Reversion to the market mean return strikes again. Between 1978 and 1982, the S&P return explained 82 percent of the return of Fund X, but between 1998 and 2002, it explained fully 97 percent. If one believes in indexing, that is not a bad thing. But from the vantage point of investors who paid fund fees and costs that totaled $3 billion during that five-year period, such a windfall for the manager is outrageous. From the standpoint of the managers who are receiving these fees, however, they are the souls of rationality: "We made the fund large, and we deserve to be paid for that success." If that argument appeals to you, welcome to the mutual fund industry.

Marketing Focus—We Make What Will Sell

An article by Friend (2003) describes Hollywood as exemplifying

> *the most joyless aspects of capitalism. The "industry," as it insists in calling itself, packages ideas and images as "products," and then values them according to how they "penetrate" markets, support "platforms" of ancillary products, and "brand" a company as a reliable purveyor of similar products. (p. 41)*

If that makes Hollywood sound like what the mutual fund industry has become, you are paying attention to the march of history.

Some 50 years ago, fund management companies were relatively small, privately held professional firms, which focused on stewardship. Marketing had yet to rear its ugly head. Those managers provided their services to just 75 mutual funds, of which 66 were essentially what today we would call large-cap blend funds, holding a widely diversified portfolio of blue-chip stocks with returns that generally paralleled the returns of the stock market, as measured by the S&P 500 Index. Most of these fund managers ran but a single stock fund. In short, funds sold what they made.

What a difference 50 years makes. Today, giant financial conglomerates that focus on salesmanship dominate the industry. There are some 3,600 equity funds large enough to be tracked by Morningstar, and only 500 of them closely resemble their blue-chip forebears. What are these other funds? Two thousand funds are diversified equity funds investing in one of the eight remaining style boxes, which make bets away from the total market—bets on large-cap growth stocks, or small-cap value stocks, and mid-cap blend stocks. Another 400 funds invest in specialized industry segments, such as technology, telecommunications, and computers. And 700 are international funds, which invest predominately in foreign markets.

In general, these other fund categories assume higher risks than the marketlike funds of earlier times. In 1951, an investor could throw a dart at the tiny list of funds and have a 9-in-10 chance of picking a fund whose returns would parallel the return of the market. Today, the investor's chances of doing so are just 1 out of 8. For better or worse, selecting mutual funds has become an art form, and fund choice rules the day.

Packaging New "Products"

The fund industry has become a business school case study in marketing. Funds package new ancillary "products" to penetrate new markets and to expand penetration of existing markets. Modern marketing has played a major role in the burgeoning profitability of investment managers, and, in that sense, it has worked. The hundreds of billions of dollars poured into these new products, along with appreciation in the value of existing products during the great bull market, created a bonanza for fund managers. From 1980 to 2002, total mutual fund assets rose 60 times over, from $115 billion to about $7 trillion. Yet despite the staggering economies of scale in this industry, fund management fees and expenses rose 90 times over, from $800 million to $72 billion. The average expense ratio of the only exception to the industry's external management structure—the Vanguard funds, operated on an "at-cost" basis—declined 54 percent during the same period, from 0.59 percent to 0.27 percent.

The reason expenses have increased is that the industry's desire for market share demands the creation of funds that the investing public wanted to buy. What the public wanted to buy, and was willing to pay higher fees for, was the hot idea of the day. In the stock bubble of the 1998 to 2000 market, it was the desire for "new economy" funds—Internet funds, technology funds, telecommunications funds, and aggressive growth funds. Indeed, these risky sectors also dominated the portfolios of even the more diversified traditional growth funds. The public had little interest in the more sedate value funds. The industry created these risky new funds and promoted them simply because they would sell.

The trends are easily measured. From 1998 through 2000, the public bought $460 billion of high price-earnings ratio *growth* funds, at ever-ascending prices, and redeemed a net total of $100 billion in lower price-earnings ratio *value* funds. Then, after the market neared its lows, investors switched gears. In 2001–2002, these growth funds experienced net redemptions of $46 billion, and value funds took in $89 billion of additional capital. Never was it clearer that the mutual fund industry had become a market-sensitive industry.

This sensitivity worked to the advantage of fund managers. That huge flow of additional capital to new-economy–oriented funds produced some $30 billion of additional management fees and investor costs between 1998 and 2000. While these costs tumbled when the bubble burst, investors paid an additional $20 billion of fees and costs to the speculative funds during 2001–2002. This total revenue of $50 billion was accompanied by only modest incremental expenditures by fund managers. The focus on marketing has been a remarkably profitable strategy for managers.

Fund and Shareholder Returns

Alas, the managers' strategy was not profitable for investors. That same marketing strategy cost shareholders hundreds of billions of dollars. Aided and abetted by the aggressive sales promotion of the managers, investors moved their money into the most vulnerable areas of the market and withdrew money from the least vulnerable areas, precisely the reverse of what they should have been doing. We now have the tools to recognize just how badly these investors fared. While mutual funds report only their "time-weighted" returns (standard measure for the return a mutual fund earns on each share), it is time that they be required also to report the "dollar-weighted" returns that measure what the fund actually has earned for its shareholders as a group.

While the suggestion for such a mandatory second measurement that I recommended a decade ago is only beginning to bear fruit, those shareholder returns can be readily calculated. It is instructive to consider the dollar-weighted returns earned by the shareholders of a whole variety of the largest and most popular growth funds during the years 1998 to 2002. Roughly speaking, the $460 billion that investors poured into this group of new-economy funds as the market reached its peak resulted in a loss of some $300 billion in the decline that followed.

It is fair to say that (1) fund managers made huge profits by their desire to make what would sell, and (2) fund investors absorbed huge losses from buying into that strategy. Put another way, the change in the mutual fund industry, in which the managers have come to consider money management a business focused on their desire for profits rather than a profession focused on the interests of their fund shareholders, could itself well be considered a certain kind of scandal. Let us look at the record.

MARKET RETURNS VERSUS FUND AND INVESTOR RETURNS

During the period 1980 to 2005, the U.S. stock market, as measured by the S&P 500 Index, provided an annual rate of return of 12.5 percent. As the trained, experienced investment professionals employed by the industry's managers compete with one another to pick the best stocks, their results average out. Thus, the average mutual fund should earn the market's return before costs. The after-cost return on the average mutual fund adjusted to take into account the (inferior) records of funds that failed to survive the period was 10.0 percent. Since all-in fund costs can be estimated at perhaps 2.5 percent per year, the difference of 2.5 percent between market and fund after-cost returns is unsurprising. Even that number overstates the fund record, because it ignores the negative impact of sales charges.

The returns that fund managers actually deliver to fund shareholders serve as the definitive test of whether investors are getting a fair deal. It is reasonable to expect the average mutual fund investor to earn a return that falls well short of the return of the average fund. Investors have paid a large timing penalty in their decisions, investing little in equity funds early in the period and huge amounts as the market bubble reached its maximum. During 1984 to 1988, when the S&P Index was below 300, investors purchased an average of just $11 billion per year of equity funds. They added another $105 billion per year when the index was still below 1100. But, after it topped the 1100 mark in 1998, they added to their holdings at an annual rate of $218 billion. Then, during the three quarters before the recent rally, with the index below 900, equity fund investors actually withdrew $80 billion. Clearly, this perverse market sensitivity poorly served fund investors.

But fund investors paid not only a timing penalty but also a selection penalty. As described earlier, the vast majority of fund investors chose to invest not in the staid middle-of-the-road old-economy funds but in the booming new-economy funds, which boasted spectacular short-term records. Unfortunately, these were the funds that would have the farthest to fall when the bubble burst.

As a result of these timing and selection penalties, during the past 25 years, while the stock market was providing an annual return of 12.5 percent and the average equity *fund* was earning an annual return of 10.0 percent, the average fund *investor* was earning only 7.3 percent a year.

Compounded over the full period, the 2.5 percent penalty incurred by the average fund was huge, as a $10,000 investment in the index would have grown to $179,200, versus just $98,200 in the average equity fund—just 57 percent of what was there for the taking. But the dual penalties of faulty timing and adverse selection were even larger, as the compound return earned by the average fund investor tumbled to $48,200, a stunning 27 percent of the return provided by the stock market.

It is the myriad existing conflicts between the interests of fund managers and the interests of fund owners that bear so much of the responsibility for this staggering gap between the stock market's return and the returns earned by fund investors, and even the returns earned by the funds themselves. The unacceptable and partly illegal market timing scandal has gained a great deal of well-deserved attention. But it pales in significance when compared with the powerful impact of high costs on reducing fund returns, the force of fund size in diminishing fund returns, and the marketing focus that tempted too many investors to purchase funds that they should never have bought.

That conflict is severe, and it is unacceptable. It can be resolved only by implementing reforms in fund structure that create a governance model that puts the shareholders in the driver's seat, where all those years ago the Investment Company Act of 1940 insisted that they belong. Such structural reform must be our highest priority, and the sooner the better.

FUND STEWARDSHIP

Truth told, even if the funds in which you have invested were not participants in the scandals, you might consider using the stewardship standards discussed here to reappraise how you think about all of the mutual funds that you favor with your trust.

We know that past performance is a highly unreliable guide to the returns funds earn in the future. So it is well worth considering selecting funds based on the extent to which they place the investment interests of their shareholders ahead of the business interests of their managers—the very principle suggested by the Investment Company Act of 1940. When the Act says that mutual funds must be "organized, operated, and managed" in the interests of shareowners rather than in the interests of "investment advisers and underwriters [distributors]," it places the stewardship of investor assets over the salesmanship of the "products" of the managers.

There are 12 measurable standards (see Exhibit 15.1) that help to reflect the degree to which mutual fund managers balance these two distinct, and often competing, interests. Before discussing these standards, a disclaimer: These elements represent the viewpoint that was the driving force in creating Vanguard, even though the highest standards of stewardship are inevitably upheld only imperfectly by us mere mortals. What is more, these standards may be self-serving, given that the Vanguard model of a fund group with a truly *mutual*, shareholder-owned structure has yet to be emulated or copied. However, these standards do carry the conviction that they are the right ones for fund investors and, in the long run, the right ones for the fund industry. Now let us examine the 12 standards.

1. Fund Costs: Management Fees and Operating Expense Ratios

Nowhere is the conflict between fund managers and fund shareholders more sharply and obviously manifested than in the level of management fees and operating expense ratios. One major aspect of stewardship, then, is the setting of management fees and reconciling the conflict between managers who seek to maximize their fees and shareholders who benefit by minimizing them. Lower fee rates, therefore, reflect a higher stewardship score. Since lower expense ratios clearly lead to higher returns, it is only common sense for fund investors to do their fund shopping in the low-cost quartile. When you select a mutual fund, you get what you do not pay for. So give 3 "stewardship" points to the tiny handful of firms with very low costs and 0 to those above the (high) industry norm.

2. Portfolio Turnover

A similar inverse relationship exists between a fund's portfolio turnover and its returns. Higher turnover correlates with lower returns. For example, the lowest-turnover quartile of equity funds (with an average turnover of 15 percent per year) earned fully 2.3 percentage points of extra annual return versus the highest-turnover quartile (an average turnover of 176 percent per year). This relationship was also remarkably strong, ranging from about 1 percent to 2.3 percent in eight of the nine Morningstar style boxes but reaching 3.9 percent in the small-cap growth group. These gaps in returns appear to reflect largely the *costs* of turnover. For taxable investors, however, turnover also increases the tax burden, and on an after-tax basis the advantage for the low-turnover quartile rises from 2.2 percentage points to fully 3.1 percentage points. Let us award 3 stewardship points for lower turnover (say, below 30 percent), and 0 points for turnover above 100 percent.

And, we showed earlier, funds in the low-cost quartile for total costs (including expense ratios and turnover costs) provide a combined cost/benefit ratio that is even stronger than its two individual parts—the highest-cost quartile, with total costs of 3.4 percent, trailed the returns provided by the lowest-cost quartile, with total costs of 1.0 percent, by 3.4 percent annually (10.2% – 6.8%). The jury is

Exhibit 15.1 Calculating Your Manager's Stewardship Quotient

Manager Name _____

Stewardship Quotient*

	SQ Scores				
	3	**2**	**1**	**0**	**Score**
1. Management Fees and Operating Expense Ratios	Very Low	Below Average	Roughly Average	Above Average	_____
2. Equity Portfolio Turnover	Under 30%	30%–60%	60%–100%	Over 100%	_____
3. Equity Diversification	Owns total market	Large cap–blend	Other style box	Sector fund	_____
4. Marketing Orientation	Sells what it makes	Gives in, but rarely	Gives in sometimes	Makes what will sell	_____
5. Advertising	None	Limited	Extensive	Performance	_____
6. Pays for Shelf Space	No	Broker-dealer Low pay	Broker-dealer High pay	Supermarkets	_____
7. Sales Commissions	Strictly no-load	No-load with small 12b-1 fee	Low-load	Substantial sales loads +12b-1 fees	_____
8. Shareholder Stability (Redemption Rate)	Under 20%	21–35%	36%–60%	Over 60%	_____
9. Limitations on Fund Size	Clear size limits	Frequent fund closings	Rare fund closings	No limits on size	_____
10. Experience, Stability of Portfolio Managers	More than 15 years	10–14 years	7–10 years	Less than 7 years	_____
11. Insider Ownership of Fund Shares	Large in many funds	Moderate in many funds	Moderate in few funds	Small or none	_____
12. Organization of Manager	Mutual	Privately owned	Publicly owned	Conglomerate subsidiary	_____
			Total Points		_____
				SQ*	_____

* Stewardship quotient for manager = (Total score / 18) x 100.

297

in, and the verdict is costs matter. Funds that are managed with a view toward low operating and turnover costs for their investors reflect a significantly higher concern for the stewardship of investor assets than their peers.

3. Equity Diversification

Even as stewardship has something to do with organizing, operating, and managing mutual funds that have low costs and low turnover, it also has something to do with mutual funds that are very broadly diversified and designed to be held for the long term. At one extreme lies the all-stock-market index fund, owning essentially all of the publicly traded equities in the United States and holding them forever. At the other extreme, we have the specialty funds, investing in narrow market sectors such as telecommunications and technology, and ultimately created for trading purposes. In the middle lie the funds following various style specialties, such as mid-cap value and small-cap growth. These funds represent a bet that from time to time they will outpace the market as a whole and can be part of a portfolio and/or traded on an opportunistic basis. In its early era of stewardship, the fund industry was dominated by broad, market-oriented funds. But in its recent era of salesmanship, such funds have found themselves in the minority, surrounded by an army of more specialized funds with narrow policies.

Vanguard admits to a strong bias toward highly diversified funds, especially low-cost index funds. These funds deliver no more or less than what they promise—as close to 100 percent of the stock market's annual rate of return as is achievable. Because of costs, beating the market is by definition a loser's game for investors as a group, so earning almost 100 percent of the stock market's annual return is, in and of itself, a virtual guarantee that the investor will, over the long-term, accumulate more assets than his neighbors. I would award 3 stewardship points for highly diversified funds (including all-market index funds) and 0 for sector funds.

4. Marketing Orientation

What is more, the record is clear that the gap between the returns earned under the highly diversified, low-cost, broad market concept relative to the more concentrated funds-as-individual-stocks concept is far larger than the cost differential. The cost differential reflects only the economic component of the investment management service. But there is also a large emotional component to the returns earned by investors. Because buying and holding the entire market is apt to entail far less trading and far less emotion, such investors actually earn the market return.

But when fund managers act as salesmen of specialized funds, investors almost universally act at the wrong time. In the expectation that investors will take the bait, these managers favor the fads that are in the momentary limelight. Partly because of their own greed, investors do exactly that, jumping in after a particular style peaks and just before it goes out of style. As a wise man once said: "The issue is not people with investment problems, it is investments with people problems."

Fund managers cannot possibly be unaware that the best time to sell an exciting new fund concept is usually the worst time to buy it, a trend so clearly illustrated by the industry's forming more and more technology funds as their prices soared. Early in the 1990s, for example, it was rare to see more than a single new tech fund created in a single year. But between 1998 and 2001, 133 new technology funds were created. After the fall in the market—led by those very funds—the number plummeted to 3 funds in 2002 to none in 2003.

The manager's range of choice between solid, diversified funds that largely reflect the stock market as a whole, rather than specialized funds whose popularity blows back and forth in the market winds, is a powerful reflection of its emphasis on stewardship versus salesmanship. The highest stewardship is reflected by those managers with the strongest discipline against pandering to the public taste for the hottest new investment ideas, especially those who limit their offerings to what they do well, which may be a single fund or even a half-dozen. Mutual fund managers who jumped on the new-economy bandwagon a few years ago and lured in, collectively, hundreds of billions of investor dollars that went up in smoke when the bubble burst were part of firms that made what would sell. No stewardship points for them; 3 points for firms that simply sold what they made.

5. Advertising

When it comes to advertising, the stewardship–salesmanship orientation is patently obvious. The existing fund shareholders pay for it, but the fund managers benefit by enticing new shareholders to invest in their funds, thus increasing their revenue. It is often argued that the manager is spending "its own money" to promote the fund, but, of course, it is the fees paid by shareholders that are the source of this money. These fees could otherwise be waived and returned to the fund shareholders. There is simply no evidence whatsoever that advertising benefits fund investors by bringing in new assets in an amount adequate to create economies of scale that offset the amounts spent.

But there is considerable evidence that building fund assets above a certain size impinges on its manager's ability to create superior performance. In generating costs to investors, advertising expenditures reflect a serious question about stewardship. Spending these dollars to promote fund growth suggests that salesmanship is in the driver's seat. For whatever reason, most fund firms find it necessary to spend shareholder dollars to promote new and existing funds. So I would award the 3-point maximum to firms that do not advertise, 2 points to those that do so only on a limited basis, and 1 point to those whose advertisements are rife.

Almost universally, fund managers advertise only their most successful funds, and they do so only after they have generated high returns. When the funds fail or when the stock market has tumbled, there is complete silence. Ads that follow this pattern are inherently misleading. Coinciding precisely with the stock market's peak, 44 funds in the March 2000 *Money* magazine advertised returns that averaged an astonishing 85.6 percent during the preceding year. Could these fund advertisers really have been thinking about stewardship? Today, it sure looks a lot more like salesmanship. Of those 44 funds, 9 no longer exist. The average return of the funds that survived was –39.5 percent, or 125 percentage points short of the gains they had touted.

6. Shelf Space

When funds pay for shelf space to build distribution, fund advertising finds a sorry counterpart. A decade ago, when the first of today's mutual fund supermarkets came into existence, it was a transforming moment for the industry. No longer would investors pay their own commissions or transaction costs when they shopped there. Rather, the managers whose funds were effectively listed for sale would pay for shelf space, a marketing concept if ever there were one. Few observers expressed concern that the apparent ability to make what appeared to be "free" transactions would lead to a rise in market timing or to a high-turnover mentality by investors. Neither was concern expressed that all of the fund's shareholders were effectively paying for the shelf space, even though few of them were actually utilizing the service.

It was not long, of course, before the national wire houses that did not view themselves as supermarkets demanded similar treatment from funds to get their sales support. As the going rate for bringing in assets for funds rose from 0.20 percent to 0.25 percent, to 0.30 percent, to what now seems to be 0.40 percent, firms that never considered their funds to be products of supermarkets soon found that sharing management fees with brokers was a requisite to receiving the broker's sales support. Somewhere along the way, an important line was crossed, and stewardship was on the wrong side of it. So, 3 points for funds that will have no part of paying for shelf space, 1 or 2 points for funds that are paying for broker-dealer space, and 0 points for funds that are spending their shareholders' resources (directly or indirectly) on supermarkets.

7. Sales Loads

It is no secret that the fund industry, like the financial services industry in general, is in many respects a marketing business. Indeed, the industry would be but a fraction of its current giant size had there not been securities brokers and salesmen to carry the message to investors who otherwise might have learned about mutual funds far later and with far less information. Although these costs obviously detract from the returns investors earn, that information service is essential and it has value. But it does not appear that we are getting the right information to investors. The focus is on past performance, despite our knowledge that, if it is not negatively correlated with future returns, the linkage is anything but causal. To earn their keep, advisers should focus their clients on factors such as sound asset allocation, broad diversification, low cost, and simplicity.

In broad generalization, no-load funds are less engaged in salesmanship than load funds. After all, the purpose of the load is to compensate a salesperson. While there are a number of good fund managers with reasonable sales charges and 12b-1 fees, the fact is that these costs are a significant drag on returns. So consider awarding no stewardship points for these funds; if you think other factors dictate, award 1 point.

8. Shareholder Stability

During the early decades in the fund business, market timing was anathema. Shareholder redemptions averaged about 8 percent of assets, suggesting a holding period of 12-plus years for the average investor. But then the redemption rate then began to steadily rise, reaching an average of 41 percent in 2002, a holding period of just 2.4 years for the average fund investor.

Part, but only part, of the increase was accounted for by illegal late trading and by the international time-zone trading. (The average redemption rate for international funds was more than 100 percent per year.) But the largest part is accounted for by the fact that we have created an industry of funds with relatively narrow styles and funds focusing on concentrated sectors. These are funds bought by investors, not to be held for an investment lifetime, but to be sold at some point along the way. Unless they are given free rides through late and time-zone trading, among other sources, investors who engage in such foolishness are playing a loser's game. The problem is that substantial trading volume generates costly portfolio turnover for the fund itself, which is a disservice to all those investors who trusted the fund managers to be their stewards.

"The proof of the pudding is in the eating." If funds are heavily focused on stewardship, they ought to have redemption rates of no more than about 20 percent. About 1,800 funds, or one-fifth of the total, meet this test. While that seems like a high number to me, let us award them 3 full stewardship points, with 2 points with rates somewhat below the current 42 percent norm—say 20 to 35 percent—and a stingy 1 point if the redemption rates stay below 60 percent. But 0 points when rates exceed that level, along with a warning that when redemptions exceed 100 percent of fund assets, there must be heavy market timing going on.

9. Limitations on Fund Size

Many, perhaps most, managers are in the business of gathering the maximum possible amount of assets, the better to increase their fee revenues. Yet it is no secret that, in the field of investment management, "Nothing fails like success." Promoted aggressively, funds with apparently superior performance records draw large amounts of capital, and eventually get muscle bound. Their investable universe shrinks, the impact of their portfolio transactions on the prices at which they buy and sell rises, and soon their ability even to strive to recover the glory of their early days has vanished. A perfect example is Fund X (discussed earlier) whose glory days in 1978 to 1983 have long since ended.

In cases like this, salesmanship is clearly in command, and any notion of stewardship seems powerless to influence the direction of the funds. While index funds and some other funds with very low turnover are relatively immune to becoming "dinosaurs," most funds are not. So I would award 3 stewardship points to firms that announce in advance any limitations on assets (and live by them!); 2 points to those that frequently close funds to new investors so as to preserve their investment characteristics for existing shareholders; just 1 point to firms that have closed funds, even if infrequently and too late, or, even worse, have announced the closing in advance, a sure-fire way to increase cash flow; and 0 points to funds that are allowed to grow without concern for the obvious consequences.

10. Experience and Stability of Portfolio Managers

A critically important part of measuring stewardship is what happens behind the scenes of fund management. Do managers act like, well, stewards? It is not easy to measure trust and confidence and integrity, but information about the age, education, professional experience, and tenure of fund executives and portfolio managers is widely available. In general, investors should go with the veterans who have worked through a market cycle or two, who can clearly articulate their philosophy and strategy, and who run portfolios that give living expression to those factors. Typically, such managers also focus on the long term, whether they emphasize what are called value stocks or growth stocks.

Morningstar reports that the typical portfolio manager runs a fund for just five years, which seems like a long way from stewardship. Consider a typical shareholder who owns five funds and holds them, however unlikely, over an investment lifetime of 50 years. Employing 50 different portfolio managers over 50 years seems much more like a choice of products than the selection of a trustee, let alone the near impossibility of those 50 managers posting returns superior to the market index. So I would reserve 3 stewardship points for managers with 15 years or so of experience and tenure, with 0 points (except under special circumstances) for those with fewer than seven years on duty.

More than incidentally, investors should not ignore funds run by teams or investment committees. We know that many seemingly well-qualified portfolio manager "stars" have turned out to be more like comets, burning out after a few years in the limelight. In a real sense, the wisdom of the collective seems more suggestive of stewardship, especially since the stars are often promoted with dazzling salesmanship. I would not hesitate to award 3 points to funds run by experienced investment committees.

11. Insider Ownership

Investors should prefer fund directors, executives, and portfolio managers who "eat their own cooking," by investing importantly in the shares of the funds they manage. A few firms even take this philosophy to a wonderful extreme, requiring their insiders to invest all of their liquid assets in their funds. Three stewardship points for them and for others who approach that goal in spirit but not quite in letter. After all, we can expect a steward to have special concern in the administration of his own investments. If there is little or no ownership by the fund insiders, 0 points.

Unfortunately, there is little solid information on this vital issue, with management company officials and portfolio managers required to disclose their holdings in broad ranges, and no requirement that they disclose their fund share transactions. As the scandals have shown, some fund managers were even engaging in market timing in the shares of the very funds they managed. Investors ought to consider investing in funds in which the stewards are not only willing, but eager, to disclose their policies, holdings, and transactions alike.

As to fund holdings by fund directors, there is also a serious, indeed inexplicable, information gap. Somehow the Investment Company Institute persuaded the SEC to exempt fund directors from disclosure of the precise number of shares they own, the standard for all other public corporations. Rather, like fund managers, fund directors need only disclose the range of their holdings, which are stated as none, $10,000 or less, $10,000 to $50,000, $50,000 to $100,000, and over $100,000. These ranges apply to the fund and for all funds in the group. What earthly good is it for an investor to learn that a trustee has spread a modest $100,000 among 100 or more funds in the group? The sooner regulations require funds to provide full and accurate disclosure, the better.

12. Organization of Managers

In the early decades of this industry, virtually all fund management companies were small partnerships or corporations, closely held by their principals. They were but a step removed from the funds they managed and looked at themselves as trustees, stewards of the assets entrusted to their care, members of the profession of investment management. By 1958, this sound structure was on the way out. Public offering of management company shares became possible, and numerous management company initial public offerings quickly followed. At that point, managers began to focus on the price of their stock and the interest of their public owners. Their earlier focus on the welfare of their fund shareholders had to compete with their focus on the welfare of their own owners, which required building the fund group's asset base, increasing revenues, marketing aggressively, and making as much profit as they could.

But that was only the beginning. Gradually, both public and private management companies were purchased by giant financial conglomerates—banks and brokers and insurance companies, U.S. and international—whose principal interest was not the return on the capital of the fund investors they served but on the return on their own capital. If a bank bought a fund manager for $1 billion, the fund had better earn its, say, 12 percent cost of capital ($120 million per year), or else. As a result, professional interest as a steward of shareholder assets was superseded by business interest in salesmanship, marketing, and revenues. Manager profits became the name of the game, and the industry's values changed accordingly.

Thirty-six of the 50 largest fund managers are owned by giant financial conglomerates. Of those remaining 14, 7 are publicly held, and 6 remain private. The remaining fund manager, Vanguard, is mutually owned by the funds it manages and therefore by shareholders. You are free to agree or disagree with my awarding 3 stewardship points to firms that choose the mutual structure, 2 point to the firms that remain private, and 1 point for those that are publicly held. And if you agree that the spirit of stewardship is vastly diminished when a fund manager is owned by a conglomerate far removed from the fund's operations, a score of 0 points seems the right judgment for funds operating under such a structure.

If you decide to leave the fund groups that have betrayed your trust, you might consider these 12 elements of stewardship in selecting replacement funds. You will be best served if you focus on those fund managers who strike a balance between stewardship and salesmanship, and hold the interest of their fund shareholders at the highest possible level.

Come to think of it, this list may have even a broader use. Rather than thinking of it only as series of checkpoints for the selection of new funds for investors who wish to move away from the scandal-riddled firms, I believe that investors would profit by thinking of the list as a series of checkpoints in selecting the firms that will be responsible for managing their shareholders' assets.

You will find, I think, few fund firms that have Stewardship Quotients higher than 150 and many that have SQs below 50. It is a very safe bet, in my hardly objective view, that during the decade that lies ahead the former group will deliver significantly higher returns to investors.

REFERENCES

Bogle, J. C. 1999. *Common Sense on Mutual Funds: New Imperatives for the Intelligent Investor.* New York: John Wiley & Sons.

Boudoukh, J., M. Richardson, M. Subrahmanyam, and R. F. Whitelaw. 2002. "Stale Prices and Strategies for Trading Mutual Funds," *Financial Analysts Journal* 58: 4 (July/August): 53–71.

Buffett, W. 1985. Chairman's Letter to the Shareholders, *Annual Report of Berkshire Hathaway*, Berkshire Hathaway, Inc.

Fink, M. P. 2003. ICI President's Report at the ICI General Membership Meeting, *Investment Company Institute*, http://www.ici.org/issues/dis/03_gmm_fink_spch.html.

Friend, T. 2003. " Remake Man," *The New Yorker*, June 2, 40.

Investment Company Institute. 2001. *Fundamentals: Redemption Activity of Mutual Fund Owners* 10: 1 (March): 1–8.

Investment Company Institute. 2003. *Mutual Fund Fact Book*, http://www.ici.org/pdf/2003_factbook.pdf.

Lowenstein, R. 2003. "The Purist," *New York Times Magazine*, December 28, p. 44.

Molitor, J. S. 2002. Letter to the AIMR Board of Governors, *Financial Analysts Journal* 58: 6 (November/December): 17.

State of New York, Office of the Attorney General. 2003. Complaint against Canary Capital Partners, LLC, September, www.oag.state.ny.us/press/22003/sep/Canary_complaint.pdf.

Strauss, L.C. 2003. "Putnam Surveys the Damage: New CEO Seeks to Rebuild Investor Confidence; Janus to Repay $31.5 Million," *Barron's*, December 22, p. F2.

ABOUT THE AUTHOR

John C. Bogle is Founder of The Vanguard Group, Inc., and President of the Bogle Financial Markets Research Center. He created Vanguard in 1974 and served as Chairman and Chief Executive Officer until 1996 and Senior Chairman until 2000. He had been associated with a predecessor company since 1951, immediately following his graduation from Princeton University, *magna cum laude* in Economics. In 2004, *TIME* magazine named Mr. Bogle as one of the world's 100 most powerful and influential people, and *Institutional Investor* presented him with its Lifetime Achievement Award. Mr. Bogle is a bestselling author, beginning with *Bogle on Mutual Funds: New Perspectives for the Intelligent Investor* (1993); *Common Sense on Mutual Funds: New Imperatives for the Intelligent Investor* (1999); *John Bogle on Investing: The First 50 Years* (2000); *Character Counts: The Creation and Building of The Vanguard Group* (2002); *The Battle for the Soul of Capitalism* (2005); and *The Little Book of Common Sense Investing* (2007). His seventh book, *Enough: True Measures of Money, Business, and Life*, was published by John Wiley & Sons in November 2008.

CHAPTER 16

Identifying Mutual Fund Stewardship

JOHN A. HASLEM, Ph.D.
Professor Emeritus of Finance, Robert H. Smith School of Business, University of Maryland

The Investment Company Act . . . places the stewardship of investor assets over the salesmanship of the. . ." products" of the advisers. [When problems occur,] the issue is not people with investment *problems, it is investments with* people *problems.*
—John C. Bogle, "Has Your Fund Manager Betrayed Your Trust?"

The year 2003 unleashed a scandal of huge proportions in the mutual funds industry. These revelations brought forth intense feelings of shareholder betrayal, anger, dismay, and financial loss to the millions whose assets were improperly and illegally diminished And, these emotions were rightly justified. *TIME* magazine's Thottam (2003) reports that 50 percent of 88 scandal-plagued funds had special arrangements allowing market timing, 30 percent assisted market timers to "cover their tracks," 10 percent reported possible late trading, and three funds approved market timing.

Former New York Attorney General Spitzer found numerous and disturbing incidents of illegal and improper behavior, which illustrated ever so graphically the need for tough reform of the industry. But the scandal did not bring forth significant reform with real sunlight on fund advisers, operations, costs, and fees. Certainly, objective students of the funds industry agree that shareholders deserve much greater protection and real transparency.

In a real sense, the need for significant change derives from the important role mutual funds play in the financial well-being of individual investors, who have their wealth and retirements at risk. And a large risk it is. *There are over 90 million fund shareholders with assets of over $10 trillion. Unhappily, the industry scandal touched funds with assets equal to 20 percent of the industry total.*

The quandary mutual fund shareholders found themselves in has an easy solution, at least as it applies to fund advisers found to engage in illegal and/or improper activities: Do not invest with any fund adviser found to violate (by omission or commission) its ethical and legal roles as shareholder steward. There are to be no second chances for tainted fund advisers.

Of even greater importance, as it involves the present and future, is the need to provide mutual fund shareholders with guidance for identifying fund advisers who are (1) superior performers and (2) serve the primary interests of shareholders (today and, it is hoped, in the future) as shareholder watchdogs. Adviser funds that are truly superior along both dimensions are identified as stewardship funds. Even if the mutual fund industry has learned its lesson, there will always be flawed advisers whose practices have escaped the sunlight, and those who change their stripes to serve their own financial interests. To the extent this is so, fund shareholders will need to continually update the list of stewardship funds.

FIVE DIMENSIONS OF ANALYSIS

The overall approach taken applies each of the four dimensions of analysis, which, when taken in their entirety, identify stewardship mutual funds. The identified funds should be superior to matched peers in financial performance (first dimension), first, and then in each of the other three dimensions. We want a superior performing fund that is also high performing in stewardship of shareholder interests. Bogle (2004) and Haslem (2005) discuss this approach. Funds identified overall as stewardship funds are likely (it is hoped) to continue as such. After all, they have done well and should not see any reason to change. But there are no guarantees and continuing assessment is essential. Further, funds identified as superior in a given dimension should also be superior to their matched peers in this regard.

1. Return, Risk, and Risk/Return Performance

The first dimension of identifying mutual fund stewardship focuses on the identification of superior return, risk, and risk/return performance. This issue is developed in Haslem (2003). The performance measures are found in Morningstar's (2007e) online fund reports. These reports include the measures discussed here plus other performance measures, including Morningstar's Star Ratings and financial analyst opinions. Morningstar's complete online package of fund research should be consulted in identifying funds that are superior financial performers, including their matched peer funds.

The five key performance measures in the first dimension are:

1. R-squared is a fund diversification measure that indicates the percentage of its variance in returns that are explained by its best-fit benchmark index, where 100 indicates that its variance matches the benchmark. Such a fund is fully diversified with only market risk and zero residual (other) risk. A fund with an eclectic investment style, and especially a concentrated portfolio, would be expected to have sizable unique risk. Smaller unique risk is found when a fund's R-squared is larger than the average of its peer group.
2. Beta measures the sensitivity of a mutual fund's returns with respect to its benchmark index, where 1.0 indicates that its sensitivity equals that of its benchmark. Beta indicates the percentage change in fund returns that is expected to accompany a given percentage change in benchmark returns.

Smaller systematic risk is found when a fund's beta is smaller than the average of its peer group.

3. Jensen's Alpha measures a mutual fund's risk-adjusted performance relative to its benchmark index over a period of time, where the benchmark's alpha is zero. Alpha represents the difference between the fund's actual and expected return, given its systematic risk (beta). An alpha that is both positive and significantly larger than zero reflects superior portfolio manager skill, as well as other factors. Therefore, positive alphas are good (the larger the more likely to be significant), and negative alphas are not. Thus, higher risk-adjusted performance is reflected when a fund's alpha is both positive and significantly larger than the average of its peer group.

4. The Sharpe Ratio measures a mutual fund's reward-to-variability performance relative to its benchmark index over a period of time. This most often cited risk/return measure relates the fund's average portfolio returns for a period of time to its total risk, measured by the standard deviation of its returns. Positive ratios are good (the larger the more likely to be significant), and negative ratios are not. Thus, higher risk-adjusted performance is reflected when a fund's Sharpe Ratio is both positive and significantly larger than the average of its peer group.

5. The standard deviation of mutual fund returns (also in the Sharpe Ratio) measures a fund's total risk over a period of time. Thus, smaller total risk is found when a fund's standard deviation of returns is smaller than the average of its peer group.

2. Diversification Risk

The second dimension of identifying mutual fund stewardship applies the concept of mutual fund diversification risk developed in Haslem (2003). Diversification risk focuses on those fund measures that reflect smaller risk (more conservative) relative to comparative funds and its peer group.

The elements of this concept are defined and discussed. As simplified here, *diversification risk* refers to the risks the fund in question has relative to those of comparative funds and its peer group. The fund's investment style, category, and portfolio manager strategies and skills, among others, determine the impacts on its risk measures. The 10 risk measures used to identify a fund's diversification risk include:

1. Value/growth investment style
2. Cash asset allocation
3. Net cash inflow
4. Market liquidity
5. Returns distribution
6. Industry sector concentration
7. Security concentration
8. *Value Line* safety
9. *Value Line* timeliness
10. Overall diversification risk

But, first, investors need to create an investment plan that allows consideration of funds within percentage allocations of three basics types of funds: (1) short maturity funds, (2) bond funds, and (3) stock funds. Once the percentage allocation among these three fund types has been determined, the next step is to consider funds to comprise the portfolio. Thus, the investment plan involves a step-by-step process that ends with portfolio asset allocations. The next step is to consider funds for each of these allocations. At this point, the funds under consideration may be analyzed using the diversification risk concept to assist in the final selection of funds for the portfolio.

To implement the mutual fund investment plan process, Vanguard (2007) provides a reasonable and easy-to-use online approach. A five-step methodology is recommended:

1. Identify investor goals and time horizon.
2. Identify investor risk preferences from completion of the investor questionnaire.
3. Select diversified portfolio asset allocations based on results of the investor questionnaire.
4. Select funds for the portfolio asset allocations.
5. Implement the plan.

No plan is forever, so an annual revisit is recommended to see if any assumptions have changed, such as a family addition.

There is also no magic formula in the investment plan, and it is important for shareholders to validate the results by self-analysis of major life experiences, core family values, and intuitive risk instincts. To this end, Baker and Haslem (1974) found three factors to be important in explaining investor perceptions of what is important in making fund decisions. In order of perceived importance they are (1) dividends, (2) future expectations, and (3) financial stability (risk).

Two distinct types ("clienteles") of investors were also found: (1) those who seek dividend income and (2) those who seek capital gains. Preferences for *dividends* are strongly, positively correlated with interest in dividend income, older investors, female investors, and service employees. Conversely, dividends are significantly, negatively correlated with acceptable risk of loss, interest in capital gains, and level of family income.

Investor preferences for *future expectations* were significantly positively correlated with interest in capital gains, portfolio size, housewives, and retired or nonemployed adults. Preferences for future expectations are significantly negatively correlated only with interest in dividend income.

Finally, investor preferences for *financial stability* were significantly positively correlated with older investors, interest in dividend income, level of expected annual returns, and female investors. Stability is significantly negatively correlated with education level and interest in capital gains. See Haslem (2003) for additional research findings.

To ensure this comparison, the fund in question must be in the same investment style category as comparative funds and its peer group. For example, if Vanguard 500 Index is the fund in question, Morningstar's (2007d) investment Style Box (nine cells) places the Index 500 in the "large-cap blend" cell, which means the fund is among those with the largest dollar capitalizations. "Blend" refers to its indexed portfolio, which combines elements of both value and growth investment styles. (For bond funds, Morningstar uses a nine-cell style box containing three investment styles and three risk classes.) The funds in the Index 500s Large Blend Morningstar Category represent its peer group.

Further, Morningstar includes the Vanguard Index 500s Morningstar Return (average), Morningstar Risk (average), and Morningstar Rating (three stars) for comparisons with other funds. These "average" classifications are to be expected for an index fund that mirrors the Standard & Poor's 500 Index.

Based on application of diversification risk across the spectrum of measures analyzed, the funds with less risk generally outperform in asset allocation, generation of net asset inflows, and generation of risk and return. The measures of diversification risk are discussed next, and Morningstar's (2007e) topic headings of the required data for the fund in question and its comparison funds are provided. In addition, but not noted in this chapter, *Morningstar Principia* (2007a) provides comparative data for the fund's peer group in its Morningstar Category.

To begin, smaller *investment-style diversification risk* is reflected if a fund's portfolio P/E Ratio (price-earnings ratio), P/CF Ratio (price-cash flow ratio), P/B Ratio (price-book ratio), P/S Ratio (price-sales ratio), and long-term earnings growth rate are each or generally smaller than those of its comparison funds. See the fund's Morningstar's Valuation and Growth Rates, specified ratios, and then compare the data to comparison funds.

Smaller *cash asset risk* is found when a fund's cash-flow ratio is larger than its comparison funds and peer group. See the fund's Asset Allocation, Cash Percentage, and then compare the data to comparison funds. Smaller net cash inflow risk is reflected if a fund's annual growth rate of net cash inflows is larger than its comparison funds. See the fund's Valuation and Growth Rates, Cash-Flow Growth, and then compare the data to comparison funds.

Smaller *market liquidity risk* is reflected if a fund's average and median percentages of combined giant- and large-capitalization securities are larger than those of its comparison funds and peer group. See the fund's Market Capitalization, Giant plus Large Percentages, and then compare the data to comparison funds.

Smaller *rate of return distribution risk* is reflected if a fund's percentage of income returns to total returns is larger than its comparison funds and peer group. If so, the fund looks to total return, not simply capital appreciation. See the fund's Historical Profile, Income Ratio (over three years), and then compare the data to comparison funds.

Smaller *industry sector concentration risk* is reflected if a fund's percentage investment in its top-three industry sectors is smaller than its comparison funds and peer group. See the fund's Portfolio Analysis, Sector Breakdown (Percentage of Stocks), Information plus Service plus Manufacturing, and then compare the data to comparison funds.

Smaller *portfolio concentration risk* is reflected if a fund's percentage investment in its top-five stocks is smaller than its comparison funds and peer group. See the fund's Percentage Assets in Top Ten Holdings, Top Five Holdings as Percentage of Net Assets, and compare the data to comparison funds.

Finally, smaller *Value Line Safety (quality) risk* is reflected if the fund's quality of its top-15 holdings is calculated to be higher than its comparison funds. Smaller *Value Line* Timeliness (next 12 months performance outlook) risk is reflected if a fund's expected performance for its top-15 holdings is calculated to be higher than its comparison funds. See the *Value Line Investment Survey* (2007) to make the calculations, and then compute and compare them to comparison funds.

The results of analyzing each of the fund's diversification risk measure are rated "excellent," "acceptable" or "unacceptable." Overall Diversification Risk reflects these results. These ratings are then assessed relative to comparison funds.

3. Management and Culture

The third dimension of identifying stewardship funds is based on the identification of fund advisers with superior management and culture, including integrity. By reading *Barron's,* Zweig in *Money* and the *Wall Street Journal,* Jonathan Clements in the *Wall Street Journal archives,* Timothy Middleton at Moneycentral.msn.com, and Morningstar's mutual fund site, among others, it is quite easy to become familiar with leading fund advisers and portfolio advisers. Management culture is also one of the five components in Morningstar's Stewardship Grades for mutual funds (to be discussed).

Setting aside the mutual fund advisers that former New York Attorney General Spitzer found to be poor shareholder stewards, what are the management and culture characteristics of stewardship funds? Based on their consistency with the preponderance of the characteristics, the identified funds are likely to be successful relative to their peers.

Stewardship funds are often managed by a small number of *long-tenured insiders,* who own the fund companies and manage the fund portfolios. They structure management fees and portfolio manager compensation consistently with fund objectives, and performance incentives require superior after-tax performance over at least three years. Importantly, *incentives* are not tied to growth in fund assets. Morningstar's Kinnel (2003) observes: "A manager's incentives tell you a lot about how a fund will be run." For examples, management of the Tweedy Browne and Longleaf Partners funds fit this description.

The fund portfolio advisers are disclosed by name and characterized by *lengthy investment experience* and *long tenure* in their current positions. Long tenure is associated both with higher performance and higher risk-adjusted performance.

Portfolio advisers are *not hired guns,* whose judgment and portfolio decisions are likely to be colored by short-term salary and bonus concerns. They are less likely to jump ship for higher compensation, ownership or hedge fund opportunities.

Insider-owned mutual fund management companies differ from companies owned by banks and investment bankers. In these cases, fund advisers and portfolio advisers are normally subjected to greater pressure to meet the aggressive profit goals set by their owners, rather than to serve as fiduciaries of shareholder interests.

Haslem (2003) finds insider-owned mutual fund advisers and portfolio managers provide shareholder letters that are well written, meaningful, informative, and frank. The letters discuss fund investment philosophy and strategy, performance, risks, and expectations. Some letters are worth reading, if only for their style and educational value.

Quality communication is important for all mutual fund shareholders, but perhaps even more so for advisers of those smaller funds who practice eclectic boutique portfolio investment styles and strategies. These portfolio advisers are more likely to value securities conservatively and seek consistency in satisfying returns over time, coupled with low risk and few unhappy surprises along the way.

Trading rooms in these mutual funds focus on *building portfolio value*, not growing the asset base for larger fees. Portfolio advisers do not attempt to "shoot the lights out" so that marketing departments can hype returns as Number 1 in some way or another. And if there is a marketing department, it does not call any of the shots, such as growing the asset base and facilitating market timing.

The mutual fund advisers and portfolio advisers are known both for *ethical behavior* and *successful careers*. In fact, Kinnel (2003) states: "When advisers believe in their funds, they tend to invest quite a lot." It is reassuring to fund shareholders that these portfolio advisers have done very well as investors and that they have serious money invested in their funds. That is, "They eat their own cooking." But this is far from the general case.

Some of these portfolio advisers have invested personal fortunes in their mutual funds and may even be the largest shareholders. The management of Longleaf Partners is known for investing with fund shareholders—guided by strict requirements for in-house investing. But this is not the general case in significant amounts.

Based on analysis of fund management and culture, the actively managed funds so identified are likely (it is hoped) to outperform their peer group averages. To confirm these results, Morningstar's revised Stewardship Grades should also be applied.

4. Morningstar's Stewardship Grades

The fourth dimension of identifying mutual fund stewardship applies Morningstar's (2007c) Stewardship Grades. These grades were introduced in 2004 following the fund scandals to provide investors with guides to make informed fund decisions. Since the imposition of fund grades, Morningstar's Lutton (2007d) reports an evolution in improved governance, with some movement toward *best practice*, more *independent board chairs*, and more movement beyond regulatory requirements in serving shareholder interests as primary. After three years' experience, the methodology was changed to improve the focus on funds with the best stewardship practices that act to serve shareholders' best interests.

Morningstar's Lutton (2006, 2007b, 2007c, 2007e) discusses Stewardship Grades in several articles that include components and methodology and some summary results from applying the grades to funds. The methodology has made it more difficult for funds to receive an overall Stewardship Grade of A. In fact, just two fund advisers received grades of A in all areas, and only 6 percent of the funds received overall grades of A. The two elite fund advisers are the Davis-advised Davis Advisers and Selected American funds, and the advisers of the Clipper Fund. The typical Fidelity fund dropped to a C because the board chairman is an insider, and the portfolio manager does not "eat his own cooking."

Lutton (2007a) and Morningstar (2007c) report mutual funds that should not be purchased based on overall Shareholder Grades. For example, Lutton reports that the Morningstar 5-star Neuberger Berman Partners fund gets an overall Shareholder Grade of C but an F in Manager Incentives "because management's own financial interests aren't well aligned with those of long-term investors."

Not all fund advisers agree with the use of particular criteria, with the result of lower area and overall Stewardship Grades. For example, Morningstar (2007b) gives the Vanguard Index 500 (and other Vanguard funds) reduced Board Quality grades partly because it marches to a different drummer. Board Quality is rated B because the chief executive officer is the board chairman, yet, historically, the other seven directors are independent. Maxey (2007) reported Vanguard's response in the *Wall Street Journal*: "We've maintained our governance structure for more than three decades, and it has served our shareholders extremely well."

In addition, Vanguard Index 500s (and most other Vanguard funds) Manager Incentives are rated C. The performance component of its long-term compensation plan does not reveal how it is calculated and over what period of time. But, more important, the Index 500s portfolio manager has just $10,000 to $50,000 invested in the fund. The result is a loss of credit for portfolio manager ownership.

The five areas that comprise Stewardship Grades remain the same, but their weights have changed:

1. Corporate culture, increased to 40 percent
2. Board quality, 20 percent
3. Manager incentives, 20 percent
4. Fees, 20 percent
5. Regulatory issues, decreased to 0 percent, with regulatory problems reflected by a negative percentage

Morningstar's analysis of fund practices involves four methods:

1. Assess, over time, the experience with fund advisers and their practices.
2. Perform in-person interviews with fund management and boards of directors.
3. Analyze years of data and Securities and Exchange Commission (SEC) filings.
4. Make field visits to fund management offices.

Each of the five areas used to compute overall fund Stewardship Grades are assessed and graded based on *specific criteria.*

Corporate Culture

These seven criteria determine fund grades:

1. Is the fund manager sales-oriented (trendy funds) to gather assets, or is it investment-oriented to serve shareholders?
2. Are shareholders treated like owners?
3. Are candid explanations of the investment process and results included in shareholder communications?
4. Are key investment personnel maintained and long tenured?
5. Are funds closed at the appropriate size, or do they allow them to balloon to increase advisory fees?
6. Are redemption fees used to discourage rapid trading (market timing)?
7. Are soft dollars prohibited?

Board Quality

These five criteria determine fund grades:

1. Does the board have an independent chairman elected by independent directors, and is there a supermajority of 75 percent truly independent directors on the board (key criterion)?
2. Does the board avoid active conflicts of interest by negotiating reasonable, well-structured advisory fees and expense contracts that benefit shareholders, rather than management (not the general case)?
3. Do board members have more money invested collectively in the funds they oversee (minimum of $100,000) than they receive in compensation?
4. Has the board taken effective action at such time shareholder interests were violated by management?
5. Does the board close funds at reasonable asset sizes?

Manager Incentives

These two criteria determine fund grades:

1. Does management invest significantly (over $1 million in most cases) in the funds they oversee (in cases where funds are appropriate for large investments)?
2. Does the fund manager's compensation package reward only long-term performance, rather than asset growth or short-term performance?

Fees

These three criteria determine fund grades:

1. Has the expense ratio declined markedly as fund assets have grown?
2. Does the advisory contract call for significant and effective fee "breakpoints" as fund assets increase?
3. Is the fund expense ratio below the 25th percentile for its peer group?

Regulatory Issues

This general criterion determines fund grades:

Have regulators cited legal violations and, if so, how pervasive and frequent are these violations of shareholder and legal trust?

5. Bogle's Stewardship Quotient

Bogle (2004) provides the fifth dimension of identifying fiduciary mutual funds. This guide includes 12 attributes and assigns numerical scores to each based on how well the fund meets his stewardship standard. Funds with the overall highest scores are "stewards of shareholder interests." Here are the 12 attributes that together identify the degree to which a fund is a stewardship fund. The list provides the method for calculating a fund's "Stewardship Quotient," based on the median score of 18. The fund with a median overall score has a Stewardship Quotient of 133.

In more general terms, mutual funds with the highest score for each of the *12 attributes* may be generalized in this way:

1. Management fees and expense ratios are very low.
2. Portfolio turnover is under 30 percent.
3. Equity diversification is broad and designed for long-term investment.
4. Marketing focuses on what the funds make, not what will sell.
5. No advertising to increase fund size or hype performance.
6. No fund payments for "shelf space" (revenue sharing) to boost distribution of fund shares.
7. "Pure no load" funds with no front-end loads and no 12b-1 fees.
8. Shareholder stability with redemption rate under 20 percent (no market timing or late trading) and strict application of redemption fees.
9. Stated limits on growth in fund assets to avoid reduction in performance.
10. Portfolio advisers act as shareholder stewards with 15 years of experience and fund tenure.
11. Insider ownership of fund management companies and fund advisers and directors invest large sums in their funds.
12. Fund management companies are organized as mutual organizations (Vanguard) or privately owned firms.

COMPLEMENTS TO BOGLE'S APPROACH

Zweig (2003) provides five additional attributes of stewardship funds that complement Bogle's 12 attributes for identifying funds with the highest Stewardship Quotient:

1. Fund advisers state what they stand for through effective and transparent communication, including informative and frank discussions of returns and expectations, inclusion of mission statements and ethics codes, and statements of governing investment principles.
2. Funds follow their stated investment philosophy and vision, and do not merely herd sheepishly around their benchmarks.
3. Funds minimize shareholder taxes by using tax management strategies based on low portfolio turnover and focusing on after-tax returns.
4. Fund mangers seek to bond with shareholders in a shared community of investors, including open and candid discussion with portfolio advisers at annual shareholder meetings.
5. Fund advisers own, and openly report they own, substantial stakes in their own funds, deliberately aligning their interests with their outside shareholders.

In addition, Middleton (2003a) provides six attributes of "great funds" and analysis of fund performance. Middleton (2003b) also discusses replacements for scandal-ridden funds and gives deserved plaudits to principals at Davis Funds, Longleaf Partners, Clipper Fund, and Tweedy Browne. With respect to the fund scandal, he quotes Bullard, president of Fund Democracy: "This is the biggest fraud in the fund industry since fund regulation began in 1940."

Schurr's (2003) interview with Bullard finds his favorite large fund families to be Vanguard, Fidelity, American Funds, T. Rowe Price, and TIAA-CREF. It is hoped that these and many more funds will be (correctly) identified as stewardship funds. However, since then, regulators have investigated American Funds' sales practices. Again, there are no guarantees.

STEWARDSHIP FUND (OR NOT)

The *Wall Street Journal*'s Lauricella (2004) identified the Bridgeway family of funds as stewardship funds. John Montgomery is president of Bridgeway Capital Management, which manages 11 funds with some $1.4 billion in assets. Montgomery is an industry maverick who discloses his salary as well as the policy limits on its size. Advisory fees are primarily based on long-term performance, and funds are closed (really) before cash inflows can hurt performance. Fund compliance budgets are also being doubled.

Montgomery believes mutual fund proxy votes should be disclosed. But, he opposes quarterly posting of portfolio securities, fearing that traders will front-run fund transactions. He states that market timing, late trading, and revenue sharing have long been common knowledge in the industry. Montgomery believes strongly that these behaviors should be prohibited, as should soft dollars, except as direct payments for research.

Montgomery favors required use of scaled regulations that would be most onerous for mutual funds with large expenses and low performance. And he states that fund directors should explain why they approved fund advisory contracts. He earlier sought to enrich his fund prospectuses with quantitative measures, but the SEC refused his request.

Montgomery also states that if the Sarbanes-Oxley certification is to be effective, it must also be applied to mutual fund trading rooms. Further, he believes fund investors need to be educated about the tremendous loss of assets from "chasing hot returns." Further, Middleton (2004) includes Bridgeway in his choice of stewardship funds.

But then, John Montgomery gets a shot to his white-hat reputation. It was revealed that three Bridgeway funds overcharged shareholders for advisory fees. The fees include both fixed and variable performance-based components, the latter a desirable quality. The fees are linked to fund performance relative to an index over a five-year period (also a desirable length of time). Under the law, these fees were supposed to be calculated using a five-year average of asset size. Instead, the fees were calculated using the latest, and largest, asset size.

Would this error have occurred if asset sizes trended downward? The SEC considered this a serious breach, and required Bridgeway to return more than $4.4 million in advisory fees to shareholders, plus interest of nearly $500,000. A $250,000 civil penalty was also imposed, and John Montgomery paid a $50,000 fine from his personal funds.

Bridgeway's overcharge of advisory fees will take more time to assess, either as a one-time stumble or a pattern. Morningstar's Hughes (2004) has a rather sympathetic reaction to this event. Others may feel that "one strike and you're out."

CONCLUSIONS

The revelations of major scandals in the mutual funds industry brought intense feelings of betrayal and financial loss to millions of fund shareholders whose assets were improperly and illegally appropriated. Shareholders need and deserve much greater protection and transparency of normative disclosure that meets their normative shareholder needs.

Investors need guidance in identifying stewardship funds that (it is hoped) will remain so. Through application of five dimensions of analysis, investors are able to make an overall identification of stewardship funds. These dimensions are (1) return, risk and risk/return performance, (2) diversification risk, (3) management and culture, (4) Morningstar's Stewardship Grades, and (5) Bogle's Stewardship Quotient. The fund scandal has shown the identification of stewardship funds to be essential now, and in the future, to sound investing.

REFERENCES

Baker, H. K., and J. A. Haslem. 1974. "Toward the Development of Client-specified Valuation Models," *Journal of Finance* 29: 4 (September): 1255–1263.

Bogle, J. C. 2004. "Has Your Fund Manager Betrayed Your Trust? Consider the 'Stewardship Quotient,'" Keynote address, AICPA Personal Financial Planning Conference, Las Vegas, January 5.

Haslem, J. A. 2003. *Mutual Funds: Risk and Performance Analysis for Decision Making*. Oxford, UK: Blackwell Publishing.

Haslem, J. A. 2005. "Investing in 'Fiduciary' Mutual Funds: How to Improve the Odds," *Journal of Investing* 14: 4 (Winter): 63–68. Accepted Paper Series, SSRN, June 18, 2008, http://ssrn.com/abstract=1143045.

Hughes, B. B. 2004. "What to Make of Bridgeway's Run-in with Regulators," Morningstar.com, September 16.

Kinnel, R. 2003. "What Is Your Fund Manager Getting Paid For?" Morningstar.com, November 20.

Lauricella, T. 2004. "Maverick Aims at Fund Business," *Wall Street Journal*, February 2, R1, R4.

Lutton, P. P. 2006. "Are Your Mutual Fund's Watchdogs Eating the Kibble?" Morningstar.com, December 14.

Lutton, P. P. 2007a. "February's Mutual Fund Red Flags," Morningstar. com, February 13.

Lutton, P. P. 2007b. "Letter to the SEC: Make Fund Boards More Independent," Morningstar.com, March 12.

Lutton, P. P. 2007c. "Takeaways from Our Stewardship Grades," Morningstar.com, May 14.

Lutton, P. P. 2007d. "Will Your Funds Pass Our Tougher Stewardship Test?" Morningstar.com, June 19.

Lutton, P. P. 2007e. "Few Funds Ace Morningstar's Stewardship Test," Morningstar.com, September 25.

Maxey, D. 2007. "Morningstar Grades Firms on Stewardship," *Wall Street Journal*, September 27, p. C15.

Middleton, T. 2003a. "Six Traits the Best Funds Share," Moneycentral.msn.com, January [undated].

Middleton, T. 2003b. "Don't Let the Crooks Manage Your Money," Moneycentral.msn.com, September 9.

Middleton, T. 2004. "Bridgeway Joins the 'Clean Funds' Ranks," Moneycentral.msn.com, January 6.

Morningstar. 2007a. *Morningstar 2006 Principia Pro for Mutual Funds,* Advanced Module (CD), January 1.

Morningstar. 2007b. "Vanguard 500 Index, Stewardship Grade Methodology," Quicktake.Morningstar.com, September 12.

Morningstar. 2007c. "Morningstar Stewardship Grades," Morningstar.com, September 27.

Morningstar. 2007d. "Vanguard 500 Index," Quicktake.Morningstar.com, September 28.

Morningstar. 2007e. "Morningstar Mutual Fund Analyst Reports," Morningstar.com. October 3.

Schurr, S. 2003. "The Good, Bad and Criminal among Mutual Funds," TheStreet.com, October 14.

Thottam, J. 2003. "Are They All Crooked?" *TIME*, November 10.

Value Line. 2007. *Value Line Investment Survey.* New York: Value Line Publishing.

Vanguard Group. 2007. "How to Create Your Investment Plan," Personal.Vanguard.com, September 28.

Zweig, J. 2003. "Funds You Can Trust," *Money* (November): 86ff.

ABOUT THE AUTHOR

John A. Haslem is Professor Emeritus of Finance in the Robert H. Smith School of Business at the University of Maryland. He served as founding academic affairs dean and founding chair of the finance department. He received the Panhellenic Association's "Outstanding Teacher Award" for his first-of-a-kind mutual funds course. Professor Haslem studied at Duke University, Harvard University, and the University of North Carolina, and he taught at the University of North Carolina and on the faculty of the University of Wisconsin. His research has appeared in the *Journal of Finance, Journal of Business, Journal of Financial and Quantitative Analysis, Journal of Money, Credit and Banking, Financial Analysts Journal,* and *Journal of Investing,* among numerous others. He also has contributed five books, including *Mutual Funds: Risk and Performance Analysis for Decision Making.* Professor Haslem served as personal financial consultant to the director of Supersonic Transport, U.S. Department of Transportation; and consultant and expert witness to two divisions of the U.S. Department of Justice (including the Supreme Court case *U.S. v. State of Louisiana*).

CHAPTER 17

Normative Transparency of Mutual Fund Disclosure

JOHN A. HASLEM, Ph.D.
Professor Emeritus of Finance, Robert H. Smith School of Business, University of Maryland

Mutual fund disclosure is dismal.
—Barbara Black, University of Cincinnati School of Law

The recent years have been a nightmare for far too many investors. After the imploding stock market bubble, investors were hit with abundant findings of conflicts of interest, greed, and fraud that pervaded too many corporate executive suites and directors' boardrooms, along with their willing participants on Wall Street. This fall from grace on Wall Street and in corporate America has fueled many legal actions to punish the perpetrators, but with limited actions to improve laws and regulations protecting investors.

Correspondingly, in 2003, mutual fund investors had to deal with widespread findings of major fund adviser misconduct and illegality that still calls for much improved regulation and disclosure. The scandal findings require a new look at the Investment Company Act of 1940 (40Act), and the role of independent directors in providing adviser oversight.

The *Wall Street Journal*'s Lauricella (2003) quoted then–New York Attorney General Spitzer as stating that the "breach of fiduciary duty is appalling." And, indeed, it was and still is. Spitzer examined the moat around the mutual fund industry's self-proclaimed "wall of trusteeship" and found it all too shallow. This was seen in the all-too-frequent findings of selective disclosure of portfolio holdings, insider market timing and front running, allowance of illegal late trading to selected traders, and more.

Following revelations of the mutual funds scandal, the fund industry was anything but early in facing up to the situation and offering real remedies. Who better knows what goes on in fund management? But then the Investment Company Institute (ICI) offered some remedies for the failings of fund governance. Moreover, the Securities and Exchange Commission (SEC) followed Spitzer in investigating problems in the fund industry it is responsible for regulating. However, initially the SEC appeared less than aware, even surprised, by the scandals.

Congressional hearings and limited legal actions followed the major uproar of
the scandals and the publicity of trials and settlements. The consensus of public
opinion and serious researchers appears to agree that fund shareholders continue to
need and deserve much more in the way of protection and disclosure. Vanguard's
John C. Bogle (2005) reports the scandal was not an isolated event but rather
involved mutual fund advisers holding $1.6 trillion in shareholder assets and
included some of the oldest, largest, and formerly most respected fund advisers.

Now that much of the corresponding furor over the lack of fiduciary behavior
in the mutual fund scandals has peaked, what is it that fund shareholders are
still owed in the way of fiduciary protections and disclosures? First, funds owe
shareholders fiduciary protection of the huge amounts they have invested in funds,
including retirement plans. The ICI (2007) reports that 96 million individuals in 55
million households hold fund assets of $10.4 trillion, and increasing. Mutual funds
thus play a key intermediation role between Main Street and Wall Street.

Second, Morningstar's Phillips (2004) observes mutual funds have foolishly
jeopardized the public's trust, their major asset. As a result:

> [I]t would behoove the industry to redouble its commitment to the effective stewardship of
> the public's assets. . . . [T]he recent scandals make it abundantly clear that too many people
> in this industry were willing to forsake their responsibility in exchange for short-term
> personal profit. Sadly, these were violations of trust that took place at the highest levels,
> including company founders, CEOs, portfolio managers, and several current or former
> members of the Investment Company Institute's Board of Governors.

Third, industry leader Bogle (2005) finds that the growth and management of
mutual funds and their practices call for major reform. He notes that the asset size
of the 25 largest fund advisers increased 3,600-fold between 1945 and 2004, while
their direct fund expenses increased 6,600-fold. This huge growth in shareholder
expenses occurred while advisers benefited from "staggering" economies of scale.

Bogle (2005) also summarizes the steps the mutual fund industry must take to
improve the lot of those who actually own the funds, the shareholders.

> To enhance the share of fund returns earned by fund shareholders, the industry needs to
> reorder its product strategies to focus once again on broadly diversified funds with sound
> objectives, prudent policies, and long-term strategies. The industry needs to take its
> foot off the marketing pedal and press down firmly on the stewardship pedal.
> At the same time, the industry must give investors better information about asset
> allocation, fund selection, risks, potential returns and costs—all with complete
> candor. To do otherwise will doom the industry to a dismal future. For whatever the
> profession, finally, the client must be served. For whatever business, finally, the customer
> must be served. [emphasis added.] (p. 24)

But in spite of the broad-based agreement that something more needs to be
done, far too much remains to be done in actually providing mutual fund shareholders with their broad protections under the Investment Company Act of 1940.

The 1940 Act states that "[t]he national public interest and the interest of
investors is adversely affected . . . when investment companies are organized, operated, or managed . . . in the interest of investment advisers." Independent mutual
fund directors are responsible for selecting (and compensating) fund advisers who

will maintain effective legal separation between themselves and shareholders. However, effective separation has not been achieved. Independent fund directors have failed as fiduciaries in their legal roles as shareholder watchdogs.

Palmiter (2006) explains that the act's "outsourcing" of regulatory oversight of mutual fund advisers to independent directors, rather than to the SEC, has not provided essential fiduciary protections to fund shareholders. Further, the outlook remains bleak for Congress and the SEC to achieve all, or even most, of what should be done for fund shareholders.

DISCLOSURE AS AN EFFECTIVE REGULATORY TOOL

Before continuing, it is important to consider whether disclosure is an effective tool of mutual fund regulation. Professor Zingales (2004) reviews and assesses regulatory theories, and analyzes the costs and benefits of financial market and fund regulation. The two most important costs are those of compliance and the burden on firms that should not be regulated. He distinguishes between disclosure requirements and other types of regulation. *Disclosure is found to be almost without question the desired form of regulation.*

Other types of regulation can be justified in particular situations, such as when it is very costly to enforce contracts, when limited liability restricts punishment, and, as in financial markets, when shareholders are too dispersed for coordinating their individual rights.

However, regulation is not designed from the ground up, but is the result of political pressure by lobbies with varying degrees of political power. The incumbent lobbies are usually the stronger and better organized, and the weaker lobbies are the customers, investors, and new market entrants. The result is regulation biased against new entrants and competition. Not all regulation is bad, but in the "real world" welfare enhancing regulation can have unintended consequences, none of them normative.

Zingales (2004) finds a conflict of interest between mutual fund advisers and shareholders. This conflict is evident in four practices: (1) "stale" price arbitrage and illegal "late trading"; (2) lack of disclosure of brokerage commissions, bid–ask spreads, custodial fees, and soft-dollar brokerage commissions; (3) large and increasing expense ratios; and (4) excessive risk taking. (The author summarizes these issues widely discussed in the literature.)

Another major source of mutual fund adviser–shareholder conflicts lies in the structure of fund adviser compensation. Shareholders are rewarded by fund performance, but advisers are rewarded primarily by the size of assets under management. The major reason for this difference lies in the adviser rewards system. The law prohibits incentive-based compensation that rewards superior performance, but does not also penalize inferior performance.

Mutual fund shareholders can "fire" fund advisers by redeeming their shares at net asset value. But in contrast to traded corporations, there is no corresponding market signal in the form of downward pressure on fund prices. Often it is the sophisticated investors who redeem their shares when fund advisers are found to misbehave, leaving the less informed shareholders to continue to receive the adviser's tender mercies. This pattern has encouraged some advisers to take perverse advantage of these typically smaller shareholders by increasing fund expenses and not improving portfolio management, all with the expectation that no further major redemptions will occur.

The threat of shareholder lawsuits is less of a deterrent to mutual fund advisers. Federal courts have refused to hear cases of excessive advisory fees. The tremendous growth in mutual fund assets, including those in retirement plans, has major implications. The growth of fund assets and economies of scale and scope have greatly benefited fund advisers in cases where large trade size has not subsumed economies of scale. The diffuse ownership of fund shares has increased the likelihood and risk of abuses, especially for unsophisticated shareholders. All of this has enabled opportunities for adviser abuse.

Zingales (2004) concludes: "*While the case for mandatory disclosure is simple, the case for other forms of regulation is not*" (p. 49). With the huge and increasing size of mutual fund assets, it is not cost effective to depend just on regulatory prohibitions. Regulations have generally failed in finding major causes and cases of fund adviser abuse. It is no accident that adviser employee whistleblowers are most effective in spotlighting abuse.

This is not to say that regulators are ignorant of the need for improved mutual fund disclosure. They have studied the disclosure issue numerous times. For example, in a presentation to Congress, R. J. Hillman (2003) states:

> *The fees and other costs that mutual fund investors pay as part of owning fund shares can significantly affect their investment returns. As a result, it is appropriate to debate whether the disclosures of mutual fund fees and fund marketing practices are sufficiently transparent and fair to investors.*

The answer to the question raised is obviously in the negative.

The SEC's P. F. Roye, in a statement to Congress, discusses the need for improved mutual fund transparency. His pre-Spitzer testimony was highly supportive of the proposed Mutual Funds Integrity and Fee Transparency Act of 2003. Roye (2003) concludes: "The Commission supports Congressional efforts to improve transparency in mutual fund disclosure, to provide mutual fund investors with the information they need to make informed investment decisions and enhance the mutual fund governance framework." However, achievement of this goal remains far from realization.

In Professor Bicksler's (2004) presentation to Congress, he identifies the major necessary dimensions of public policy: (1) individual choice, (2) competitive markets, and (3) *transparency*. He explains:

> *The role of government, including government regulation, is limited except when ... parties have sufficient market economic power preventing the functioning of competitive markets. Further, individual choice and its end results, the efficiency of resource allocation is strengthened if there is firm* transparency *where relevant investor informational parameters are provided. This will, in turn, enhance investor awareness and improve investor choice of mutual funds. Hence, individual rational choice of mutual funds and competitive markets are intertwined. Further, rational investor choice of mutual funds is dependent upon* transparency *of relevant investor choice parameters provided by mutual funds. [emphasis added.] (p. 6)*

Bicksler (2004) also provides three specific mutual fund agent–principal questions:

1. Do independent directors act in the best interests of fund shareholders when negotiating the investment advisory fee contract?
2. Is it in the best interest of shareholders for fund advisers to pay for broker distribution to "grow" fund assets?
3. Are the fund industry's soft-dollar practices in the best interests of fund shareholders?

He answers each question in the negative. Further, he reports that excessive mutual fund fees cost shareholders an additional $10 billion per year. Fund advisers are able to sell funds with excessive marketing expenses because there are many less sophisticated investors who provide advisers with financial incentives to sell inferior funds. Financial incentives also drive advisers to use soft-dollar trades and similar arrangements that involve undisclosed, unnecessary, improper, and excessive costs.

NORMATIVE TRANSPARENCY OF DISCLOSURE

In the broader scheme of things, transparency has become accepted in its own right as an inherent component of good public and private governance, and thus reinforces the need for independence, accountability, and policy consistency among financial regulators. The key issue is no longer whether transparency is desirable but rather how can domestic and foreign publicly traded firms, nonprofit organizations, and governments better achieve transparency.

At minimum, improvements in mutual fund transparency are called for if only to be comparable to the requirements for corporate disclosure. To accomplish this minimum disclosure and then to move toward normative transparency, lawmakers and regulators and fund advisers and independent directors must give shareholders their due as fund owners.

The transparency issue assumes particular importance because of the principal–agent problem, which arises where work is delegated to others. That is, a principal hires an agent to perform tasks on his behalf, but he cannot be sure that the agent performs the tasks precisely as the principal would like. The agent's decisions and performance are expensive to monitor, and the incentives of the two parties may well differ. The principal–agent problem also exists in the mutual fund world, where fund shareholders are principals and fund advisers their agents.

The general concept of transparency that applies to public and private and domestic and international institutions and governments also applies to mutual fund disclosure. The World Bank's Vishwanath and Kaufmann (1999) define *transparency* as the "increased flow of timely and reliable economic, social and political information, which is accessible to all relevant stakeholders."

The World Bank's Bellver and Kaufman (2005) add that for information to be transparent it must be accessible, relevant, reliable, and of good quality. Transparency thus captures institutional openness, which for mutual funds requires that shareholders be able to monitor and evaluate the actions of fund advisers. However, current fund disclosure falls far short of meeting this transparency test. Fund shareholders cannot adequately monitor and evaluate the actions of advisers.

While one of the major objectives of the 1940 Act is to ensure mutual fund shareholders receive adequate and accurate information, they have yet to receive either in a normative fashion. It is "normative transparency of disclosure" that provides a focus for the regulatory reform required to facilitate identification of stewardship funds.

There are some exceptions to the need for normative transparency of disclosure. Mutual fund sales loads (up front and deferred) are relatively transparent on shareholder accounts. Investment advisory fees, 12b-1 fees, and "other" expenses, however, are less readily transparent, being included in fund expense ratios.

Transaction costs, which approximate expense ratios in size, are not at all transparent. Transaction costs add to the costs of securities purchased and reduce the net proceeds of securities sold, thereby adversely affecting fund assets. Further, fund industry practice and regulatory disclosure requirements all too often result in incorrect accounting and incomplete, missing, misleading, or perfunctory disclosure.

Positive transparency of disclosure is the first as-is approach to mutual fund disclosure. The term refers to the relative degree of a particular fund's disclosure under current laws and regulations. A fund's actual transparency in disclosure must be identified relative to the industry composite, which, of course, requires a transparency analysis of each fund. The adequacy of positive transparency has long been debated, but the recent fund scandal provides strong evidence that much more than positive disclosure under current laws and regulation is required.

The second and necessary approach to defining mutual fund transparency of disclosure is normative ("should be"). As defined, *normative transparency of disclosure* refers to the degree of mutual fund voluntary and proactive disclosure and also new and revised legal and regulatory disclosure required for shareholders to be able to make information-efficient fund investment decisions. The acceptance and requirement of this disclosure concept in public policy should also be the guiding principle in fund disclosure. This disclosure is essential if fund shareholders are to be able to identify stewardship funds—those stewards of shareholders and their money.

The definition of normative transparency of disclosure provides a goal consistent with the classic finance proposition of maximization of share value. The goal of normative transparency is to provide information efficient disclosure that enhances the ability of mutual fund investors to make wealth-enhancing buy/sell decisions. Normative transparency also requires prohibition of disclosures that impede investors from making information-efficient fund decisions.

If Congress and the SEC were to enact laws and regulations that provide normative transparency of disclosure, these mandates would provide much of what is required. While additional regulatory disclosure may be forthcoming, it is most unlikely that the political process will achieve normative transparency.

However, the political obstacles to normative transparency of disclosure are much more likely to be overcome if individual mutual fund advisers, their directors, and the fund industry work vigorously, proactively, and collectively in conjunction with Congress and the SEC to achieve normative transparency. This effort is unlikely because of the political influence of the large number of advisers who benefit from poor disclosure.

The achievement of normative transparency by individual mutual funds should not be as difficult or expensive as they and the industry are likely to claim. Funds are now required to have regulatory compliance officers. And much of what is required for normative transparency is, or should be, available in written or oral form, or such that it may be reasonably generated within the scope of fund operations.

The record of the topics, deliberations, and decisions of mutual fund directors and committees should include much of the information needed to provide normative transparency of disclosure. What more that may be needed in the way of disclosure information includes the analysis and explanations for the decisions made.

Normative transparency of mutual fund disclosure will not prevent shareholders from making investment mistakes, but it will at least enhance their potential for making informed buy/sell decisions. Normative transparency is also conducive to attracting investors who are prone to be patient, long-term shareholders.

Mutual fund shareholders need to know whether portfolio managers and independent directors are actually investing with them. In turn, patient shareholders are more likely to favor funds with long-term focus and transparency in disclosure. The result is that these funds are likely to have fewer share redemptions during times of poor returns and when the inevitable surprises occur along the way.

American Century Mutual Funds (2003) provides an example of a mutual fund adviser on the right path to normative transparency. The statement of additional information is well organized with solid, informative disclosure printed in readable-size font. American Century also makes effective use of templates in numerous topic discussions:

- Investment policy
- Interested and independent directors (detailed and very well done)
- Fund committees
- Director compensation
- Director ownership in each fund (dollar range)
- Principal shareholders
- Investment adviser (rates and dollars)
- Multiple share classes (shareholder and distribution services and dollars of fees)
- Capital loss carry-forwards and before- and after-tax returns
- Ratings of fixed income securities

More funds should join American Century in providing improved disclosure.

Improved mutual funds transparency is also called for if only to be more comparable to that disclosure required and provided by major publicly held corporations. In a real sense, a fund's degree of normative transparency effectively projects how much confidence its managers have that they are operating in the best interests of their shareholders as owners. Many fund advisers oppose disclosure of portfolio manager holdings in their portfolios based on the argument that shareholders cannot make effective use of this information.

DISCLOSURE TEMPLATE

A disclosure template designed for each mutual fund should be posted and regularly updated on the fund's Web site, where it would be readily accessible to thousands of investors. Among other benefits, online access would facilitate investor searches for funds that are most dedicated to their shareholders.

The disclosure template provides a tool to guide mutual fund advisers on the road to absolute and normative transparency of disclosure to investors. First, the template seeks to provide disclosure in an absolute sense, not limited to current best practice. Second, it seeks to provide transparency of disclosure in a normative sense, not limited to current laws, regulations, fund practice, and disclosure. Some of the normative disclosure may even be beyond that currently recognized as needed by objective students of funds. The template thus seeks to provide item-by-item normative transparency of that data and information that is essential for meeting the information-efficient decision needs of fund investors.

The disclosure template is broadly organized around seven categories:

1. Guide to Use
2. Disclosure of the Board of Directors
3. Board of Directors Disclosure: Actions and Approvals
4. Audit Committee Disclosure
5. Other Committee Disclosures
6. Portfolio Manager Disclosure
7. Portfolio Performance Disclosure

There are 69 numbered disclosure items in categories 2 to 7. Here is a list of the first disclosure item (generalized) in each numbered category:

2. Thirteen descriptors of each director
3. Selection of fund chief executive officer (CEO)
4. Members of audit committee
5. Members of other committees
6. Eight descriptors of portfolio managers
7. Shareholder performance reports

For each disclosure item in the prospectus or financial reports to shareholders, mutual fund managers are called on to cite each and explain. For full disclosure in the statement of additional information, fund advisers are requested to copy each item and explain it.

However, if a mutual fund adviser declines to disclose a particular item, it is requested that the item be cited and the reasons explained. The decision not to disclose a particular item assumes, of course, that there is no legal requirement to do so. But it is hoped that fund adviser refusals to disclose will decline over time as they:

- Become more enlightened and responsible as shareholder fiduciaries
- Experience that not doing so increasingly places them at competitive disadvantage
- Decide that disclosure beyond the requirements of current laws and regulation benefits all participants

To that end, the disclosure template reflects judgment concerning what represents normative transparency of disclosure for mutual fund shareholders. The disclosure items are not written in stone but rather provide a current guide to what constitutes normative transparency. But the maintenance of normative transparency also requires constant monitoring by the SEC and the fund industry to ensure it reflects changes in shareholder needs, fund practices (proper and improper), and regulation.

NORMATIVE TRANSPARENCY AND THE EXPENSE RATIO

The expense ratio and its stated components provide the primary disclosure for shareholders to obtain needed cost information. Because of its importance, this imperfect measure calls out urgently for disclosure that provides normative transparency. The needed major changes include not only expense ratio components but their categories and subcategories as well. Current expense ratio components should be restated and defined, and several new components should be added. Properly excluded are fund sales loads (front end and back end) that are relatively transparent and paid directly by investor purchasers.

The normative transparency and *total* expense ratio concepts and regulatory and cost issues discussed herein evolved in Haslem (2003, 2004, 2006, 2007, 2008a, 2008b, 2008c, 2009a, 2009b). Stewardship funds were developed in Bogle (2004) and further in Haslem (2005).

CURRENT SEC EXPENSE RATIO

Current mutual fund regulatory requirements call for three expense ratio categories: (1) management fees, (2) distribution (12b-1) fees, and (3) "other" expenses. But, in practice, strict uniformity in disclosure within is lacking and requires urgent attention.

Management fees are the major category in the expense ratio. They include investment advisory fees, but may include also administrative and other fees paid to the fund adviser or affiliates.

Distribution (12b-1) fees are paid out of mutual fund shareholder assets and partly used by fund distributors to pay brokers for sales of fund shares and distribution expenses, which include market support services and servicing of customer accounts. Adviser payments of sales fees and/or asset fees (discussed later in the chapter) and smaller front-end loads have generally replaced traditional single use of front-end loads to reward brokers for sales. Another use of 12b-1 fees is to pay for fund advertising and promotion, printing and mailing prospectuses, and printing and mailing sales literature.

"Other" expenses are residual expenses paid for transfer agent fees, custodian fees, legal fees, accountant fees, auditor fees, legal counsel fees, directors' fees, shareholder brokerage fees, and perhaps also some 12b-1 customer service fees.

THE *NEW* TOTAL EXPENSE RATIO

The *New* Total Expense Ratio construct with normative transparency of disclosure of its four "behind the mutual fund curtain" payment categories with sub-categories is designed as normative additions and improvements in the components of the current SEC expense ratio, which does not provide this inside view of payments.

The dollar amounts of the *New* Total Expense Ratio categories and sub-categories should be computed as percentages that provide contrast with the regulatory expense ratio and its categories. The required use of this construct would also provide standardized descriptors for uniform reporting among funds.

Based on the *New* Total Expense Ratio, the categories and sub-categories of fees follow:

Management Fees (%)
- Investment advisory fees
- Administrator expenses
- Service provider fees to adviser and affiliates
- Adviser fall-out benefits from revenue sharing payments (see distribution fees)
- Adviser rebates from soft-dollar trades (see distribution fees)

Distribution Fees (%)
- Selling group payments
  - Dealer (broker) concessions
  - Account servicing fees
- Revenue sharing payments net of adviser fall-out benefits
  - Broker marketing pools
  - Broker bonus compensation
  - Syndicated distributions
  - Sub-transfer agency fees
  - Networking fees
- Soft-dollar trades net of rebates

"Other" Expenses (%)
- Service provider fees to *other* than adviser and affiliates
- "Residual" direct fund fees and expenses

Transaction Costs (%)
- Total transaction costs net of adviser rebates from soft-dollar trades
- Net "flow induced" trade transaction costs
- Net "discretionary" trade transaction costs

The *New* Total Expense Ratio provides additional categories to those provided by the current SEC expense ratio. Further, *distribution fee* sub-categories are modeled after actual adviser/distributor accounts from which payments are made. The stated sub-categories are generalized and can be matched by their descriptions to "inside" sub-category labels used by specific advisers. "Inside" distribution fee sub-categories and descriptions thus provide much more disclosure than the current SEC total expense ratio.

A brief discussion of the normative disclosure sub-categories of each fee category follows:

Management Fees (%)

Investment advisory fees include payments to the fund adviser (including any sub-adviser) for research and portfolio management expenses consistent with fund investment objectives, policies, and stated limitations.

Administrator expenses include fund management and regulatory oversight, evaluation of performance of other affiliates, and perhaps fund expenses and general accounting services.

Service provider fees to adviser and affiliates include:

- *Fund distributor* for direct fund expenses, including advertising and promotion
- *Custodian* for safeguarding fund assets and settling portfolio and shareholder transactions
- *Auditor* for fund accounts
- *Legal counsel* for legal services and regulatory oversight
- *Transfer (servicing) agents* for fulfilling shareholder transactions, receiving and disbursing monies, and providing customer services and communications, and
- *"Other" adviser and affiliate fees*

Adviser fall-out benefits from revenue sharing payments (see distribution fees).
Adviser rebates from soft-dollar trades (see distribution fees).

Distribution Fees (%)

Selling group payments are fund distributor payments to brokers to reward sales of adviser fund shares. "Brokers" include financial advisers, traditional brokers, wire house brokers, broker-dealers, and bank trust departments.

- *Dealer (broker) concessions* are fund distributor payments to brokers based on front-end loads of broker sold adviser fund shares.
- *Account servicing fees* are fund distributor payments to brokers stated for providing *continuing customer service* to accounts holding adviser fund shares. Distributor payments of usually 5–15 basis points are computed as percentages of allocated broker *sales targets* of annual dollar sales "sales fees" and/or dollar holdings "asset fees" of adviser fund shares.

Revenue sharing payments net of adviser "fall-out" benefits are stated to defray broker costs of providing marketing support services for customers holding adviser fund shares. But, in fact, fund distributor payments are *based on or result from* broker sales of adviser fund shares.

Adviser fall-out benefits are broker agreed rebates paid directly to fund advisers from "excess" revenue sharing payments. These conflicted rebates should be repaid to the source, fund assets, which would negate use of revenue sharing payments with fall-out benefits. Better, revenue sharing payments with adviser fall-out benefits should be prohibited.

The first three types of revenue sharing payments are *based on* broker sales of adviser fund shares.

- *Broker marketing pools* are fund distributor allocated payments to each high selling broker of adviser fund shares.
- *Broker payments* from marketing pools are based on broker annual dollar sales "sales fees" and/or dollar holdings "asset fees" of adviser fund shares.
- *Broker (bonus) compensation* is fund distributor payments of "bonus" compensation to very *top selling* brokers of adviser fund shares.

Syndicated distributions are investment banker allocations of shares of initial public offerings to fund advisers based on purchase history. Advisers may assign their allocations to brokers to reward sales of adviser fund shares (and in this way are related to revenue sharing payments).

The final two types of revenue sharing payments *result from* broker sales of adviser fund shares.

- *Sub-transfer agency fees* are fund distributor payments to brokers for providing transfer agency payments to customer accounts holding adviser fund shares.
- *Networking fees* are fund distributor payments to brokers for transmission of customer account and transaction data through the Networking Securities Clearing Corporation. Networking fees are usually $6–10 for each customer account holding adviser fund shares.

Soft-dollar trades net of rebates require funds to pay "premium" brokerage commissions, and perhaps higher trading costs than provided by "best execution" trade brokers. Thus, soft-dollar trades are more costly to fund assets and shareholders than routine trades.

Soft-dollar trades provide *advisers* with broker agreed rebates of some 70% of the premium brokerage commissions that are paid in and limited to in-kind investment products and services—the "soft dollars." Brokers also benefit from the higher net brokerage fees. Soft-dollar trades provide financial benefits to both fund advisers and brokers parties, which encourages additional soft-dollar trades. Soft-dollar trades are thus conflicted as they are paid from shareholder assets and performance and should be prohibited.

"Other" Expenses (%)

Service provider fees to other than fund advisers and affiliates (see management fees for types of payments).
  "Residual" direct fund fees and expenses.

Securities Transaction Costs (%)

Total transaction costs net of adviser soft-dollar rebates represent total fund portfolio transactions, net of adviser rebates from soft-dollar trades (see management fees).

Flow-induced trade portions of total transaction costs net of adviser rebates from soft-dollar trades arise from fund shareholder purchases/sales "flow" of fund shares. These "operational trades" have higher transaction costs than "discretionary" trades (below). Net flow-induced trades relate to any unlikely soft-dollar trades.

Discretionary trade portion of total transaction costs net of adviser rebates from soft-dollar trades arise from fund portfolio manager execution of trades designed to implement fund strategy. These unforced trades are less costly than operational trades.

12b-1 FEES AND MULTIPLE SHARE CLASSES

Rule 12b-1 fees facilitated the creation of multiple mutual fund share classes. Each share class has a different mix of loads and 12b-1 fees, which often makes investor choices of share classes a confusing and costly exercise. Brokers have also used this confusion to their own advantage.

Class A shares typically have 5.75 percent front-end loads and perpetual annual 0.25 percent shareholder servicing fees. In general, Class A shares have the lowest cost to shareholders for holding periods in excess of eight years. The front-end loads can be lowered if current shareholder purchases or previous holdings are large enough to qualify for lower load breakpoints.

Class B mutual fund shares do not have front-end loads, but rather they have 5.00 percent contingent deferred sales charges that decline to zero after eight years, and annual 1.00 percent 12b-1 fees that decline to 0.25 percent annually after eight years. Brokers have often sold Class B shares as "no load" when, in fact, they are only free of front-end loads and have higher annual 12b-1 fees. Under pressure, Class B shares now normally convert to Class A shares after eight years to reduce costs to long-term shareholders.

Class C shares do not have front-end loads but they have 1.00 percent contingent deferred service charges that decline to zero after one year and perpetual annual 12b-1 fees of 1.00 percent. In general, Class C shares have the lowest cost to shareholders for up to an eight-year holding period.

Further, mutual fund shareholders who buy so-called no-transaction-fee funds on fund supermarkets actually pay higher expense ratios, either as fund 12b-1 fees or expenses.

TRANSACTION COST ISSUES

The mutual fund industry often opposes the disclosure of transaction costs as too difficult to measure and, in any case, these costs need not be disclosed. But this opposition is wrong on both counts. Normative disclosure of transaction cost components should be a regulatory or, at least, an industry "best practices" requirement, with definitional and measurement standards of each cost, along with use of lowest-cost trading strategies.

The definitions and measurements of trading costs is an active field for research and service to mutual funds. As progress continues, the SEC and the fund industry should follow with defined and specified trading cost subcategories. Transaction costs are not "expenses," but they do reduce shareholder assets by adversely affecting the actual cost of security purchases and the realized price of security sales. Transaction costs are major costs and are often larger than management fees and expense ratios.

Measurement of the various components of transaction costs has long been a challenge, but now much of this information is available. Kissell (2006) discusses how proper assessment of trading costs requires an understanding of its components and how they influence trading. Nine cost components are defined in detail: brokerage commissions, trade taxes, trade fees, bid–ask spreads, delayed trade cost, price appreciation, market impact, timing risk, and opportunity cost. Of these, brokerage commissions and trade taxes are fixed costs and the remaining are variable costs. The only visible components are brokerage commissions, bid–ask spreads, and trade taxes.

Kissel (2006) classifies transaction costs as *investment costs* (trade taxes and trade delay cost), *trading costs* (brokerage commissions, trade fees, and bid–ask spreads, price appreciation, market impact and timing risk), and *opportunity costs.* Classification assists in determining where and when each cost appears in the trade process, which then assists in determining the party to the trade that is responsible for managing each cost. Importantly, classification provides funds with the basis for managing these costs so that trade execution strategies are consistent with fund investment objectives.

Gastineau (2005) reports a Plexus Group transaction cost study. The institutional costs of trading a $30 stock are estimated to include brokerage commissions of 17 basis points per share (bps) and implicit trading costs of 140 bps. Implicit trading costs comprise market impact costs of 34 bps, delayed-trade costs of 77 bps, and missed-trade costs of 29 bps. The largest cost, delayed trades, is 52 percent of total trading costs.

Chalmers, Edelen, and Kadlec (2008) investigate mutual fund expense ratios and direct trading costs, the latter defined to include bid–ask spreads and brokerage commissions. As percentages of fund assets, these costs are estimated as: expense ratio (1.07 percent), spread costs (0.47 percent), brokerage commissions (0.31 percent), and total fund expenditures (1.85 percent). Direct trading costs are thus estimated as 73 percent of the size of the expense ratio and 42 percent of total expenditures.

In a major study, Edelen, Evans, and Kadlec (2008) find that scale effects in mutual fund trading are the primary cause of diminishing returns to scale. Trading costs are larger on average than expense ratios and have a higher cross-sectional variation related to trade size. Annual average fund trading costs are 1.44 percent while expense ratios are 1.21 percent.

Mutual fund trades of relatively large (small) size have a negative (positive) impact on performance. By adjusting for trading costs, fund performance is not related to fund asset size, which says that trading costs are the major source of diseconomies of scale.

Flow-induced trades arise from cash inflows/outflows from investor purchases/sales of mutual fund shares. These operational trades are much more costly than discretionary trades, which portfolio managers plan to execute fund investment strategy. However, operational trades do not explain all negative effects of trade size on mutual fund performance. By controlling for flow and scale effects, discretionary trades have a small positive impact on fund performance, but relatively large trades have a negative relation.

Relatively large mutual fund trade sizes are beyond the point of cost recovery. Two motives for excess trading are flow and agency conflicted soft-dollar trades, the latter benefiting fund advisers and brokers at the expense of shareholders. However, neither flow nor soft-dollar trades explains all excess trading.

The negative impact of large size trades on fund performance is due to trade size scale diseconomies and also to operational flow trades and agency-related soft-dollar trades.

CONCLUSIONS: NORMATIVE DISCLOSURE, THE *TOTAL* EXPENSE RATIO, AND REGULATORY CHANGE

The 40 Act states that the interests of shareholders are compromised when mutual funds are operated in the interest of fund advisers. In this regard, one of the act's major objectives is to ensure investors receive adequate and accurate information. They do not. For this reason, Congress, the SEC, fund advisers and independent directors, and the fund industry must focus on the goal of requiring across-the-board normative transparency of disclosure. This disclosure includes adoption of "best practices" over the current focus on rule-making, which allows incorrect accounting and incomplete, missing, misleading and perfunctory disclosure.

Adoption of the *Total* Expense Ratio construct and its components would provide a major portion of what is needed in the way of normative transparency of disclosure by placing up front its four major categories of fees and their subcategories. In so doing, payments by advisers/distributors would no longer be behind the mutual fund curtain. There would also be continual need to benchmark.

By making these payments behind the mutual fund curtain up front and transparent, there will be increased pressure on fund advisers and independent directors, the fund industry, Congress, and the SEC to prohibit inappropriate fund practices and actions, most important of which includes selling group payments of dealer concessions and 12b-1 fees, the several types of revenue-sharing payments, and costly soft-dollar trades. If successful, there would also be continual need to benchmark normative transparency if it is to be maintained with future changing conditions.

But while improvements in regulatory disclosure are likely to occur over time, it is most unlikely that the political process will achieve complete normative transparency of disclosure. However, industry and political obstacles for reform are more likely to be overcome if major shareholder-friendly fund advisers and dedicated independent directors work collectively, vigorously, and proactively for congressional and SEC legal and regulatory action. However, such success will be difficult to attain because of the powerful influence of many major mutual fund advisers who benefit greatly from the regulatory status quo, and at the great expense of fund shareholders.

REFERENCES

American Century Mutual Funds. 2003. Statement of Additional Information, March 31.

Bellver, A., and D. Kaufmann. 2005. " 'Transparenting Transparency': Initial Empirics and Policy Applications." Working Paper, The World Bank, Washington, DC.

Bicksler, J. L. 2004. "Mutual Funds Debacle: Economic Foundations, Fundamental Problems and First Step Governance Reforms." Working Paper, School of Business, Rutgers University, New Brunswick, NJ.

Black, B. 2008. "Are Retail Investors Better Off Today?" University of Cincinnati College of Law, Research Paper Series, January 15.

Bogle, J. C. 2004. "Has Your Fund Adviser Betrayed Your Trust? Consider the 'Stewardship Quotient.'" Keynote address, AICPA Personal Financial Planning Conference, Las Vegas, January 5.

Bogle, J. C. 2005. "The Mutual Fund Industry 60 Years Later: For Better or Worse?" *Financial Analysts Journal* 61 (January/February): 15–24.

Chalmers, J. M. R., R. M. Edelen, and G. B. Kadlec. 2008. "An Analysis of Mutual Fund Trading Costs." Working Paper Series, SSRN, September 4, http://ssrn.com/abstract=195849.

Edelen, R.M., R.B. Evans, and G.B. Kadlec. 2008. "Scale Effects in Mutual Fund Performance: The Role of Trading Costs." Working Paper Series, SSRN, September 4, http://ssrn.com/abstract=951367.

Gastineau, G. L. 2005. *Someone Will Make Money on Your Funds—Why Not You?* Hoboken, NJ: John Wiley & Sons.

Haslem, J. A. 2003. *Mutual Funds: Risk and Performance Analysis for Decision Making*. Oxford, UK: Blackwell Publishing.

Haslem, J. A. 2004. "A Tool for Improved Mutual Funds Transparency," *Journal of Investing* 13: 3 (Fall): 54–64. Accepted Paper Series, SSRN, June 12, 2008, http://ssrn.com/abstract=1143498.

Haslem, J. A. 2005. "Investing in 'Fiduciary' Mutual Funds: How to Improve the Odds," *Journal of Investing* 14: 4 (Winter): 63–68. Accepted Paper Series, SSRN, June 18, 2008, http://ssrn.com/abstract=1143045.

Haslem, J. A. 2006. "Indecent Disclosure (What Mutual Funds Investors Should Have: Normative Transparency of Disclosure)," *Journal of Indexes* 8: 4 (July/August): 35–40. Working Paper Series, SSRN, October 22, 2008, http://ssrn.com/abstract=1287483.

Haslem, J. A. 2007. "Normative Transparency of Mutual Fund Disclosure and the Case of the Expense Ratio," *Journal of Investing* 16: 4 (Winter): 167–173. Accepted Paper Series, SSRN, June 6, 2008, http://ssrn.com/abstract=1137003.

Haslem, J. A. 2008a. "An Idea Whose Time Has Come (Should the SEC Rid Mutual Fund Investors of 12b-1 Fees?)," *Journal of Indexes* 11: 3 (May/June): 42–45, 47. Working Paper Series, SSRN, June 15, 2008, http://ssrn.com/abstract=1114922.

Haslem, J. A. 2008b. "What Independent Directors Should 'Request' of Mutual Fund Advisers." Working Paper Series, SSRN, November 16, 2008, http://ssrn.com/abstract=1302373.

Haslem, J. A. 2008c. "Why Have Mutual Fund Independent Directors Failed as 'Shareholder Watchdogs'?" Working Paper Series, SSRN, November 16, 2008, http://ssrn.com/abstract=1140320.

Haslem, John A. 2009a. "The *Total* Expense Ratio: The Reality of Distribution Fees 'Behind the Mutual Fund Curtain.'" Working Paper Series, SSRN, January 10, 2009, http://ssrn.com/abstract=1325612.

Haslem, John A. 2009b. "Investor Learning and Mutual Fund Advertising and Inside Distribution Fees.'" Working Paper Series, SSRN, June 18, 2009, http://ssrn.com/abstract=1422245.

Investment Company Institute. 2007. *Investment Company Fact Book, 47th Ed*. Washington, DC.

Kissell, R. 2006. " The Expanded Implementation Shortfall: Understanding Transaction Cost Components," *Journal of Trading* 1: 1 (Summer): 6–16.

Lauricella, T. 2003. "Probe Hits Strong's Chairman," *Wall Street Journal*, October 30, pp. C1, C12.

Palmiter, A. R. 2006. "The Mutual Fund Boards: A Failed Experiment in Regulatory Outsourcing," *Brooklyn Journal of Corporate, Financial and Commercial Law* 1: 161–205.

Phillips, D. 2004. "Phillips' Senate Testimony: Morningstar Proposes 10 Steps to Reform the Mutual Fund Industry," Morningstar.com, February 25.

Schack, J. 2005. "Sins of Commissions," *Institutional Investor* 39 (December): 36–45.

Steil, B., and D. Perfumo. 2003. *The Economics of Soft-Dollar Trading*. New York: Efficient Frontiers LLC.

U. S. General Accounting Office. 2003. Testimony Before the Subcommittee on Capital Markets, Insurance and Government Sponsored Enterprises, Committee on Financial Services, House of Representatives. Mutual Funds: Additional Disclosures Could Increase Transparency of Fees and Other Practices. Statement by R. J. Hillman. Washington, DC, June 18.

U. S. Securities and Exchange Commission. 2003. Testimony Before the Subcommittee on Capital Markets, Insurance, and Government Sponsored Enterprises, Committee on Financial Services, House of Representatives. The Mutual Funds Integrity and Fee Transparency Act of 2003, H. R. 2420. Statement by P. F. Roye. Washington, DC, June 18.

Vishwanath, T., and D. Kaufmann. 1999. "Towards Transparency in Finance and Governance." Working Paper, The World Bank, Washington, DC.

Zingales, L. 2004. "The Costs and Benefits of Financial Market Regulation." Law Working Paper, European Corporate Governance Institute, Brussels, BE.

ABOUT THE AUTHOR

John A. Haslem is Professor Emeritus of Finance in the Robert H. Smith School of Business at the University of Maryland. He served as founding academic affairs dean and founding chair of the finance department. He received the Panhellenic Association's "Outstanding Teacher Award" for his first-of-a-kind mutual funds course. Professor Haslem studied at Duke University, Harvard University, and the University of North Carolina, and he taught at the University of North Carolina and on the faculty of the University of Wisconsin. His research has appeared in the *Journal of Finance, Journal of Business, Journal of Financial and Quantitative Analysis, Journal of Money, Credit and Banking, Financial Analysts Journal,* and *Journal of Investing*, among numerous others. He also has contributed five books, including *Mutual Funds: Risk and Performance Analysis for Decision Making*. Professor Haslem served as personal financial consultant to the director of Supersonic Transport, U.S. Department of Transportation; and consultant and expert witness to two divisions of the U.S. Department of Justice (including the Supreme Court case *U.S. v. State of Louisiana*).

CHAPTER 18

A Design for the Mutual Funds of the Future

JOHN C. BOGLE
Founder, The Vanguard Group, Inc., and President, The Bogle Financial Markets Research Center

THE VANGUARD VISION

I have a dream for the design of the mutual fund of the future. I did my best to provide this design when I created Vanguard in 1974, and nothing has happened in the nearly 35 years since then to shake my conviction that it is the right design. It seems timely to examine that design, the structure of Vanguard, the strategy that structure demanded, and the results it delivered. It is also high time to expand that narrow mandate and consider a comparable design—new to the other firms in this industry—for the mutual fund of the future.

Vanguard was created in 1974, the result of the "mutualization" of the Wellington Management Company mutual funds, then with just $1.4 billion of assets. Under this structure, the first step we took was to have our funds employ their own officers and staff; assume responsibility for operational, administrative, legal, and shareholder record-keeping services; and operate on an at-cost basis. Wellington continued its responsibility for all investment management and marketing services. This initial structure was designed to place Vanguard in a position to be the low-cost provider in an industry where, as we saw it then—and see it now—cost was the ultimate competitive weapon.

Following approval by the Securities and Exchange Commission (SEC) and our fund shareholders, we began operations on May 1, 1975. We were hardly unaware, however, that if our new firm was to shape its own destiny, we had to move quickly to control our investment management services and distribution services as well. We immediately began that process. Within six months, we had gained our board's approval for the world's first index mutual fund and entered the investment arena. Now known as Vanguard Index 500, its initial public offering (IPO) took place on August 30, 1976. The new index fund ("Bogle's folly") began with a frustratingly tiny asset base of only $11 million.

Adapted from J. C. Bogle, 2007, Keynote Address, "Designing a New Mutual Fund Industry," 25th Anniversary Conference, National Investment Companies Service Association, Miami, February 20.

When Vanguard began in 1975, this was an 80 percent equity fund business. But money market funds and bond funds were on the rise, and by 1981, they would constitute 83 percent of industry assets. It was obvious that in these two income-driven industry segments, as well as in index funds, the impact of our low-cost advantage was even greater. Our strategy would focus largely on these three cost-sensitive investment segments. But, in principle if not in materiality, gaining permission from our board to manage these funds was our second giant step forward, for it enabled us to assume responsibility for supervising fund investments for the first time.

Within months after the IPO, we took the third necessary step to complete our control over the triangle of mutual fund services, which included administrative services, investment services, and marketing services. In February 1977, we converted our distribution system overnight from a commission-based, broker-dealer–old, demand-push system that had been our practice for 50 years to a no-load, investor-purchased, supply-pull system.

It took until February 1981—four years later—in what remains the longest Investment Company Act hearing in history, for the SEC finally to approve our internalization. Conducting business under this cloud of uncertainty had been a challenge. But we never lost confidence that the Commission would eventually support our application. Finally, of course, it did.

The SEC (1981) not only approved our plan, it did so in a decision that was unanimous, sweeping, and robust. Indeed, it was so positive that we ran this excerpt in the 1981 annual reports of our Vanguard funds:

> *The Vanguard plan actually furthers the (1940) Act's objectives by ensuring that the Funds' directors are better able to evaluate the cost and performance of the funds; improves disclosure to shareholders; and clearly enhances the Funds' independence. It also benefits each fund within a reasonable range of fairness, promotes a healthy and viable mutual fund complex within which each fund can better prosper; enables the Funds to realize substantial savings from advisory fee reductions; promotes savings from economies of scale; and provides the Funds with direct and conflict-free control over distribution functions. (p. 18)*

All of those words have been borne out in the years that followed. In fact, the Commission's powerful endorsement marked the very moment that the uninterrupted ascendancy of Vanguard began. From then to today, our market share has never declined, rising on balance from 1.7 percent of industry assets to 10.6 percent currently.

The major reason that what we once called "The Vanguard Experiment" in mutual fund structure and governance has worked in the marketplace is obvious. Check almost any independent rating of mutual fund investment performance, and you will see that the returns we have earned for our shareowners have consistently ranked at or near the top among all fund complexes. The lion's share of that superiority in returns is accounted for simply by our lower costs. The jury is in, and our system has proven itself to be an artistic success for our shareholders and a commercial success for our firm. *The simple system worked.*

Economic theory assumes that ideas that prove themselves in competitive capitalism quickly spawn legions of competitors. That is not true in Vanguard's case. Despite outstanding performance for our fund shareholders and our unremitting rise in market share—which alone accounts for nearly $1 trillion of our $1.25 trillion asset base—not a single other fund manager has adopted the Vanguard model. Our structure, of course, results in the profits from organizing, operating, and managing mutual funds being returned to fund owners rather than to fund managers. So it seems at least possible, and perhaps even likely, that in today's fund industry, making money for fund investors carries a lower priority than making money for fund managers. Whether the Vanguard model is emulated or not, I expect that the values that drive the Vanguard agenda will gradually work their way into our industry.

A DESIGN FOR THE FUTURE

I have five goals for redesigning the mutual fund industry in the years to come. The first is fair pricing of mutual funds. The second is a focus on lifetime investing. The third is a policy of long-term investing for mutual fund managers. The fourth is a new design for "product development," and the fifth is a new governance structure that puts fund shareholders in the driver's seat.

1. A Fair Shake for Fund Shareholders

My first goal is to design a new industry that gives shareholders a fair shake in terms of costs. In 1977, we predicted that investors would come to focus far more heavily on fund costs, evaluating "total price—or total cost-effectiveness over time, including any initial sales charges and fund operating and advisory expenses." But, by 1987, we could only grade ourselves F on that prediction. Over the decade then ended, the expense ratio of the average equity fund had risen from an average of 0.96 percent to an estimated 1.38 percent, a 44 percent increase. Despite the fact that total industry assets had grown from $37 billion to $588 billion, expense ratios actually increased, and the amount of annual fund costs had risen 4,000 percent, from $232 million to $4.2 billion.

We stubbornly held our ground, predicting in 1987 that the industry pricing structure would improve. We challenged the industry "to regain our bearings, and return to the principles that got us to our present eminence in the first place." But in 1998 the expense ratio of the average equity fund continued to rise, to 1.43 percent. However, with industry assets rising to $3.5 trillion, the total expenses borne by fund shareholders soared from $4.2 billion to $27 billion. We awarded ourselves another F. "Despite my 20 years of unfulfilled expectations," I said then, "I'm confident that the excessive costs paid by fund investors would at last begin to decline."

Today, the outcome is unequivocal: Yes and no. No, because while equity fund expense ratios on average seem to have leveled off, they remain 50 percent higher than 30 years ago. This increase occurred despite the staggering increase in assets under management. With industry assets now over $10 trillion, compared to $37 billion in 1977, fund costs are now some $75 billion a year, which includes sales charges but not portfolio transaction costs. This amount is more than 30 times the costs of $232 million in 1977. Rather than sharing the huge economies of scale that derive from managing other people's money with shareholders, fund managers have taken it for themselves.

Nonetheless, there has recently been a hint of "yes" in the air. While the industry still refuses to compete on price, there is evidence that the industry's shareholders are increasingly investing where they are offered a fair shake on cost and value. Consider the five firms that dominated our industry's cash flow last year (2006). Together, American Funds, Vanguard, Barclays, Dodge and Cox, and Dimensional Fund Advisors (DFA) drew net investor capital of nearly $200 billion, fully two-thirds of the $300 billion flow into all long-term mutual funds. Three of these firms are giant complexes known both for their ultra-low costs and their index funds, and the other two have costs that are significantly below industry norms.

As investors increasingly choose lower-cost firms, we are confident that no matter how powerful the negative impact on their huge profit margins of 40 to 50 percent, higher-cost firms will be driven to conform. So, in this first part of my grand design for the future, I expect that the march toward a fair shake for fund investors will be inexorable and that investor costs will come down in the years ahead.

2. Serving Investors for a Lifetime

My second goal is that we design an industry that will serve investors for a lifetime. Retirement planning, of course, is central to this goal. In 1977, this was a business that ran money for investors who already had money. But even then, we confidently predicted that mutual funds would become the preferred vehicle for those who wanted to build their wealth, especially through retirement planning. At that time, retirement plans held only about 7 percent of fund shares, but we were confident that they "would become extremely important to our industry's future growth."

But, when 1987 rolled around, ownership of fund shares by retirement plans had actually fallen to 4 percent of assets. So we graded the earlier prediction a D. But we held our ground, noting that "the recent trend from traditional defined benefit pension plans toward defined contribution plans such as 401(k) savings plans will open vast new markets for mutual funds."

By 1998, the jury was in again. Our 1987 forecast was "a home run." Led by 401(k) plans, retirement plan investments in funds had grown some 30 times over from $30 billion to $900 billion. We predicted again that "the institutional uptrend should persist," and that prediction, too, proved accurate. Today, defined contribution thrift plans hold more than $1.1 trillion of fund shares, and defined benefit pension plans hold some $500 billion. Adding individual retirement accounts (IRAs) of $1.4 trillion brings our industry's retirement plan assets to more than $3 trillion, more than 40 percent of all long-term mutual fund assets.

Our industry's ability to handle the complex record keeping for nearly 50 million participants in multifaceted defined contribution plus plans has been something of a triumph. But the vast menus of funds provided and the wide array of investment strategies offered have come nowhere near that high standard. We have too many investors who are too aggressive. The 401(k) plan participants working for Fortune 100 companies allocate an average of 36 percent to company stock, which concentrates their investment risk and aligns it with their career risk. We also have too many investors who are too conservative. Those investors who have stable value and money market funds as investment options allocate nearly 24 percent to these funds.

What is more, 401(k) investors are notorious for performance chasing, and we seem not to care. Traditionally, the most popular funds in our retirement plans have been those with extraordinary past performance, but these returns are destined to revert to the market mean at best and more likely below it. Magellan Fund, for example, was by far the most popular choice of retirement plan investors during the 1990s. But since 1993, it has failed by a wide margin to achieve the average returns turned in by the unmanaged Standard & Poor's 500 Index, trailing the index by a cumulative total of 91 percentage points. Yet Magellan remains the third most popular option.

Today's favorites, of course, also have provided excellent past performance. But it is not clear is that these leaders—American Growth, American Washington Mutual, Fidelity Contrafund, and Fidelity Low-Priced Stock—can replicate the records they achieved when their assets were fractions of these levels, no mean task when each fund has assets ranging from $40 billion to more than $100 billion. However, we can be confident that Vanguard 500 Index, ranking among the top four choices, will continue to deliver roughly the stock market's future return, just as it is guaranteed to do.

In this industry, we offer too many choices to retirement plans and thereby sow considerable confusion among participants. We allow too much borrowing, and fully 45 percent of those who leave their jobs simply take their money and run. We often also offer participants a self-managed brokerage account, even though it makes it too easy for employees to invest in a manner that is directly contrary to their long-term interests. Yes, automatic enrollment is a good enhancement, and target retirement funds, properly used, are a relatively new and wonderful option. But we have no monopoly on the affections of retirement plan investors. It is therefore in our industry's interest to provide far more investment discipline and lower-cost funds in the choices that we offer and to make crystal clear the importance of these two elements not only to employees but to plan sponsors as well.

Most important of all, we need to recognize that mutual funds are now a central element in the nation's retirement system, including corporate, federal, state, and local government plans. Rather than looking after the parochial interests of our own industry, we ought to be leading the way to rationalizing the entire retirement services system. So, my goal of providing lifetime services to investors includes a vision that our industry leaders will at last step forward with proposals and designs to help accomplish cradle-to-grave retirement security for our citizens. We owe it to ourselves and to society to do no less.

3. Long-Term Investment Horizons for Fund Managers

My third goal is that our money managers turn back the clock, reverting to our traditional focus on long-term investment strategies. During my first 15 years in this industry, the typical equity mutual fund turned its portfolio over at about 16 percent per year. As a result, the average fund held its average stock for an average of about six years. We can define that strategy as *long-term investing.*

Today, by way of contrast, we turn our portfolios over six times as rapidly. The average fund portfolio turns over at an annual rate of 100 percent, which is a holding period of just one year for the average stock. Our larger funds turn over at a somewhat slower rate, perhaps a necessity given their size, and our index funds portfolios barely turn over at all. Whatever the case, last year our actively managed equity funds, with assets of $4.6 trillion, bought $3.2 trillion of stocks and sold another $3.3 trillion, an amazing total of $6.5 trillion in transactions. We calculate that turnover rate at about 70 percent, since the accepted turnover formula is to divide the asset base into the lesser of portfolio purchases or sales. Even using this lower turnover rate, however, suggests that our average stock is now held for only 17 months. We can define that not as long-term investing but as short-term speculation.

Since most fund trading takes place with other mutual funds, all of this turnover cannot possibly serve the interests of our fund shareholders as a group. In fact, such substantial trading activity actually dilutes the returns of our owners. After the trading costs of our Wall Street croupiers are deducted, the inevitable zero-sum game when stocks are traded from one investor to another becomes a loser's game. It must be obvious that short-term speculators lose to long-term investors. The fund industry's conversion from yesteryear's focus on the long-term to today's focus on the short-term has been, by definition, detrimental to the interests of our shareholders.

There is another great benefit in becoming, once again, an own-a-stock industry. We would be forced to recognize that the interest of our shareholders demands that we act as responsible corporate citizens, carefully examining company financial statements, making our views known on matters such as stock options, executive compensation, and corporate governance, and encourage the corporations whose shares we hold to operate in the interests of their shareholders rather than their managers. In today's rent-a-stock industry, where stocks are treated as mere pieces of paper to trade back and forth, governance issues are too often ignored. My goal is that we return to our roots as investors. Not only because this return will be to the economic benefit of our shareholders, but because we can play the determining role in returning corporate America to its roots of democratic capitalism.

4. Serving Long-Term Investors

My fourth goal is that we again serve long-term investors. This is not how it works today. For even as the investment horizons of our fund managers diminished, so, too, have the horizons of fund investors. Small wonder, since we have shaped our business to meet the demands of short-term investors. When I came into this business, the rate of fund redemptions to fund assets was about 6 percent annually, suggesting an average holding period of 16 years for our average shareholder.

By the late 1990s, this shareholder turnover rate had soared to nearly 50 percent, suggesting an average holding period of only 2 years. One reason for this huge leap was that funds were widely used as vehicles for illicit market timing and time-zone trading, in which certain fund managers conspired with certain favored short-term speculators. There were 300 hedge funds using this strategy, trading directly contrary to the interests of fund long-term investors. But even with the elimination of much of that abuse, the redemption rate remains at a remarkably high level of 24 percent, a holding period of a bit more than 4 years. This is a far cry from the 16-year holding period of our early tradition.

The underlying reason for this excessive rate of investor turnover lies in our mad rush to offer funds designed to be traded rather than funds designed to be held for a lifetime. The contrast of yesteryear's fund industry of largely market-like portfolios holding blue-chip stocks to today's offerings of narrowly focused portfolios could hardly be starker. Our industry thinks in terms more suggestive of high fashion than investing. Morningstar has popularized nine style boxes, with one axis focused on large- or medium-, or small-cap U.S. stocks; and the other axis, funds focused on growth stocks, or value stocks, or a blend of the two. In addition, we offer hundreds of funds focused on industry segments (technology, precious metals, telecommunications, etc.) as well as international stocks, including the total non-U.S. market. The international market represents about one-half of the world's market capitalization and is surely a legitimate investment choice. But there are also scores of funds whose investments are concentrated in individual regions and countries bearing considerable risk.

It is no secret that this radical change in our industry's focus reflects the rise of gathering assets as our highest priority. Once an industry that sold what we made, we became an industry that made what would sell, determined to give the public whatever it wants. Alas, the public seems to like the exciting and the new rather than the tried and the true. In the speculative new-economy market bubble of the late 1990s, for example, we created some 240 new technology-based funds, which collapsed in the bear market that followed. Producing "products" based on evanescent market funds has seriously jeopardized the financial goals of our fund shareholders.

That failure can now be measured statistically. Financial services firms are at last beginning to differentiate the rates of return they *report* (time-weighted returns) from the rates of return shareholders actually *achieve* (dollar-weighted returns). This difference provides clear evidence that investors have chosen unwisely among the funds we have unwisely created. For example, of the 200 funds with the largest inflows of investor capital during 1997 to 2000, the average annual return earned by investors was 64 percentage points per year below that reported by funds, a cumulative loss of 107 percentage points. Not surprisingly, the more specialized funds had the largest shortfalls.

In recent years, we have taken our focus on a bewildering array of highly specialized fund choices, designed for traders rather investors, to new heights. The stampede into exchange-traded funds (ETFs) has been dominated by highly specialized funds that, in the words of an ETF advertisement, "can be traded in real time, all day long." Among 690 ETFs, 678 are narrowly focused, some on individual foreign countries (Korea, Germany, whatever you wish) or industry sectors (technology, small-caps, even health shares and "emerging cancer"). Only 12 ETFs are highly diversified index funds holding the entire U.S. stock market or the entire non-U.S. stock market, close cousins to our diversified blue-chip funds of yore. Of course, such ETFs, held for the long term, are fine investments. But ETFs that actively pursue narrow investment strategies, too often chasing past performance, will surely be hazardous to the wealth of our investors. In the long run, that cannot be good for our industry. So my fourth goal is to return to our roots in providing broadly diversified funds that can be bought and held forever.

5. Fund Investors in the Driver's Seat

My fifth goal is to place investors in the driver's seat of fund governance. Only in this way can we honor the demand of the Investment Company Act of 1940, the statute that governs our industry, that mutual funds be "organized, operated, and managed in the best interests of their shareholders rather than in the interest of their advisers and underwriters." Yet, for all of the act's noble intentions, that is simply not the principle under which our industry operates today. Once focused on management and investment, we are now focused on marketing and asset gathering.

Of course, our managers are eager to earn a fair return on the capital entrusted to them by their fund shareholder/clients. But they also are in business to earn the highest possible return on their capital. That is what we call a conflict of interest. So long as the gross returns earned by fund investors as a group are reduced by the costs of fund investing (management fees, operating costs, marketing costs, portfolio turnover costs, and excessive taxes imposed on shareholders by short-term investment policies), investor net returns will be far less. It is but a truism to state of this industry that in the aggregate, "The more that fund managers *take,* the less that fund investors *make.*"

The coming of public ownership of fund management companies in the early 1960s bears an important share of the responsibility for many of the problems described. These problems include:

- Rising costs for investors from the failure to deliver our huge economies of scale to shareholders
- Failure to make the most of our opportunity in retirement planning
- The move away from long-term investment in favor of short-term speculation
- The asset-gathering mentality
- The focus on fads like size and style, all of which have meant staggering profits for fund managers, at great cost to fund shareholders

Time is money. Yet shareholder education is glacially slow, and time is money. The conglomerates that own 32 of the 50 largest fund complexes will not soon accept eroded returns on their capital, nor will they willingly return their profits to their fund shareholders. There is no recourse but to put fund shareholders in the driver's seat of fund governance, thereby at last honoring both the letter and the spirit of the 1940 Act.

What is necessary is that the governance of mutual funds comports with just what the act calls for, and that is a board of directors that is beholden first and foremost to the shareholders who elected them. We must eliminate the blatant conflict of interest that exists when the chairman of the fund board is the same person as the chairman of the management company board. As Warren Buffett (1985) says: "Negotiating with one's self seldom produces a barroom brawl." For the same reason, we need a board wholly independent of the manager. At Vanguard, our outside advisers have no board representation, but this has had no adverse consequences for our fund shareholders. The requirement that 75 percent of the directors must be independent is a good beginning. Regulations already require independent legal counsel and a chief compliance officer for the funds themselves. For the larger fund complexes, we must require that an independent staff, responsible directly to the board, provide objective and unbiased information on fund costs, performance, marketing, capital inflows and outflows, portfolio turnover, and other aspects of fund operations.

My goal of fund independence means more than implementing these board reforms, however. It means ultimately laying the groundwork for an industry that at last acts under the spirit and letter of our federal statute, an industry in which fund shareholders, through their elected representatives, are placed in the driver's seat of fund governance.

CONCLUSIONS

Broadly stated, my goal is an industry that is focused on stewardship, the prudent handling of other people's money solely in the interests of our investors—an industry that is of the shareholder, by the shareholder, and for the shareholder. An industry that has both vision and values—a vision of fiduciary duty and shareholder service, and values rooted in the principles of long-term investing and of trusteeship that demands fair management costs and integrity in serving our shareholders.

Ultimately my goal is that Vanguard's mutual at-cost model will find its first follower. And then a second, third, and more followers as we move away from today's management company–oriented and increasingly conglomerate-dominated structure. This will happen not because the fund industry wants to change, but because intelligent investors who "vote with their feet" will drag this industry into a Brave New World. But even if that sea change to a new structure—a change that has clearly worked so effectively both for our investors and for our firm—does not happen, the industry will finally move, at least philosophically, in the direction of the Vanguard model.

How close will we get to these lofty goals in the coming decade? So far, one of the major goals I have expressed—lower costs—still remains unrealized. We are well on the way to the second goal, our industry's primacy in retirement planning, although it took decades to come to fruition. It also may take years for the other three goals to come to pass: long-term portfolio strategies, shareholders who invest with us for the long-term, and our shareholders sitting firmly in the driver's seat of fund governance. It may even take decades, though I fervently hope that change will come much sooner, for it is high time that our legions of investors be served efficiently, economically, and honestly. Only time will tell.

REFERENCES

Bogle, J. C. 1977. Marketing Mutual Fund Shares in the 1980's: Speech at a Meeting of the National Investment Company Service Association, *The Vanguard Group of Investment Companies* March 10, 1977.

Bogle, J. C. 1987. Mutual Funds in 1987: A $700 Billion Trust Keynote Speech Before the Annual Meeting of the National Investment Company Services Association, *The Vanguard Group of Investment Companies*, February 16, 1987.

Bogle, J. C. 1998. Honoring Our $4 Trillion Trust: Mutual Funds in the 21st Century Keynote Speech Before the National Investment Company Service Association, *The Vanguard Group of Investment Companies*, February 24, 1998.

Buffett, W. 1985. Chairman's Letter to the Shareholders, *Annual Report of Berkshire Hathaway*, Berkshire Hathaway, Inc.

U. S. Securities and Exchange Commission. 1981. "In the Matter of the Vanguard Group," 47 SEC 450, February 28.

ABOUT THE AUTHOR

John C. Bogle is Founder of The Vanguard Group, Inc., and President of the Bogle Financial Markets Research Center. He created Vanguard in 1974 and served as Chairman and Chief Executive Officer until 1996 and Senior Chairman until 2000. He had been associated with a predecessor company since 1951, immediately following his graduation from Princeton University, *magna cum laude* in Economics. In 2004, *TIME* magazine named Mr. Bogle as one of the world's 100 most powerful and influential people, and *Institutional Investor* presented him with its Lifetime Achievement Award. Mr. Bogle is a bestselling author, beginning with *Bogle on Mutual Funds: New Perspectives for the Intelligent Investor* (1993); *Common Sense on Mutual Funds: New Imperatives for the Intelligent Investor* (1999); *John Bogle on Investing: The First 50 Years* (2000); *Character Counts: The Creation and Building of The Vanguard Group* (2002); *Battle for the Soul of Capitalism* (2005); and *The Little Book of Common Sense Investing* (2007). His seventh book, *Enough: True Measures of Money, Business, and Life*, was published by John Wiley & Sons in November 2008.

Index

-

Printed in the United States
Bookmasters